SDI
TECHNOLOGY,
SURVIVABILITY,
and
SOFTWARE

SDI

TECHNOLOGY, SURVIVABILITY, and SOFTWARE

Princeton University Press, Princeton, New Jersey

Published by Princeton University Press, 41 William Street, Princeton, New Jersey 08540
In the United Kingdom: Princeton University Press, Guildford, Surrey

First Princeton University Press edition, 1988
LCC 87-619857
ISBN 0-691-07747-9 (alk. paper)   ISBN 0-691-02270-4 (pb.)

Reprinted by arrangement with the Office of Technology Assessment, Congress of the United States,
Washington, D.C. 20510

Publisher's Note: Undertaken by the Office of Technology Assessment at the request of the House
Armed Services Committee and the Senate Foreign Relations Committee, and made public in June
1988, *SDI* was published by the Government Printing Office in a limited quantity. It is our purpose
in republishing this report to make it more readily available to students, scholars, and the general
public.

Clothbound editions of Princeton University Press books are printed on acid-free paper, and binding
materials are chosen for strength and durability. Paperbacks, while satisfactory for personal collec-
tions, are not usually suitable for library rebinding.

Printed in the United States of America.

Foreword

In its 1985 report, *New Ballistic Missile Defense Technologies*, OTA attempted to place those technologies against a useful policy background for the Congress. While that report introduced the major subject areas of Strategic Defense Initiative research, the amount of detailed technical evaluation it could offer was limited. The chief limitations were the relative newness of the SDI program and the lack of specific BMD system architectures to examine. Since that report, the SDIO has conducted enough additional research and, in particular, identified a sufficiently specific system architecture that a more detailed OTA review of the relevant technologies should be helpful to Congress.

Public Law 99-190 (continuing appropriations for fiscal year 1986) called for the Office of Technology Assessment to conduct a ". . . comprehensive classified study . . . together with an unclassified version . . . to determine the technological feasibility and implications, and the ability to survive and function despite a preemptive attack by an aggressor possessing comparable technology, of the Strategic Defense Initiative Program." In addition, the accompanying Conference Report specified that . . . "This study shall include an analysis of the feasibility of meeting SDI computer software requirements."

This unclassified report completes OTA's response to that mandate. It puts SDI technologies in context by reporting the kinds of ballistic missile defense (BMD) system architectures that the SDI organization has considered for "phased deployment." It reviews the status of the various SDI technologies and system components. It analyzes the feasibility of producing dependable software of the complexity that advanced BMD systems would require. Finally, it summarizes what is now known—and unknown—about the probable survivability of such systems against concerted enemy attacks of various kinds.

The study found that major uncertainties remain concerning the probable cost, effectiveness, and survivability of the kinds of BMD system (which rely on kinetic rather than directed-energy weapons) that might be deployable in the "phase-one" proposed for the mid to late 1990s. In addition, OTA believes several more years of SDI research would be needed to determine whether it is feasible to construct the kinds of directed-energy weapons contemplated as follow-ons to SDIO's "phase one" BMD system. The survivability of both short-term and longer-term BMD systems would depend heavily on the outcome of a continuing competition in weapons and countermeasures between the United States and the Soviet Union. Finally, developing dependable software for advanced BMD will be a formidable challenge because of the difficulty of testing that software realistically.

OTA gratefully thanks the hundreds of individuals whose contributions of time and effort helped make this report possible. OTA, of course, bears the final responsibility for the contents of the report.

JOHN H. GIBBONS
Director

Advisory Panel on SDI: Technology, Survivability, and Software

H. Guyford Stever, *Chairman*
Foreign Secretary, National Academy of Engineering

Robert Clem
Director of Systems Sciences
Sandia National Laboratories

Malcolm Currie
Executive Vice President
Hughes Aircraft Company

Gerald P. Dinneen
Corporate Vice President for Science &
  Technology
Honeywell, Inc.

Peter Franken
Professor
Optical Sciences Center
University of Arizona

John Gardner
Vice President for Engineering &
  Operations
McDonnell Douglas Astronautics Co.

Richard L. Garwin
IBM fellow
IBM T. J. Watson Research Center

O'Dean Judd[1]
Chief Scientist for Defense Research &
  Applications
Los Alamos National Laboratory

Michael M. May
Associate Director at Large
Lawrence Livermore National Laboratory

Stephen Meyer
Associate Professor
Center for International Studies
Massachusetts Institute of Technology

David Parnas
Department of Computing and Information
  Science
Queens University

Charles Seitz
Professor
Computer Sciences
California Institute of Technology

John Shore
Director
Washington Research Lab
Entropic Processing, Inc.

Jeremiah D. Sullivan
Professor
Department of Physics
University of Illinois

Samuel Tennant
Vice President
The Aerospace Corporation

Victor Vyssotsky
Director
Cambridge Research Laboratory
Digital Equipment Corporation

Gerold Yonas
Vice President
The Titan Corporation

Charles A. Zraket
President
The MITRE Corporation

Invited Observer:
Chief Scientist
Strategic Defense Initiative Organization

---

[1]Currently, Chief Scientist, Strategic Defense Initiative Organization.

NOTE: OTA appreciates and is grateful for the valuable assistance and thoughtful critiques provided by the Advisory
  Panel members. The views expressed in this OTA report, however, are the sole responsibility of the Office
  of Technology Assessment. Participation on the Advisory Panel does not imply endorsement of the report.

OTA Project Staff—SDI: Technology, Survivability, and Software

Lionel S. Johns, *Assistant Director, OTA*
Energy, Materials, and International Security Division

Peter Sharfman, *International Security and Commerce Program Manager*

Thomas H. Karas, *Project Director*

Anthony Fainberg
C. E. "Sandy" Thomas
David Weiss

Administrative Staff

Jannie Coles   Cecile Parker   Jackie Robinson

Acknowledgments

The following organizations generously made their personnel available to provide OTA with information and ideas

Aerospace Corporation
American Physical Society,
AT&T Bell Laboratories
Avco Systems/Textron
Boeing
Booz-Allen & Hamilton
Ford Aerospace and Communications
General Research Corporation
Hughes Aircraft Company
Lawrence Livermore National Laboratory
Lockheed Missiles & Space Company
Los Alamos National Laboratory
LTV
Martin-Marietta
McDonnell-Douglas
M.I.T. Lincoln Laboratory
MITRE Corporation
Nichols Research

Rockwell International
SAIC
Sandia National Laboratory
Sparta
Strategic Defense Initiative Organization
System Planning Corporation
TRW
University of Texas, Center for Electro-
    Mechanical Engineering
U.S. Air Force Electronic Systems
    Division
U.S. Air Force Space Division
U.S. Air Force Weapons Laboratory
U.S. Army Strategic Defense Command
U.S. Naval Research Laboratory
U.S. Naval Sea Systems Command
W. J. Schafer & Associates
Westinghouse Marine Division

Workshop on Soviet Response to SDI, January 1987

Sidney Graybeal, *Chairman*
Vice President, System Planning
 Corporation

Alex Gliksman, *Convener/Rapporteur*
Consultant

Arthur Alexander
The RAND Corporation

Mark M. Lowenthal
Director, INR/SFA
US Department of State

Arthur F. Manfredi, Jr.
Assistant National Intelligence Officer
Central Intelligence Agency

John A. Martens
ITA/Office of Foreign Availability
U.S. Department of Commerce

Stephen Meyer
Professor
Center for International Studies
Massachusetts Institute of Technology

Robert Nurick
Co-Director RAND-UCLA, Soviet Studies
 Center
The RAND Corporation

Sayre Stevens
President, System Planning Corporation

Keith Taggart[1]
Assistant Director/Countermeasures
Strategic Defense Initiative Organization
U.S. Department of Defense

Robert D. Turnacliff
Principal Director, Threat Analysis Office
The Aerospace Corporation

Vann H. Van Diepen
INR/SFA
U.S. Department of State

---

[1]Currently with SAIC, Inc.

Workshop on SDI Software, January 1987

Larry Druffel, *Chairman*
Director, Software Engineering Institute
Carnegie-Mellon University

Speakers

William Ainsley
Logicon, Inc.

Mack Alford
Senior Software Scientist
General Electric Corporation

Karl Dahlke
Technical Staff
AT&T Bell Laboratories

Discussants

Bruce Arden
Dean of Engineering & Applied Science
University of Rochester

Richard Kemmerer
Department of Computer Science
University of California, Santa Barbara

Butler Lampson
Corporate Consulting Engineer
Digital Equipment Corporation

Brian Reid
Consulting Engineer
Digital Equipment Corporation

Panelists

David Parnas
Professor
Department of Computing and Information
 Science
Queens University

John Shore
Director, Washington Research Lab
Entropic Processing, Inc.

Victor Vyssotsky
Director, Cambridge Research Laboratory
Digital Equipment Corporation

Office of Technology Assessment

The Office of Technology Assessment (OTA) was created in 1972 as an analytical arm of Congress. OTA's basic function is to help legislative policymakers anticipate and plan for the consequences of technological changes and to examine the many ways, expected and unexpected, in which technology affects people's lives. The assessment of technology calls for exploration of the physical, biological, economic, social, and political impacts that can result from applications of scientific knowledge. OTA provides Congress with independent and timely information about the potential effects—both beneficial and harmful—of technological applications.

Requests for studies are made by chairmen of standing committees of the House of Representatives or Senate; by the Technology Assessment Board, the governing body of OTA; or by the Director of OTA in consultation with the Board.

The Technology Assessment Board is composed of six members of the House, six members of the Senate, and the OTA Director, who is a non-voting member.

OTA has studies under way in nine program areas: energy and materials; industry, technology, and employment; international security and commerce; biological applications; food and renewable resources; health; communication and information technologies; oceans and environment; and science, education, and transportation.

Contents

Preface

This report is the unclassified version of a classified document delivered to Congress at the end of August 1987. In attempting to reach agreement with the Department of Defense on what information could be included in an unclassified report, OTA found the wheels of bureaucracy to turn very slowly—when they turned at all. Only through the active intervention of the Strategic Defense Initiative Organization, beginning in late in November 1987, and extending to the end of March, 1988, was a partial resolution of the problem achieved.

OTA, with assistance from SDIO staff, revised the entire report to produce a complete version that both agreed should not be considered classified. The Department of Defense concurred on all but the final three chapters. These latter chapters deal—in a general way and without the kind of specific detail that might be useful to an adversary—with a variety of potential countermeasures to BMD systems. In particular, chapters 11 and 12 deal with defining and countering threats to the survivability of space-based BMD systems.

Chapter 1 offers a brief review of the "bottom lines" of chapters 10 through 12. But apparently some in the Defense Department wish to assert that it is *impossible* to present an unclassified analytical discussion that would enable the reader to understand the issues and form his own judgments. In OTA's judgment, this position does not deprive potential adversaries of any information they do not already have: rather, it stifles rational public debate in the United States over the pros and cons of proceeding with ballistic missile defense. To give the reader at least some appreciation of the scope of the deleted material, the tables of contents of chapters 10 through 12 appear at the end of this volume. In addition, the major conclusions of these chapters (without, of course, the supporting analysis) are summarized in chapter 1.

OTA thanks the SDIO for the additional substantive comments and information it provided on the final drafts of the report. Thus, despite the many months of delay since original completion of the report, this unclassified version is reasonably up to date. OTA, not SDIO, is responsible for the contents and conclusions of the report.

A further note on the subject of classified information is in order. Any report which attempts to analyze the feasibility and survivability of prospective ballistic missile defense systems must refer to possible measures an adversary could take to counter the system. OTA sought the views of a variety of experts on Soviet military research, development, and deployment about potential responses to the SDI. It also sought to understand the technical feasibility of various countermeasures. It did not seek out or report on the official judgments of the U.S. intelligence community on what countermeasures the Soviet Union would or could take against SDI-derived systems. *Therefore, nothing said in this report should be construed as an "intelligence" judgment of Soviet intentions or capabilities.*

SDI
TECHNOLOGY,
SURVIVABILITY,
and
SOFTWARE

Chapter 1
Summary

CONTENTS

Box

Figures

Tables

Summary

PRINCIPAL FINDINGS

The Strategic Defense Initiative Organization (SDIO) currently advocates planning for a three-part "phased deployment" of ballistic missile defense (BMD) systems, with each phase providing an increment of strategic benefits while preparing the way for the next phase. The first phase would be intended to ". . . compel Soviet operational adjustments and compromises by reducing the confidence of Soviet planners in predicting the outcome of a ballistic missile attack." The second phase would be intended to negate Soviet abilities to destroy many strategic targets, and the third to "eliminate the threat posed by nuclear ballistic missiles." The exact composition and timing of each phase are still under study, but some tentative system "architectures" have undergone preliminary analysis.

Finding 1: After 30 years of BMD research, including the first few years of the Strategic Defense Initiative (SDI), defense scientists and engineers have produced impressive technical achievements, but questions remain about the feasibility of meeting the goals of the SDI. The SDIO has identified most of the gaps between today's technology and that needed for highly effective ballistic missile defenses; it has initiated programs to address those gaps. It should surprise no one that many technical issues remain unresolved, especially when one considers that the SDI has so far had time and authorization to spend only a fraction of the money that the Fletcher Commission estimated would be necessary to assess BMD feasibility. The SDIO argues that application of sufficient resources will resolve the outstanding issues.

Finding 2: Given optimistic assumptions (e.g., extraordinarily fast rates of research, development, and production), the kind of first- phase system that SDIO is considering might be technically deployable in the 1995-2000 period. Such a system might include:

- space-based hit-to-kill vehicles for attacking missile boosters and post-boost vehicles (PBVs) and
- ground-based rockets for attacking warheads before reentry into the atmosphere.

Depending on whether U.S. deployment schedules could be met, the effectiveness of countermeasures that should be available to the Soviets in that period, the numbers of offensive weapons they had deployed, and the nature of the attack, such a system might destroy anywhere from a few up to a modest fraction of attacking Soviet intercontinental ballistic missile (ICBM) warheads.

Again depending on the effectiveness of Soviet countermeasures, the BMD system might be able to carry out a strategy of "adaptive preferential defense," allowing it to protect successfully a useful fraction of certain sets of U.S. military targets.[1]

Additional defense capabilities would soon be needed to sustain this level of defense against either increased or more advanced, but clearly feasible, Soviet offenses.

One key to sustaining and improving defense capabilities in the 2000-10 period would be development of technologies to discriminate between missile warheads and decoys so that ground- and satellite-based rockets could effectively attack warheads in space. **Assuring functional survivability of space-based systems would also be essential (see Finding 4).**

Note: Complete definitions of acronyms and initialisms are listed in Appendix B of this report.

---

[1]SDIO officials argue that denial to the Soviets of high confidence of destroying as many of these targets they would like (as estimated by U.S. planners) would enhance deterrence of an aggressive nuclear attack.

As the Soviets phased in faster burning, faster weapon-dispensing ballistic missiles, it would probably be necessary to develop and deploy directed-energy weapons to intercept missiles in the boost phase and post-boost phases.

Given higher annual funding levels than so far appropriated, the SDI research and technology program might establish in the mid-to-late 1990s whether the components needed for warhead/decoy discrimination in a second-phase system would be feasible for deployment in the 2000-10 period. Also assuming higher funding levels than in the past, by the mid-to-late 1990s the SDI may determine the technical feasibility of deploying BMD directed-energy weapons in the 2005-15 period. The cost and survivability of such weapons will be among the key issues.

Finding 3: A rational commitment to a "phase-one" development and deployment of BMD before the second and third phases had been proven feasible, affordable, and survivable would imply: a) belief that the outstanding technical issues will be favorably resolved later; b) willingness to settle for interim BMD capabilities that would decline as Soviet offenses improved; or, c) belief that U.S. efforts will persuade the Soviets to join in reducing offensive forces and moving toward a defense-dominated world.

Finding 4: The precise degree of BMD system survivability is hard to anticipate, because it would depend on the details of measures for offensive attack on the BMD system and defensive countermeasures, on the tactics employed by each side, and on the inevitable uncertainties of battle. **It appears that direct-ascent nuclear anti-satellite weapons (DANASATs) would pose a significant threat to all three defense system phases, but particularly to the first two.** Numerous DANASATs could be available to the Soviets in the mid-1990s (e.g., ballistic missiles relying on mature technology, could probably be adapted to this role.) **Such weapons deployed in quantity, especially with multiple decoys, would threaten to degrade severely the performance of a first- or second-phase BMD system.** SDIO officials say, however, that adequate survivability measures could meet this threat. If the Soviets chose to attack the U.S. BMD satellites during emplacement, they might prevent full system deployment and operation altogether.

Finding 5: There has been little analysis of any kind of space-based threats to BMD system survivability. SDIO analyses assume that U.S. BMD technologies will remain superior to Soviet technologies (although such superiority would not necessarily guarantee U.S. BMD system survivability). **In particular, SDIO and its contractors have conducted no serious study of the situation in which the United States and the Soviet Union both occupy space with comparable BMD systems.** Such a situation could place a high premium on striking first at the other side's defenses. The technical (as well as political) feasibility of an arms control agreement to avoid such mutual vulnerability remains uncertain.

Finding 6: The survivability of BMD systems now under consideration implies unilateral U.S. control of certain sectors of space. Such control would be necessary to enforce "keep-out" zones against Soviet anti-satellite weapons or space mines during and after U.S. BMD deployment. Most BMD weapon technologies would be useful in an anti-satellite role before they reached the levels of power and precision needed for BMD. **Thus, the Soviets would not need to achieve BMD capabilities to begin to challenge U.S. control of, or even access to, space.**

Finding 7: The nature of software and experience with large, complex software systems indicate that there may always be irresolvable questions about how dependable BMD software would be and about the confidence the United States could place in dependability estimates. Existing large software systems, such as the long-distance telephone system, have become highly dependable only after extensive operational use and modification. In OTA's judgment, there would be a significant probability (i.e., one large enough to take seriously) that the first (and presumably only) time the BMD system were used in a real war, it would suffer a catastrophic failure.[1] The complexity of BMD software, the changing nature of system requirements, and the novelty of the technology to be controlled raise the possibility that the system may not even be able to pass the more realistic of the peacetime tests that could be devised for it. **The relatively slow rate of improvement in software engineering technology makes it appear unlikely to OTA that this situation will be substantially alleviated in the foreseeable future.** SDIO officials assert, however, that SDI software problems will be manageable, that adequate testing will be possible, and that previous military systems have been deployed without complete system testing (e.g., the Minuteman missile system, the Navy's AEGIS ship defense system.)

Finding 8: No adequate models for the development, production, test, and maintenance of software for full-scale BMD systems exist. Systems such as long-distance telephone networks, early missile defense systems such as SAFEGUARD, the AEGIS ship defense system, and air traffic control all differ significantly from full-scale BMD.

The only kind of BMD system for which the United States has software development experi-

---

[1]In ch. 9 catastrophic failure is arbitrarily defined as a decline of 90 percent or more in system performance, and there is a discussion of alternative approaches to the concept.

ence is a terminal defense system. Incorporating a boost-phase defense would add complexity to the software and require the inclusion of technologies hitherto untried in battle. Adding a mid-course defense would probably increase the software complexity beyond that of any existing systems.

Experts agree that new methods for producing and safely testing the system would be needed. Evolution would be key to system development, requiring new methods of controlling and disseminating software changes and assuring that each change would not increase the potential for catastrophic failure. OTA has found little evidence of significant progress in these areas.

Finding 9: There is broad agreement in the technical community that significant parts of the research being carried out under the SDI are in the national interest. There is disagreement about whether or not this research is best carried out within a program that is strongly oriented toward supporting an early 1990s BMD deployment decision, and that includes system development as well as research elements. This question was outside the scope of OTA's mandate and is not addressed in this report.

INTRODUCTION

Origin of This Study

The appropriations continuing resolution for fiscal year 1986 (Public Law 99-190) called for the Office of Technology Assessment to produce a "comprehensive classified study . . . together with an unclassified version . . . to determine the technological feasibility and implications, and the ability to survive and function despite a preemptive attack by an aggressor possessing comparable technology, of the Strategic Defense Initiative Program." In addition, the conference report accompanying this legislation specified that "this study shall include an analysis of the feasibility of meeting SDI computer software requirements." This report responds to that legislation.

After 30 years of BMD research, including the first few years of the Strategic Defense Initiative, the dedication and ingenuity of thousands of U.S. scientists and engineers have produced many impressive technical achievements. Such achievements may someday cumulate to form the basis for a highly effective BMD system. For now, however, many questions remain about the feasibility of meeting SDI goals.

Goals of the SDI

According to SDIO's annual report to Congress:

From the very beginning, the SDIO has maintained the same goal—to conduct a vigorous research and technology development program that could help to eliminate the threat of ballistic missiles and provide increased U.S. and allied security. Within this goal, the SDIO's task is to demonstrate SDI technology and to provide the widest range of defense options possible to support a decision on whether to develop and deploy strategic defenses.[2]

Such defenses might, to a greater or lesser degree, protect the American population from nuclear weapons. **But, contrary to the perceptions of many, SDIO has never embraced the goal of developing a leakproof shield against an unconstrained Soviet nuclear weapon threat.** It is the position of SDIO that President Reagan has not embraced that goal either.[3]

Rather, the organization, in its first 4 years, worked out a scenario that it argues could lead to President Reagan's stated "ultimate goal of eliminating the threat posed by strategic nuclear missiles . . . [which could] . . . pave the way for arms control measures to eliminate the weapons themselves."[4] The scenario, paraphrased from the SDIO report, is as follows:

1. a research and development program continues until the early 1990s, when a decision could be made by a future President and Congress on whether to enter into full-scale BMD engineering development;
2. the Defense Department begins full-scale development of a "first-phase" system while continuing advanced technology work;
3. the United States begins "phased deployment" of defensive systems, "designed so that each added increment of defense would enhance deterrence and reduce the risk of nuclear war"; although this "transition period" would preferably be jointly managed by the United States and the Soviet Union, U.S. deployments would proceed anyway; then

4. the United States completes deployment of "highly effective, multilayered defensive systems," which "could enhance significantly the prospects for negotiated reductions, or even the elimination, of offensive ballistic missiles."

Figures 1-1 and 1-2 are SDIO graphic representations of its development and deployment policies. Figure 1-1 illustrates that, as time goes on, newer, more capable BMD systems would be necessary to respond to advanced Soviet missile threats. Alternatively, it is argued, the *prospect* of such new systems might persuade the Soviets to accept U.S. proposals for joint reductions of offensive forces which might, in turn, obviate the need for new systems.

Figure 1-2 lists the kinds of information SDIO seeks to provide for BMD development decisions. According to this figure, SDIO does not see "complete understanding" of *later* system phases as prerequisite to *initial* commitments to develop and deploy BMD. Instead, it proposes to seek a "partial understanding" of the issues surrounding the follow-on phase and provide "reasonable estimates" that the necessary systems could be available as needed.

SDIO has affirmed the so-called "Nitze criteria" as requirements for the BMD options it offers: that the defenses be militarily effective, adequately survivable, and "cost-effective" at the margin, that is, "able to maintain their defensive capabilities more easily than countermeasures could be taken to try to defeat them."[5]

[5]SDIO, op. cit., footnote 2, p. IV-3.

[2]Strategic Defense Initiative Organization, *Report to the Congress on the Strategic Defense Initiative* (Washington, DC: April 1987), p. II-13.

[3]Lt. General James Abrahamson, personal communication to OTA staff, July 7, 1987.

[4]Ronald Reagan, televised speech, Mar. 23, 1983.

Figure 1-1.—The Path to "Thoroughly Reliable" Defenses

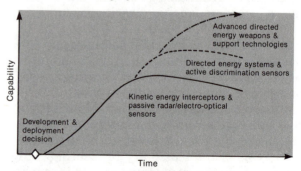

SOURCE: Department of Defense, Strategic Defense Initiative.

Figure 1-2.—Development Decision Content

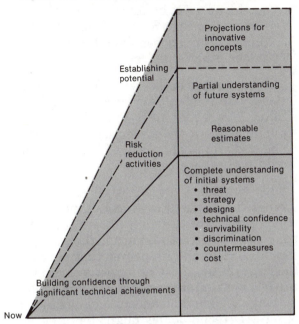

- Major Political Decision
- First of Several

SOURCE: Department of Defense, Strategic Defense Initiative.

Figure 1-3.—Mission Effectiveness Improves With Phased Deployment

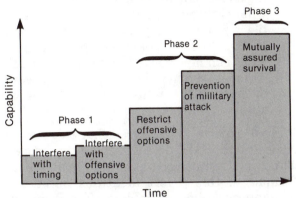

SOURCE: Department of Defense, Strategic Defense Initiative.

The SDIO has identified three "phases" of BMD deployments that might extend from the mid-1990s well into the 21st century (see figure 1-3). In mid-1987, SDIO proposed to proceed with a series of "technology validation experiments" to build and test hardware that might demonstrate the feasibility of components of a "first-phase" system. These experiments would require SDI budgets substantially above the levels appropriated by Congress in the first 4 years of the SDI.

In deciding about funding and directing the SDI program, then, Congress must decide whether to accept, modify, or reject the phased research and deployment scenario proposed by SDIO. Options for Congress include:

- accept the SDIO phasing scenario and plan now to decide in the early 1990s whether the full-scale engineering development of a first-phase system is feasible or attractive, but with only a "reasonable estimate" at that time of whether the second and third phases would later prove feasible; such a decision would imply an

intention to deploy the first phase in the mid-1990s while beginning full-scale development of the second phase, but the actual mid-1990s decisions would depend on the progress made;

- decide soon to begin immediately to develop whatever technologies may be available for deployment in the early 1990s, bearing in mind that space-based weapons are, in any case, unlikely to be deployable in quantity until 1995 or beyond;
- plan to delay a decision on a first phase of development and deployment until advanced research confirms that the second and third phases would be feasible;
- return to the pre-SDI BMD research program intended to hedge against technological surprise and to deter Soviet BMD deployment, but not intended to work toward a specific deployment scenario; or
- add to the previous option a new emphasis on terminal defense systems designed specifically to protect elements of U.S. strategic nuclear retaliatory forces.

Nature of This Report

To assist Congress in making these choices, this report surveys the technologies under research in the SDI and reports, as of early 1988:

- which technologies might be available for each of the projected deployment phases;
- what is known and what remains to be learned about the feasibility of develop-

ing those technologies and manufacturing and deploying weapons based on them;
- what can now be said about how survivable against enemy attack space-based BMD systems themselves may be; and
- what can now be said about the feasibility of producing the computer software of the requisite performance and dependability.

Most experts would agree that the technical issues for BMD present severe challenges. Thus, in attempting to provide the above information, this report identifies numerous demanding technical problems. The technical challenges to the SDI have been variously interpreted:

- **From the point of view of SDI officials and contractors, questions of feasibility are challenges that the application of sufficient time and resources can overcome.** They are working on most, if not all, the issues identified in this report.
- **In another view, the obstacles to effective BMD are great, and may not be overcome for several decades; nevertheless, the kind of research SDIO is sponsoring will have some long-term military and economic benefits for the United States whatever the SDI outcome.** In addition research on BMD is necessary to avoid technological surprise and to hedge against Soviet breakout from the Anti-Ballistic Missile (ABM) Treaty.
- **From a third point of view, the obstacles to accomplishment of the SDI's ultimate goals are so complex and so great that SDIO's goals are simply implausible.** Therefore, although the United States should conduct some BMD research to avoid technological surprise and to hedge against Soviet break out from the ABM Treaty, research needed for other military or civilian purposes should be carried out under other auspices.

OTA attempts in this report to present realistically the available evidence about SDI feasibility. The reader must decide how optimistic or pessimistic the evidence should lead one to be and which approach to BMD research would be best for the nation.

This summary organizes OTA's findings around the kinds of system designs, or "architectures," for the three phases that SDIO has recently been studying and discussing. **It should be recognized, however, that, except for the first phase, these architectures are illustrative, not definitive.** They provide a means of thinking about and understanding how various BMD technologies might be integrated into working systems and in what time frames. **Only the first represents SDIO's proposal for actual systems to develop and deploy.**

Table 1-1 outlines SDIO's suggested first phase of deployment; the time frame 1995-2000 is strictly an OTA assessment of a very optimistic but arguably plausible period for the beginning and completion of deployments of the various elements of the system phase. Table 1-2 outlines OTA's projections of the second and third phases of BMD deployment, based on SDIO descriptions of the technologies it is researching. The overlapping time frames (2000-10 and 2005-15) reflect OTA assessments of very optimistic but arguably plausible periods for the beginning and completion of deployments of the various elements of each system phase.

FIRST-PHASE TECHNOLOGIES AND SYSTEMS
(OTA Estimates Approximately 1995-2000)

Goals of a First-Phase System

In the fall of 1986 SDIO and its contractors began to study options for "first-phase" deployment of BMD. They attempted to design systems that the Nation might select in the late 1980s for initial deployments in the early 1990s. OTA estimates that as a practical matter—given the development, manufacturing, and space transportation needs—deployment

Table 1-1.—SDIO's Phase One Space- and Ground-Based BMD Architecture

Component	Number	Description	Function
First phase (approximately 1995-2000):			
Battle Management Computers	Variable	May be carried on sensor platforms, weapon platforms, or separate platforms; ground-based units may be mobile	Coordinate track data; control defense assets; select strategy; select targets; command firing of weapons
Boost Phase Surveillance and Tracking Satellite	Several at high altitude	Infrared sensors	Detect ballistic or ASAT missile launches by observing hot rocket plumes; pass information to tracking satellites
Space-based Interceptor Carrier Satellite	100s at several 100s of km altitudes	Each would carry about 10 small chemical rockets or "SBIs"; might carry sensors for tracking post-boost vehicles	On command, launch rockets at anti-satellite weapons (attacking BMD system), boosters, possibly PBVs.
Probe	10s	Ground-launched rocket-borne infrared sensors	Acquire RV tracks, pass on to ERIS interceptors
or			
Space Surveillance and Tracking System	10s	Satellite-borne infrared sensors	
or			
Space-based Interceptor Carrier Satellites	100s	Satellite-borne infrared sensors	
Exo-atmospheric Interceptors (ERIS)	1000s on ground-based rockets	Rocket booster, hit-to-kill warhead with infrared seeker	Cued by satellite-borne or rocket-borne infrared sensors, home in on and collide with RVs in late mid-course

SOURCE: Office of Technology Assessment, 1988.

of the systems discussed could not begin until 1995 or later and would probably take at least until the end of the 1990s to complete.

The first-phase options generally exclude *space-based* attack on Soviet reentry vehicles in mid-course (see table 1-1). While limiting the effectiveness of a BMD system, this omission eases the sensing, discrimination, and battle management tasks.

Depending on the nature of the Soviet attack assumed, and depending on the effectiveness of Soviet countermeasures, the kind of system described by SDIO officials system might destroy anywhere from a few up to a modest fraction of the (now predicted number of) Soviet reentry vehicles in a full-scale attack. The SDIO has suggested such a system as only the first phase of what in the longer term would expand to a more effective system. However, the organization cites as "an intermediate military purpose"

. . . denying the predictability of Soviet attack outcome and . . . imposing on the Soviets significant costs to restore their attack confidence. These first phases could severely restrict Soviet attack timing by denying them cross-targeting flexibility, imposing launch-window constraints, and confounding weapon-to-target assignments, particularly of their hard-target kill capable weapons. Such results could substantially enhance the deterrence of Soviet aggression.[6]

SDIO officials assert that the military effectiveness of the first-phase system would be higher than indicated by the percentages of reentry vehicles intercepted. They envisage a strategy of "adaptive preferential defense." In this strategy, first the space-based layer of defense disrupts the structure of the Soviet attack. Then the ground-based layer defends only those U.S. targets of the highest value *and* un-

---

[6]Ibid., footnote 2, p. II-11.

Table 1-2.—OTA's Projections of Evolution of Ground- and Space-Based BMD Architecture

Component	Number	Description	Function
Second phase (approximately 2000-2010) replace first-phase components and add:			
Airborne Optical System (AOS)	10s in flight	Infrared sensors	Track RVs and decoys, pass information to ground battle management computers for launch of ground-based interceptors
Ground-based Radars	10s on mobile platforms	X-band imaging radar	Cued by AOS, track RVs as they enter atmosphere; discriminate from decoys, pass information to ground battle managers
High Endo-atmospheric Interceptors	1000s	Rocket with infrared seeker, non-nuclear warhead	Collide with RVs inside atmosphere, but before RV nuclear detonation could cause ground damage
Space Surveillance and Tracking Satellite (SSTS)	50-100 at few 1000s of km.	High-resolution sensors; laser range-finder and/or imaging radar for finer tracking of objects;	Track launched boosters, post-boost vehicles, and ground or space-launched ASATs; Track RVs and decoys, discriminate RVs from decoys;
		May carry battle management computers	Command firing of weapons
Space-based Interceptor Carrier	1000s at 100s of km altitudes	Each carries about 10 small chemical rockets or "KKVs"; at low altitude; lighter and faster than in phase one	On command, launch rockets at anti-satellite weapons (attacking BMD system), boosters, PBVs, and RVs
Space-based Neutral Particle Beam (NPB)	10s to 100s at altitude similar to SSTS	Atomic particle accelerator (perturber component of interactive discrimination; additional sensor satellites may be needed)	Fire hydrogen atoms at RVs and decoys to stimulate emission of neutrons or gamma rays as discriminator
Detector Satellites	100s around particle beam altitudes	Sensors to measure neutrons or gamma rays from objects bombarded by NPB; transmitters send data to SSTS and/or battle management computers	Measure neutrons or gamma rays emitted from RVs: heavier objects emit measurable neutrons or gamma rays, permitting discrimination from decoys
Third phase (approximately 2005-2115), replace second-phase components and add:			
Ground-based Lasers, Space-based Mirrors	10s of ground-based lasers; 10s of relay mirrors; 10s to 100s of battle mirrors	Several laser beams from each of several ground sites bounce off relay mirrors at high altitude, directed to targets by battle mirrors at lower altitudes	Attack boosters and PBVs

SOURCE: Office of Technology Assessment, 1988.

der attack by the fewest reentry vehicles remaining after the winnowing by the space-based layer (see box 1-A). In this way, a meaningful fraction of a large set of "point targets" (e.g., missile silos or command posts) might be protected. Such a strategy, however, would require successful discrimination of RVs and decoys by the first-phase system sensors—a technology that remains to be proven. In addition, the Soviets could counter the strategy if they could modify their current offensive systems and deploy substantial numbers of maneuvering reentry vehicles.

Figure 1-3 presents SDIO's description of how the phases of SDI deployment might satisfy a spectrum of strategic goals. In evaluating the desirability of the goal of enhancing

Box 1-A.—Adaptive Preferential Defense

The SDIO has proposed that a first-phase ballistic missile defense system (see table 1-1) employ a tactic of "adaptive preferential defense." If successfully executed, this tactic could give an outnumbered defense some leverage against a large attack.

"Preferential defense" means defending only a selected set of high-value targets out of a larger number of targets under attack, thus concentrating the defensive forces. In essence, some targets would be sacrificed to increase the chances of survival of others.

"Adaptive preferential defense" means deciding during the course of the battle which targets to defend by adapting to the distribution of the attacking RVs (missile warheads) that survive earlier layers of defense. Of the high-value targets under attack, those with the fewest RVs coming at them are defended first.

Two Layers of Defense

A first-phase Strategic Defense System (SDS) would include orbiting interceptors and land-based interceptors. The orbiting interceptors would first destroy a small fraction of the rising Soviet missile boosters and post-boost vehicles. Since the SDS could not at this stage predict the targets of the Soviet missiles, the defense would not be preferential: instead, it would merely subtract at random some warheads from the Soviet attack. Even if the Soviets had initially aimed the same number of RVs at each target, some would have been filtered out by the first layer of defense.

Land-based rockets would carry other interceptors into space to destroy RVs that survived the space-based attack. Tracking sensors would determine the targets of the RVs to within several kilometers. Battle management computers would determine which high-value targets were under attack by only one RV and launch ground-based interceptors against them first, until all were covered. Then the computers would determine which targets were under attack by two RVs and assign interceptors to them, and so on. In this way, few interceptors would be wasted defending targets that would later be destroyed anyway by additional, unintercepted RVs.

A Simple Example

Suppose, for example, that 2000 RVs were attacking 1000 targets, with 1 RV aimed at each of 500 targets and 3 RVs aimed at each of another 500 targets. Assume that the defense had only 1000 interceptors (each with a 100 percent chance of interception). If the defense assigned interceptors randomly to 1000 of the 2000 attacking RVs, about 312 targets would be expected to survive (50 percent of those under single-RV attack and 12.5 percent of those under 3-RV attack). But if it assigned 500 interceptors to defend the targets under a single-RV attack, and then assigned 3 interceptors each to defend the next 166 targets, a total of 666 targets might be saved.

The SDI Case

Analysts for SDIO have concluded that a first-phase system applying this tactic could protect a useful fraction of selected U.S. targets against the kind of attack the Soviets are predicted to be able to carry out in the mid-1990s.

Some Qualifying Considerations

If feasible, an adaptive preferential defense would be suitable mainly for protecting fractions of redundant, single-aimpoint targets, such as missile silos, command posts, or other isolated military installations. Large-area, soft targets (such as cities or large military installations), would present so many potential aimpoints that defending, say, a third or a half of the aimpoints in a given area would be unlikely to assure survival of the that area. In addition, the aimpoints that could be defended would be small enough that the blast and fires from exploding nuclear weapons would affect neighboring "soft" target areas.

Serious questions also remain about whether SDIO's proposed phase-one BMD system could, in fact, successfully execute a strategy of adaptive preferential defense. In particular, if the infrared sensors of the tracking system could not discriminate between Soviet RVs and decoys, many of the ground-launched interceptors would be wasted on decoys. And if the Soviets could deploy many maneuvering reentry vehicles during the operational period of the first-phase defense system, the targets could not be accurately predicted and defended.

deterrence by forcing modification of Soviet attack plans, Congress should also be aware of the counter-arguments to that position:

- Many believe that, given the awesome consequences of nuclear war for the Soviet Union as well as for the United States, deterrence does not require enhancement because the U.S. threat of nuclear retaliation is already strong enough and can be kept so with timely strategic offensive modernization.
- Soviet military planners already face operational uncertainties, such as the unreliability of some percentage of deployed missiles.
- Other, less costly, more clearly feasible, methods of complicating Soviet attack plans, such as increased mobility for U.S. strategic forces, may be available.
- A corresponding Soviet deployment of BMD would impose uncertainties and costs on U.S. retaliatory attack plans.

The context for evaluating the goal of complicating Soviet attack plans changes, however, if one accepts the point of view that it is only the first benefit on a long-term path toward "mutual assured survival." In OTA's view, figure 1-4 illustrates, somewhat more realistically than figure 1-1, the *relative* levels of defense capability over time to be expected from phased BMD deployments, assuming their feasibility. **Whether or not initial capabilities could be sustained or improved upon depends on information not likely to be available by the early 1990s.**

Figure 1-4.—OTA Understanding of Projected Roles of BMD Deployment Phases

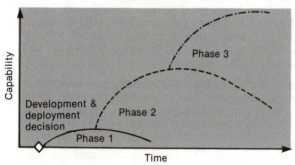

SOURCE: Office of Technology Assessment, 1988.

Technical Feasibility of Sensors and Weapons

In a first-phase system, space-based interceptors (SBI), also known as "hit-to-kill" or "kinetic kill" vehicles, would attack missile boosters and post-boost vehicles (PBVs), but not their dispensed reentry vehicles (RVs). The only mid-course interception would be near the end of that phase of missile trajectory by ground-based, exo-atmospheric interceptors.

Boost-Phase Surveillance and Tracking System (BSTS)

It appears feasible to develop by the mid 1990s high altitude satellites that would tell lower altitude satellites, or possibly SBIs themselves, where to look for rising missile boosters. Complex communications links among the satellites may be necessary to avoid enemy interference.

Carrier vehicles ("garages") for space-based hit-to-kill interceptors could receive data from the BSTS and track the boosters and post-boost vehicles with their own infrared sensors and laser range-finders.

Space-Based Interceptors (SBI)

A few hundred SBI carriers that would carry a few thousand kill vehicles (rocket interceptors) might destroy a modest fraction of Soviet missile warheads in the boost and post-boost phases. Such a system might be feasible to deploy starting in the projected first-phase period, but questions of engineering and cost remain unresolved. For example, considerable miniaturization of components for propulsion, guidance, and sensors would be needed to make a rocket fast enough to reach boosting missiles and light enough to be affordably launched into space. **Recent progress toward such miniaturization appears promising.** Substantial testing of prototype weapons would be necessary to show system feasibility. Once these technologies were proven, the affordable mass production of rocket-carrier vehicle systems for space deployment maintenance would remain a major challenge.

Exo-atmospheric Reentry Interceptor System (ERIS)

The Homing Overlay Experiment of 1984 and subsequent development work suggest that it is feasible to design a ground-launched interceptor capable of homing in on objects in space under favorable conditions. Such weapons could make up an Exo-atmospheric Reentry Interceptor System, or ERIS. More research, testing, and engineering remain to be done before the United States will know if the interceptor homing warheads can be produced cheaply enough to be affordable in large numbers. The ERIS, however, is likely to be deployable before space-based BMD interceptors.

Under study are both space-based and ground-launched infrared sensor systems and ground-based radars to direct ERIS interceptors to the vicinity of their targets. Both the satellite and ground-based systems remain to be developed, tested, and affordably produced. Upgraded versions of now existing ground-based radars might also provide initial tracking information to the interceptors.

In this first-phase architecture, the ERIS would rely on radars or on passive infrared detection and tracking of potential targets. **Whether or not these sensors could adequately discriminate between decoys and RVs disguised as decoys remains to be demonstrated. Without such discrimination, decoys could probably cause serious problems for this late mid-course layer of defense. Developing a decoy system like this is within Soviet capabilities.** Even with good discrimination by external sensors, the homing sensor on the interceptor itself would need to find the genuine RV if it were traveling within tens of meters of other, closely spaced objects. In general, many scientists and engineers working on the SDI have agreed that such countermeasures may well be feasible for the Soviets in the near term. However, both within and outside SDIO there is some dissent on the potential type, quality, number, and deployment times of Soviet countermeasures.

There is widespread agreement that much more experimentation is needed on missile "penetration aids" such as decoys. Very little SDI money has gone to the design, construction, and testing of penetration aids, although a full understanding of their potential and limitations would be key to developing and evaluating the effectiveness of a BMD system.

Besides decoys, ERIS interceptors could face many other false targets, particularly those generated by debris from PBV activity, from intercepts made earlier in the boost phase by the SBIs, or from deliberate Soviet countermeasures. Warm objects in the field of view of the ERIS interceptor's sensors might distract it from its target RV, even if it had originally been correctly pointed toward the RV by a probe or Space Surveillance and Tracking System (SSTS) sensor.

Software Feasibility

In the first-phase system designs now under consideration for SDI, hundreds of satellites would have to operate automatically and, at the same time, coordinate their actions with those of other satellites. The battle management system would have to track hundreds of thousands of objects and decide when and how to attack thousands of targets with little or no human intervention.

Among the most challenging software tasks for such a first-phase system would be designing programs for the largely autonomous operation of hundreds of satellites. But even for ground-based components of the system, the number of objects, the volume of space, and the brevity of time would preclude most human participation in battle management. **Humans would decide at what alert status and state of activation to place the system. Once the battle began, computers would decide which weapons to use when, and against what targets.**

A first-phase system would have the advantage of a simpler battle management problem than that of more advanced BMD systems. In particular, the space-based segment of the system would not attempt to track and discriminate among hundreds of thousands of mid-course objects, or to assign weapons to any of them. The distribution of SBI carrier vehicles would be so sparse that the targets within its range would not be in the range of neighboring carrier vehicles. It could, for the most part, safely shoot at a target within its own range without the risk that some other vehicle had shot at the same target. Some coordination among carrier vehicles would still be necessary because the continual relative motion of carriers and targets would leave some ambiguities about which targets were most appropriate for each carrier to fire interceptors at.

Although a first-phase system would have simpler tasks than a later system, its software would still be extremely complex. **The nature of software and experience with large, complex software systems, including weapon systems, together indicate that there would always be irresolvable questions about how dependable BMD software was, and also about the confidence we could place in dependability estimates.** Existing large, complex software systems, such as the U.S. long-distance telephone system, have become highly dependable only after extensive operational use and modification.

Extrapolating from past experience with software, it appears to OTA that the complexity of BMD, the uncertainty and changeability of the requirements it must meet, and the novelty of the technology it must control **would impose a significant probability of software-induced catastrophic failure in the system's first real battle.** The issue for SDI is the degree of confidence in the system that simulations and partial testing could provide. **SDIO officials argue that such tests will permit adequate confidence and that this issue is no more serious for the SDI than for all advanced military systems developed to date.**

Computer simulations would play a key role in all phases of a BMD system's life cycle. Battle simulations on a scale needed to represent realistically a full battle have not yet been attempted. Whether or not sufficiently realistic simulations can be created is a hotly debated

question. In particular, it is difficult for OTA to see how real-world data could be gathered to validate simulations of the phenomena that must be accounted for, such as multiple enemy missile launches, nuclear explosion-induced backgrounds, and enemy choices of countermeasures. **The differences between BMD software and previous complex software that is considered dependable suggests to some experts that BMD software might never be able to pass even its peacetime tests.** It should also be noted, however, that both the United States and the Soviet Union now base deterrence on an offensive nuclear delivery system that has never been operationally tested either.

While the United States could not be certain that a BMD system would work as intended, the Soviets could not be certain that it would not.[7] If they had at least some reason to believe the U.S. BMD system might be effective, they might be more deterred from attacking than before. On the other hand, the United States would not want to base a major change in its nuclear strategy on a BMD system in which it had little confidence. In the case of a first-phase system, whose effect on the strategic balance would be small anyway, the risk of software-induced system failure might seem acceptable.

The SDIO sees software problems as challenges to be overcome rather than as insurmountable obstacles to effective BMD. It is supporting some software research intended to address the challenges. Others argue that the limitations of software engineering technology and its relatively slow rate of improvement make it unlikely that dependable BMD software could be produced in the foreseeable future. Thus far, no new software engineering developments have appeared to contradict the latter view.

Survivability of a First-Phase System

The survivability of any BMD system will not be an all-or-nothing quality. The question

---

[7]Unless they had high confidence in the potential effectiveness of a secretly deployed countermeasure (perhaps a software bug planted by a saboteur programmer).

will be whether enough of a system's assets would survive for it to carry out its mission. The issue would then turn on whether the defense could make attacking the BMD system too costly for the offense, or whether the offense could make defending the BMD system to costly for the defense. (On the other hand, if the United States and the Soviet Union agreed to coordinate offensive weapon reductions and defensive deployments, they might do much to ameliorate BMD survivability problems.)

To protect satellites, the defense might employ combinations of such techniques as evasive maneuver, tracking denial, mechanical shielding, radiation hardening, electronic and optical countermeasures, and shoot-back. **Categorical statements that these techniques will or will not make any BMD system adequately and affordably survivable are not credible.** Judgments on specific cases would depend on the details of entire offensive and defensive systems and estimates of the techniques and tactics that the opponent would employ.

Space Mines

A space mine is a satellite that would trail another satellite and explode lethally either on command or when itself attacked. Space mines may or may not prove a viable threat to space-based BMD systems. Although *nuclear* space mines would be a very stressing threat, much more analysis would be needed to clarify the question of the viability of space mines. **After repeated attempts to locate such analysis within the SDIO or among its contractors, OTA concludes that it has not yet been adequately performed.**

Anti-Satellite Weapons (ASATs)

There is widespread agreement among experts on Soviet military practices that the initial Soviet response to U.S. BMD deployments would not be to try to develop and deploy systems based on similar technology. They would instead attempt a variety of less sophisticated countermeasures. These might include extensions of their current co-orbital, pellet-warhead anti-satellite weapon (ASAT), or else a ground-launched nuclear-armed ASAT (or "DANASAT," for "Direct Ascent Nuclear Anti-satellite" weapon).

The susceptibility of a BMD satellite system to degradation by DANASAT attack would depend on many complex factors, including:

- the maneuvering and decoying capabilities and the structural hardness of the BMD satellites;
- the precision and reaction time of Soviet space surveillance satellites; and
- the speed, numbers, decoying capabilities, and warhead power of the DANASATs.

Depending on target hardness, the radius of lethality of a nuclear warhead could be so great that the ASATs might need only inertial guidance (they need not home in on or be externally guided to the BMD asset). Thus they would not be susceptible to electronic countermeasures against homing sensors or command guidance systems. It appears that, at practical levels, maneuvering or radiation shielding of low-altitude satellites would not suffice against plausible numbers of rapidly ascending nuclear ASATs.

There appears to be no technical reason why the Soviets, by the mid-1990s, could not deploy DANASATs with multiple decoys among the nuclear warheads. Multiple decoys would likely exhaust the ability of the defenders to shoot back at the attack—unless extremely rapid discrimination of decoys and warheads were possible. It would be difficult to deny tracking of or to decoy near-earth satellites, especially large sensor platforms, if they were subjected to long periods of surveillance. If deployed while the satellites were under attack, satellite decoys would frequently not have time to lure DANASATs far enough away from the real targets.

If several SSTS satellites were a key element of a first-phase BMD system, they would be the most vulnerable elements. Otherwise, the most vulnerable elements of a first-phase BMD system would be the carrier vehicle satellites for the interceptors. The carrier vehicles, or CVs, as well as sensor satellites (BSTS and

SSTS) might employ combinations of various defense mechanisms against the ASAT threat. The SDIO argues that such combinations of measures potentially offer a high degree of survivability to space-based BMD system components.

For the near-term, however, no prototypes exist for carrier vehicles with these characteristics; the issue for SDI is whether in the 1990s such satellites could be developed, produced, and deployed. The Soviets, on the other hand, have already demonstrated the ability to field DANASATs by deploying rapidly accelerating, nuclear-armed anti-ballistic missiles near Moscow over 15 years ago and recently upgrading that system. Newer ballistic missiles, relying on mature technology, might also be adapted to this purpose. More advanced DANASATs appear feasible for the Soviets by the mid-1990s.

DANASATs would be a stressing threat against first-phase BMD systems and could probably degrade severely the performance of such systems. The SDIO argues, however, that strong survivability measures in the defensive system could successfully counter this threat.

The Soviets might also consider gradual attrition of the system in "peacetime." They might use co-orbital, non-nuclear ASATs or ground-based laser ASAT weapons to take "potshots" at the carrier vehicles.

Attack During Deployment

Should the Soviets deem U.S. space-based BMD deployments to be sufficiently threatening to their national security, they might resort to attack before the system was fully deployed. Whether they waited for full deployment or not, in the first-phase architecture SBI carrier vehicles would be so sparse that they would probably have only limited abilities to help defend one another, although each might to some extent defend itself. Other survivability measures, however, might offer some protection.

Attacks on Ground-Launched Systems

Insofar as the ERIS ground-launched interceptor relied on fixed, ground-based early warning radars for launch-commit information, its effectiveness could be greatly reduced by nuclear or jamming attacks on those radars.

Use of Comparable Technologies

Responses to threats from comparable Soviet weapon systems have not been defined by the SDIO or its contractors. Indeed, a working assumption of SDIO research and analysis has been that the United States could and would maintain a consistent lead over the Soviet Union in BMD technologies for the indefinite future. Because the Soviets lag in some of the technologies required for a space-based BMD system, it seems unlikely that they would attempt to deploy SBIs for BMD in the 1990s. A more attractive option for them might be to deploy kinetic-kill vehicles as a *defense suppression* system rather than as a *BMD* system—a less difficult task.

They could then choose orbital configurations designed to give their weapons temporary local numerical advantages over the U.S. BMD system. In a shoot-out between the systems, at a time of their choosing, the Soviets might then eliminate or exhaust those SBI carrier vehicles within range of a Soviet ICBM launch salvo. **Effective non-nuclear ASATs would, however, require good space surveillance capabilities.** If a BMD system were to cohabit space with a competent defense suppression system (possibly embodying a lower technical capability), the side that struck first might eliminate the other.

The fact that a lower level of technology would be needed for defense suppression than for BMD could drive a race to control access to space as soon as possible. For example, U.S. space-based ASATs might be needed to prevent Soviet ASAT deployments that could in turn interfere with U.S. BMD deployments.

SECOND-PHASE TECHNOLOGIES AND SYSTEMS
(OTA Estimates Approximately 2000-10)

Goals

The goal of a phase-two system would be to "enhance deterrence," first by imposing uncertainty on Soviet strategic attack plans, then by denying the Soviets the ability to destroy "militarily significant" portions of important sets of targets (such as missile silos or command and control nodes) in the United States. As a result, **the Soviets would retain the ability to inflict massive damage on the U.S. economy and population, but would lack the ability to accomplish certain precise military objectives.** At least, such denial should decrease whatever incentives may now exist for the Soviets to commit nuclear aggression (though analysts disagree on whether such incentives do now exist); at best, the Soviets might be induced to negotiate away their militarily obsolescent missiles.

If the Soviets believed they could restore their compromised military capabilities at an acceptable price, they might attempt to do so by adding new offensive weapons and by attempting both active and passive countermeasures against the U.S. BMD system. Even if they did not believe they could recapture lost military capabilities, but only believed that they were in danger of losing any credible nuclear retaliatory power against the United States, they might still attempt to employ BMD countermeasures. **If, however, they concluded that countermeasures would be futile, they might, as conjectured in the "SDI scenario," agree to mutual offensive arms reductions as a way of containing the U.S. threat.** In that case, BMD combined with effective air defenses might offer much higher levels of protection of military and even civilian targets.

Currently available BMD technology for nuclear-armed, ground-based interceptors would probably allow the United States to build a system that could deny the Soviets confidence in destroying substantial fractions of certain sets of hardened or mobile targets.[8] An SDI "phase-one," non-nuclear system may also be able to provide such protection. This is more likely to be the case if the defense could be configured to defend subsets of targets preferentially, and in such a way that the Soviets could not detect which targets were defended more heavily. Moreover, if the Soviets continued to aim weapons at highly defended targets, they would have fewer weapons left over to aim at softer military and civilian targets.

There is less evidence that the United States could deny the Soviets the ability to strike with high confidence at many other kinds of militarily valuable, but more vulnerable, targets. There are, however, many ideas and some promising technologies for pursuing this goal.

Achieving the strategic goals of this kind of system implies air defenses of comparable potential. Otherwise, except for the most urgent targets, the Soviets could shift strategic missions from ballistic to cruise missiles.

Technical Feasibility

Airborne Optical System (AOS)

An airborne infrared sensor system would tell ground-based radars where to look for reentering objects. **Such a system appears technically feasible during the 1990s.** The infrared sensors, however, might be subject to confusion by high-altitude light-scattering ice crystals created as debris reentered the atmosphere, or by nuclear detonations intended to blind the system.

Ground-Based Radar (GBR)

Imaging radar systems would observe lighter decoys slowing down more quickly than gen-

---

[8]See U.S. Congress, Office of Technology Assessment, *Ballistic Missile Defense Technologies*, OTA-ISC-254 (Washington, DC: U.S. Government Printing Office, September 1985), pp. 33-34.

uine RVs. Computers using this information would launch very high acceleration rockets (HEDI) with infrared homing sensors toward the RVs. **Tests to date indicate that such radars are feasible, but unresolved questions include their susceptibility to interference from nuclear burst, to jamming by radio-frequency jammers on incoming warheads, to signal-processing overloads created by many simultaneously reentering objects, and to deception by carefully designed RV's and decoys.**

High Endo-atmospheric Interceptor (HEDI)

A rocket-borne high endo-atmospheric defense interceptor would attack incoming RVs after they had begun to reenter the atmosphere.

Because the rising interceptor's friction with the atmosphere would cause it to heat up, a cooled crystal window would have to protect its homing sensor. Experiments suggest that such windows are feasible, although researchers have not yet established whether they could be rapidly mass-produced.

Because the HEDI would have a limited "divert" capability, the sensor system would need to give it a very accurate target track. A relatively short-range ground-based radar, using the upper atmosphere as a discriminant against decoys, might be the easiest way to provide such a track. This tracking method, however, would restrict each interceptor to protecting a relatively small area. Intensive coverage of all U.S. territory would demand too many thousands of missiles. Instead, the HEDI mission would be to "mop up" small numbers of warheads leaking through the earlier defensive layers. Thus the most useful mission for HEDI might be to protect specific, localized targets, such as ICBM silos.

SDIO officials point out, however, that passive infrared sensors or long-range radars may be able to discriminate between RVs and decoys in space. Then the High Endo-Atmospheric Interceptor could be committed earlier and thus defend a much larger area. Nevertheless, in order to avoid the impression of providing a defense designed primarily to protect hardened strategic targets, rather than U.S. terri-

tory in general, the SDIO elected to omit the HEDI and its associated sensors (AOS and a terminal imaging radar or TIR) from its proposals for a first-phase BMD system.[9] Technically, however, initial deployments in the late 1990s period appear plausible.

SSTS and RV/Decoy Discrimination

A phase-two system would add to the first-phase architecture dozens of space-based sensors that could accurately track thousands of RVs and decoys from the moment of their deployment from the PBVs. Such sensors would require electro-optical focal planes of unprecedented size, or high-resolution laser radar systems, and considerable signal processing ability.

It seems likely that, by the time a substantial U.S. BMD system could be in place, the Soviets could deploy many reentry vehicle decoys and RVs disguised as decoys. Unless these RVs and decoys could be destroyed on their boosters and post-boost vehicles, some means of distinguishing between them would have to be developed. Otherwise, the defense's ammunition would be quickly exhausted.

In the terminal, "endo-atmospheric" phase of interception, the atmosphere might filter out all but the heaviest and most sophisticated decoys. But too many reentering objects might overwhelm local defensive sensors and weapons. **In sum, effective discrimination in the mid-course of ballistic missile trajectories would be necessary to a highly effective BMD system.**

One proposed technique for RV/decoy discrimination is a laser radar system that might observe the movements of RVs and decoys as, or after, they were dispensed from PBVs. Subtle differences in the behaviors of the less massive decoys might give them away. Concealing deployments off PBVs or other tactics might counter this technique, but much research both on decoy technologies and spaceborne laser radars will be needed to judge the potential of either.

---

[9]Lt. General James Abrahamson, personal communication to OTA staff, July 7, 1987.

Various methods of passive and active discrimination have been suggested, including multiple wave-length infrared sensors, laser radar, and microwave radar. But if the Soviets could build sufficiently sophisticated decoys, differentiating decoys and RVs might be impossible without some means of externally perturbing all the objects being tracked and observing differences in how they react to such perturbations. This technique is known as "interactive discrimination."

So far there is no proven candidate system for the task of interactive discrimination. The program receiving the most funding has been the neutral particle beam (NPB). In this concept, a space-based atomic accelerator would fire high-energy neutral hydrogen or deuterium atoms at suspect objects. A sensor would then detect the neutrons or gamma rays emitted from heavier objects struck by the hydrogen atoms. A hundred or more NPB platforms, and perhaps several hundred sensor satellites, would be needed for a complete system. It may be more appropriate to consider such a system for a phase-three, rather than phase-two, BMD architecture.

A space test of a subscale NPB platform was scheduled for the early 1990s, although recent budget cutbacks have made the experiment's status unclear. Key issues determining the feasibility of NPB systems will include cost, the rapid and precise ability to point the beams at thousands of objects in a few tens of minutes, and the ability to gather and correlate the return information.

Other interactive discrimination ideas include, for example, space-based high energy lasers that would "tap" target objects. The greater recoil of lightweight decoys would give them away.

Kinetic Energy Weapons

Missile boosters that completed their boost phase in about 120 to 140 seconds—slightly faster than current modern ICBMs—would greatly reduce the effectiveness of rocket-propelled SBIs in the boost phase. They could still intercept post-boost vehicles. However,

fast RV dispensing technologies could reduce kill in the post-boost phase. On the other hand, if such countermeasures had forced the Soviets to greatly reduce missile payloads, mid-course discrimination might become easier: then the Soviets could only afford to deploy fewer, less sophisticated decoys. Improved SBIs, even though ineffective against boosters, could be useful in the mid-course. They would require long-wave infrared sensors for homing in on small, cold RVs. Alternatively, laser designators on sensor satellites might illuminate RVs with light that SBI sensors could see and track.

It seems likely that by roughly the period projected for the first phase ERIS (Exo-atmospheric Reentry Interceptor System) missiles could be refined to the specifications now envisioned. Provided that the challenge of RV-decoy discrimination had been overcome, they would begin to provide an important layer of missile defense. **If the discrimination problem could not be solved, ERIS interceptors would be of doubtful utility. If it could be solved, ERIS effectiveness in phase two would be much greater than in phase one.**

The question for HEDI in the phase-two period is whether the Soviets could deploy many maneuvering reentry vehicles to evade the system and sophisticated reentry decoys to deceive it. The more effective the earlier defensive layers might be, the less the Soviets could afford to use precious missile payload weights on heavier RVs and decoys. **However, numerous, even slightly, maneuvering reentry vehicles, especially with depressed missile trajectories, could probably evade HEDIs unless the interceptors were equipped with nuclear warheads.**

Software Feasibility

A phase-two BMD system such as envisaged here would need to account for hundreds of thousands (or more) of objects as they were dispensed into space. It would require a highly complex communications net for keeping track of all BMD space assets, boosters, PBVs, RVs, decoys, and space debris, then assigning weapons to intercept the selected targets. Concepts, but so far no genuine designs, exist for "partitioning" the battle space into local networks of sensors and weapons (taking into account that different combinations of satellites would be constantly shifting in and out of given regions of space).

In terms of sheer computing power, continued advances seem likely to provide the processing capacities needed for advanced BMD. The most difficult hardware engineering task will be to combine the qualities of high capacity and radiation hardness in space-qualified electronics.

A BMD designed for boost, post-boost, midcourse, and terminal battle is likely to be the most complex system ever constructed. In OTA's judgment, there would be no precedents for estimating the likelihood of the BMD software system's working dependably the first time it was used in a real battle. Moreover, no adequate models for the development, production, test, and maintenance of software on the scale needed currently exist. The system's complexity, coupled with the need to automate the use of technologies previously unused in battle, might result in unforeseen problems dominating the software life cycle. For example, large, complex systems that undergo continuous change sometimes reach states where new changes introduce errors at a greater rate than they remove errors.

A BMD system—as has been the case with other strategic nuclear systems—could be tested only with computer simulations and some piecemeal hardware exercises. **Furthermore, no existing systems must operate autonomously (without human intervention) in the face of deliberate enemy attempts to destroy them.**

Whether the risks of catastrophic BMD failure resulting from the inevitable software errors in a system of this magnitude would be unacceptable is a policy decision, not a technical one, that the President and the Congress would ultimately have to make. They would have to weigh those risks against the perceived risks and benefits of *not* building a BMD system but deploying national resources elsewhere. **As with a first-phase system, another consideration would be the likelihood that the Soviets could not be confident that the BMD system would not work as advertised, and that they might be deterred from trying to find out by attacking.** (On the other hand, if the Soviets found a way to break into and tamper with the software system without U.S. knowledge, they might be confident that they *could* defeat it.)

Phase-Two Survivability

More advanced BMD systems would be designed and deployed with more advanced self-protection or survivability measures. Ground-launched, nuclear-armed ASATs (DANASATs) would continue to be a threat. The additional SBI carriers available after the year 2000, however, could begin to provide mutual defense for one another, which would not be possible in the first-phase architecture.

By that time, on the other hand, the Soviets could develop more advanced anti-satellite weapons and space surveillance sensor systems. **Most BMD weapon technologies for use in space or against targets in space are likely to achieve ASAT capabilities before they become applicable to BMD missions.**

Direct-Ascent Nuclear ASATS

As with phase one, **DANASATs would be particularly threatening to a "phase-two" system.** The U.S. Space Surveillance and Tracking System and any associated interactive discrimination platforms would now be primary targets for Soviet defense suppression attacks. Since many of these satellites would be at higher altitudes than the SBI garages, they would have more time to maneuver away from attackers. But they would also be heavier and therefore more fuel-costly to maneuver. They would be more difficult to shield against nuclear radiation.

Space Mines

The United States would have to consider the possibility of Soviet attempts to co-orbit nuclear or non-nuclear space mines with these platforms as they were being deployed. Such "mining" might be carried concurrently with the deployment of the BMD system assets. System designers have proposed "keep-out" zones to keep potential attacking weapons outside their lethal ranges. Whether the United States (or any power) could achieve this kind of dominance of near-earth space remains to be seen. **In any case, very little analysis has as yet been carried out by the SDIO or its contractors on interim and long-term space-based threats to BMD systems.**

Comparable Technologies

If the Soviets could develop technologies comparable to those of the United States, three might be of special concern. One would be advanced space-based surveillance systems permitting better-timed, more accurate ASAT attacks. Second would be the development of space-based neutral particle beam weapons, which could be very effective anti-satellite weapons from great range. **Third, even though laser weapons might not have achieved the power levels necessary for the BMD missions, laser ASATs could begin to pose substantial threats to U.S. space assets.** If only for self-defense, the United States might have to consider deploying directed-energy ASATs in the phase-two architecture period.

THIRD-PHASE TECHNOLOGIES AND SYSTEMS
(OTA Estimates Approximately 2005-15)

Goals

In the SDI scenario, the first goal of a phase-three BMD system would be to sustain the capabilities of the second-phase system as more advanced Soviet countermeasures came on line. Eventually, the system might achieve still higher levels of protection. As originally presented by the Administration, the SDI was to identify a path to the "assured survival" of the U.S. population against nuclear attack. An intermediate step on this path would be to design a BMD system that would make nuclear ballistic missiles "impotent and obsolete." In this scenario, the Soviets would then be confronted with the choice of negotiating away obsolescent missiles or engaging in a costly defensive-offensive arms race that would sooner or later leave their offensive missiles unable to penetrate U.S. or allied territory. Either way, in the end few or no nuclear ballistic missiles could reach U.S. territory.[10]

As with a second-phase system, extremely effective air defenses would be an essential complement to an extremely effective BMD system. And, as with earlier phases, deep reductions in offensive forces (by arms control agreement) could increase the effectiveness of the system.

Technical Feasibility

Directed-Energy Weapons

Directed-energy weapons for boost-phase interception are still far in the future. **It is unlikely that confidence in their feasibility could be established by the early 1990s even with requested SDIO budgets.** OTA judges that experimental evidence of the feasibility of BMD directed-energy weapons (DEW) is at least a decade away.[11] It is extremely unlikely that confidence in DEW could be established in the next several years, given continuation of the actual appropriation pattern.

---

[10]SDIO reports to Congress make no mention of "assured survival," and cite as the ultimate objective of the SDI to "secure a defense-dominated strategic environment in which the U.S. and its allies can deny to any aggressor the military utility of ballistic missile attack." SDIO, op. cit., footnote 2, p. II-11. Other SDIO documents, however, do still refer to the goal of "mutually assured survival" (see figure 1-3).

---

[11]A similar conclusion was reached by a committee of the American Physical Society in 1987. *Science and Technology of Directed Energy Weapons: Report of the American Physical Society Study Group* (April 1987), p. 2.

Ultimately however, directed-energy weapons may be necessary to intercept long-range ballistic missiles and direct-ascent ASAT weapons in the boost and post-boost phases. **If the Soviets could, over 15 or 20 years, develop and begin to deploy very fast-burn, laser-hardened boosters with single (or few) warheads (and associated decoys) and if they deployed those boosters at concentrated launch sites, the burden even on directed-energy weapons would be great.** In that case, the time available for attacking each booster might be so short as to drive very high the requirements for power levels, retargeting speed, and numbers of directed-energy weapons. (However, PBVs would continue to be vulnerable to DEWs.)

Fast-burning Soviet boosters appear technically plausible—the main issue would be cost. The Soviets would have to deploy enough of these boosters to continue to deliver hundreds of thousands of RV decoys into the mid-course, and they would have to be aware that, for example, if U.S. DEWs achieved significant improvements in retargeting time, they might neutralize a good fraction of the Soviets' expensive fast-burning fleet.

Although some work has continued on chemical lasers, and proposed future budgets would increase the share going to them, most SDI laser funding in 1987 went to the free electron laser (FEL). The most likely way to deploy such lasers would be on the ground, with orbiting relay and battle mirrors to focus laser beams on Soviet boosters and PBVs. **Scientists have made significant progress in FEL research, but they are a long way from having established the feasibility of a weapon.** The SDIO has sponsored construction of laboratory versions of FELs and plans a major test facility at White Sands Missile Range. Among the outstanding issues to be studied with these experimental lasers are whether FELs can be made bright enough at useful wavelengths and the feasibility of optical techniques for successfully passing very high energy laser beams out of and back into the atmosphere. Other outstanding issues include: whether large, agile beam directing optics can be affordably manufactured and reliably based in space; the cost of building and maintaining several large laser ground station complexes; and the survivability of space mirrors and ground stations against defense suppression attacks.

Other directed-energy concepts are under consideration. Neutral particle beams (NPBs), which do not penetrate the atmosphere, might engage those missile boosters and PBVs that operated above about 120 kilometers. Advanced booster and warhead dispensing technologies, however, might evade NPBs. (Unlike most lasers, however, NPBs could penetrate and destroy reentry vehicles in the mid-course.) Another directed-energy weapon may be the nuclear-explosion pumped x-ray laser, which also could not penetrate far into the atmosphere. For various reasons, the x-ray laser appears more promising as an anti-satellite weapon than as an anti-missile weapon.

Software Feasibility

If an interactive discrimination system were added in the phase-two architecture, the phase-three architecture would not pose significantly different software challenges and prospects from the second phase. The very fine pointing and tracking needed for laser weapons could impose significant additional computing requirements on sensors.

As time went on, Soviet defense suppression threats—weapons aimed at the BMD system itself—could grow more intense. The additional burdens of self-defense for the BMD system against advanced ASAT threats would add to the complexity of software requirements. The challenges to producing dependable software cited above would persist in phase three.

Phase-Three Survivability

If large directed-energy weapon platforms were deployed in space (whether these were laser generators with beam directors or only relay and battle mirrors for ground-based lasers), they would themselves become prime high-value targets for defense suppression attacks. Unless they were powerful enough to be deployed at rather high altitudes, they would have a difficult time either denying tracking to enemy sensors or maneuvering out of the way of attacks. They would probably have to defend themselves (and one another) as well as depend on "escort" interceptors. Third-phase directed-energy weapons systems could be survivable against the current or first-phase Soviet DANASAT threat; the question is, would they be survivable against a later DANASAT threat that might be in place by the time the directed-energy weapons were deployed?

Directed-Energy ASATs

Long before directed-energy weapons such as lasers or particle beams achieve the capabilities they would need as BMD weapons, they could be effective anti-satellite weapons. Anti-satellite laser weapons, if placed in space before more capable BMD laser weapons, might successfully attack the latter as they were being deployed.

In some cases, such as the nuclear bomb-pumped x-ray laser, the most likely application of an advanced directed-energy weapon would be as an ASAT. What little analysis has been done so far indicates that x-ray laser ASATs launched from the ground to fire from the upper atmosphere would be difficult, if not impossible, to counter. However, the feasibility of x-ray laser weapons remains to be demonstrated.

Soviet Possession of Comparable Technologies

As one attempts to project various combinations of survivability techniques and various modes of anti-satellite attack into the far term, the situation becomes even hazier. **It does appear that two DEW ballistic missile defense systems occupying space could pose risks of crisis instability.** The side that struck first in a simultaneous attack on all the other's DEWs might seize an advantage. Much would depend on each side's tactics and its ability to jam, spoof, or disable the sensors on the other side. At best, each side might neutralize the other's BMD system, leaving both defenseless but with nuclear retaliatory capabilities (as is the case today). At worst, the side striking first might unilaterally neutralize the other's BMD (and other military space assets), leaving him open to nuclear blackmail. Mutual fears of this possibility might lead to crisis instability.

On the other hand, if the two sides could define precisely balanced deployments and rules for ensuring the mutual survivability of their systems, and then arrive at verifiable arms control agreements providing for them, they might avoid such instability.

IMPORTANT GENERAL ISSUES

Costs

Some experts in space systems argue that the major cost driver of space-based BMD would be the manufacture of hundreds or thousands of novel, yet highly reliable, spacecraft. The SDIO suggests that its research into new production techniques would result in substantially reduced costs. Until such techniques have actually been demonstrated in practice, this suggestion will be difficult to verify.

In any case, space transportation cost would be a major challenge. The SDIO has spoken of ultimately requiring launch operating costs one-tenth those existing today (not counting the costs for development of such a system). For the nearer term (late 1990s) the goal appears to be a threefold operating cost reduction. **For the very near term, planners are being told to design systems that could evolve into less costly ones, but there is little expectation of immediate first-phase savings.**

Components today are conceptual, so reliable cost estimates are not possible. Efforts to improve "producibility" and operations costs for SBIs, ERIS, and HEDI are also conceptual.

System architects' estimates put the costs of designs comparable to the second-phase architecture in the low hundreds of billions of dollars. Given that the United States would have to engineer, build, and deploy entirely new classes of space systems, cost estimates today are shaky at best. For any given component, unanticipated difficulties might increase costs, or technical breakthroughs might decrease costs. **The SDIO has produced a rough estimate for the cost of a phase-one system: $75 billion to $150 billion.**

Phase-three architectures are now so loosely defined and understood that few if any contractor cost estimates exist.

Nobody now knows how to calculate, let alone demonstrate to the Soviets, the cost-exchange ratio between offense and defense. Detailed defensive system designs and a thoroughly researched understanding of potential offensive countermeasures may help. But unless the ratio appears obviously to be much greater than one-to-one, it will be extremely difficult to determine whether the criterion of "cost-effectiveness at the margin" has been met by any proposed BMD system. At least in the first phase, it appears that the Soviets would have a strong incentive to add missiles, warheads, and countermeasures to attempt to restore their strategic nuclear capabilities. **The question would be whether the Soviets were persuaded that in the long run the defense system would evolve into one that cost less per Soviet RV destroyed.**[12]

Timing and Evolution

The Strategic Defense Initiative Organization (SDIO) has not pursued the SDI as an open-ended research program to be concluded only when a certain level of knowledge was attained. Instead, the research has been strongly oriented toward trying to provide the basis for

an "informed decision" on BMD full-scale engineering development by the early 1990s (the exact year, although it appears widely in the press, is classified). Nevertheless, **implied in the SDI program was that whatever information might be available by the early 1990s, proposals for deployment would be offered.**

Congress, however, has not funded the SDI at the level that the SDIO asserted was necessary to permit an informed decision about such proposals by the early 1990s. Nevertheless, by cutting back parallel technology programs and longer-term research while preserving programs believed to have near-term promise, the SDIO has attempted to maintain the goal of making detailed deployment proposals by only 1 year later than the appointed date.

In late 1986 and in 1987 the SDIO began developing the "phase-one" BMD system architecture described above. In its 1987 annual report to Congress, the SDIO said that its **study of the first phase of a phased deployment ". . . does not constitute a decision to deploy. Such a decision cannot be made now."**[13] OTA concurs. First, the required space transportation system is unlikely to be available for early 1990s deployment. Second, the reductions in SBI weights essential to deploying significant numbers of effective weapons are not yet available. Third, the U.S. aerospace industry would have to engineer, mass produce, and deploy entire new classes of satellite systems. Fourth, cost estimates for all these steps today are shaky at best. The SDIO does argue that the first-phase option would lay the groundwork for the deployment of subsequent phases. This could be true if the subsequent phases were in fact known to be feasible, affordable, survivable, and cost-effective at the margin— and if the first-phase system retained some capability against a responsive Soviet threat.

Every part of the complex development, production, and deployment scheme would have to work well and on schedule. Otherwise, the Soviets could be well on the way to neutralizing the first-phase architecture before it was

---

[12]This discussion does not address whether the Soviets would accept the cost/exchange ratio criterion for their own decisions or whether they might simply do their best at improving their offense and hope the United States might not follow the ensuing offensive-defensive arms race through to its expensive conclusion.

[13]SDIO, op. cit., foot note 2, p. II-10.

fully in place. Countermeasures could have greatly degraded SBI capabilities. For example, as the booster rocket burning times of Soviet missiles decreased (a process already occurring as the Soviets move to solid-fueled boosters), fewer SBI's could reach the boosters before their post-boost vehicles had separated and begun to dispense reentry vehicles and decoys. New post-boost vehicles, which would in any case be harder to track and hit than boosters, could also dispense their payloads more rapidly. Without altering their rocket technologies, the Soviets could concentrate their ICBM bases so that fewer SBIs would be in range when many ICBMs were launched at once (that is, the "absentee ratio" would be higher). **While the Soviets would not find all such countermeasures cheap and easy, one should compare their cost and difficulty to those of developing and deploying a vast new space-based BMD system.**

Adding more SBIs to the BMD constellation would allow attacks on more boosters, but the numbers of SBIs needed would become increasingly prohibitive as the Soviet ICBM force evolved. On the other hand, if the Soviets could not soon reduce the burn-times of their post-boost vehicles, SBI effectiveness might endure for some time—assuming that the first-phase SBI infrared sensors could effectively home in on the colder PBVs.

Although a phase-one architecture may be presented to Congress as the first step of a "phased deployment," research on the later phases is far from demonstrating that those succeeding phases will be feasible, affordable, and compatible with first-phase systems. The feasibility of fully trustworthy battle management software systems may never be entirely demonstrable. The feasibility of directed-energy weapons and interactive discrimination systems remains to be demonstrated, and persuasive evidence one way or the other will probably not be available until after 1995. The feasibility of a new, post-2005 generation of Soviet fast-burn boosters that could stress even directed-energy weapons remains plausible and cannot be discounted.

Thus a "phased deployment" in which only the first phase was shown to be feasible would not necessarily be able to evolve and adapt to

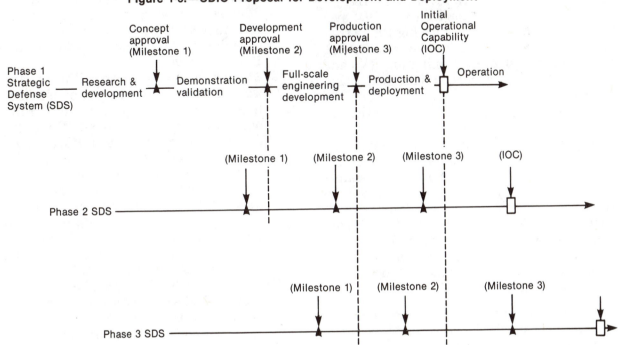

Figure 1-5.—SDIO Proposal for Development and Deployment

SOURCE: Office of Technology Assessment, adopted from Department of Defense information on the Strategic Defense Initiative.

a responsive Soviet threat. The SDIO plan calls for completing "demonstration and validation" of phase-two concepts before actual production and *deployment* of phase one. **Therefore,**

- **commitment in the early 1990s to a phase-one development would imply confidence that phases two and three will ultimately prove feasible, and**
- **commitment in the mid-1990s to phase-one deployment would require an act of faith that phase three would prove feasible.**

Otherwise, depending on how long deployment actually took and how effective the Soviet response was, either the first- or second-phase systems could be reduced to only modest effectiveness or impotence even before deployment was completed.

SDIO officials and contractors have surmised that the technologies needed to maintain and extend the defensive capabilities of first- and second-phase systems into the farther term will in fact become available. If a continuing, vigorous research and development program produced the necessary technologies, and if Soviet offensive developments could not keep pace, the first-phase concept **might** evolve into a more advanced BMD system. If the Soviets responded to the SBI system by developing faster-burning PBVs that could carry only much reduced payloads, then the ultimate task of discriminating RVs and decoys in the mid-course could be greatly simplified. (This conclusion assumes that the Soviets could not afford at the same time to double the size of their missile fleet.) The United States could add sophisticated SSTS satellites and SBIs with improved sensors. If Soviet decoys were few enough and simple enough, the sensor satellites might be able to track and discriminate RVs and decoys in mid-course, thus allowing improved hit-to-kill weapons to attack RVs individually after they were dispensed. Or, interactive discrimination techniques might turn out to make RV/decoy discrimination feasible.

OTA concludes that, if shown to be technically feasible and desirable, second-phase system production and deployment could not begin until around the year 2000 or be completed much before 2010. Soviet countermeasures coming into deployment by then could include more missiles, advanced RVs (possibly including maneuvering RVs or "MaRVs") and decoys, faster rocket boosters and post-boost vehicles, concentrated launch-sites for boosters, and advanced anti-satellite weapons. The utility of space-based SBIs for boost-phase interception would then be severely limited. Depending on whether and when the Soviets could field faster-dispensing PBVs, the SBIs might be of some utility for PBV interception. Overall system effectiveness, however, would probably depend heavily on how well the mid-course discrimination challenge had been met.

If the Soviets developed high-payload, fast-dispensing PBVs, the United States might have to add laser weapons to the defense system to increase boost- and post-boost intercepts to reduce the mid-course discrimination burden. As is noted below, however, even this step might not suffice.

As of 1988, three uncertainties about the viability of a second-phase system especially stand out:

1. evidence demonstrating effective and affordable technology for discriminating Soviet nuclear warheads from decoys will probably not be available before the mid-1990s, if then;
2. a follow-on, directed-energy BMD system would be needed to restore or maintain defense effectiveness once faster-burning boosters were able to evade SBIs; but directed-energy weapons for BMD may or may not be technically feasible; such feasibility is very unlikely to have been determined by the early 1990s; if the Soviets were able to field a few thousand very fast-burning boosters with one warhead and several decoys each, even directed-energy weapons might not suffice to maintain a high level of defense effectiveness;
3. the survivability of a space-based system itself against a defense suppression attack by Soviet weapons likely to be available after the year 2000 may not have been determined by the early 1990s.

Ballistic missile defense deployments of dubious long-term effectiveness could stimulate the Soviet Union to offensive countermeasures and weapon deployments rather than to negotiations to reduce mutual offensive threats.

Competition in Anti-satellite Weapons

As noted above, the technologies applicable in exo-atmospheric weapons are, in most cases, liable to be applicable in ASAT weapons before they are applicable in BMD. Thus there will be pressures from the military establishments on both sides to field such weapons as they become feasible, whether or not they prove to have BMD potential. For example, the first mission for space-based SBIs may be as defensive satellites, or DSATS, to protect the BMD system as it is being deployed. Space lasers may be attractive ASATs and DSATs whether they are adopted as BMD weapons or not. Neutral particle beam discriminators could be powerful ASAT weapons. If the nuclear-pumped x-ray laser can be developed as a weapon—which is far from proven—its most promising application may be as an ASAT. No credible answer to the x-ray laser as a BMD suppression weapon has been developed.

As the United States or the Soviet Union began to deploy subtantial numbers of BMD weapons on the ground or in space, these weapons would greatly increase the anti-satellite threat to the other's space assets. (Space-based weapons themselves would, of course, be among those space assets.) Neither side is liable to permit the other the kind of unilateral control of space that such unchallenged ASAT capabilities would provide. **Therefore, in the absence of arms control agreements to the contrary, we should expect from the beginning of BMD space deployments an intense competition between the superpowers for control of near-earth space.**

A frequently proposed survivability measure for U.S. space-based BMD assets is the enforcement of keep-out zones against any potentially threatening Soviet satellites. **Whether, when, and how the Soviets might challenge such assertions of U.S. exclusionary zones in space has not been analyzed by those proposing this tactic. Indeed, the whole question of the mutual occupation of space by weapons of comparable capability has not yet been adequately addressed by SDIO or its contractors.**

Chapter 2
Introduction

CONTENTS

ORGANIZATION OF THIS REPORT

This report identifies questions to be answered before the technical feasibility of achieving the goals set for the Strategic Defense Initiative (SDI) can be determined. The report also offers a snapshot of how far researchers have come toward answering these critical questions and how much remains unknown.

Chapter 1: Summary

Chapter 1 summarizes and explains the principal findings of this OTA study.

Chapter 2: Introduction

This introductory chapter devotes considerable attention to goals for the SDI, since this subject continues to be a source of confusion and debate in the country. Various leaders in the Administration and in Congress have at one time or another emphasized different goals, and which goals will ultimately prevail remains uncertain. Clearly, some goals would be easier to reach than others. This discussion does not include a critical analysis of the goals nor does it attempt to resolve the debate about them. Instead, this chapter tries to provide a context for the issues of technical feasibility.

Chapter 3: Designing a Ballistic Missile Defense (BMD) System: Architecture and Trade-off Studies

To assess the feasibility of a potential BMD system, the United States needs to know both what the system's elements and the system as a whole might look like. To this end, the Strategic Defense Initiative Organization (SDIO) has awarded a series of contracts to several teams of defense companies to try to define some candidate "system architectures" for BMD. Drawing on these studies, SDIO synthesized its own "reference architecture" to help SDI researchers understand the requirements that the technologies being developed eventually must meet.

Late in 1986 and in the first half of 1987, system architecture analysis was in a state of flux as SDIO instructed its contractors to conceptualize the early stages of a BMD deployment. In mid-1987, the SDIO proposed a first-phase architecture to the Defense Acquisition Board and in September the Secretary of Defense approved a program of "demonstration and validation" for this architecture. The process of evolving system architecture analysis and design is likely to continue throughout the life of the program and into the period during which defenses are actually deployed, if they are. There should be continuing feedback between system designers and technology developers, balancing the desirable and the possible. This chapter introduces that process, discusses its importance, and describes where it has led so far.

Chapter 4: Status and Prospects of Ballistic Missile Defense Technologies, Part I: Sensors

Chapter 5: Status and Prospects of Ballistic Missile Defense Technologies, Part II: Weapons, Power, Communication, and Space Transportation

These chapters are organized as reference works on several of the key technologies under research in the SDI program—describing them, surveying the requirements they must ultimately meet, and reporting their status (including key unresolved issues) as of early 1988. The chapters also examine the requirements for combining those technologies into working components of a BMD system, with emphasis on the kinds of components needed for recent SDIO "reference architecture" formu-

Note: Complete definitions of acronyms and initialisms are listed in Appendix B of this report.

lations. Chapter 4 reviews technologies for finding, tracking, and pointing weapons at missile boosters, post-boost vehicles, and reentry vehicles and for discriminating between genuine targets and decoys. Chapter 5 reviews the weapon technologies for delivering lethal doses of energy (kinetic or electromagnetic) to targets. It also addresses the key technologies of space transportation, communication, and power supplies for space assets.

Chapter 6: System Development, Deployment, and Support

If BMD is to play a role in U.S. national strategy, the technologies described in the previous chapters must be incorporated into working weapon components. Those components must be integrated into effective weapon systems that are affordable, maintainable, and adaptable over time to possible adversary responses. By focusing on some particularly challenging issues, such as the development and engineering of a space-based space surveillance system and the logistics of space transportation, chapter 6 attempts to give an appreciation of the steps involved in these processes.

Chapter 7: System Integration and Battle Management

With variations on SDIO's reference architecture for a BMD system as models, this chapter shows how the various components of such a system would have to work together to intercept a ballistic missile attack in its several phases. The chapter attempts to give an appreciation of the complexities of integrating BMD system components into a quickly reacting system. It does so by presenting an overview of the tasks a BMD system would have to perform and examples of how it would perform them. It also examines the concept of BMD battle management and the roles of humans and computers in such a battle.

Chapter 8: Computing Technology

Computers would be crucial to any BMD system, from simulation testing of theoreti-

cal designs, through operation of most of the hardware, to management of the battle. Chapter 8 focuses on the roles of computers in BMD and on the computation capabilities needed to satisfy SDI requirements. Computing technology encompasses both hardware and software. This chapter, however, emphasizes hardware questions while chapter 9 focuses on software.

Chapter 9: Software

The legislation mandating this study instructed that it include an analysis of the feasibility of meeting SDI software requirements. Chapter 9 examines the question of whether the complex computer programs that BMD will require could be made sufficiently dependable. It analyzes the concepts of software trustworthiness and reliability, as well as other important software issues. It compares requirements and characteristics of BMD software to existing, trusted software systems. The chapter ends with conclusions about the prospects for producing trustworthy software for the SDI.

NOTE: Chapters 10, 11, and 12 are now available only in the classified version of this report. The descriptions here are for reference.

Chapter 10: Nondestructive Countermeasures Against Ballistic Missile Defense

Ballistic missile defense systems must be designed to cope with the kinds of countermeasures the Soviets might deploy against them. These include modified or new ballistic missiles, devices intended to make reentry vehicles harder to find or shoot at, and weapons that could attack the BMD system. This chapter examines the first two types of countermeasure, while chapter 11 describes the latter, or "defense suppression" technologies and their counters. Estimates of physically possible countermeasures must be refined by estimates of what is technically, economically, and strategically feasible for the Soviet Union. The chapter concludes with a review of the technologies that might provide responses to the potential Soviet countermeasures.

and the technologies and tactics that might counter them.

Chapter 11: Defense Suppression and System Survivability

The legislation instructing OTA to carry out this study placed special emphasis on the survivability of an SDI-produced BMD system in the face of an enemy attack on the system itself. The chapter reviews the technologies that might be applied to defense suppression

Chapter 12: Defense Suppression Scenarios

In a variety of "scenarios," chapter 12 identifies the most stressing attack threats that various BMD elements would be likely to face and the methods a BMD system might use to defend itself, actively or passively.

THE GOALS OF THE STRATEGIC DEFENSE INITIATIVE

According to the Strategic Defense Initiative Organization in 1986:

> The goal of the SDI is to conduct a program of vigorous research and technology development that may lead to strategic defense options that would eliminate the threat posed by ballistic missiles, and thereby:
> - support a better basis for deterring aggression,
> - strengthen strategic stability, and
> - increase the security of the United States and its Allies.
>
> The SDI seeks, therefore, to provide the technical knowledge required to support an informed decision in the early 1990s on whether or not to develop and deploy a defense of the U.S. and its Allies against ballistic missiles.[1]

What does the phrase, "eliminate the threat posed by ballistic missiles," mean, and how

---

[1]Strategic Defense Initiative Organization, *Report to the Congress on the Strategic Defense Initiative*, June 1986, p. IV-1. In its 1987 report, SDIO dropped "in the early 1990s" from its goal; it also dropped the "not" from the phrase "whether or not" in the above quotation.

might doing so enhance deterrence, stability, and security? Proponents of BMD have argued that increasing levels of defense could offer increasing benefits. Fairly modest levels of BMD, they say, might improve deterrence of a Soviet nuclear attack by increasing Soviet military planners' *uncertainty* about the effectiveness of such an attack. Higher levels of defense capability might actually *deny* the Soviets even the possibility of achieving whatever military goals they might have for attack. Finally, extremely good defenses against all types of nuclear attack—including attacks by ballistic missiles, cruise missiles, bombers, and other means of delivery—might essentially *assure* the *survival* of the U.S. population and society no matter what the Soviets tried to do. Then U.S. security would no longer rely on the threat of retaliation to deter a nuclear attack.

SDIO officials emphasize that currently the preponderance of their attention is focused on systems and technologies intended to lead to early accomplishment of the first goal of enhancing deterrence.

THREE GOALS FOR STRATEGIC DEFENSE

Increase Attacker Uncertainty

Working with assumptions about the accuracy, explosive power, and reliability of weapons systems as well as the nature of in-

tended targets, Soviet military planners can make some predictions about Soviet ability to destroy a chosen set of targets. Just how confident Soviet planners would or should be about the validity of their assumptions is extremely difficult for U.S. analysts to determine.

Relatively modest amounts of strategic defense,[2] some argue, might add to the uncertainties that the potential attacker already faces.[3] He would be forced to make additional assumptions about how—and which—of his warheads would be intercepted by the defenses. Insofar as a Soviet decision to launch a nuclear attack on the United States might depend on Soviet confidence in their ability to destroy a given set of targets, the protection added by modest U.S. strategic defenses might help deter such a decision.[4] Presumably, the larger factor in a Soviet decision on whether to strike first is the current high probability that a U.S. retaliatory attack would devastate much of the Soviet Union.

In its 1987 report to Congress, SDIO suggested that relatively modest levels of defense might begin to add to Soviet uncertainties by "denying the predictability of Soviet attack outcome . . . and imposing on the Soviets significant costs to restore their attack confidence."[5]

There are ways the Soviets might try to reduce the uncertainties added by U.S. defenses. They might deploy offensive countermeasures designed to restore their previous level of confidence in their weapons' ability to reach and destroy assigned targets. They might deploy

additional weapons intended just to exhaust the defenses, assuring that some weapons face no defensive screen. They might attempt to circumvent the BMD system by adding more bombers and cruise missiles to their arsenal.

On the other hand, the Soviets would have to make new assumptions about how well these responses would work. The Soviets might also choose to give up some weapon capabilities to preserve others: for example, some countermeasures intended to assure that a given number of nuclear warheads could penetrate the defense might be traded against sacrifices in the number, accuracy, or yield (explosive power) of those warheads. If only because the offensive task had become more complicated, at least some more uncertainty would exist than if the United States had no defenses at all.[6] Opinions vary, however, on what margin of additional uncertainty the Soviets would face and whether there might be other, less costly, and earlier ways to complicate Soviet attack problems.

Deny Military Objectives

Some analysts have argued that an increase in attacker uncertainty as described above is itself a sufficient enhancement of deterrence to justify deploying ballistic missile defenses. The SDIO, however, places a more rigorous requirement on defense:

> A defense against ballistic missiles must be able to destroy a sufficient portion of an aggressor's attacking forces to deny him the confidence that he can achieve his objectives. In doing so, the defense should have the potential to deny that aggressor the ability to destroy a militarily significant portion of the target base he wishes to attack.[7]

The goal here is not just to reduce the attacker's confidence in achieving some set of goals, but to *deny* him any reasonable pros-

---

[2]This section addresses strategic defense generically—i.e., goals for defense against all means of delivering nuclear weapons, not just against ballistic missiles. Since the SDI is directed at developing defenses only against ballistic missiles, we quickly turn to that particular task for strategic defenses. Where relevant, the report will call attention to the relationships between ballistic missile defense and other kinds of strategic defense.

[3]These would include uncertainties about: the accuracy of missiles over untested trajectories; the vulnerabilities of some kinds of targets, such as command and control systems; whether the victim of the attack would launch his own missiles "on warning," thus defeating the most critical objective of the attack; and the nature and results of the retaliation carried out by submarine-launched missiles, bombers, and cruise missiles that escaped the attack.

[4]For a more detailed discussion of deterrent strategy, see U.S. Congress, Office of Technology Assessment, *Ballistic Missile Defense Technologies*, OTA-ISC-254 (Washington, DC: U.S. Government Printing Office, September 1985), pp. 67-132.

[5]Strategic Defense Initiative Organization, *Report to the Congress on the Strategic Defense Initiative*, April 1987, p. II-11.

[6]Alternatively, some would argue that the Soviets might find a secret countermeasure that they were certain was capable of totally disabling the U.S. BMD system; if they combined this countermeasure with expanded offensive forces, their net certainty of attack success might be increased over what it is today.

[7]Strategic Defense Initiative Organization, *op. cit.*, p. IV-2.

pect of doing so. Suppose, for example, that the Soviets have set for their strategic forces the goal of destroying 75 percent of a particular target set. A U.S. strategic defense that could predictably allow them to destroy only 50 percent of this set would therefore deny the Soviets their goal. If the difference between the Soviets' choosing to attack and refraining from attack rested on their confidence in their ability to destroy 75 percent of the targets, they would be deterred.

An attack of thousands of nuclear weapons that failed in its purely military objectives, whatever they might be, would still wreak great, perhaps irreparable, damage on U.S. society. Such damage would include not only the direct effects of nuclear weapons exploding near U.S. cities, but the longer-term effects of nuclear fallout and economic and social disruption.[8] Moreover, for purposes of intimidation or deterrence, the Soviets might change their target plans to retain their ability to destroy U.S. cities intentionally. Thus we would still need to rely on the threat of retaliation to deter Soviet or other attacks (or, perhaps more to the point, threats of attack) on our economy and society.

Assured Survival

In his speech of March 23, 1983, inaugurating the SDI, President Reagan set an even higher goal for strategic defenses:

> What if free people could live secure in the knowledge that their security did not rest upon the threat of instant U.S. retaliation to deter a Soviet attack, that we could intercept and destroy strategic ballistic missiles before they reached our own soil or that of our allies?[9]

This goal goes beyond denying the Soviets an ability to destroy a "militarily significant portion" of some target base; it would be to

protect people. As the President said over 3 years later:

> Our research is aimed at finding a way of protecting people, not missiles. And that's my highest priority and will remain so.[10]

The goals of increasing attacker uncertainty, denying military objectives, and assuring national survival imply progressively more capable defensive systems, and correspondingly more difficult technical challenges. The following survey of the Soviet missile threat and the kinds of targets the United States would need to defend against that threat illustrates the scope of the strategic defense problem.

The Soviet Ballistic Missile Threat

The Soviets now have about 1400 intercontinental ballistic missiles (ICBMs) carrying about 6300 nuclear-armed re-entry vehicles (RVs). They also have about 944 submarine launched ballistic missiles (SLBMs) with about 2800 nuclear-armed RVs (see figure 2-1). The Soviets also have several hundred intermediate-range ballistic missiles based in the Soviet Union that can reach all or part of Europe and Asia with about 1400 nuclear RVs— but these are to be eliminated under the Intermediate Nuclear Forces (INF) agreement signed in December 1987. Several hundred shorter-range missiles can deliver single warheads from tens to hundreds of kilometers; many are based in Soviet Bloc countries and can reach important targets in NATO countries. Under the terms of the INF agreement, the Soviets are also to eliminate their other missiles with ranges above 500 km.

The composition of the Soviet ballistic missile force will change over the years during which BMD might be developed and deployed

---

[8]See, for example, U.S. Congress, Office of Technology Assessment, *The Effects of Nuclear War*, OTA-NS-89 (Washington, DC: U.S. Government Printing Office, May 1979), esp. ch. 4, pp. 109-118.

[9]Ronald Reagan, televised speech, Mar. 23, 1983.

[10]President Ronald Reagan, "SDI: Progress and Promise," briefing in Washington, D.C. on Aug. 6, 1986, Current Policy No. 858, U.S. Department of State, Bureau of Public Affairs, Washington, DC, p. 2. Secretary of Defense Caspar Weinberger has said, "When the President says that we are aiming at a strategic defense designed to protect people, that is exactly what he means." Speech at Harvard University, Sept. 5, 1986, quoted by David E. Sanger, "Weinberger Denies Antimissile Shift,"*The New York Times*, Sept. 6, 1986, p. 9.

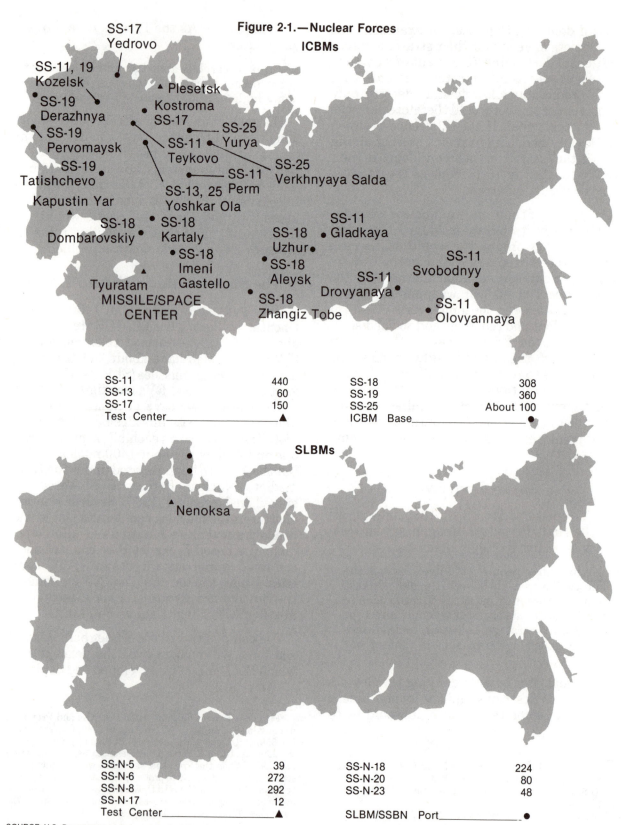

Figure 2-1.—Nuclear Forces

ICBMs

SS-17 Yedrovo

SS-11, 19 Kozelsk

SS-19 Derazhnya

▲ Plesetsk

Kostroma

SS-17

SS-19 Pervomaysk

SS-11 Teykovo

SS-25 Yurya

SS-19 Tatishchevo

SS-13, 25 Yoshkar Ola

SS-11 Perm

SS-25 Verkhnyaya Salda

Kapustin Yar ▲

SS-18 Dombarovskiy

SS-18 Kartaly

SS-11 Gladkaya

SS-18 Uzhur

SS-18 Imeni Gastello

SS-18 Aleysk

SS-11 Svobodnyy

Tyuratam MISSILE/SPACE CENTER ▲

SS-18 Zhangiz Tobe

SS-11 Drovyanaya

SS-11 Olovyannaya

SS-11	440	SS-18	308
SS-13	60	SS-19	360
SS-17	150	SS-25	About 100
Test Center_____▲		ICBM Base_____•	

SLBMs

▲ Nenoksa

SS-N-5	39	SS-N-18	224
SS-N-6	272	SS-N-20	80
SS-N-8	292	SS-N-23	48
SS-N-17	12		
Test Center_____▲		SLBM/SSBN Port_____•	

SOURCE: U.S. Department of Defense, *Soviet Military Power* (Washington, DC: U.S. Government Printing Office, 1987).

(see figure 2-2). **The changes would be more dramatic if the Soviets attempted to counter the effectiveness of prospective U.S. defenses.** Anticipating this "responsive threat" is a major challenge for BMD planners. The SDIO has not been assigned to address the Soviet ability, present and forecast, to deliver nuclear weapons with aircraft and ground-, sea-, or air-launched cruise missiles. The Air Force is conducting an "Air Defense Initiative" (ADI) that is studying the interception of air-breating weapons. The ADI, however, is operating at much lower funding levels than the SDI.

Targets To Be Defended

The three goals of uncertainty, denial, and assured survival remain abstract and ambiguous until we consider the *kinds* of targets to be defended against nuclear attack. Soviets attack objectives might include four broad categories of targets:

1. *strategic retaliatory forces*—ICBM silos (or, in the future, mobile ICBMs), bombers (and refueling tankers) at their bases, submarines in port, command posts, and communications nodes;
2. *other military targets*—including military headquarters, barracks, nuclear and con-

ventional ammunition dumps, supply depots, naval ports and shipyards, airfields, and radars;
3. *economic targets*—industrial facilities, fuel reserves, research centers, transportation nodes, and cities; and
4. *political targets*—non-military government facilities, and civil defense shelters.

Each of these sets of targets (for further explanation, see box 2-A) has different implications for strategic nuclear offensive and defensive operations.

Strategic Retaliatory Forces

The purpose of a Soviet nuclear attack on U.S. strategic nuclear forces—a so-called "counterforce" attack—would be to reduce the ability of those forces to carry out a retaliatory nuclear attack on the Soviet Union. In 1986 the Department of Defense estimated that by attacking each of 1000 U.S. Minuteman missile silos with two SS-18 warheads, the Soviets could destroy about 65 to 80 percent of U.S. land-based ICBMs.[11]

An attack would have to succeed quickly and destroy a high percentage of the targets. Otherwise, U.S. weapons could be launched against the Soviet Union (assuming they had not already been launched on warning, before the first Soviet missiles arrived). The objective of substantially reducing the retaliatory damage inflicted on the Soviet Union would not be met. Thus slower bombers and cruise missiles would be less suitable than ballistic missiles for this kind of disarming attack.

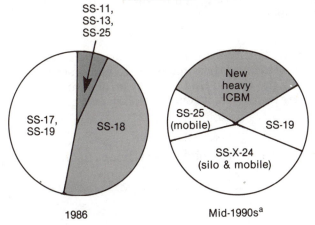

Figure 2-2.—Modernization of Soviet ICBMs Warhead Mix

aEstimates based on current trends.
SOURCE: U.S. Department of Defense, *Soviet Military Power* (Washington, DC: U.S. Government Printing Office, 1987).

[11]U.S. Department of Defense, *Soviet Military Power 1986* (Washington, DC: U.S. Government Printing Office, 1986), p. 25. The United States maintains several hundred Poseidon and Trident missiles at sea at all times and is adding sea-launched nuclear cruise missiles to its arsenal. It also maintains bombers (many with cruise missiles) on alert for rapid escape on warning. The President's Commission on Strategic Forces (the "Scowcroft Commission") argued in 1983 that, in view of overall U.S. retaliatory capabilities, ICBM vulnerability did not warrant ABM (anti-ballistic missile) defense of missile silos in the near term. Some argue that future Soviet anti-submarine warfare developments might compromise the survivability of U.S. ballistic missile submarines, and that defense of land-based missiles might compensate for that eventuality. Others argue that if both the United States and the Soviet Union were to deploy BMD, U.S. retaliatory missiles would be less able to fulfill their missions, whether launched from land or sea.

Box 2-A.—Potential Targets for a Soviet Nuclear Ballistic Missile Attack

Strategic Retaliatory Forces

Land-based ICBMs.—The United States has about 1,000 intercontinental ballistic missiles in hardened silos. In the 1990s it may deploy "Midgetman" missiles on road-mobile carrier vehicles. It may deploy some MX "Peacekeeper" ICBMs on railroad cars within U.S. military lands. An attack on land-based ICBMs would have to be swift, well-coordinated, and accurate. Otherwise, many of the missiles would remain available for striking back at the Soviets. (The Soviets would also have to consider the risk that the United States would launch its ICBMs while they were under attack, with many escaping destruction to retaliate against the Soviet Union.

Bomber Bases.—About 350 strategic bombers, able to carry several thousand nuclear bombs and cruise missiles, are based at some tens of airfields around the United States. Additional aircraft are needed to refuel the bombers in flight. Normally, a substantial number of the U.S. strategic aircraft are on standby alert and might be expected to escape a Soviet missile attack given several minutes of warning; in times of crisis, more bombers would be placed on alert. A Soviet attack might try to catch as many as possible of the U.S. bombers (and their refueling tankers) on the ground or just after take-off.

Submarine Bases.—Thirty-odd submarines with several hundred underwater-launched ballistic missiles are based at just a few U.S. ports. By plan, in peacetime somewhat more than half these submarines, with 2,500-3,000 nuclear warheads, are always at sea. Those in port would be easy, inviting targets for a Soviet strategic counterforce attack. During a crisis, some of the submarines in port could be sent to join those already at sea.

Communications, Command, and Control Facilities.—Linking the above forces to U.S. National Command Authorities is a network of underground command posts, mobile command posts, mobile communications (air, ground, and space) relays, and fixed communications transmitter and receiver stations. A Soviet nuclear attack is likely to try to disrupt this network by direct nuclear destruction of the fixed land facilities or by means of nuclear-generated electromagnetic pulses intended to interfere with the functioning of electronic devices.

Other Military Targets

Military Headquarters; Barracks, Nuclear and Conventional Ammunition Dumps, Supply Depots, Naval Ports and Shipyards, and Airfields.—Many other military facilities, while not directly supporting U.S. rapid-response strategic nuclear forces, would be essential to the conduct of conventional warfare or tactical nuclear warfare abroad. Many of these targets are "soft" . . . difficult to shelter from the effects of even relatively inaccurate nuclear weapons.

Economic Targets

Factories, Power Plants, Fuel Supplies, and Transportation Nodes.—These are sometimes called "economic recovery" targets. The military purpose of attacking them might be to eliminate the economic base that supports U.S. military power. While the United States might be able to carry out a strategic nuclear retaliatory attack if its cities were destroyed, it could not carry on a conventional war abroad very long.

Political Targets

Government Facilities and Civil Defense Shelters.—The Soviets might also attempt to disrupt government to hinder economic and political recovery.

The purpose of a U.S. ballistic missile defense against such an attack would be to preserve enough missiles and bombers to retaliate successfully against the targets in the Soviet Union designated by U.S. military planners.[12] At a minimum, the United States might wish defenses to add to current Soviet uncertainties about how well they could prevent those offensive weapons from reaching the Soviet Union. If these redundant, hardened targets could be defended *preferentially*, that is, if defensive resources could be devoted to protecting a sub-set of them that is unknown to Soviet planners, then Soviet confidence in being able to destroy the whole force might be reduced to a very low level.[13]

At best, we would want defenses that persuaded the Soviet Union of the *certainty* of *failure* of any preemptive attack on our strategic forces that had the purpose of reducing significantly the damage we could do to the Soviet Union.

Other Military Targets

The purpose of attacking U.S. military targets other than those connected with strategic nuclear forces would be to weaken or eliminate the ability of the United States to project military power abroad (to fight conventional or limited nuclear wars in Europe, Asia, or elsewhere), or even to defend its own territory against invasion. Unlike sheltered ICBMs, most of these other military targets are relatively soft—each could be easily destroyed by one or a few moderately accurate nuclear weapons. Nor must they be destroyed instantaneously, since they cannot be used for a prompt nuclear retaliation against Soviet territory.

Since these other military targets can be destroyed more or less at leisure, strategic delivery vehicles other than ballistic missiles can

be used against them—bombers and cruise missiles in particular. Therefore, a strategic defense intended to protect these targets must be highly effective against "air breathing" weapons as well as against ballistic missiles.

The purpose of defending such targets would be to decrease the probability that a nuclear attack on them could significantly weaken our military power; at best we would want the Soviets to be certain that such an attack would fail.

It is important to note that many of these "other military targets" are located in or near urban complexes, and an attack on them might be hard to distinguish from a punitive city attack. Fallout would reach extensive areas of the United States and millions of people might die.

Urban Economic and Political Targets

The main military purpose of attacking the U.S. industrial and political infrastructures would be to remove the base from which the United States exerts military and economic power abroad. Another purpose, however, might simply be to inflict punishment. Before a war occurred, the purpose of having such an ability to punish would be to deter actions (e.g., nuclear or nonnuclear attacks) by threatening to impose a cost higher than the expected gain of such actions. For example, Britain and France maintain nuclear deterrent forces that they believe help deter the Soviet Union from attacking them, even though the effects of those forces on Soviet military capabilities might be more indirect than direct.[14]

Even a few tens of nuclear weapons landing on U.S. cities would cause unprecedented destruction in this country. Extensive use of civil defense measures, if feasible, might ameliorate the effects of such destruction (e.g., if city populations could be evacuated and sheltered from radioactive fallout and if industrial machinery could be sheltered). But even more so than the

---

[12]Opinions vary greatly on how many of what kinds of targets the Soviets would have to believe they would lose in such a retaliation before they would be deterred from launching an attack on the United States. See OTA, *Ballistic Missile Defense Technologies, op. cit.*, pp. 68-76.

[13]For a more detailed explanation of the concept of preferential defense, see OTA, *Ballistic Missile Defense Technologies, op. cit.*, pp. 94-98.

---

[14]It might be noted, however, that the Moscow area has many military facilities; attacks on them would have widespread military as well as civilian consequences.

kinds of "soft" military targets described above, cities are vulnerable to attacks over hours and days by bombers and cruise missiles as well as by ballistic missiles. Defending cities, then, would require extremely effective air defenses as well as missile defenses.

The purpose of defending against attacks on urban industrial targets would be primarily to save lives, property, and civilized society. Militarily, the purpose of having such defenses would be to persuade potential attackers that we could so limit damage to our Nation that we would not have to constrain our own actions out of fear of the effects of an enemy nuclear attack.

From the standpoint of deterrence, various considerations may affect just how much we believe we need to limit damage to our Nation. One consideration might be relative damage: would the damage the United States is likely to suffer in a nuclear war be more or less acceptable to us than the damage the Soviets are likely to suffer would be to them? Another measure might be absolute: regardless of how much damage we could inflict on the Soviets, under what conditions would we be willing to accept the amount of damage they could inflict on us (and vice-versa)?

An open question is just how limited the potential damage would have to be before the United States would decide to give up entirely its own ability to carry out a nuclear retaliation against potential attackers. That is, at what point would we decide to rely on defense rather than the threat of retaliation for our own security?

The Special Case of Defense of Allies

Part of the stated mission of the SDI is to design defenses to protect U.S. allies against ballistic missiles. But the purposes and technical problems of doing so differ somewhat from those of defending the continental United States.

In the case of North Atlantic Treaty Organization (NATO) allies, for example, the Soviet ability to deliver nuclear weapons onto Western European soil is massive and diverse.

Besides their land- and sea-based long-range ballistic missiles, the Soviets might use hundreds of short-range ballistic missiles (intermediate- and medium-range missiles with ranges above 500 km are to be eliminated under the terms of the INF Treaty signed in December 1987). Thousands of Soviet and Warsaw Pact tactical aircraft are credited with the ability to strike Western Europe. Air- and ground-launched cruise missiles are or will be available.

The probability of being able to defend Europe's densely populated territory against *all* the potential kinds of nuclear attacks on cities and industries seems low. Therefore, most proponents of BMD for the European theater of war focus on the defense of what are above called "other military targets"—command posts, communications nodes, sheltered weapons-storage sites (nuclear and nonnuclear), and airfields. Ballistic missile defenses might at least disrupt and reduce the effectiveness of Soviet nuclear missile attacks on such targets (though other means of delivery would also need to be dealt with).

Moreover, some believe that as Soviet ballistic missile accuracies increase, the Soviets might use those missiles to attack military targets with nonnuclear explosive or chemical warheads. Stopping moderately high (and in some cases even modest) percentages of the warheads in such attacks might make a military difference.[15] Others argue, however, that the conventional tactical ballistic missile threat, if it exists, is minor compared to others NATO will have to contend with in the future.[16]

Another mission for Soviet "theater" ballistic missiles might be the delivery of chemical weapons intended to incapacitate NATO troops. Again, the interception of a significant percentage of such missiles might make the difference between some troops surviving a chemical attack or not.

---

[15]See Manfred Woerner, "A Missile Defense for NATO Europe," *Strategic Review*, Winter 1986, pp. 13ff.

[16]For a detailed technical analysis, see Benoit Morel and Theodore A. Postol, "A Technical Assessment of The Soviet TBM Threat to NATO," to be published by the American Academy of Arts and Sciences, Cambridge, MA.

The shorter range Soviet ballistic missiles differ in flight characteristics from their larger relatives: their trajectories are shorter and confined to lower altitudes. While they travel more slowly, their shorter flight times also leave less time for them to be intercepted. On the other hand, because these missiles spend a greater part of their flight time inside the atmosphere, reentry vehicle decoys present less of a problem to the defense. Space-based BMD (especially of the kinetic kill variety) would be of limited utility, and ground-based rocket-interceptors would be the likeliest BMD candidates.

The SDI Scenario

Various statements by Reagan Administration officials over the first 4 years of the Strategic Defense Initiative can be combined to form a scenario about how successively more ambitious goals for strategic defenses might be achieved.[17] The expectation of the Administration is that SDI research will show that deployment of ballistic missile defenses is feasible and desirable. As President Reagan has said, "When the time has come and the research is complete, yes, we're going to deploy."[18]

In the early stages of deployment, according to the Administration scenario, Soviet attack uncertainties would increase, thus reducing the probability of a Soviet first-strike decision (though not the damage they might inflict should they choose to attack). At first, minimal defense capabilities would only complicate Soviet attack plans. As strategic defenses became more capable, the Soviets ought to be more persuaded that the military purposes of any attack would fail. Nevertheless, as long as a substantial number of targets in the United States were still vulnerable to attack, we would have to continue developing and deploying offensive strategic nuclear weapons. As Secretary of Defense Weinberger has written:

> From the outset, we have insisted that progress toward an effective SDI will have to proceed hand in hand with regaining an effective offensive deterrent . . .[19]

The Administration hopes, however, that ultimately offensive deterrence can be abandoned:

> As the United States has repeatedly made clear, we are moving toward a future of greater reliance upon strategic defense. The United States remains prepared to talk about how—under what ground rules and process—we and the Soviet Union can do this cooperatively. Such strategic defenses, coupled with radical reductions in offensive forces, would represent a safer balance and would give future statesmen the opportunity to move beyond it—to the ultimate elimination of nuclear weapons from the face of the Earth.[20]

The key to this ultimate goal is seen to be the development and deployment of defenses that are unequivocally cheaper than corresponding amounts of offense. As SDIO puts it:

> We seek defensive options—as with other military systems—that are able to maintain capability more easily than countermeasures could be taken to try to defeat them. This criterion is couched in terms of cost-effectiveness. However, it is much more than an economic concept.[21]

---

[19]Caspar W. Weinberger, "U.S. Defense Strategy," *Foreign Affairs,* Spring 1986, p. 678.

Earlier in the same article Weinberger explained his concept of a multi-leveled deterrent:

If the adversary calculates that his aggression is likely to fail in its own terms, he will not attack. Further, he must know that even if his aggression should succeed in achieving its immediate objectives, he faces the threat of escalation to hostilities that would exact a higher cost than he is willing to pay. In addition to defense and escalation, the third layer is retaliation: if the adversary confronts a credible threat that aggression will trigger attacks by a surviving U.S. retaliatory capability against the attacker's vital interests that result in losses exceeding any possible gain, he will not attack.

Ibid., p. 678.

[20]President Ronald Reagan, Speech to the U.N. General Assembly, Sept. 22, 1986, reprinted in *The Washington Post*, Sept. 23, 1986, p. A16.

[21]Strategic Defense Initiative Organization, *Report to the Congress on the Strategic Defense Initiative*, April 1987, p. IV-3. It should be added that not only should capability be maintainable at the margin, but that our initial acquisition of defense capability needs to be affordable in comparison with the cost to the Soviets of upgrading their current offensive capabilities to counter our defenses. The offense, being already in place, has a head start on defenses yet to be built.

---

[17]For a list of statements prior to August, 1985, see OTA, *Ballistic Missile Defense Technologies,op. cit.,* App. I, pp. 308-309.

[18]President Ronald Reagan, "SDI: Progress and Promise," briefing in Washington, DC, on Aug. 6, 1986, Current Policy No. 858, U.S. Department of State, Bureau of Public Affairs, Washington, DC, p. 2.

Such a favorable "cost-exchange" ratio between defenses and offenses would be intended to persuade the Soviets of the futility of continuing a competition in offensive arms. The SDIO has stated that:

Program success in meeting its goal should be measured in its ability both to counter and discourage the Soviets from continuing the growth of their offensive forces and to channel longstanding Soviet propensities for defenses toward more stabilizing and mutually beneficial ends . . . It could provide new and compelling incentives to the Soviet Union for serious negotiations on reductions in existing offensive nuclear arsenals."[22]

Agreements on mutual offensive reductions could make defensive tasks easier for each side. Thus the Soviets could be offered both a carrot (possibility of their own effective defenses) and a stick (threat of losing an arms race between offenses and defenses) as incentives to subscribe to the U.S. scenario.

Current SDI Goals

The scenario shown in table 2-1 for the SDI suggests the following official attitudes toward the three goals of uncertainty, denial, and assured survival.

Uncertainty

Imposing greater uncertainty on Soviet attack planners would be an initial benefit of deploying BMD, but, presumably is not in itself sufficient to justify the SDI.

Denial

Denial of Soviet military objectives in a ballistic missile would, in itself, justify deploying BMD. Secretary Weinberger has said:

. . . our strategic defense need not be 100 percent leakproof in order to provide an extraordinary amount of deterrence. Even a partially effective defense would convince Moscow that a first-strike was futile. And once we have rendered a Soviet first-strike obsolete and unthinkable, we will have dramatically increased

Table 2-1.—Strategic Defense Initiative Scenario

Stage 1: SDI Research	Leads to national decision in early 1990's to proceed to full-scale engineering development aimed at deployment of BMD (reference to early 1990s date dropped by SDIO in 1987)
Stage 2: Development and production of BMD systems	Preparation for deployment in mid-to-late 1990s (earlier initial deployments raised as possibility by Secretary Weinberger in 1987)
Stage 3: Initial BMD deployments	Introduces uncertainty into Soviet strategic nuclear attack planning; deployments preferably coordinated by agreement with Soviets on transition to defenses, but proceeds in any case
Stage 4: Extensive deployment of highly effective BMD	Denies Soviet strategic forces ability to achieve military objectives; demonstrates to Soviets futility of competition in offensive strategic missiles
Stage 5: Deployment of advanced BMD systems, combined with agreed deep reductions in offenses	Deep reductions in all types of offensive strategic nuclear forces plus defenses allows abandonment of threat of nuclear retaliation for security: assured survival achieved

SOURCE: Compiled from U.S. Department of Defense, *Report to the Congress on the Strategic Defense Initiative, June 1986*, p. IV-12 and other Administration statements.

stability and rested deterrence on a rock-solid basis. But bear in mind that our goal remains to make ballistic missiles—the most destabilizing and dangerous weapons known to man—obsolete.[23]

Assured Survival

The goal of assured survival may well require Soviet cooperation in offensive nuclear disarmament. A perfect defense against all ballistic missiles may not be possible, and:

Even a thoroughly reliable shield against ballistic missiles would still leave us vulnerable to other modes of delivery, or perhaps even to other devices of mass destruction. De-

[22]Ibid., pp. IV-1-2.

[23]Remarks before the Ethics and Public Policy Center, Washington, DC, Sept. 26, 1986.

spite an essentially leakproof missile defense, we might still be vulnerable to terrorist attacks against our cities. Our vision of SDI therefore calls for a gradual transition to effective defenses, including deep reductions in offensive nuclear weapons.[24]

In the expressed Administration view, then, the SDI should aim ultimately for ballistic mis-

sile defense systems that are nearly leakproof. One way of achieving assured survival might be to build defenses so effective that they would succeed no matter what the Soviets might throw at them. Another way might be to build defenses that promise to be so effective that the Soviets would prefer to negotiate offenses on both sides away rather than embark on an offense-defense race that they have been persuaded they would lose technically or economically.

---

[24]Weinberger, "U.S. Defense Strategy," *op. cit.*, p. 684.

THE CRITERIA OF FEASIBILITY

Supporters and critics of the SDI would probably both agree that proposals for deploying ballistic missile defense should meet at least the four following criteria:

1. effectiveness,
2. affordability,
3. favorable cost-exchange ratio, and
4. survivability.

Note that in each case, meeting the criterion will be at least partly dependent on *Soviet* decisions and actions: the Soviets can make the job harder or easier for the defense. In an unconstrained arms race, they would do what they could to make the job harder. In a cooperative regime of mutual defensive deployments and offensive reductions and controls, each side might make the BMD job easier for the other.

Effectiveness

Obviously, before deciding to deploy a BMD system we would want to be confident that it would be effective—that it would work well enough to achieve the goals set for it. Effectiveness needs to be evaluated on two complementary levels. One level is technical performance: how well can the proposed BMD system perform against the missile threat expected at the time of defense deployment? On a higher level, would such performance provide a better basis for deterrence, strengthen strategic stability, and increase U.S. and Allied

security—the goals stated by SDIO? This second level of analyses received considerable attention in the 1985 OTA report on *Ballistic Missile Defense Technologies*, so it will receive much less attention in this report.

On the level of technical performance, it is difficult to decide what "effectiveness" means. For example, one frequently used criterion of BMD effectiveness is "leakage rate": what percentage of a specified Soviet missile attack would we expect to penetrate our defenses and what percentage could we stop? Given the enormous destructive power of nuclear weapons, though, leakage rates may only tell part of the story. A leakage rate of 10 percent might sound worthwhile, and for some purposes it may be. But under an attack of 10,000 nuclear warheads, a 10 percent leakage rate would mean 1000 nuclear detonations on U.S. territory.

Another problem with leakage rate as a measure of effectiveness is that it is likely to vary with the size and nature of attack. For example, a system that could stop only 50 percent of a massive, nearly instantaneous attack might stop 100 percent of an attack consisting of two or three missiles. On the other hand, a system that could stop 50 percent of an attack of a certain size might not be expandable in such a way that it could stop 50 percent of an expanded enemy missile force. In addition, to maintain damage at a fixed level, the defense would have to stop, for example, 75 percent of a doubled attack.

A slightly better indicator of effectiveness, then, might be the absolute number of nuclear warheads penetrating the defense under the severest plausible attack. Such an estimate would give a better indication of the maximum damage a Soviet attack might inflict.

An even better indicator would be the numbers of different types of targets that the United States would expect to survive a missile attack. This approach would take into account the numbers of attacking weapons, the numbers of penetrating weapons, the numbers and types of targets attacked, and the numbers and types of targets protected. These numbers might be translated into percentages of types of targets surviving—e.g., 70 percent of the land-based missile force.[25] We might carry the analysis further by weighing the values of different types of targets. For example, one underground strategic command post might be worth 10 missile silos.

All of the above indicators would be difficult to apply with precision. And the more factors an indicator has to take into account, the more imprecise it is likely to be. Indeed, there would be no direct way to measure the potential effectiveness of a BMD system: only an actual nuclear war would do so. Instead, we would have to rely on estimates, based on assumptions about:

- enemy offensive technical capabilities (numbers of weapons, accuracy, explosive yields, ability to penetrate defenses);
- enemy target attack plans;
- defensive technical capabilities;
- vulnerability of targets defended; and
- the objective and subjective relative values of targets defended.

These factors would be difficult for U.S. planners to assess. They would also be difficult for Soviet planners to estimate. Therefore, if the U.S. goal is mainly to introduce uncertainties into Soviet strategic calculations, precise measures of BMD effectiveness might not be necessary. On the other hand, if we wished to be certain of *denying* Soviet attack objectives, we might need higher confidence in our estimates.

At the same time, if the Soviets decided, along with the United States, that defenses were desirable, then each side could help make them more effective by agreeing to deep cuts in offensive weapons and to restrictions on countermeasures against defenses.

Affordability

If and when the Department of Defense eventually presents its proposals for deploying BMD, the country will have to decide whether the expected benefits would be worth the expected costs. Part of the SDI research program is to estimate costs for the proposed systems. For various reasons, the initial cost estimates for complex weapon systems tend to be inaccurate, and usually too low. Producing reliable cost estimates for future BMD systems will be a challenging task.

Another part of the SDI program is to attempt to develop new, cheaper ways to manufacture weapons and to deploy them in space.[26] The ultimate weighing of costs and benefits will be a political judgment made by the President and Congress. But a critical part of the demonstration of technical feasibility of BMD will be that the proposed systems can be built at a cost the country would, at least arguably, find reasonable.

As mentioned above, Soviet actions could make effective BMD more or less affordable. If they chose to invest heavily in offensive countermeasures timed to take effect about when our defenses might be deployed, they could make those defenses much more expensive than if they stabilized the threat they pose at today's levels. Alternatively, in a cooperative regime they could make defenses cheaper by agreeing to decrease their offensive threat

---

[25]Note that planning to penetrate defenses may require the offense to concentrate his attacks on higher-value targets. In that case, the targets which he no longer has enough weapons to strike can be considered "saved" by the defense.

[26]Until a re-organization in 1987, the SDIO Systems Engineering Directorate was in charge of this program, among others. The Systems Engineering program element of the SDI budget received $20.2 million in fiscal year 1987; $39 million was requested for fiscal year 1988.

in exchange for reductions in the U.S. offensive threat.

Favorable Cost-Exchange Ratio

The Nation must decide not only that a particular defense system proposed at a particular time is affordable, but whether the potential long-run competition of U.S. defenses against Soviet offenses is likely to be affordable in the future. In the absence of a long-term U.S. commitment to sustaining defensive capabilities, the Soviets would have incentives to stay in the "game" until the United States' will to spend flagged.

One way to try to persuade the Soviets to abandon efforts to maintain offensive capabilities would be to demonstrate clearly that additional increments of offense would be more costly to the Soviets than corresponding increments of defense would be to the United States. Therefore, a corollary goal of the SDI is to design defenses that are cheaper "at the margin" than offenses. If the "cost-exchange" ratio were favorable to defenses, and if the two sides invested equal resources in defenses and offenses respectively, then the side investing in offenses should find its capabilities inexorably declining.

Achieving this favorable cost-exchange ratio will be technically challenging. Accurately estimating the costs of defensive systems would be difficult enough. Attaining high confidence that the ratio of U.S. defensive costs to Soviet offensive costs would be favorable, even before the United States deployed its defenses and before Soviet offensive countermeasures were known would be even more difficult. Neither side may actually know the relative costs of additional increments of defense and offense until they actually buy them.[27]

Because the United States and the Soviet Union have such different economies, it will be difficult to quantify the cost-exchange ratio. Moreover, the effective cost-exchange ratio may differ from the technical one. That is, the ratio depends not only on what things cost, but also on what people are willing to pay. If the Soviets are willing and able to pay for an increment of offense that is more costly than our corresponding increment of defense, for practical purposes the cost-exchange ratio is at least even. **The SDI objective, then, is to persuade the Soviets that the defenses we can afford will more than offset the offenses they can afford.** Thus the offense/defense cost-exchange ratio may have to be not just 1.5:1 or 2:1, but several-to-one.

On the other hand, if the Soviets were to agree with the United States that a mutual reduction of offensive missile capabilities was worthwhile and that defenses were desirable, then the technical challenge could be reduced. In effect, mutual political decisions could improve the cost-exchange ratio by mandating reductions—rather than enhancements—of offensive capabilities, along with limitations on other offensive countermeasures.

Survivability

One of the many possible types of countermeasures against a BMD system is to attack the system itself—which will be called "defense suppression" in this report. Obviously, to carry out its defensive mission, the BMD system must survive such attacks. "Survivability" does not mean the ability of every element—each satellite, e.g.—to survive any attack. Rather, it means the ability of the system as a whole to perform acceptably despite attacks that may disable some elements.

No BMD system will be *either* survivable *or* not survivable. The question will be, "How survivable, at what cost?" The cost-exchange ratio between defense and offense will have to be calculated on the basis of the costs of all kinds of offensive response, including defense suppression, compared to the costs of all kinds of defensive counter-countermeasures, including "survivability" measures.

[27]It might be argued that, faced with these uncertainties, the Soviets would accede to the U.S. proposal for a negotiated transition that regulated offensive and defensive deployments. On the other hand, drafting such an agreement that both sides would find equitable, given the asymmetries in forces and technologies on the two sides, would be a formidable task.

The remainder of this report surveys what was—and was not—known as of April 1988 about the potential of the SDI for developing systems that would meet the effectiveness, affordability, cost-exchange, and survivability criteria.

Designing a BMD System: Architecture and Trade-off Studies

CONTENTS

Tables

Designing a BMD System: Architecture and Trade-off Studies

THE IMPORTANCE OF BMD ARCHITECTURE STUDIES

Researchers have performed proof-of-principle experiments for some Strategic Defense Initiative (SDI) technologies. But many of the basic technologies for the SDI are still in an experimental, or even theoretical, stage. Therefore it might seem premature to be designing full-scale ballistic missile defense (BMD) systems for deployment not only in the mid-1990s, but in the 21st century. In fact, such designs are key to assessing the feasibility of achieving U.S. strategic goals through ballistic missile defense. National decisionmakers can only fully evaluate proposed systems on the merit of system architectures, not on the promise of one technology or another. **If called upon to appropriate funds for BMD development and deployment, Congress will be asked to decide upon an architecture—a specific system design comprising many technologies and components.**

Attempting such designs, or "system architectures," as the Strategic Defense Initiative Organization (SDIO) calls them, compels systematic analysis of all the factors that will affect SDI feasibility. In the near term, such analysis helps guide the technology research effort. In the long term, it will provide the substance of the national debate over whether to deploy BMD.

System architecture analysis, if done well, will provide some of the key elements of information upon which to base decisions about whether to commit the Nation to deploying any proposed BMD system:

- **Specification of Goals.** Explicit identification of the particular strategic goals that BMD system designs will be expected to achieve (e.g., impose uncertainty on So-

Note: Complete definitions of acronyms and initialisms are listed in Appendix B of this report.

viet strategic planners); understanding of those goals in the larger context of U.S. national security; and cost-effectiveness comparisons of alternate means, if any, of achieving the goals.
- **Specification of Threat.** Projections of future Soviet missile and BMD countermeasures that BMD system designs would be expected to overcome.
- **System Requirements.** Specification of the missile-interception tasks and sub-tasks that effective BMD systems would have to perform to meet the project threats; specification of passive and active survivability measures for the system.
- **System Designs.** Proposals for integrating sensors, weapons, and command and control arrangements into BMD systems that would likely meet system requirements and that could be practically modified to meet changing threats; and specification of how technologies under research would be incorporated into a BMD system—such a design is called a system architecture.
- **Technology Requirements.** Specification of the technologies needed to build the weapon systems required by the overall system design, by the deployment and maintenance plans, and by plans for adaptive evolution of the system to meet changes in the threat; and plan for bringing all technology developments to fruition when needed (full-scale engineering development plan).
- **Manufacturing Requirements.** Specification of the materials, manufacturing facilities, tools, and skilled personnel needed to manufacture all system elements.
- **Deployment and Operations Analyses.** Proposals for how the designed system can be put into place and maintained (in-

cluding space transportation requirements); and schedules for doing so.

- **Cost Estimates**. Estimates for what development, procurement, deployment, and operation of the proposed system design will cost; and proposals for reducing system costs.

This chapter will focus on two particular topics:

1. the ways in which system architects for SDIO have related strategic goals to BMD system performance needs, and
2. the general characteristics of the system architectures studied for SDIO.

The concluding sections of the chapter will identify areas of analysis within those topics where important work remains to be done.

It would be highly unrealistic now to expect system architecture studies to be definitive. Each category of analysis is subject to considerable uncertainty, some of which may never be resolved by analysis and limited experimentation. The architecture analysis will necessarily be tentative and iterative: as new information and ideas emerge, modifications will be inevitable. Moreover, the findings from analyses in each category will and should affect the findings in other categories. For example, meeting a particular technology requirement may be judged possible, but too expensive. The system architecture design may have to be modified to utilize another technology to carry out the same function. On the other hand, new technological developments may make it cheaper to carry out a function in a way that previous analyses had shown to be too costly. For that reason, the system architects attempt to design "evolutionary" architectures into which advanced technical developments could be phased as they became available.

Even after a commitment had been made to develop a particular technology into a weapon system, the process of full-scale engineering development might prove more difficult than anticipated: alternate systems might have to be designed and developed. Moreover, while it is the goal of the architecture analyses to provide options for meeting a range of potential changes in the offensive missile threat, a fully deployed BMD system might still have to be modified in unanticipated ways if the Soviets were to deploy unforeseen countermeasures.

Despite the necessarily tentative nature of system architecture analyses, they compel a coherence in thinking about BMD that would otherwise be missing. They also bring into the open the assumptions implicit in the arguments for and against deploying BMD. Because these analyses will inevitably include assumptions and projections that reasonable people may disagree about, it is important that they be carried out *competitively*, by more than one group of analysts. Such competition will give both the Administration and Congress a basis for identifying the uncertainties, varying assumptions, and alternative projections of the future that will underlie decisions about BMD. **It will also be important, when these analyses are offered in justification of major decisions, that they be independently evaluated.**

Recognizing the importance of system architecture studies, SDIO late in 1984 awarded contracts to 10 teams of military systems analysis contractors to provide competing analyses at a price of $1 million each. On the basis of that competition, five teams were chosen for $5-million, "Phase II" architecture studies, which were largely completed in mid-1986. In addition, a sixth contractor provided SDIO with analytic support to synthesize the findings of the five competitors into a "reference architecture" to help guide SDI research. As of this writing, the five Phase II teams had been awarded additional contracts to continue some analytic work common to all and to perform some tasks unique to each. Their reports were due at the end of January 1988.[1] It had

---

[1] Three other sets of "architecture" contracts should also be noted. First, through the Air Force Electronic Systems Division, contracts were awarded to three firms to design battle management and communications systems for a BMD system with land- and space-based elements. This work necessitated definitions of more or less complete BMD system architectures, thus to some extent paralleling the work of the general system architecture contractors. The SDIO has subsequently attempted

been planned that the five would be narrowed to two competitors in a final phase, but that decision was postponed through 1987. Eventually a single contractor team will be chosen to design a BMD system in detail.[2]

to better coordinate the parallel work of the battle management systems analyses and the main system architecture studies.

Second, the Army Strategic Defense Command awarded three other contracts for study of the battle management and communications systems for BMD composed primarily of ground-based components. Third, late in 1986 SDIO awarded seven contracts to teams composed of U.S. and European firms to begin designs of system architectures for European theater defense against intermediate-, medium-, and short-range ballistic missiles.

[2]For the future, SDIO has proposed two new organizations for carrying out work on system architectures. One organization would be an "SDI Institute," a federally (and, specifically, SDIO) funded "think tank" to monitor the work on the actual system architecture to be proposed for deployment by SDIO. The Institute would be independent of particular defense contractors, thus reducing the possibility that the interest of current defense firms in selling hardware to the government would play a role in architecture designs.

A second new organization is to be a "National Test Bed," which would be a network of computers, communications links, and some sensor hardware for simulating ballistic missile defenses. In some cases, the simulations would be purely conceptual, creating a computer "world" of BMD systems and offensive systems, and testing various assumptions about each. In other cases, this imaginary world might, with simulated incoming and outgoing data, test computer software actually intended for use in a real BMD system. In yet other cases, actual BMD

This report will offer numerous examples from the findings of the system architecture contractors and of SDIO adaptations of such findings. With a few exceptions, we will not cite specific contractor sources for those examples. OTA has not undertaken a systematic analysis and comparison of all the dozens of documents that emerged from the several contractor studies. Therefore, a few selected citations might give an unfair impression of the overall performance of any given contractor. Our purpose here is to convey an understanding of the system architecture analysis process and to report some of the results—not to conduct management oversight of any Department of Defense (DoD) contractor. In addition, the system architecture work is continuing, and constant revision of previous findings is both necessary and desirable. Thus any given conclusion might not reflect the current views of the particular contractor.

hardware tests might be conducted, with data from the computers being fed into an actual test sensor system, and the sensor system sending processed signals back into the computer simulation. If a full-scale BMD system were deployed, the National Test Bed might then be used for simulated battle exercises of the system.

OVERVIEW OF SYSTEMS ARCHITECTURE ANALYSES

Initially, each of the system architects undertook the same general task of designing BMD systems whose deployment might begin in the mid-1990s and that might evolve into more advanced systems after the year 2000. Each group produced designs that it believed could, when fully deployed, provide near-perfect interception of Soviet ballistic missile reentry vehicles (RVs) forecast for deployment in the mid-1990s.[3] Each also argued, however,

[3]A mid-1990s threat posed against a BMD system that could not be fully deployed until after the year 2000 is unrealistic. Not all architects used the same threat numbers for the same time frames. The architects did, however, project this "baseline" threat into larger numbers of reentry vehicles and decoys for later years. They also ran "excursions" on the baseline threat to explore the impacts of larger and smaller threats on defense effectiveness. The excursions into larger threats, with one exception, do not generally appear in the summary documents produced by the contractors.

that lesser percentages of interception would achieve desirable military goals along the lines described in chapter 2 of this report.

Goal Specification

As part of their analyses, the architects used computerized strategic nuclear exchange models (see next section on this topic) to simulate the numerical results of hypothetical nuclear wars between the United States and the Soviet Union. These simulations assumed various levels of defense capability on the two sides (in general the projected offensive capabilities for the mid-1990s were assumed at this stage) for the purpose of showing what differences those defenses might make.

From these simulations, the analysts drew conclusions about how defenses might contribute to the goals of security and strategic stability. In chapter 2, we described the kinds of measures used to define BMD effectiveness. In this chapter we will further describe some of the assumptions that went into and conclusions that came out of these strategic exchange simulations.

Threat Definition

A preliminary step to running the strategic exchange simulations was to state the Soviet offensive threat that BMD systems would be designed to counter. The starting point was an SDIO-supplied projection of the offensive missile forces the Soviets might have in the mid-1990s. From this starting point, the architects made varying "excursions," positing possible future Soviet missile developments and deployments. In addition, they hypothesized various types and numbers of anti-satellite weapons that the Soviets might conceivably deploy to attack space-based components of BMD systems.

Subsequently, and under different program managers, SDIO began a "Red Team" program to attempt to anticipate possible Soviet responses to U.S. BMD deployments. A major project of this program has been to bring together groups of experts to attempt to design plausible Soviet countermeasures to the technologies under consideration in other parts of SDIO. These potential countermeasures are then presented to SDIO "Blue Teams" so that they can adapt their technology research and system designs accordingly.

In mid-1987, SDIO presented to the Defense Acquisition Board a proposal to proceed with "concept demonstration and validation" ("Milestone I") for the first phase of a "Strategic Defense System" (BMD system) to be deployed in the mid-1990s. This presentation included an officially approved "threat" description for that period.

In reviewing DoD proposals for any BMD system, Congress should understand whether the officially assumed Soviet threat is "responsive" —i.e., whether it reflects plausible countermeasures that the Soviets could have taken by the time the BMD system were full deployed.

System Requirements

In showing what numbers of nuclear weapons would have to be intercepted to provide various levels of protection for different types of targets (cf. ch. 2), the strategic exchange models also yielded basic requirements for strategic defense system performance. Additional "end-to-end" computer simulations helped define requirements for interception at each stage of flight.

(In SDIO presentations accompanying mid-1987 proposals for an initial, less effective BMD system, this process was reversed. First, a number of warheads to intercept was established, then the strategic goals that might be served analyzed afterward.)

Systems Designs

The system architecture contractors designed BMD systems intended to intercept a very high percentage of the projected missile threat. The working assumption was that early stages of BMD deployment would be stepping stones to the ultimate goal of protecting cities and people from nuclear ballistic missile attack. The designs were not optimized to less ambitious goals. For example, systems that might protect hardened missile silos but could not serve as elements of city defenses were not considered. Systems designed from the outset to preserve nuclear deterrence might well look materially different from those designed to replace it altogether.

Each architect was asked to design:

1. a system that was both space-based and ground-based;
2. one that was primarily ground-based; and
3. one that was intended primarily for defense of U.S. allies against intermediate and shorter range ballistic missiles.

In the second phase of system architecture contracts, analysts placed greatest emphasis on the first type of system, somewhat less on the second, and least on the third. Each architect considered systems that might be deployable in the mid-1990s, but each also offered concepts for more advanced systems that might be deployed against more advanced Soviet offensive systems out to the year 2015 or so. For each case, analysts identified counter-countermeasures intended to neutralize Soviet attempts to penetrate or directly attack the BMD system.

The details of the systems designs (for example, a given type and number of space-based rocket interceptors) were built into simulation models that expanded on the nuclear exchange models described above. These "end-to-end" simulations represented the details of intercepting ballistic missiles throughout all phases of flight, from rocket boost to warhead reentry. Some of the results of these "end-to-end" simulations are discussed below. These models also aided "trade-off" analyses of various types of BMD system components arranged in various configurations. The models were also used to evaluate excursions in the technological requirements forced by particular types of Soviet anti-BMD countermeasures.

Technological Requirements

The architects quantitatively analyzed the relative costs and effectiveness of various approaches to each defensive task. For example, an analysis might examine trade-offs between highly capable missile-tracking sensors on a few high altitude satellites and less capable sensors on many more low-altitude satellites.

Many of these "trades" are discussed in subsequent chapters of this report.

Operational Requirements

Because system designs are still preliminary, it is difficult to specify their exact operational requirements. The system architects did attempt to estimate the continuing space transportation and maintenance requirements for space-based systems over their lifetime. Other SDI programs are conducting research on the logistics of maintaining various space-based and ground-based systems.

Costs

In general, system architects estimated costs for their nearer-term, "interim" designs— those not including directed-energy weapons for boost-phase missile interception. These systems were estimated to cost on the order of $200 billion, depending on the projected need to respond to various types of Soviet countermeasure. Costs of complementary air defense systems were not included. It should be recognized that, given the conceptual nature of the architectures, accurate cost-estimating is virtually impossible at this stage. It does appear that, with thousands of space platforms envisaged, considerable changes would be needed in the way such equipment is now designed and manufactured if space-based BMD systems were ever to be affordable. In addition, a major new space transportation system would have to be designed, developed, manufactured, and deployed.

NUCLEAR FORCE EXCHANGE MODELS: DERIVING REQUIREMENTS FROM GOALS

The SDI system architects—and several other groups as well—have run several types of strategic nuclear exchange computer simulations to try to show how defenses might affect the U.S.-Soviet nuclear balance. These simulation models assume various U.S. and Soviet offensive nuclear force levels, beginning with U.S. Government estimates for 1995. Then they assume various strategic targeting plans on the two sides and analyze how the attempted execution of those plans might be affected by various levels of defense capability on the two sides.

The intermediate measure of defense effectiveness is usually the percentage of nuclear warheads intercepted or its complement, the number of "leakers." The models translate the numbers of leakers in various cases into numbers or percentages of different types of targets surviving the attack. (For examples of such target types, see ch. 2, box 2A.) Each type of target, in turn, is given a different weight based on judgments about how U.S. and Soviet leaders might value them. Thus the numbers of different types of targets surviving are translated into "surviving strategic value."[4] The percentage of surviving strategic value on the two sides is then linked with particular strategic goals. (For a discussion of goals for BMD and ways of measuring BMD effectiveness, see ch. 2.) In some cases, "leakage" rates were linked (via asset survival expectations) to strategic goals to show what kind of BMD system performance would be needed given a particular assumed level of offensive threat (for example, see table 3-1).

Some Conclusions Drawn From Nuclear Exchange Models

Strategic Goals and Defense Leakages

The system architects' strategic nuclear exchange simulations provide a useful basis for studying BMD performance goals. However, because each architect used a different computer model and different assumptions for the sizes and compositions of future U.S. and Soviet offensive nuclear forces, the results are difficult to compare.

With that important qualification, here are some conclusions drawn frequently (but not universally) by the different system architects. First, for a mid-1990s Soviet strategic nuclear

threat, a BMD system that allowed a few thousand Soviet RVs to penetrate into the United States might complicate Soviet attack plans, but probably would not stop them from destroying most of their chosen targets.[5]

In support of SDIO's mid-1987 proposal for an initial BMD system, other SDIO contractors argued that a strategy of "adaptive preferential defense" might prevent the Soviets from destroying as high a percentage of certain sets of targets as they would wish (as estimated by U.S. analysts).

A system that allowed fewer Soviet RVs to leak through would begin to deny the Soviets certainty of destroying many of the military targets that their planners might have designated. But if the Soviets chose to concentrate on economic targets in the United States, they might still be able to deny the United States the possibility of economic recovery from the nuclear war. (Compare this finding with the second set of projections in table 3-1.)

With yet lower leakage, the Soviets could still inflict immense damage on the United States. Note, for example, that 10 percent of an attack with 10,000 nuclear weapons would still result in 1,000 nuclear weapons exploding in the United States. But since the Soviets could not be sure which 1,000 of the 10,000 launched would reach which targets, confidence in achieving precise attack goals on a given set of targets would be low.

Analyses also seem to show that if the United States had a relatively highly effective BMD system against a mid-1990s Soviet threat while the Soviets had no BMD, the Soviets would improve their relative strategic situation more by adding defenses to limit damage to themselves than by adding offensive weapons in hopes of increasing the damage they could inflict on the United States.[6] In attempt-

---

[4]In these models the Soviets are assumed to have a larger number of strategic targets than the United States, and the Soviet targets are assumed to be harder to destroy. Part of the difference is due to the existence of numerous nuclear-hardened shelters for Soviet political leaders; see *Soviet Military Power, 1987*, (Washington, D.C.: Department of Defense) p. 52.

[5] The exact percentages in this conclusion and the others below were apparently classified by the system architecture contractors because the computer simulations from which they were derived include classified estimates of U.S. and Soviet military capabilities.

[6] This conclusion assumes that the addition of offenses could not improve the leakage rate—the same percentage of every added group of warheads would be intercepted. This is not necessarily a valid assumption: much would depend on the composition of the offensive and defensive forces on the two sides.

Table 3-1.—Two Perspectives on BMD Effectiveness and Strategic Goals

Soviet warheads leaking through	Expected strategic consequences

A. One system architect's strategic exchange model and conclusions[a]

Many

Increase in Soviet attack planning uncertainties. They are forced to launch all their strategic forces at once or reduce their military objectives. A strategic exchange would result in more losses to Soviets than to the United States.

The Soviets could no longer reliably achieve the military goals of a strategic nuclear attack while maintaining a secure reserve of missiles for later attacks. Preserves full range of U.S. strategic offensive force retaliatory flexible response options. Each new Soviet ballistic missile has only a fractional chance of being useful.

Survival of a large portion of the population and industrial base, a high proportion of military targets other than strategic offensive forces, and sufficient strategic offensive forces to preserve full range of U.S. retaliatory flexible response options. If Soviets attack only other military targets (not strategic offensive forces), medium-high survival of those assets.

Fewer

Would preserve the full range of U.S. "flexible response" options in war with the Soviets even if Soviets devoted entire attack to U.S. strategic offensive forces (presumably only if Soviets do not have comparable BMD capability—OTA).

Assured survival of the Nation as a whole: 3 to 5% U.S. casualties in population attack.

Extremely few

Assured survival: Soviet ability to put U.S. population at risk is negligible; the United States needs no strategic nuclear retaliatory capability.

Assumptions:
- Mid-1990s projections of Soviet and U.S. strategic forces.
- Effectiveness of Soviet BMD not specified.
- Status of air defenses not specified.

Alternate analysis: As U.S. strategic defenses improved, an option for the Soviets would be to change their offensive target priorities to maintain a deterrent "assured destruction" capability. Instead of concentrating their forces on hardened missile silos, for example, they might concentrate them on key military industries or other economic targets; they might even focus on cities per se. Various non-SDIO analysts have previously calculated potential consequences of such nuclear attacks, as indicated below.

B. If the Soviets retargeted to maintain assured destruction

10%

The Soviets attack industries in the 71 largest U.S. urban areas; the equivalent of 500 1-megaton and 200 to 300 100-kiloton weapons get through. Of the U.S. population, 35 to 45 percent is killed or injured; 60 to 65% of U.S. industry is destroyed.[b]

3%

The Soviets attack industries in the 71 largest U.S. urban areas; the equivalent of 100 1-megaton and 200 to 300 100-kiloton weapons get through. From prompt blast and radiation effects, 20 to 30% of U.S. population is killed or injured; 25 to 35% of U.S. industry is destroyed.[c]

1 to 2%

Case 1: The Soviets attack 77 U.S. oil refineries; the equivalent of 80 1-megaton weapons get through. From prompt blast and radiation effects, 5 million Americans die. The U.S. economy is crippled.[d]

Case 2: The Soviets attack 100 key military-industrial targets with the equivalent of 100 1-megaton weapons. Three million die of blast and radiation effects, another 8 million from fires; dead and injured total 10 to 16 million.[e]

Case 3: The Soviets attack 100 U.S. city centers with the equivalent of 100 1-megaton weapons. Fourteen million die from blast and radiation effects alone, a total of 42 million die from blast, radiation, and fires; total dead and injured are 32 to 51 million.[f]

Assumptions:
- Total Soviet strategic attack of 10,000 weapons.
- Air defenses equally effective as BMD.

[a]Adapted from Martin Marietta Aerospace analyses. Percentages of weapons leaking and assets surviving deleted for security classification reasons.
[b]From U.S. Congress, *Economic and Social Consequences of Nuclear Attacks on the United States*, A Study Prepared for the Joint Committee on Defense Production, Published by the Committee on Banking, Housing, and Urban Affairs, U.S. Senate (Washington, D.C.: U.S. Government Printing Office, 1979), pp. 4-14.
[c]Ibid.
[d]From U.S. Congress, Office of Technology Assessment, *The Effects of Nuclear War* (Washington, D.C.: U.S. Government Printing Office, May, 1979), pp. 64-75. Calculations on casualties were performed for OTA by the the U.S. Defense Civil Defense Preparedness Agency. About 125 500-kiloton weapons would have the same blast effects as 80 1-megaton weapons, but the pattern of distribution of blast might in fact do more damage.
[e]William Daugherty et al., "The Consequences of 'Limited' Nuclear Attacks on the United States," *International Security*, spring 1986 (vol. 10, No. 4), p. 5. Findings based on the authors' computer simulations. About 160 500-kiloton weapons have about the same blast effects as 100 1-megaton weapons.
[f]Ibid.

ing to assess the effect on deterrence of various levels of defense, the strategic analysts compared the amount of damage the Soviets might suffer (as a weighted percentage of given types of targets) with the amount the United States might suffer. Differences in surviving (value-weighted) percentages of military targets were assumed to confer strategic advantages or disadvantages that would affect Soviet decisions about how to respond to U.S. weapon deployments, whether to go to war, or whether to escalate a conflict to nuclear exchange.

Even very low leakage of the BMD system (and assuming comparable leakage of air-breathing nuclear weapon delivery vehicles) could still kill several million Americans, if that were the Soviet objective. (Note that the alternative projections in table 3-1 suggest higher possible casualties.) This level of protection (given the mid-1990s projected nuclear threat) *might* assure survival of the United States as a functioning nation, but would not assure survival of the whole population. Most of the system architects appeared to believe that in the long run they could design systems capable of keeping out a very high percentage of Soviet ballistic missile RVs (assuming the mid-1990s projected threat); none appeared to believe that leakage levels compatible with "assured survival" of the U.S. population would be possible without negotiated limitations of Soviet offensive nuclear forces.

U.S.-Soviet Asymmetries

With varying degrees of clarity, the system architects' use of nuclear exchange models brought out the current—and likely future—asymmetries between U.S. and Soviet offensive nuclear forces. The Soviet Union has more ballistic missile RVs than the United States. More of the Soviet RVs are based on land than on submarines, while the reverse is true of the U.S. RVs. The United States has more strategic nuclear bombers and air- and sea-launched cruise missiles than the Soviet Union, while the Soviet Union has a more extensive air defense system than the United States.

If the Soviet Union had ballistic missile defenses comparable to those of the United States, the net effect of trying to defend our land-based missiles against a Soviet strike would be to *reduce* the U.S. ability to carry out planned retaliatory missions. Here is why. If defended, a sizable number of U.S. land-based missiles that might otherwise have been destroyed on the ground might survive a Soviet offensive strike. On the other hand, they would then have to survive *defensive* attacks as they attempted to carry out their retaliatory missions against Soviet territory. In addition, the U.S. submarine-launched missiles (SLBMs), which would not benefit from the defense of land-based missiles, would also have to face Soviet defenses. Furthermore, if the intercepted SLBMs were aimed in part at Soviet air defense assets, such as radar sites, the ability of U.S. bombers and cruise missiles to carry out their missions might also be impaired.

Besides the asymmetries in weapons, there are asymmetries in targets on the two sides. The Soviet Union, for example, reportedly has more than 1,500 hardened bomb shelters for its political leadership. The Soviets also are said to spend copious sums on other types of civil defense. The combination of passive defense measures and BMD might do more to protect valued Soviet targets than BMD alone would to protect valued U.S. targets.

Given the asymmetries in U.S. and Soviet weapons and defenses, then, the net effect of mutual deployments of comparable levels of defense could be to weaken, not strengthen deterrence—if deterrence were still measured primarily by the penalty that we could impose on Soviet aggression through nuclear retaliation. (If deterrence were measured by denial to the Soviets of some attack goals other than reducing damage to the Soviet Union, then deterrence might be strengthened.)

The United States might compensate for U.S.-Soviet asymmetries in three ways:

1. The United States could attempt to build and maintain BMD that was notably su-

perior to that of the Soviet Union, so that a greater proportion of the smaller U.S. ballistic missile force could be expected to reach its targets. This was the recommendation of at least one of the SDI system architects, who argued that until very high defense effectiveness levels had been reached, equal defensive capabilities on the two sides might confer an exploitable strategic advantage on the Soviet Union (SDIO officials disagree with this assessment).

2. The United States could attempt to maintain and improve the ability of its air-breathing weapons (bombers and cruise missiles) to penetrate Soviet air defenses so that the loss in effectiveness of our ballistic missiles was offset by the other means of nuclear delivery. This course was assumed in the calculations of a second system architect.

3. If U.S. strategic defenses against all types of nuclear threat (air-breathing as well as ballistic missile) could be made extremely effective, we might not care about imbalances in punitive abilities on the two sides; the Soviets would have little or nothing to gain by threatening nuclear attack. Then, even a minimally destructive retaliatory ability on the U.S. side should fully deter the Soviets from even contemplating attack. This was the ultimate goal hypothesized by all the system architects. (It should be noted that most, though not all, analysts believe that this kind of deterrence now exists. If so, BMD would not significantly reduce the risk of nuclear war.[7])

However, some would argue that future Soviet "counterforce" capabilities, plus Soviet civil defense and perhaps active (BMD and air defense), could reduce prospective Soviet damage to levels acceptable to them. A U.S. BMD system, it is argued, would either maintain the survivability of the U.S. deterrent, or equalize the prospective damage on the two sides, or both.

In sum, the force exchange models employed by some of the SDI system architects seem to show that BMD performance levels must be high to substantially alter the current U.S.-Soviet strategic nuclear relationship:

- Some increments of uncertainty could be imposed on Soviet planners by defenses able to intercept about half the Soviet missile force. If an "adaptive preferential defense" strategy could be executed, significant fractions of some sets of "point" targets might be protected.
- The ability to intercept a high percentage of *all* Soviet strategic nuclear weapons including air-breathing ones (assuming threats projected for the mid-1990s) might actually deny the Soviets the ability to destroy many military targets.
- However, at such levels of defensive capability, because of asymmetries in U.S. and Soviet strategic postures, U.S. missile and air defenses might have to perform conspicuously better than Soviet defenses to prevent the Soviets from holding an apparent strategic advantage.[8]
- The design of a system that could, in the long term, protect U.S. cities from potential nuclear destruction seems infeasible without sizable, presumably negotiated, reductions in Soviet offensive forces.

At the conclusion of this chapter, we return to the subject of nuclear force exchange models to indicate the scope of future work OTA believes should be carried out if a decision on BMD development and deployment is to be considered fully informed.

---

[7]That is, given the threat of retaliatory punishment, it would be highly irrational for the Soviets to start a nuclear war. In this view, whatever calculations the Soviets may make about the "military effectiveness" of their ballistic missiles, the price (in damage to the Soviet Union) would be too high to justify a nuclear attack.

---

[8]However, if the United States maintained a substantial bomber-cruise missile threat, if Soviet air defenses were ineffective, and if the Soviets did not pose a substantial bomber-cruise missile threat to the United States, such a Soviet advantage might be avoided.

Limitations of Nuclear Force Exchange Models

Although force exchange analysis is important, applying the results of the analyses requires extreme caution. The greatest danger lies in accepting the numbers generated by the computer as representing reality: they do not. The verisimilitude of a computer simulation can only be checked by comparisons with measured results in the real world that the model is trying to simulate. **There has never been—and we all hope there will never be—a real nuclear war to calibrate the correctness of nuclear force exchange models.**

Instead, such models combine what is known or estimated about the characteristics of weapons and potential targets on each side with a myriad of personal, even if carefully considered, judgments about how nuclear attacks would take place and what the immediate physical results might be. If national leaders are to make wise use of the outcomes of such analytic models, they need to judge whether they agree with the assumptions that go into the models (see table 3-2).

Aside from the many subjective judgments that must go into force exchange models, there are other aspects of the real world that cannot be included in a quantitative computer simulation. The models generally include estimates of prompt casualties from nuclear attacks, but they do not even attempt to account for the longer term medical, social, political, and eco-

Table 3-2.—Judgmental Assumptions in Nuclear Force Exchange Models

- Soviet valuation of Soviet targets
- Estimation of U.S. targets selected by Soviet planners
- Priorities Soviets would attach to destroying particular targets
- Soviet estimates of the reliabilities and capabilities of their weapons
- Soviet estimates of the reliabilities and capabilities of U.S. weapons
- U.S. estimates of the reliabilities and capabilities of U.S. weapons
- U.S. estimates of the resistance or vulnerability to nuclear attack of various Soviet targets
- Estimates of casualties on both sides from nuclear attacks

SOURCE: Office of Technology Assessment, 1988.

nomic consequences of nuclear war. Computer simulations also abstract strategic calculations out of political context. We can only guess, with varying degrees of informed judgment, under what circumstances the Soviets would contemplate starting or risking nuclear war. We do not know how leaders on either side would actually behave in a real nuclear crisis. We do not know, in particular, how and to what degree their decisions would be affected by military planners' strategic exchange calculations.

In sum, nuclear force exchange models can serve as a useful tool for thinking about the goals we might use BMD to pursue. But they cannot demonstrate as scientific fact that those goals will be accomplished, nor can they offer certainty that the effects of deploying BMD would fulfill predictions.

SYSTEM DESIGNS AND END-TO-END MODELS

Force exchange models such as those described above can help analysts estimate how many nuclear weapons a BMD system must intercept to achieve various levels of protection. In this way, decisionmakers can set the overall requirements for BMD performance. Much more detailed analysis is needed to evaluate systems designed to meet those requirements.

This kind of analysis begins, as do force exchange analyses, with projections of the Soviet missile threat during the period for which one expects to have BMD deployed. In this case, however, analysts must consider more than the destructive capabilities of the offensive missile threat. Analysts must also estimate the precise technical performance of the missiles, the numbers of each type, and the tactical plans under which the Soviets might launch them. **In addition, the analysis has to include possible changes in Soviet offensive forces[9] in response to U.S. BMD deployments.** Among the techniques used for this kind of analysis are "end-to-end" computer simulations, which model both the offensive attack and the roles of each type of BMD component, from the sensor that first detects an enemy missile launch to the last layer of interceptors engaging reentry vehicles as they approach their targets.

As table 3-3 indicates, an ICBM flight includes four broad phases: the boost, post-boost, mid-course, and reentry or terminal. System architects for SDI have proposed ways of attacking ballistic missiles in all phases.

Space- and Ground-Based Architectures

Suggested components and functions of a multi-phase BMD system are outlined in tables 3-4 and 3-5. (Chs. 4 and 5 examine the technology for many of these components in considerable detail.) The SDI system architects subdivided the primarily space-based architectures into nearer- and farther-term BMD sys-

tems, with the nearer-term systems envisaged as evolving into the farther-term systems as the Soviet missile threat grows and as more advanced BMD technologies become available. Except for the projected timing, the architecture in table 3-4 reflects SDIO's proposal in mid-1987 for a first-phase "Strategic Defense System." The design would also be intended to lay the basis for expansion into phase two and three systems.

The architectures in table 3-5 draw on information provided by SDIO, but do not constitute their—or anyone else's—specific proposal for what the United States should plan to deploy. Instead, the examples provide a framework for analyzing how the parts of a future BMD system would have to fit together to try to meet the requirements set for it. The tables do include the leading candidates for sensors, discrimination, and weapons described by the system architects. The projected dates in the tables reflect OTA rather than SDIO estimates for the earliest plausible periods over which each phase might be deployed **if it were proven feasible.**

The SDI system architects subjected their various BMD constructs to detailed computer simulations. (These are called "end-to-end" simulations because they attempt to model

[9]Including offensive countermeasures such as decoys and defense suppression measures such as anti-satellite weapons.

Table 3-3.—Phases of Ballistic Missile Trajectory

Phase	Duration	Description
Boost	Several 10s to 100s of seconds[a]	Powered flight of the rocket boosters lifting the missile payload into a ballistic trajectory
Post-boost	10s of seconds to 10s of minutes[b]	Most ICBMs now have a "post-boost vehicle" (PBV), an upper guided stage that ejects multiple, independently targetable reentry vehicles (MIRVs) into routes to their targets. If these RVs are to be accompanied by decoys to deceive BMD systems, the PBV will dispense them as well.
Mid-course	About 20 minutes (less for SLBMs)	RVs and decoys continue along a ballistic trajectory, several hundred to 1,000 kilometers up in space, toward their targets.
Reentry	30 to 60 seconds	RVs and decoys reenter the Earth's atmosphere; lighter decoys first slow down in the upper atmosphere, then burn up because of friction with the air; RVs protected from burning up in friction with the air by means of an ablative coating; at a preset altitude, their nuclear warheads explode.

[a]Now in the hundreds of seconds, in the future boost times may be greatly reduced.
[b]Post-boost dispersal times may also be shortened, though perhaps with penalties in payload, numbers of mid-course decoys, and accuracy.

SOURCE: Office of Technology Assessment, 1988.

Table 3-4.—SDIO's Phase One Space- and Ground-Based BMD Architecture

Component	Number	Description	Function
First phase (approximately 1995-2000):			
Battle Management Computers	Variable	May be carried on sensor platforms, weapon platforms, or separate platforms; ground-based units may be mobile	Coordinate track data; control defense assets; select strategy; select targets; command firing of weapons
Boost Phase Surveillance and Tracking Satellite	Several at high altitude	Infrared sensors	Detect ballistic or ASAT missile launches by observing hot rocket plumes; pass information to tracking satellites
Space-based Interceptor Carrier Satellite	100s at several 100s of km altitudes	Each would carry about 10 small chemical rockets or "SBIs"; might carry sensors for tracking post-boost vehicles	On command, launch rockets at anti-satellite weapons (attacking BMD system), boosters, possibly PBVs.
Probe	10s	Ground-launched rocket-borne infrared sensors	Acquire RV tracks, pass on to ERIS interceptors
or			
Space Surveillance and Tracking System	10s	Satellite-borne infrared sensors	
or			
Space-based Interceptor Carrier Satellites	100s	Satellite-borne infrared sensors	
Exo-atmospheric Interceptors (ERIS)	1000s on ground-based rockets	Rocket booster, hit-to-kill warhead with infrared seeker	Cued by satellite-borne or rocket-borne infrared sensors, home in on and collide with RVs in late mid-course

SOURCE: Office of Technology Assessment, 1988.

BMD performance from booster launch to final RV interception.) Such simulations help show the interdependence of the system components and the requirements posed for the technologies that go into them. These analyses show that, at least in the long run, intercepting a substantial portion of the missiles in the boost phase and early post-boost phase would be essential to a highly effective BMD system. This conclusion follows from the fact that 1,000 to 2,000 boosters could dispense hundreds of thousands of decoys that would greatly stress mid-course interception.[10]

The system architects noted that this boost-phase interception task would eventually (barring sizable offensive arms limitations) have to be accomplished by means of directed-energy weapons, rather than by the space based interceptors (SBIs) envisaged for the first stage of BMD deployments. The speed-of-light velocity of directed energy would be needed because the development of faster-burning rocket boosters and faster-dispensing post-boost vehicles (PBVs) would eventually permit Soviet missiles to finish their boost phases before the space-based interceptors (SBIs) could reach them.

The SDIO contends, however, that interception of PBVs may suffice to meet SDI goals. Although a fast-burn booster would burn out inside the atmosphere, the PBV must clear the atmosphere to dispense light-weight decoys. It then would be vulnerable to SBIs. If SBI interception of PBVs were adequate, directed-energy weapons might not be necessary. If successfully developed, though, they might prove more cost-effective.

The interplay of offensive and defensive technologies is discussed in more detail in chapters 6, 10, and 11 of this report.

[10]SDIO officials point out that an arms control agreement reducing offensive forces would make the defensive job easier and cheaper. On the other hand, the Soviets may not be persuaded to enter into such an agreement unless they can be shown that potential defensive options would make offensive countermeasures on their part futile.

Table 3-5.—OTA's Projections of Evolution of Ground- and Space-Based BMD Architecture

Component	Number	Description	Function
Second phase (approximately 2000-2010) replace first-phase components and add:			
Airborne Optical System (AOS)	10s in flight	Infrared sensors	Track RVs and decoys, pass information to ground battle management computers for launch of ground-based interceptors
Ground-based Radars	10s on mobile platforms	X-band imaging radar	Cued by AOS, track RVs as they enter atmosphere; discriminate from decoys, pass information to ground battle managers
High Endo-atmospheric Interceptors	1000s	Rocket with infrared seeker, non-nuclear warhead	Collide with RVs inside atmosphere, but before RV nuclear detonation could cause ground damage
Space Surveillance and Tracking Satellite (SSTS)	50-100 at few 1000s of km.	High-resolution sensors; laser range-finder and/or imaging radar for finer tracking of objects;	Track launched boosters, post-boost vehicles, and ground or space-launched ASATs; Track RVs and decoys, discriminate RVs from decoys;
		May carry battle management computers	Command firing of weapons
Space-based Interceptor Carrier	1000s at 100s of km altitudes	Each carries about 10 small chemical rockets or "KKVs"; at low altitude; lighter and faster than in phase one	On command, launch rockets at anti-satellite weapons (attacking BMD system), boosters, PBVs, and RVs
Space-based Neutral Particle Beam (NPB)	10s to 100s at altitude similar to SSTS	Atomic particle accelerator (perturber component of interactive discrimination; additional sensor satellites may be needed)	Fire hydrogen atoms at RVs and decoys to stimulate emission of neutrons or gamma rays as discriminator
Detector Satellites	100s around particle beam altitudes	Sensors to measure neutrons or gamma rays from objects bombarded by NPB; transmitters send data to SSTS and/or battle management computers	Measure neutrons or gamma rays emitted from RVs: heavier objects emit measurable neutrons or gamma rays, permitting discrimination from decoys
Third phase (approximately 2005-2115), replace second-phase components and add:			
Ground-based Lasers, Space-based Mirrors	10s of ground-based lasers; 10s of relay mirrors; 10s to 100s of battle mirrors	Several laser beams from each of several ground sites bounce off relay mirrors at high altitude, directed to targets by battle mirrors at lower altitudes	Attack boosters and PBVs

SOURCE: Office of Technology Assessment, 1988.

Battle Management Architecture

Specifying Battle Management Architecture

Any BMD system architecture will contain a kind of sub-architecture, the "battle management architecture." The battle management design shows how BMD system components would be integrated into a single coordinated operating entity. The battle management software, which would direct the battle manage-

ment computers and control the actions of the system, would carry the burden of integration. A communications system would transmit data and decisions among the battle management computers and between the computers and the sensors and weapons.

The system would probably divide the volume in which the battle would be fought into a set of smaller battle spaces. A regional or local battle manager would consist of the battle management software and computer with responsibility for controlling the resources used to fight within a particular battle space. The battle manager and the resources it controlled would be known as a battle group. The battle management architecture specifies the following:

- the physical location of the battle management computers and the nodes of the communications network;
- the method for partitioning resources into battle groups so that battle management computers have access to and control over appropriate numbers and kinds of sensors and weapons;
- a hierarchical organization that specifies the authority and responsibility of the battle managers, similar to a military chain-of-command;
- the role of humans in the battle management hierarchy;
- the method used for coordinating the actions of the battle managers through the battle management hierarchy and across the different battle phases so that handover of responsibility, authority, and resources between boost, post-boost, midcourse, and terminal phases would take place smoothly and efficiently; and
- the organization of and the method used for routing data and decisions through the communications network, probably organized as a hierarchy that would govern how the nodes of the network were connected.

Battle management architectures proposed so far have varied widely in their approach to these issues. For example, some architects proposed placing their space-based battle management computers on the same satellite platforms as the Space Surveillance and Tracking System (SSTS), some on the carrier vehicles, and some on separate battle management platforms; some proposed that the battle managers exchange track information only among neighbor battle managers at the same level of the battle management hierarchy, while others proposed that the same data also be exchanged between upper and lower levels; some architects permitted humans to intervene in the midst of battle to select different battle strategies while others allowed humans only to authorize weapons release.

Table 3-6 describes two different battle management architectures that are representative of those proposed. It shows the physical locations of the battle managers, the criteria used for partitioning resources into battle groups, the data exchanged by the battle managers, the methods used for coordinating responsibility and authority between phases of the battle, the degree to which human intervention would be allowed during battle, and the structure of the communications network.

Interaction Between Battle Management and System Architecture

Battle management architectural decisions would strongly affect the size, complexity, and organization of the battle management soft-

Table 3-6.—Two Representative Battle Management Architectures

Design by location of battle managers	Partitioning criterion	Data exchanged by battle managers	Method of coordinating between battle phases	Degree of human intervention	Communications network organization
Design I: SSTS	Local battle groups assigned to cover specific Earth-based geographic areas	Object tracks	Regional battle managers control hand-over between phases	Humans authorize weapons release at start of battle; can switch strategies during battle	Two-tiered hierarchy
Design II: Carrier vehicles	Initially geographic, then by threat tube (the path along which a group of missiles travels)	Health (weapon status) information	All battle managers use same criteria for target allocation, taking into account locations of other battle managers	Humans authorize weapons release at start of battle	All nodes in line-of-sight of each other are interconnected

SOURCE: Office of Technology Assessment, 1988.

ware. Because of the close relationship between the battle management computers and the communications network, such decisions also would strongly affect the software that controlled the computers forming the nodes of the communications network. A good example of the interaction among system architecture, battle management architecture, and battle management and communications software is represented by the controversy over how widely distributed battle management should be. The two extremes of completely centralized and completely autonomous battle managers and a range of intermediate options are discussed in both the Fletcher and Eastport group reports and considered in all the architectural studies.[11]

Physical Organization v. Conceptual Design

Analyses often have reflected confusion between the *physical* organization and the *conceptual* organization of the battle managers. The physical organization may be centralized by putting all of the battle management software into one large computer system, or be distributed by having battle management computers on every carrier vehicle. Similarly, the software may be designed as:

1. a single, central battle manager that controls the entire battle;
2. a hierarchy of battle managers, with local battle managers each responsible for a small battle space, regional battle managers responsible for coordinating among local battle managers, and a central battle manager coordinating the actions of the regional battle managers; or
3. as a set of completely independent battle managers with no coordination among each other.

Any of these three software designs might be implemented using either a centralized or distributed physical organization. Variations on the three designs, e.g., introducing more levels into the battle manager hierarchy, are possible, but infrequently considered.

The physical organization and the conceptual design would impose constraints on each other, and factors such as survivability and reliability would drive both. A widely distributed physical design, involving many independent computers, would impose too heavy a synchronization and communications penalty among the physically distributed components of the software to permit use of a centralized conceptual design: the attendant complications in the software would make the battle manager unreliable and slow to react. Physical distribution requires the battle management software on each computer to be relatively autonomous. A system with completely autonomous battle managers would perform less well than a system with communicating battle managers. Accordingly, even a widely distributed physical organization would likely require some communications and synchronization among the battle managers.

A centralized physical design might not provide sufficient computer processing power for acceptable performance, but would significantly improve communications among the battle managers. The result might simplify the software development, and lead to greater software reliability. On the other hand, such an organization might result in a poorly survivable system: if the central computer were disabled, the remainder of the system could not function.

Integrating Battle Management Architecture With System Architecture

Since the system architecture, physical battle management organization, and battle management software design affect each other, all should be considered together. The relationships and interfaces among the battle managers should be defined either prior to or together with definition of the physical organization of the battle managers and their requirements for communication with each other and with sensors and weapons. As the Fletcher report

---

[11]*Report of the Study on Eliminating The Threat Posed by Nuclear Ballistic Missiles, Vol. V, Battle Management, Communications, and Data Processing,* October 1983. This was the only unclassified volume of the Fletcher commission report. See also "Eastport Study Group—A Report to the Director, Strategic Defense Initiative Organization" (Eastport Study Group, Marina Del Rey, CA, 1985).

stated, "The battle management system and its software must be designed as an integral part of the BMD system as a whole, not as an appliqué."[12]

Most of the SDI architectures proposed so far have shown little evidence of an integral design. Software design has been largely ignored, giving way to issues such as the location of the battle management computers and the criteria for forming battle groups. The SDIO has reported that it is attempting to better integrate overall system architecture studies and battle management studies in its current phase of system architecture contracting. However, the system proposed in mid-1987 for "demonstration and validation" seemed to reflect no such integration.

Some Important Results of the System Requirements and Design Work

Systems analysis for SDI is still, necessarily, at a preliminary stage. Its most valuable contribution so far has probably been the identification of key issues that research would have to resolve satisfactorily before the Nation could make a rational decision to proceed to development and deployment of BMD. In particular, the analyses have shown the following:

Boost-Phase Interception

Adequate boost-phase interception of missiles is essential to make the mid-course and terminal interception problems manageable; otherwise, the offense has the opportunity to deploy so many decoys and other penetration aids that they could swamp the other defensive layers. However, an adequate boost-phase interception may, over time, be countered by new offensive weapons and still have done its job: after deploying all the faster burning boosters and PBVs it could afford to counter the boost-phase defense, the offense may not be able to deploy enough decoys to overwhelm the mid-course defense.

[12]Ibid.

Ultimate Need for Directed-Energy Weapons

As a corollary to the need for effective boost-phase interception, it will be important to have a credible long-term system design which includes directed-energy weapons based in space to carry out boost-phase interception against boosters and PBVs that are too fast to be reached by kinetic energy weapons. Without such a credible plan, the boost-phase interceptors would face fairly predictable obsolescence. (It is possible, however, to imagine the development of new SBIs able to penetrate the upper atmosphere; if launched quickly enough, they could then reach some boosters.)

Need for Interactive Discrimination

Because of the potential for Soviet deployment of hundreds of thousands of decoys that passive sensors may not be able to differentiate from RVs disguised as decoys ("anti-simulation"), mid-course interception is likely to require means of perturbing RVs and decoys and highly capable sensors to detect the differences in the ways the two kinds of objects react. Such means of "interactive discrimination" have been conceived but not yet built and tested.

Interdependence of Defensive Layers

Ideally, independent layers of sensors and weapons would carry out interception of each phase of ballistic missile trajectory, thus eliminating common failure modes and common nodes of vulnerability to hostile action. In fact, for practical reasons, the system architects generally produced designs with considerable degrees of interdependence. In addition, as noted above, even if the functions of each layer were performed entirely independently, failure in one phase of interception (the boost-phase, for example) can severely affect the potential performance of succeeding phases.

Importance of Integrated Battle Management Architecture

Initially, system architecture and battle management architecture studies were separately contracted for, producing large discrepancies among those who had studied each subject the most. The two sets of studies are apparently now being better integrated, and presumably subsequent designs will reflect that integration.

Distributed Battle Management

Although considerable work on designing BMD battle management remains, analysis so far makes clear the importance of a battle management system that make decisions in a distributed, as opposed to centralized, fashion. Attempting to centralize the decisionmaking would both impose excessive computing, software engineering, and communications requirements and make the system more vulnerable to enemy disruption.

Heavy Space Transportation Requirements

The system architecture designs now permit better forecasts of the requirements imposed by space-based systems for space transportation capabilities—capabilities far beyond those the United States now possesses. (Primarily ground-based architectures do not share this problem.)

Requirements for Assured Survival

There appears to be general agreement on the importance of significantly reducing offensive force developments if one hopes to provide mutual assured survival for the U.S. and Soviet populations.

IMPORTANT SYSTEMS ANALYSIS WORK REMAINING

The SDI architecture studies have just begun to address the complex problems of designing a working, survivable BMD system with prospects for long-term viability against a responsive Soviet threat. Thus far, the architecture studies have served the useful purpose of helping to identify the most critical technologies needing further development. Future system designers would have to integrate the technologies actually available—and mass producible—into deployable and workable weapon systems.

Given that the system architects and SDIO are just over 2 to 3 years into an analytic effort that will take many more years, it is not a criticism to say that much work remains. However, it appears to be the case that the analysis supporting the first-phase architecture that SDIO proposed in mid-1987 simply did not address many key questions. The following are further tasks that analysts should carry out to help both the executive and legislative branches judge the potential effects of decisions on BMD.

Further Strategic Nuclear Force Exchange Work

The strategic nuclear exchange modeling done so far by the SDI system architects pro-

vides a useful beginning to the larger and lengthier task of developing the information that will be needed for a national decision on whether to deploy BMD. **If the limitations of these kinds of simulations are borne carefully in mind,** they can help one to understand how BMD might affect the calculations of U.S. and Soviet national leaders, both in decisions about peace and war and in decisions about long-term strategic policies. They can also help to clarify the assumptions all participants bring to the U.S. national debate about BMD.

Introduce Comparability Among Analyses

It is desirable to have competing sets of computer simulation models for analyzing the same questions. In that way, decisionmakers could compare differing conclusions and identify the underlying assumptions of each. (Comparisons could also uncover errors in implementation of the models.) Analysts should run different models using the same sets of data about the Soviet missile threat, the same configurations of defensive systems, and the same offensive and defensive strategies and tactics. Thus far, differences in these elements have made the analyses of the system architects difficult to compare and judge.

Further Analyses of Soviet Offensive Responses

The simulations run so far have examined only limited variations on Soviet attack plans in the face of growing U.S. defensive capabilities: the assumption is made that the Soviets have an inflexible list of targets. The Soviets are assumed to optimize their exact attack plan to destroy the highest possible number of those targets at some level of confidence. Suppose, however, that if defenses drastically reduced Soviet confidence in their ability to destroy hardened military targets, they concentrated on softer military and economic targets. Analysts must carry out further exploration of this possibility if decisionmakers are to understand the full implications of BMD for all types of deterrence (see table 3-1).

Assumptions About Deterrence

An analytic focus on an inflexible Soviet target plan seems to be related to a simplified model of potential Soviet motives for attack. The usual working assumption seems to be that the Soviets would decide to launch a nuclear strike on the United States on the basis of calculations about the probabilities of destroying certain percentages of various types of targets. In this view, above a certain threshold for one or more of these probabilities, the Soviets would be willing to strike, and below it they would not because they could not accomplish their military purposes. One target set would be the weapons and command-and-control facilities that would permit a U.S. nuclear retaliation. But the exact role in Soviet decisionmaking attributed to fear of retaliation—as opposed to accomplishment of other military objectives—remains unclear. **The nuclear exchange models should make more explicit their assumptions about the weightings given to denial of military objectives as opposed to the likelihood and intensity of U.S. retaliation as enforcers of deterrence.**

Analysts should attempt to identify the *increment* of uncertainty added to the Soviet calculus of nuclear war provided by levels of defensive capability that might increase Soviet uncertainty about achieving attack objectives, but that could not assure denial of those objectives. Many things could go wrong with a nuclear attack precisely scheduled to achieve a specific set of goals (such as knocking out a given percentage of U.S. retaliatory capability). *How much* uncertainty would a given level of BMD add to that which already exists? What are the potential Soviet responses to this additional uncertainty?[13] To what extent would the increment of uncertainty strengthen deterrence? At what cost per increment of strengthened deterrence?

Strategic Stability Analyses

Closely related to the question of Soviet attack motivations is the question of strategic stability. In its 1985 report on BMD, OTA emphasized the importance of exploring this question thoroughly.

A simplified approach to crisis stability is as follows: in a military confrontation with the United States, Soviet decisionmakers would calculate whether or not they could achieve a given set of military objectives by launching a strategic nuclear first strike. If the objectives seemed attainable, they would strike; if not, they would refrain. The system architects have considered this scenario.

Another possibility they should address, however, is that Soviet *perceptions* of a likely *U.S.* first strike might affect Soviet behavior. System architects have been understandably reluctant to run or to report extensively on simulations in which the United States is assumed to strike first. Such analyses might imply to some that a change is being contemplated in U.S. policy not to launch a preemptive strategic nuclear first strike. Nevertheless, such analysis needs to be done, not because the United States *would* launch such an attack, but because the Soviet Union might not *believe* that it would not.

---

[13]A possibility suggested by one reviewer of the OTA study is that the Soviets discover, unbeknownst to the United States, a way of disabling the U.S. BMD system (perhaps by spoofing its command and control system). Further, the Soviets validate their countermeasure with undetected techniques before actually launching an attack. Certain that their technique will work, and their offensive forces augmented in response to the U.S. defensive deployments, the Soviets in this scenario end up *more* certain about the probable success of their attack than before.

It is conceivable, for example, that Soviet strategic exchange calculations could show that a U.S. first strike, backed up by U.S. BMD, might allow the United States to reduce significantly the damage from a Soviet "ragged" retaliation.[14] On the other hand, a Soviet first strike might have an analogous effect. If the Soviets believed that the United States, expecting a Soviet strike, might strike first, then the Soviets might try to get in the first blow. Thus, they would not make their decision to strike on the basis of accomplishing a clear set of military objectives, but instead on the basis of choosing the less terrible of two catastrophic outcomes.

Even if the Soviet Union and the United States avoided a nuclear crisis in which such calculations might play a role, the calculations could still influence the longer-range Soviet responses to U.S. BMD deployments. The Soviets might decide that it was extremely important to them to maintain a "credible" nuclear threat against the United States, and therefore be willing to spend more on maintaining offensive forces than "cost-exchange" ratios would seem to justify.

Administration officials have repeatedly stated their desire to negotiate (or find unilaterally) a "stable transition" path to a world in which strategic defenses play a large role. Finding such a path would require careful analysis of the incentives presented to Soviet leaders by *U.S.* actions. Estimating the consequences of a hypothetical U.S. attack is one key part of such an analysis. Only then might U.S. analysts identify offensive and defensive force levels that *both* sides could believe served their security. Some of this analytic work has been started, but more is necessary.

U.S. Responses to Soviet BMD

It is entirely possible that the Soviet Union will not wait until the United States decides whether deploying BMD is a good idea or not, but instead will unilaterally choose to expand its own BMD system.[15] The United States conducts BMD research in part to be able to respond in kind to such a decision. The system architects for SDI have conducted simulations to show how a responding U.S. BMD deployment might restore the U.S.-Soviet strategic balance. Before the United States chose such a response, however, two other kinds of analysis are desirable. First, analysts should compare the BMD option with the option of circumventing Soviet BMD by means of increasing U.S. air-breathing, low-flying cruise missile forces. Second, researchers should determine the ability of U.S. technology to find adequate offensive countermeasures to Soviet BMD.

These questions are partly amenable to the strategic exchange modeling technique. In the first case, the model could assume various numbers of cruise missiles with varying levels of probability of penetration in battle scenarios in which Soviet BMD was degrading the ability of U.S. ballistic missiles to get through. Analysts could compare these outcomes to those of similar scenarios in which the U.S. deployed BMD instead of additional cruise missiles. Then they could estimate quantities of BMD and cruise missiles required to produce similar outcomes. This information could provide the basis for cost-effectiveness comparisons between BMD and cruise missiles once data on the actual costs of the two types of systems became available.

Similarly, analysts could plug into the simulations the increases in warhead penetration of Soviet defenses caused by U.S. offensive countermeasures. Once estimates were available for the costs of these countermeasures, analyses could develop some idea of the relative cost-effectiveness of offense and defense.

---

[14]A "ragged" retaliation is one carried out after the first strike has destroyed at least portions of the nation's strategic forces and possibly degraded its command and control system, resulting in a relatively unstructured, diluted counter-attack.

[15]As permitted by the ABM Treaty, the Soviets have retained a limited, nuclear-armed ballistic missile defense system in the Moscow area; they are currently expanding the system to the full 100 interceptors permitted by the treaty, and could conceivably replicate the system elsewhere. They have also constructed a series of phased array radars around the Soviet Union which would provide warning and limited battle management capabilities for such an expanded system.

Analysis of Alternate Defensive Measures

The lesser goals of strategic defense—that is, enhancing deterrence by increasing Soviet uncertainty or denial of various military objectives—have thus far been considered as preliminary benefits on the way toward extremely high degrees of population protection. Therefore, alternate means of achieving the lesser goals as ends in themselves have not been analyzed. A few examples might clarify this point.

Defense of Land-Based ICBMs.—If strengthening deterrence by increasing the survivability of U.S. land-based retaliatory forces, especially ICBMs, were the goal of deploying BMD, then the system designs done for the SDI might not be optimal.[16] Instead, ground-based, low-altitude interceptors located relatively near the missiles to be defended might be less expensive (unlike cities, hardened missile silos or capsules might withstand low-altitude nuclear explosions). In addition, the United States would want to consider how it could use various forms of mobile or deceptive basing of ICBMs in conjunction with limited BMD to make the enemy's cost of attacking the missiles prohibitive.

Careful analysis of the goal of protecting strategic bomber bases from SLBMs launched not far off U.S. shores might also yield different BMD designs combined with different bomber basing tactics.

Defense of Command, Control, and Communications Facilities.—Similarly the strategic goal of increasing the survivability of the U.S. command and control system for nuclear forces might be achieved by some form of BMD, but the United States should also compare the cost and effectiveness of BMD with those of other measures for making the system more resistant to nuclear attack. Further analysis might show that some combination of passive survivability measures *and* BMD would be more cost-effective than either alone.

Defense Against Accidental or Terrorist Missile Launches.—Protecting the country against 10 or so incoming reentry vehicles is a much different task than protecting it against thousands. **While SDI-designed systems might offer such protection as a side-benefit, if this kind of defense were to be the major goal of deploying BMD, one would consider different, much simpler and cheaper architectures than those designed for the SDI.[17]**

Further System Requirements and Design Work

Analyze Additional Threats to BMD System Survivability

The SDI system architects recognized that survivability would be a critical feature of any BMD system. They devoted considerable effort and ingenuity to inventing ways to reduce system vulnerability to Soviet attack. The chief threat to survivability they examined was ground-based, direct-ascent anti-satellite weapons—rockets that the Soviets could "pop up" from their territory to attack U.S. space-based BMD assets with nuclear or non-nuclear warheads. This was a reasonable first approach to the survivability problem: such weapons probably represent the kind of defense suppression weapon most immediately available to the Soviets. If the defense could not counter this threat, then there would be no point in exploring other, more sophisticated threats.

In the second round of their "horse race" competition the system architects did very little analysis of other potential threats to BMD system survivability, particularly longer-term space-based threats. The threat of "space mines," satellites designed specifically to shadow and destroy the various space-based BMD components, was not considered in depth. **Moreover, no analysis assumed that the Soviets might deploy in space a BMD system**

---

[16]See U.S. Congress, Office of Technology Assessment, *MX Missile Basing*, OTA-ISC-140 (Washington, DC: U.S. Government Printing Office, September 1981).

[17]For example, a few ground-based, long-range interceptors like the Exo-atmospheric Reentry Interceptor System (ERIS)—see ch. 5—could cover the continental United States; existing early-warning radars could give initial track information and a few "pop-up" infrared sensor probes provide final track information.

comparable to that of the United States; thus the potential vulnerabilities of such weapon systems to one another were not considered. Instead, it was assumed that the United States would, for the most part, militarily dominate near-Earth space. From the statement of work provided to the SDI system architecture contractors late in 1986, it remained unclear whether this assumption would be changed in the follow-on studies to be completed early in 1988.

Develop Realistic Schedules

The system architects were originally instructed to design systems that might enter full-scale engineering development in the early 1990s and be deployed beginning in the mid-1990s. The systems they designed would have required challenging technical achievements even under the originally requested SDI budgets. For example, one system architect pointed out that a vigorous technology program did not yet exist for an active space-based sensor crucial to an "interim" defense intended for deployment in the mid-1990s. Or, to take another example, deployment in the mid-1990s of the space-based systems identified by the architects would require that the United States decide almost immediately to begin acquiring the massive space transportation system that deployment would require.[18]

Given the actual levels of SDI funding appropriated by Congress thus far, mid-1990s deployment of the kinds of systems initially proposed by the system architects is clearly not feasible. Even with the requested funding, it is unlikely that researchers could overcome *all* the technological hurdles in time to permit confident full-scale engineering decisions in the early 1990s. Nor is it clear that the full-scale engineering process, including establishment of manufacturing capabilities for the complex systems involved, could be completed in just 3 or 4 years. (For example, the most optimistic expert estimate OTA encountered for engineering full-scale SDI battle management soft-

ware was 7 years.) In short, the systems designated as "interim" (similar to those labeled "Second Phase" in table 3-5) by the system architects would not be likely to reach full operational capability until well after the year 2000.

Late in 1986, SDIO called on its contractors to orient their work to a much scaled-back system architecture, with scaled-back strategic goals (see the "First Phase" in table 3-4). Speculations emerged in the press about "early deployment" options under consideration. Analysis of the "phase one" designs, however, suggests that even they could not be ready for initial space deployment until at least the mid-1990s. Nor could they be fully in place much before the end of the century.

In the meantime, the Soviet Union might well deploy practical countermeasures against such systems. Specifically, many in the defense community believe that the Soviets could deploy decoys along with their reentry vehicles that would greatly stress the minimal mid-course discrimination capability of a phase-one system. In addition, the Soviets could at least begin to deploy new booster rockets that would drastically reduce the effectiveness of space-based interceptors (SBIs) in boost-phase defense.

Even if the United States could deploy SBIs beginning in the mid-1990s, another question remains: how confident do U.S. decisionmakers wish to be in the long-term viability of BMD before they decide to deploy such systems? Given the state of research on directed-energy devices for BMD, it is highly unlikely that U.S. leaders could have sufficient information by the early 1990s to determine whether full-scale engineering development of phases two and three would be feasible in the following decade. Thus, an early 1990s decision implies a commitment to a space-based BMD whose obsolescence would be made highly probable by the prospect of faster burning Soviet missile boosters, but whose replacement would remain unproven.

Develop Credible Cost Estimates

The SDIO has properly pointed out that trying to estimate total life-cycle costs for an un-

---

[18]The SDIO requested $250 million in supplemental funds for fiscal year 1987 to develop technology for low-cost space transportation.

precedented system is difficult. The aerospace industry would have to manufacture new components and weapons in new ways. The Nation would need a new space transportation system for a space-based system. The SDIO has agreed to estimate "cost goals" to indicate the kind of investment that the Nation would have to make in proposed BMD architectures. The system architects were instructed to develop cost estimates in their 1987 studies.

Develop Methods for Estimating Cost-Exchange Ratios Between Defense and Offense

As this report pointed out in chapter 2, one key criterion for the technical feasibility of the SDI scenario of transition to a "defense-dominated" world is that there be a favorable cost-exchange ratio between defense and offense. The system architects did try to address this issue in various ways, but there still seems to be no systematic approach toward it. The problem will be intrinsically difficult, because estimating in advance the costs of the U.S. BMD system will be difficult, estimating the costs of Soviet responses will be more difficult, and predicting *Soviet* estimates of these quantities will be most difficult of all. Nevertheless,

analyses should at least begin to specify what information would permit sufficient confidence that the defense/offense cost-exchange ratio is high enough to justify going ahead. The system architecture contractor teams were instructed to address the problem in their 1987 work.

Assess the Role and Costs of Complementary Air Defenses

The Strategic Defense Initiative Organization is specifically limited to defense against ballistic missiles. The Air Force has undertaken an "Air Defense Initiative," though at funding levels far below that of the SDI. Nevertheless, at least at the systems analysis level, U.S. decisionmakers need an integrated understanding of the role that air defense would have to play if ballistic missile defense were to achieve such goals as increasing Soviet uncertainty about attack success, denying Soviet abilities to destroy high percentages of certain types of targets, or protecting the population from nuclear attack. Moreover, insofar as BMD requires air defense to accomplish its purposes, the feasibility and affordability of air defense against possible Soviet attempts to circumvent BMD need to be included in any ultimate analysis of the feasibility of BMD.

Chapter 4

Status and Prospects of Ballistic Missile Defense Sensor Technology

CONTENTS

Box

Figures

Tables

Status and Prospects of Ballistic Missile Defense Sensor Technology

INTRODUCTION

Much of the public debate on ballistic missile defense (BMD) technologies centers on futuristic weapon systems such as lasers, rail guns, and particle beams. The Strategic Defense Initiative Organization's (SDIO) initial BMD system design, however, does not include any of these exotic weapons.[1] Rather, it calls for space-based interceptors (SBI) to collide with Soviet intercontinental ballistic missile (ICBM) boosters and post-boost vehicles (PBVs), and for high acceleration ground-based missiles to destroy Soviet reentry vehicles (RVs) by direct impact. The sensor systems required to detect, identify, and track up to several hundred thousand targets may be more challenging than the actual kinetic energy weapons: it may be more difficult to track targets than to destroy them, once tracked.

The technical feasibility of a first-phase deployment, then, may depend primarily on major technical advances in the areas of sensors and chemically propelled rockets, and less on the availability of rail-gun or laser weapons systems. Accordingly, this report emphasizes these more conventional technologies.

Nonetheless, the more exotic weapons technologies could become important in second- or third-phase BMD systems deployed in response to Soviet countermeasures. For example, if the Soviet Union deployed fast-burn boosters that burned out and deployed their RVs (and decoys) before they could be attacked by slow-moving chemically-propelled rockets, then laser weapons might be essential to attack ICBMs in their boost phase. These directed-energy weapons (DEW) would require even more accurate sensors, since their beams would have to be directed with great precision. Thus, the required sensor technology improvements might continue to be at least as stressing as weapons technology requirements.

Some of the major sensor and weapon components proposed by Strategic Defense Initiative (SDI) system architects for both near- and far-term deployments are listed in figure 4-1 (also see ch. 3). This chapter describes sensors; weapons, power systems, communications systems, and space transportation required to implement a global BMD system are described in chapter 5. For each technology, chapters 4 and 5 discuss:

- the type of system suggested by SDI architects,
- the technical requirements,
- the basic operating principles,
- the current status, and
- the key issues for each technology.

The systems aspects of an integrated BMD system are discussed in chapter 6. Computing technologies are discussed in chapter 8. Technologies for offensive countermeasures and counter-countermeasures are deferred until chapters 10 through 12 (as of this writing, available only in the classified version of this report).

---

[1]Some BMD architecture contractors did, however, call for rather exotic beam sources for "interactive discrimination," in which targets would be exposed to sub-lethal doses of particle beams or laser beams and their reactions measured to distinguish between reentry vehicles and decoys. See section on interactive discrimination.

Recently, SDIO officials have spoken of "entry level" directed-energy weapons that might constitute part of second-phase BMD deployments. The utility of such weapons would depend on the pace and scope of Soviet countermeasures.

Note: Complete definitions of acronyms and initialisms are listed in Appendix B of this report.

Figure 4-1.—Major SDI Sensors and Weapons

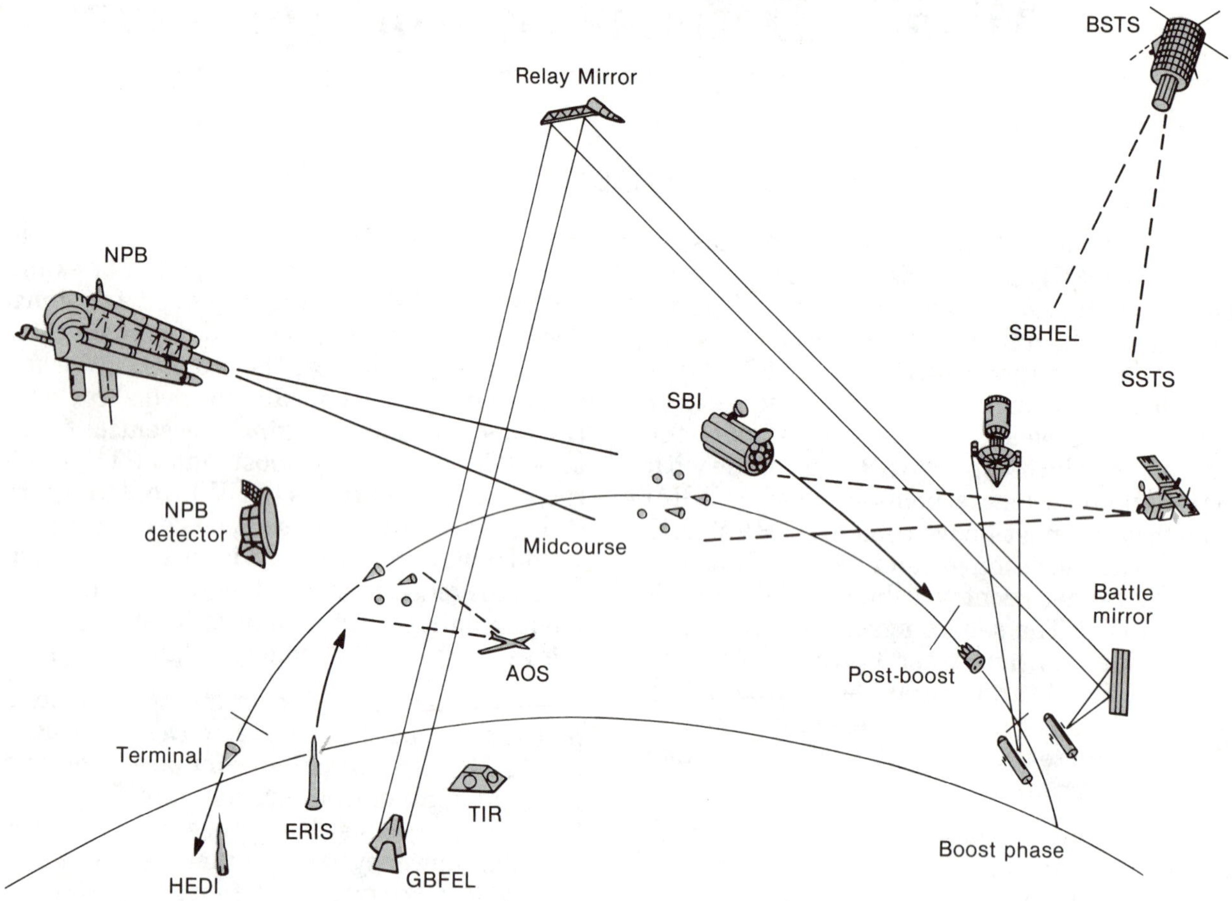

SDI sensor systems:

BSTS–Boost Surveillance and Tracking System (infrared sensors)
SSTS–Space Surveillance and Tracking System (infrared, visible, and possibly radar or laser radar sensors)
AOS–Airborne Optical System (infrared and laser sensors)
TIR–Terminal Imaging Radar (phased array radar)
NPB–Neutral Particle Beam (interactive discrimination to distinguish reentry vehicles (RV's) from decoys; includes separate neutron detector satellite)

SDI weapons systems:

SBI–Space-Based Interceptors or Kinetic Kill Vehicles (rocket-propelled hit to kill projectiles)
SBHEL–Space-Based High Energy Laser (chemically pumped laser)
GBFEL–Ground-Based Free Electron Laser (with space-based relay mirrors)
NPB–Neutral Particle Beam weapon
ERIS–Exoatmospheric Reentry vehicle Interceptor System (ground-based rockets)
HEDI–High Endoatmospheric Defense Interceptor (ground-based rockets)

SENSORS

Sensors are the eyes of a weapons system. In the past the human eye and brain have constituted the primary military sensor system. A soldier on the battlefield would:

- look over the battlefield for possible enemy action (surveillance);
- note any significant object or motion (acquisition);
- determine if the object was a legitimate target (discrimination);
- follow the enemy motion (tracking);
- Aim his rifle (weapon direction), fire;
- look to see if he had killed the target (kill assessment); and
- if not, reacquire the target (retargeting), aim, and shoot again.

Ballistic missile defense entails these same functions of target surveillance, acquisition, discrimination, tracking, weapon direction, kill assessment, and retargeting. BMD sensors, however, must have capabilities of resolution, range, spectral response, speed, and data storage and manipulation far beyond those of the human eye-brain system.

Proposed SDI Sensor Systems

The following sections describe five representative sensor systems. Most of the five SDI system architecture contractors (see ch. 3) recommended some variation of these sensor systems. The primary attack phase and recommended sensor platforms for each type are summarized in tables 1-1 and 1-2.

Boost Surveillance and Tracking System (BSTS)

The BSTS would have to detect any missile launch, give warning, and begin to establish track files for the individual rockets. Most system architects proposed a constellation of several satellites in high orbit.

Typical BSTS characteristics are summarized in the classified version of this report. Each BSTS would carry a sensor suite that would monitor infrared (IR) emissions from the

Figure 4-2.—Relations Between Temperature and Electromagnetic Radiation

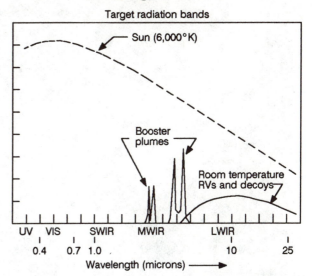

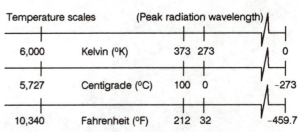

Very hot sources such as the sun radiate primarily in the visible portion of the spectrum. The hot exhaust gases from missile booster engines radiate primarily in the short and mid-wave infrared (SWIR & MWIR), while colder bodies such as reentry vehicles, the booster body, and the earth radiate at much longer wavelengths in the infrared (LWIR). Therefore different sensors would be required to detect different targets.

rocket plumes (see figure 4-2). From their very high altitude, these sensors would have relatively poor optical resolution. Track files could be started, but the Space Surveillance and Tracking System (SSTS) or other sensors at lower altitude might be required to achieve the track file accuracy needed for some BMD functions.[2]

---

[2]Space-based interceptors (SBIs), formerly called "space-based kinetic kill vehicles" (SBKKV), which have their own homing sensors, could operate with the resolution given by a BSTS sensor.

Photo credit: Contractor photo released by U.S. Department of Defense

Artist's concept of boost surveillance and tracking system (BSTS) satellite. During an intercontinental ballistic missile's (ICBM) boost phase—which lasts up to five minutes on some current ICBMs but which may be much shorter on future ones—the missile's first- and second-stage engines emit intensely hot gases. Space-borne infrared sensors can detect these plumes. A BSTS sensor might monitor, detect, and track the rocket plumes and signal ground- or space-based battle management computers to order attacks against the boosters.

Space Surveillance and Tracking System

For their equivalent of an SDIO phase-two BMD system, all five system architects proposed some type of SSTS at lower altitudes to furnish finer-resolution missile tracking and to detect cold RVs and warmer post-boost ve-hicles (PBVs) against a space background. Most of the SSTSs would be out of range for observing Soviet ICBM launches at any given time. Therefore several tens of SSTS satellites would be needed to provide continuous, redundant coverage of the missile fields, which also would supply adequate coverage around the world for submarine-launched missiles.[3] Redundancy would be necessary for survivability and for stereo viewing of the targets. These SSTS satellites might be essential for much of the mid-course battle, so some SSTSs must survive at most locations.[4]

The SSTS satellites would carry one or more long-wave infrared (LWIR) sensors for tracking the somewhat warm PBVs and cold RVs. These LWIR sensors could not detect RVs by looking straight down against the relatively warm earth background. Rather, they would look only above the horizon, in a conical or "coolie hat" pattern which would afford the necessary cold space background for the IR detectors. Thus each SSTS would monitor targets that were far from the satellite. Those targets closest to each SSTS would pass below its sensors, undetected; they would have to be observed by more distant SSTS satellites (see figure 4-3). This problem could be alleviated if sensing at other wavelengths, e.g., in the visible range, were to be feasible.

For some missions, such as cueing DEW sensors, the SSTS might include short-wave infrared (SWIR) and medium-wave infrared (MWIR) sensors to track booster exhaust plumes. This would duplicate to some extent the BSTS function, but with much better resolution.[5] These sensors might have limited fields of view, so that each SSTS platform would require several IR sensors to cover all the threats. These SWIR/MWIR sensors could look down against the Earth background, since they would be monitoring the hot plumes.

Several architects recommended placing laser systems (and some suggested microwave radars) on the SSTS. Lasers might be needed

Figure 4-3.—Scanning Pattern for Satellite Sensor

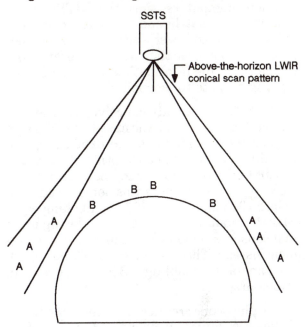

"Coolie hat" above-the-horizon scan pattern for the LWIR sensors on the SSTS which could only detect the cold RV's against the cold background of space. The targets labeled "A" could be detected by this SSTS platform, whereas the closer targets labeled "B" could not be detected against the warm earth background. These "B" targets would have to be tracked by another, more distant SSTS satellite.

to designate or illuminate targets for homing space-based interceptors (SBIs). Laser radar (Ladar) systems might be required for all of the interactive discrimination systems, just to determine the target's position with sufficient accuracy. This would be particularly true for tracking cold RVs, which could be passively detected mainly by LWIR sensors with inherently poor resolution,[6] or for discriminating and designating an RV in the presence of closely spaced objects (that often are decoys). In any case, a laser radar could supply the range to the target, which is necessary to generate three dimensional track files from a single platform.

---

[3]More recent SDI studies have recommended fewer satellites.

[4]Alternatively, pop-up IR probes on ground-based rockets could observe the midcourse battle. These probes would have to be based at high latitudes to get close enough to observe the beginning of mid-course missile flight. Otherwise, they could be based in the northern United States to view the late midcourse.

[5]An SSTS could not achieve the pointing accuracy needed by DEW satellites; each DEW platform would have to carry its own high-resolution optical sensor. An SSTS constellation might aid the battle manager in designating targets for DEWs.

[6]The resolution angle of a sensor is directly proportional to wavelength; long wavelengths such as LWIR produce large resolution spots in the sensor focal plane, or large uncertainty in the target's location. Therefore shorter wavelength laser radars may be needed to accurately measure target position.

The SSTS might also carry some battle management computers, since the SSTSs would be above the battle and to some extent less vulnerable than lower altitude weapons platforms, and because they would generate most of the track-file information essential for assigning targets to weapon platforms.

The SSTS originally conceived by the system architects for ballistic missile defense now appear too complicated, too expensive, and possibly too far beyond the state of the art of sensor technology for deployment in this century. As a result, there was some discussion in late 1986 and early 1987 of launching early SBIs without any SSTS sensor, placing minimal sensor capability on each SBI carrier vehicle instead. There would probably be no sensor capability enabling SBIs to kill RVs in mid-course.

The phase-one architecture submitted to the Defense Acquisition Board in June and July of 1987 was vague about mid-course sensors: there was a "Midcourse Sensor" (MCS) program, but no system concept. The MCS might consist of SSTS sensors, or ground-based surveillance and tracking (GSTS) rockets or "probes," or SWIR/MWIR (or other) sensors on some of the kill vehicle carrier satellites. These sensors would apparently locate targets for the ground-based exo-atmospheric reentry vehicle interceptor system (ERIS) interceptors. More recently, an MCS study proposed a combination of the three sub-systems.

The SDIO ended development work on the original SSTS program and let new contracts in mid-1987 to design a less complex SSTS system. The classified version of this report contains the range of parameters specified by the original, more comprehensive system architectures. The new designs could not by themselves furnish precise enough data to direct SBIs to RV targets.

Airborne Optical Adjunct (AOA)

The AOA would test technology for a new sensor addition to terminal defensive systems. The SAFEGUARD BMD system, operated in partial form in the 1970s, relied exclusively on large, phased-array radars to track incoming warheads. There were no optical detectors. The resolution and range of these ground-based radars was adequate (assuming they survived) to direct nuclear-tipped Spartan and Sprint missiles to the general vicinity of target RVs. Such radars would not be adequate as the only guidance for the non-nuclear, hit-to-kill vehicles proposed for SDI: these interceptors would require on-board homing guidance systems.

The AOA would test LWIR technology similar to that in the SSTS program, but deploy it on an aircraft flying over the northern United States. The sensor system has been designed and is being fabricated. Above most of the atmosphere, this sensor could look up against the cold space background and track RVs as they flew through mid-course. Resolution would be relatively coarse: a follow-up system based on this technology might eventually be able to direct ground-based radars, which in turn would hand target track data over to high speed hit-to-kill projectiles. These projectiles would derive their final target position from on-board homing sensors. The AOA aircraft might also include laser range-finder systems to supply accurate estimates of the distance to each target—and possibly to discriminate

Photo credit: Strategic Defense Initiative Organization

Airborne Optical Adjunct (AOA)

In a strategic defense system, airborne sensors might be used to help identify and track targets and to guide ground-based interceptors to them. The AOA will validate the technology to acquire targets optically at long ranges, and to track, discriminate and hand data over to a ground-based radar. It will also provide a data base that would support future development of airborne optical systems. Sensors have been fabricated and tested and test flights will take place soon. The model shows the sensor compartment on top and the crew stations in the interior of the aircraft.

decoys from RVs by measuring minute velocity changes caused by drag in the upper atmosphere.

System architecture contractors proposed tens of AOA-like aircraft as part of a sensor system. Some proposed rocket-borne, pop-up probes with LWIR sensors for rapid response in a surprise attack until the aircraft could reach altitude.

There is some uncertainty regarding the infrared background that an airborne sensor such as AOA would see. Sunlight scattered from either natural or (particularly) man-made "noctilucent clouds" might obscure the real RV targets. These clouds form at altitudes from 60 to 100 kilometers (km). During a battle, the particles ablating from debris reentering the atmosphere would form nucleation centers. Long-lived ice crystals would grow at these centers, possibly creating a noisy infrared background that would obscure the real targets arriving later. Intentional seeding of these clouds is also a possibility.[7]

Ground-Based Radar (GBR)

Large phased-array, ground-based X-band (8-12 GHz frequency) radars might work in conjunction with optical sensors to track and discriminate incoming warheads from decoys. These radars could receive target track data from those sensors and then use doppler processing to create a pseudo-image of the warheads by virtue of their spinning motion. Non-rotating decoys or decoys with different shapes or rotation rates would produce different radar signatures.

Ground-based radars would also measure the effects of the atmosphere, identifying light decoys that would slow down more than the heavy RVs. These radars might guide or cue the endoatmospheric HEDI and FLAGE-like interceptor rockets and the ERIS exoatmospheric interceptors (see ch. 5).

The GBR concept very recently supplanted the proposed Terminal Imaging Radar (TIR) system in SDIO planning. The latter would have had a much shorter range (thereby not being useful for cueing the ERIS interceptor) and much less resistance to anti-radar countermeasures, such as jamming. Some radar concepts call for deployment on railroad cars to evade enemy attack.

Neutral Particle Beam (NPB) Interactive Discrimination

While several interactive discrimination techniques have been proposed (see section below on interactive discrimination), the NPB approach has thus far received the most attention and development funds.

A series of full space-based tests was planned for the early 1990s, but has been subjected to budgetary cutbacks. A 50-MeV[8] NPB source was to be placed in orbit along with a sensor satellite and a target satellite to measure beam characteristics and to begin interactive tests. The primary detection method would be to monitor the neutrons emmitted by the target after irradiation by the NPB, although gamma rays, x-rays, and ultraviolet radiation might also be useful for indicating whether targets had been hit by the neutral particle beam. The NPB accelerator might be located 1,000 km from the target. The neutron detectors might ride on separate detector satellites closer to targets, although they could be collocated on the NPB platform under some circumstances. A single NPB discrimination accelerator system might weigh 50,000 to 100,000 kilograms (kg), making it the heaviest element proposed for a second-phase BMD.[9] Over 100 NPB satellites and several hundred neutron detector

---

[7]See M.T. Sandford, II, *A Review of Mesospheric Cloud Physics*, Report No. LA-10866 (Los Alamos, NM: Los Alamos National Laboratory, October 1986.)

[8]The energy of a beam of particles is measured in "electron volts" or "eV," the energy that one electron would acquire traveling through an electric field with a potential of one volt. The energy of beam weapon particles would be so high that it is measured in millions of electron volts, or "MeV." One MeV is equal to 1.6×10^{-13} joules; each particle carries this amount of energy.

[9]A far-term, robust BMD system might also include very heavy directed-energy weapons.

platforms might be required for a global discrimination system.[10]

Sensor System Requirements

Technical requirements for BMD sensors are discussed below for each sensor function: surveillance, target acquisition, identification, tracking, and kill assessment.

Surveillance and Target Acquisition Requirements

A surveillance and target acquisition system would have to detect the launch of any missile, either ground-based or submarine-based, and render accurate positional information to the BMD weapon system. Some SDI weapon systems would require very high resolution sensors. A laser beam, for example, would have to be focused down to a spot as small as 20 to 30 cm in diameter to produce the lethal intensity levels for projected hardened missiles.[11] A DEW sensor must therefore determine the missile location to within a few tens of cm so as to keep the laser focused on one spot on the target.

As an illustration of what is practical or impractical, note that if the sensor were placed in geosynchronous orbit at 36,000 km, just a few sensor satellites could survey the entire earth. But at this high altitude the sensor's angular resolution would have to be better than 8 nanoradians, or one part in 125,000,000.[12]

This high resolution is clearly beyond the realm of practical sensor systems.[13]

Resolution improves directly with reduced distance to the target. Therefore a reasonable alternative—one being examined—would be to place many sensor satellites at lower altitudes. Even a constellation of sensor satellites at altitudes around 4,000 km would not be adequate for directed energy weapons: positional uncertainties for sensor satellites combined with vibration and jitter would preclude the transmission of target positions to weapon platforms with 10-cm accuracy. Therefore each DEW satellite would need its own sensor to provide the final pointing accuracy. Sensor satellites might supply broad target coordinates to each weapon platform.

Homing kinetic energy weapons (KEW) would require less accurate information from a remote sensor: a homing sensor on an SBI itself would give the fine resolution needed in the last few seconds to approach and collide with the target. Still, the SBI must be fired toward a small volume in space where the intercept would occur several hundred seconds after it had been fired. The sensor system must locate each target in three dimensions.

Target Identification or Discrimination Requirements

Ballistic missile defense (BMD) sensors would not only have to detect missile launches, but they would also have to identify targets. Identification requirements would vary considerably during missile flight. During the boost phase, a sensor would first distinguish between missile exhaust plumes and other natural or man-made sources of concentrated heat. Given adequate spatial resolution, a smart sensor with memory could separate moving missiles from stationary ground-based sources of heat. The location of the missile launcher and the missile's dynamic characteristics (acceleration and burn time for each stage, pitch ma-

---

[10]Between 100 to 200 flights of the proposed Advanced Launch System (ALS) might be required to lift a full constellation of 100 NPB discriminators into space. For a discussion of the number of elements in a useful NPB system, see American Physical Society, *Science and Technology of Directed Energy Weapons: Report of the American Physical Society Study Group*, April 1987, pp. 152 and 335.

[11]For example, a 90 MW laser operating at one micrometer (μm) wavelength would require a mirror as large as 10 m in diameter to achieve the very high brightness 10^{21} W/sr required to destroy hardened (i.e., able to resist 20 KJ/cm^2) targets. A 10 m mirror would project a 20-cm diameter spot at 2,000 km or 40 cm at 4,000 km, which are typical ranges for the proposed directed energy platforms. See chapter 5 on directed energy weapons for more details.

[12]One radian is equal to 57.3 degrees; one nanoradian is 1×10^{-9} radian or one billionth of a radian.

---

[13]For example, even an ultraviolet sensor, which would have the best resolution due to its short wavelength, would require a 45-m diameter mirror to achieve 8 nanoradian resolution.

neuvers, stage separation timing, etc.) should permit identification of missile type and probable mission. Eventually a low altitude sensor would have to identify the booster body (as opposed to the hot plume), either by geometric extrapolation or by generating an IR image of the booster tank.[14]

The post-boost phase is more complicated. Most missiles carry a PBV or "bus" which may include 10 or more individual warheads in RVs. These RVs are individually aimed at separate targets: the PBV maneuvers and mechanically ejects each RV, one at a time, along a different trajectory. A BMD sensor system might detect heat from a PBV propulsion system as it made these multiple maneuvers. However, PBV propulsion energy is far less than main booster engine energy, making tracking (at least in the SWIR/MWIR range) more difficult in the post-boost phase. Once ejected, cold RVs would be even more difficult to detect and track.[15]

This reduced signal level could be partially offset by arranging the sensor satellite to view its targets against the cold space background instead of the warm and noisy Earth background, as in the boost phase. The sensors would have to look above the horizon, generally limiting detection to distant targets over the Earth's limb. Since detection becomes more difficult at longer ranges, this above-the-horizon (ATH) detection of cold RVs would be more difficult than sensing very hot booster plumes against the earth background.

If the United States deployed a BMD system, Soviet missiles would probably disperse decoys along with nuclear-armed RVs. Decoys might be simple, aluminum-covered balloons weighing 1 kg or less, or they might be somewhat more sophisticated decoys shaped like an RV with similar infrared and radar signatures. Simple decoys might be tethered to an RV within a few tens of meters: defensive sensors would then require higher resolution to separate decoys and RVs. Alternately, an RV could be placed inside a large balloon, a technique known as "anti-simulation": the RV is made to look like a decoy.

The most sophisticated decoys, called thrusted replicas (TREPs) might even have propulsion so they could push into the atmosphere during reentry to simulate the heavy RV's reentry characteristics. The total post-boost and mid-course threat cloud could contain something like 10,000 RVs, hundreds of thousands of decoys, and thousands of burnt-out rocket stages and PBVs, all traveling through space at 7 km/s. In the same trajectories might be literally millions of fragments from boosters destroyed by SBIs in the boost and post-boost phases.[16]

In principle, a BMD weapons system could fire at all of these objects, but the costs would be prohibitive. Therefore the sensors for a second- or third-phase BMD system with mid-course capability would have to *discriminate* effectively between RVs and the many decoys and debris.

In the post-boost phase, there would be some basis for discrimination. A sensor could, in theory, monitor PBV motion during deployment of RVs and decoys. Decoys would produce less PBV motion than the heavier RVs as they were ejected from the PBV. This distinctive motion might be detected, assuming that the Soviets did not cover the PBV with a shroud to conceal the dispersal of decoys, or that they did not appropriately alter the thrust of the PBV as its RVs dispersed.

In the mid-course phase, discrimination would become even more difficult. All the objects would travel together in a ballistic, free-fall flight. Light decoys would not be slowed down by atmospheric friction until they descended to the 100-150 km altitude range—the same altitude range that constrains deploy-

---

[14]A booster body, at 300° K is cold compared to its hot plume, but it is still warmer than the cool upper atmosphere at about 220° K. An LWIR sensor could therefore image the booster body against the Earth background at fairly long ranges, using wavelengths which were absorbed by the upper atmosphere.

[15]ICBM boosters typically radiate millions of watts per steradian (W/sr), PBVs hundreds of W/sr, and RVs a few W/sr. (A "steradian" is the measure of a solid angle, defined as the ratio of the surface area subtended by a cone divided by the square of the apex of that cone.)

[16]See chapter 10 for details on countermeasures to BMD.

Photo credit: U.S. Department of Defense

COBRA JUDY Radar

A new radar had been developed and installed on the COBRA JUDY ship. This improves the capability of the U.S. for making measurements on reentry vehicles in flight.

ment of rising decoys in the post-boost phase. If decoys had the same signatures or characteristics of RVs as seen by conventional infrared and radar detectors, then conventional discrimination of RVs from decoys would become extremely difficult. **Mid-course discrimination is one of the most crucial challenges facing the SDI technology development program.**

The BMD sensors would also have to detect and track defense suppression threats such as direct-ascent anti-satellite (DAASAT) missiles or space-based ASATs which might attack BMD defensive assets in space. The sensors should therefore keep track of all of the BMD weapons platforms in a given battle space, allowing the battle manager to determine which objects were likely targets and which weapons should engage the threat.

Target Tracking Requirements

Passive IR sensors on a single BSTS or SSTS satellite could only measure the target position in two angular coordinates. Each target must be located in three dimensions to al-

low the battle management computer to calculate the expected collision point of weapon and target.

Three techniques could furnish three dimensional data: stereo imaging, ranging, or ballistic trajectory prediction (see figure 4-4). Two or more separated sensor satellites could generate stereo data. This would require a computer to correlate data from multiple sensors and could become very complicated with 40 or 50 sensors generating data from thousands or hundreds of thousands of targets.

Alternatively, a laser range-finder and a passive IR two-dimensional imager together on one satellite could generate three dimensional information. A laser range-finder would determine the distance to the target. With a direct, one-to-one correlation between two target angles from a passive sensor and a third range coordinate from a laser, computational requirements would be reduced by eliminating the need to correlate data from separate platforms.

Finally, for objects traveling in space on a ballistic, free-fall trajectory, Kepler's equations

Figure 4-4. — Illustration of Three Techniques for Estimating the Three-Dimensional Position of a Target in Space

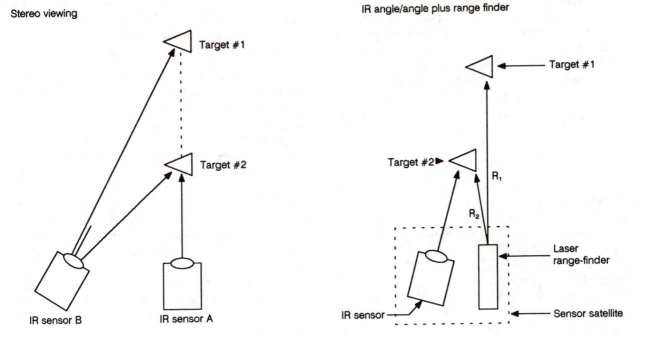

Stereo viewing

IR angle/angle plus range finder

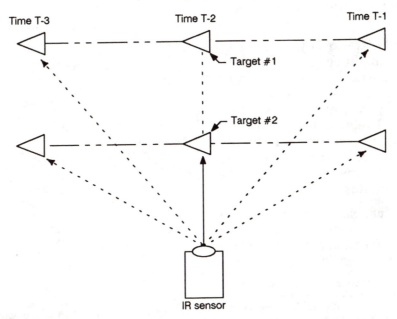

Ballistic trajectory estimation
(from one passive sensor)

In the first view Sensor A could not distinguish between Target #1 and Target #2. Stereo viewing from two or more separate satellites with passive IR sensors eliminates this ambiguity. Relatively complicated software is required to correlate data from each sensor. The other two techniques can predict three dimensional information from one platform, eliminating the requirement for multiple satellite sensor data correlation; a laser range finder determines the range or distance to a target by measuring the travel time for a pulse of light from the platform to the target and back, uniquely determining position with one measurement. The ballistic trajectory prediction approach uses only the passive IR sensor, but requires three or more measurements at different times to compute the target's path through space.

of motion may be applied: a passive sensor could determine the path of an RV in three dimensions by measuring its two-dimensional position three or more times. This trajectory prediction approach requires more time (hundreds of seconds) to build up an accurate track: this would be adequate for the mid-course phase. It would require more data storage and processing than the laser range-finder technique, but only one passive sensor.

Kill Assessment Requirements

Sensors would also have to determine whether a missile or RV had been disabled or destroyed. Missed targets would have to be retargeted, and disabled targets should be ignored throughout the remainder of the battle. Kill assessment should be straightforward for most KEW projectiles, since their impact would smash targets into thousands of pieces. However, some SBIs might partially damage a booster by clipping a non-critical edge, leaving the bulk of the missile intact. In this case the sensor might judge a missile "killed" if it veered sufficiently off-course to a non-threatening trajectory.

Damage to targets attacked by laser or particle beam weapons might be more difficult to diagnose. A laser beam might conceivably burn through a critical component without detectable damage, yet divert a missile from its intended course. More likely, the laser would disintegrate the missile body, which is highly stressed during acceleration—as demonstrated by a ground-based high-energy laser test at the White Sands Missile Range.[17]

Damage due to particle beams or electron beams might be more difficult to detect. Neutral particle beams, for example, might penetrate several cm into a missile or RV, destroying critical electronic components without any apparent external damage. An RV might be effectively "killed" with respect to its mission at much lower particle beam energy than that necessary to show detectable damage.

On the other hand, NPB system designers could increase particle beam fluence to levels that would assure electronics destruction (say 50 joules/gram (J/g)—only 10 J/g destroys most electronics) as long as the target were hit. Kill assessment would then become "hit assessment": if the beam dwelled on the target long enough to impart 50 J/g, then the electronics could be judged "killed." With this approach, NPB weapons would be effectively lethal at lower energy levels than that needed for melting aluminum or causing structural weakness (500 to 1,000 J/g). Relying on this indirect kill assessment would require confidence that the Soviets had not shielded critical internal electronic components from NPB radiation.

---

[17]The mid-range infrared advanced chemical laser (MIRACL) at White Sands Missile Range in New Mexico was aimed at a strapped-down Titan missile second stage. The missile was mechanically loaded with 60 psi of nitrogen gas to simulate the 4-g load and propellant conditions that it would experience in an actual flight. After approximately 2 seconds of exposure to the laser beam, which had a power greater than 1 megawatt, the Titan booster completely ruptured, shattering into fragments as heating of a roughly 1 m² area destroyed the mechanical integrity of the booster skin.

Table 4-1.—Summary of Typical Sensor Requirements

Surveillance:

Coverage . . . . Global
Targets . . . . ICBM's, SLBM's, direct ascent ASAT's, space mines, and one's own BMD assets, including all sensor and weapons satellites and launched SBIs

Target Discrimination:

Boost Phase . . . . ICBM/SLBM/DANASAT
Post-boost & mid-
course . . . . PBV, RV, light decoy, replica, thrusted replica, & debris
Terminal . . . . RV & thrusted replica

Tracking:

Targets	
ICBM's	1,400-2,000
SLBM's	1,000-1,500
DANASAT's:	1,000-16,000
PBV's	2,400-3,000
RV's	8,000-15,000
Decoys	hundreds of thousands

Track file . . . . position, velocity, & acceleration in 3-D

Kill assessment:

KEW . . . . destruction
Laser . . . . destruction
NPB . . . . hit assessment or other

SOURCE: Office of Technology Assessment, 1988.

Sensor Technology

Three types of sensors might satisfy portions of these BMD requirements: passive, active, and interactive. Passive sensors rely on natural radiation emitted by or reflected from the target. Active sensors, such as radars, illuminate the target with radiation and detect the reflected signal. "Interactive sensors" (a term unique to the SDI) would use a strong beam of energy or cloud of dust-like particles to perturb targets in some measurable way (without necessarily disabling it) so that RVs could be discriminated from decoys. For example, the cloud might slow down light decoys much more than heavy RVs, or penetrating particle beams might create a burst of neutrons or gamma rays from RVs but not from balloons.

Passive Sensors

How Passive Sensors Work.—Passive sensors detect military targets either by measuring their natural emission, or by detecting natural light reflected from the targets. A typical sensor is similar to an ordinary camera. An optical element (the lens) forms an image, and a light sensitive surface records that image (the film).

In BMD infrared sensors, the optical lens would be replaced by a system of reflecting mirrors and the camera film by an array of discrete optical detectors in the focal plane which convert the optical image into electronic signals for immediate computer processing. Many detectors are required to record a detailed image. In a sense each detector substitutes for one grain of photographic film. Some sensors use a stationary two-dimensional "staring" array of detectors, in direct analogy to photographic film. Others mechanically scan the image across an array of detectors that may be either two-dimensional or linear.

Infrared Sensors.—Ordinary photographic cameras record the visible light reflected from a scene. For BMD, the IR energy emitted by the target (particularly the hot exhaust gases ejected from a missile booster engine) is a better source of information.[18] The sensor images the infrared radiation from the target and background onto a photosensitive array of detectors. These detectors generate a series of electrical signals that are processed by computers to detect and track the target.

There are three distinct target classes for the BMD mission: missiles with their rocket engines firing, post-boost vehicles with much lower power engines, and cold objects such as RVs and decoys in space.[19] Each type of target demands different IR sensors. Hot exhaust gas from a booster engine radiates primarily in relatively narrow bands of short wavelength IR. The exact wavelength of this radiation is

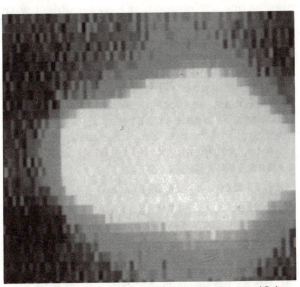

Photo credit: U.S. Department of Defense, Strategic Defense Initiative Organization

Infrared image of the moon from SDIO's Delta 181 experiment. That experiment took measurements of a rocket booster and other objects in space to gather information about the kinds of sensors that would be needed in a space-based ballistic missile defense system. This may be the first long-wave infrared image acquired from a platform in space.

---

[18]All objects with a temperature above absolute zero ($-273°$ C) emit energy in the form of electromagnetic waves, such as light waves, infrared waves, microwaves, etc. For example, the human body continuously radiates infrared waves. To an infrared camera, we all "glow in the dark": our bodies would be recorded on infrared film as a group of "hot spots," even if the picture were taken in absolute darkness. Similarly, any target emits energy which can, in principle, be detected with appropriate sensors, provided only that the target is warmer (or colder) than the background scene.

[19]The RVs do heat up from friction as they enter the atmosphere.

determined by the particular gas constituents. The primary emission bands for gas plumes are near the water vapor and carbon dioxide lines at 2.7 micrometers[20] (in the short wave IR or SWIR) and at 4.26 μm (in the middle wave IR or MWIR).[21]

Other specific radiation lines may help identify some Soviet booster plumes: this will be investigated in the SDI research program. These plumes radiate hundreds of thousands to millions of watts per steradian (W/sr) of energy. Post-boost vehicles also have propulsion systems, but their smaller motors radiate only hundreds of W/sr.

Reentry vehicles remain near "room temperature" (20° C or 293° K) in mid-course, until they are heated by the friction of the atmosphere on reentry. The maximum radiation for room temperature objects is near 10 μm in the LWIR. Infrared detection of RVs is difficult because of their low level of radiation (typically a few W/sr) and poor contrast against the earth background. That is, the earth is also near "room temperature," with strong emission in the 10-μm band. An IR sensor cannot "see" a red target against a red background. The sensor would generally have to wait until the target RV was above the horizon to view it against the cold (4° K) temperature of space. The sensor system would also have to filter out the IR energy from planets or bright stars in the field of view.[22]

The technical feasibility of detecting relatively cold RVs against a space background was demonstrated on June 10, 1984, when an LWIR sensor on board the Army's Homing Overlay Experiment (HOE) missile successfully detected a simulated RV over the Pacific

Ocean.[23] The sensor guided the HOE projectile into a collision course, destroying a target launched earlier from Vandenberg AFB in California. This test demonstrated an ability to detect and track a single approaching RV in space at relatively close range. (The initial HOE missile trajectory was specified by radar signals from Kwajalein until the missile LWIR sensor could acquire the target.)

Tracking thousands of RVs and possibly hundreds of thousands of decoys with space-based sensor satellites from distances of 5,000 to 10,000 km would be more challenging, particularly if the RVs were encapsulated in balloons and decoy balloons were tied (tethered) together or to an RV.

Three-Color Infrared Sensors.—Depending on the offense's countermeasures, discrimination of RVs from decoys might be improved if the object temperatures could be measured accurately. Long-wave IR sensors that detect one narrow wavelength band cannot determine temperature. That is, a warm object with low IR emissivity[24] could produce the same radiance at one wavelength as a cooler object with high emissivity, as illustrated in figure 4-5. However, the shape of the blackbody (nonreflecting object) radiation curve as a function of wavelength is distinct for objects at different temperatures. This suggests that two or more LWIR sensors operating at different wavelength bands within the 8- to 24-μm region could estimate the temperature of space objects, independent of their general emissivities.

Most SDI architects recommended three-color LWIR detectors to measure energy in three separate wavelength bands or "colors." Note that this complicates sensor design and

---

[20]One micrometer (μm) is one millionth (10^{-6}) of a meter.

[21]Atmospheric water vapor and carbon dioxide attenuate most of the IR radiation from a missile plume in the early stages of flight. However, the higher temperature and pressure of the water and CO_2 in the plume produce a broader IR spectrum than the atmospheric absorption bands. Infrared energy will therefore leak through on both sides of the 2.7 and 4.3 μm lines, even from rockets close to the surface of the Earth.

[22]The Air Force has used a star as the "target" for tests of the U.S. F-15 launched ASAT, which uses a LWIR sensor to home on its target.

[23]To place this experiment in perspective, it should be noted that this RV was significantly brighter than the radiance expected from current RVs, while the Soviets may take steps to further reduce IR emissions.

[24]The emissivity of any object indicates its ability to radiate energy. Emissivity is defined as the ratio of the energy radiated at any wavelength to the amount of energy radiated by a perfect blackbody at the same temperature. (A "blackbody" absorbs all energy reaching its surface.) Thus an object with low emissivity will radiate less energy than a higher emissivity object, even though they are both at the same temperature.

Figure 4-5.—Spectral Response of Two Objects at Different Temperatures

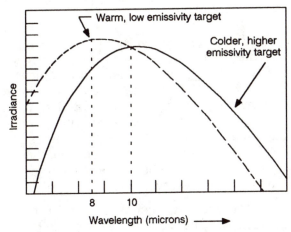

One LWIR sensor measuring only the 10 micron energy would record the same signal intensity for both targets; they could not be distinguished. The different temperatures can be detected by adding a second color measurement at 8 microns, revealing more of the shape of the spectral emission curves. Three-color LWIR sensors are recommended for even better temperature discrimination capability.

Photo credit: U.S. Department of Defense, Strategic Defense Initiative Organization

Cryocooler for space applications. Many of the advanced "heat-detecting" infrared sensors necessary to identify and track missiles and warheads in space must be cooled to work properly. Special refrigerators called cryocoolers would produce the needed very low temperatures. Cryocooler life, reliability, and performance experiments designed to demonstrate the ability to cool long-wave infrared detectors have been conducted.

construction. Each "pixel" must be measured by three different detector elements. Detector manufacturing and signal processing tasks are increased.

Cooling.—If an LWIR camera were operated at room temperature, then the entire camera enclosure would radiate LWIR energy and fog the film or saturate the IR detectors with noise. Sensitive IR cameras must therefore be cooled to reduce stray radiation. In particular, the mirrors that form the IR image must usually be cooled to keep IR noise generated by mirror radiation small compared to other background radiation. Cooling further complicates the task of building large, light-weight mirrors for space-based sensors. The degree of cooling necessary depends on the temperature and radiation levels of the expected targets.

Some detectors themselves must also be cooled—typically to the range from 4° K to 78° K—to reduce the self-generated thermal noise that would mask photon-generated signals from targets of interest. One key SDI task is therefore to develop space-qualified cryogenic coolers that could operate for many years in space. The current goal is to reach life-times

of 7 years, and at least one type of cryogenic refrigerator has demonstrated this ability in accelerated life tests.[25]

UV/Visible Sensors.—Some SDI contractors have proposed the use of visible or even ultraviolet (UV) sensors, primarily to achieve better resolution with realistic optics dimensions.[26] For example, a 28-cm diameter UV mirror at 0.3 μm could achieve the same resolution as a 400-cm (4-m) diameter mirror operating at 4.3 μm. However, this gain is not free: reducing the wavelength increases the fabrication difficulty. Mirrors must be polished to within one-tenth to one-twentieth of the operating wavelength. Thus an MWIR mirror at 4.3 μm must be polished to within at least 0.43 μm of the prescribed surface figure, while a UV mirror must be polished to an accuracy of 0.03 μm or better.

[25]Hughes Aircraft has demonstrated operation of a magnetic gas cooler system with an accelerated test simulating 7 years life.
[26]The resolution of a sensor is limited by diffraction spreading of the optical image. This diffraction spreading is proportional to the wavelength of light used to form the image; shorter wavelengths produce less image spreading, yielding better resolution or sharper images.

Visible or UV sensors might detect energy from rocket plumes, although the visible radiation from liquid-fueled missiles is minimal. The atmosphere attenuates UV below an altitude of a few tens of km, but a post-boost vehicle propulsion system may generate adequate UV radiation. To see RVs, however, these sensors would have to rely on the reflection of natural radiation (sunlight, moonlight, or Earthlight). Alternatively, they could be used in an active mode with a laser designator illuminating the target (see next section).

Current Status of Passive Sensors.—Passive infrared sensors operate today in early warning satellites. A few satellites at geosynchronous orbit, some 36,000 km above the earth, monitor the entire globe, searching for missile launches from the Soviet land mass or from the oceans. Several heat-seeking tactical missiles such as the air-to-air Sidewinder and the ground-to-air Maverick missile also employ infrared sensors. This same sensor technology supplied the terminal guidance for two successful space hit-to-kill experiments: the anti-satellite (ASAT) experiment in which a missile fired from an F-15 aircraft destroyed a satellite in space and the Homing Overlay Experiment.

Today's operational infrared sensors have relatively small optical systems, typically 20 cm or less in diameter, and focal plane arrays of a few thousand detectors. Most detectors are fabricated from bulk silicon and could not survive in a nuclear environment. Relatively few large detector arrays are built each year,

and the United States does not yet have the manufacturing technology to build large arrays economically.

Key Issues for Passive Sensors.—This report has identified five key issues for passive sensor technology development (see table 4-1). While driven by the space-based system requirements, these same sensor functions would be required for effective ground-launched weapons systems. Whether the sensors rode on airborne or space-based platforms, these issues would have to be resolved to produce a robust BMD system.

Mirror Size.—A sensor system mirror must be large to collect enough energy, to resolve closely spaced objects, and to accurately direct weapons systems (see box 4-A). The mirror size needed is determined by sensor operating wavelength, distance to target, and target positional accuracy required by the weapon system. The resolution of any optical system is given approximately by the wavelength divided by the diameter of the aperture multiplied by the range.

Typical mirror sizes for adequate *spot* resolution from a passive sensor at 3,000 km altitude are shown in figure 4-6.[27] To provide adequate aiming information to homing kinetic energy weapons, sensor resolutions from 10 m

[27]Fig. 4-6 assumes a perfect, diffraction limited optical system. In practice other factors—such as vibration, imperfect mirror quality, and thermal distortions—would degrade resolution. This figure, therefore, represents the minimum allowable mirror size for a spot. Tracking resolution may only require mirrors a factor of 10 smaller, as noted in the text.

Table 4-2.—Key Issues for Passive Sensors

	KEW	DEW	Current status
Mirror size (m)	about 0.1	about 1 (UV/visible)	0.1-2.4
Number of detector elements (resolution limited)			
Geo/staring	10^6-10^8	N/A	many tens of thousands
Geo/scanning	10^4-10^6	N/A	
3,000km/staring (1°FOV)	10^3-10^5	10^8	
3,000km/scanning	10^3	10^5-10^6	
Detector manufacturing capacity	10^8-10^9/yr	10^7-10^8/yr	10^6/yr
Signal processing			
Rates	10^9/s	10^{10}/s	several $\times$ 10^7/s
Memory	1×10^7	1×10^8	8×10^7

SOURCE: Office of Technology Assessment, 1988.

Box 4-A.—Sensor Resolution Limits

The resolution of any electromagnetic sensor (or its ability to separate two closely spaced objects) is limited by two factors: diffraction and detector element size. The image formed by the sensor optics cannot faithfully reproduce the actual scene. An infinitesimally small point in the scene will have a finite size in the image due to diffraction or spreading of the light beam. This spreading increases with distance, so diffraction will limit the useful range of any sensor as shown in figure 4-6a.

The optical system projects an image of the scene onto the detector array. The size of each detector element in this array must be equal to or preferably smaller than the optical resolution size to preserve the diffraction-resolution of the figure in the electronic signal. If the detector elements are too large, then they will further limit the system resolution.

For a fixed field-of-view, as the distance between the scene and the sensor increases, then each detector element covers a larger area in space: the resolution decreases with range, the same dependence as diffraction spreading of the optical image.

Figure 4-6a. — Diffraction-Limited Range for Ten-Meter Resolution

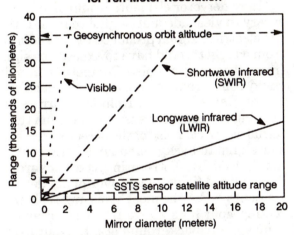

Sensor range as a function of mirror diameter to produce a 10-meter resolution element at the target, for three different wavelength sensors. Two point targets separated by 10 meters at these ranges could just be resolved by mirrors of these sizes.

Figure 4-6b. — Range Limited by Number of Detectors for Ten-Meter Resolution

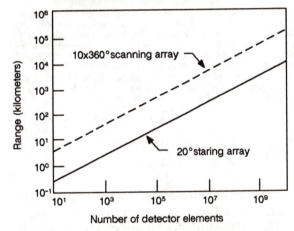

Range of LWIR sensors as limited by the number of detector elements in the focal plane array. The staring array is a fixed, two-dimensional array with a 20° field-of-view. The scanning array covers a 10° by 360° "coolie hat" pattern, with 10 rows of elements scanning each point in the image. Both arrays detect three different LWIR bands. The scanning array could use just one row of detectors to sweep out the image. However, to improve signal-to-noise ratio, most designs utilize more than one row and "time delay and integrate" (TDI) circuits to average the signals from many rows.

up to 1 km may be adequate, depending upon the sensors and the divert capability of the interceptor. As shown in figure 4-7, mirrors of 1-m diameter or less are adequate for any visible or IR wavelength. Furthermore, a 1-m mirror operating at 2.7 μm would yield 10-m target accuracy from 3,000 km.[28]

Track resolution, however, imposes a less stringent requirement than the spot resolution for a single "look." Data from many "looks" can be combined, using statistical techniques, to achieve up to a tenfold improvement. Therefore, proportionately smaller mirrors are needed for predicting tracks.

Directed-energy weapons would require much better resolution than SBIs, since they

---

[28]The primary water vapor emission line from missile exhaust plumes is at 2.7 μm.

Figure 4-7.—Mirror Size Plotted v. the Operating Wavelength of a Sensor System

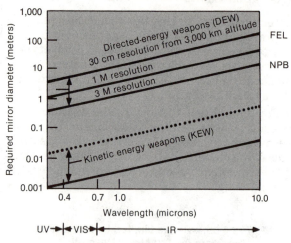

Mirror size plotted v. the operating wavelength of the sensor system, assuming a 3,000 km range to the most distant target, for indicated *spot* resolution. Note that the *tracking* resolution can be up to a factor of 10 better than the resolution calculated for one "look," based on diffraction limits. Therefore, the tracking may only require mirrors up to 10 times smaller than indicated in the figure.

For homing kinetic energy weapons, moderate-sized mirrors (well under 1 meter in diameter) would be adequate for all wavelengths. Directed-energy weapons such as high power lasers would require sensors with very large mirrors operating in the visible or even ultraviolet region of the spectrum. Thus all DEWs would have to use a low-resolution LWIR sensor to point a second UV/visible active sensor or laser on each weapons platform to achieve the necessary accuracy.

SOURCE: Office of Technology Assessment, 1988.

must be focused to a small spot without the benefit of a homing sensor at close range. LWIR sensor mirrors to direct DEWs would have to exceed 10 m in diameter. Therefore a DEW sensor would probably have to operate in the SWIR or MWIR, visible, or even ultraviolet (UV) wavelengths.[29] Laser beam weapons would demand the highest accuracy to take full advantage of their small spot size and therefore high intensity on target, typically on the order of 30 cm at 3,000 km or 0.1 microradian. Neutral particle beams, as currently envisaged, would have about one microradian

divergence, producing a 3 m spot at 3,000 km, so NPB sensors could be about 10 times less accurate than laser beam sensors.

Number of Detector Elements per Array.— Each passive sensor would need many detector elements for both adequate resolution and high signal-to-noise ratios. For example, a staring array sensor on a BSTS satellite at geosynchronous orbit (36,000 km) could need well over a million detector elements to afford coarse resolution at the surface of the Earth. This requirement could be reduced to hundreds of thousands of detector elements by scanning the IR image over a smaller array of detectors, so that each detector sampled many resolution elements in the IR image.

Many detector elements would also be necessary to yield adequate signal-to-noise ratios: the electrical signal produced by IR radiation from a target would have to exceed the signal from all sources of noise. Competing IR noise could come from the background scene such as the Earth or stars, from the mirrors and housing of the sensor system, and from the internal electrical noise of the detector elements. The signal-to-background-noise ratio could be maximized by distributing the background from a fixed field-of-view over many detector elements.[30] For the most stressing task of detecting cold RVs above the horizon against atmospheric background at a tangent height of 50 to 80 km, sensors would need at least several hundred thousand detector elements to generate adequate signal-to-noise ratios.[31]

Current IR focal plane arrays on operational military sensors for tactical elements have up to 180 detector elements. Some other operational systems have several thousand, and experimental arrays with many more than 10,000

---

[29]This might be satisfactory for boost-phase kills, but cold RV's in mid-course could only be detected with LWIR sensors. Hence a future laser BMD system designed to attack RV's would have to use a coarse LWIR sensor for detection, then a separate laser designator at shorter wavelength to illuminate targets for tracking by a second UV or visible-light sensor. This complexity, combined with the durability of RV's as a result of their ablative shield needed for reentry, makes the use of laser beams for killing RV's in mid-course very doubtful.

[30]Ideally, each detector element should be the same size as that of the target image. If the elements were twice this ideal size (half the total number of detectors in the array), then each element would collect twice the background noise with no increase in signal: the signal-to-noise ratio would be cut in half. For many long-range BMD missions, the detector element would be much larger than the target image.

[31]These numbers of detectors are based on the assumption that the sensor mirrors are cooled to the 80° to 100° K range so that IR radiation from those mirrors does not dominate the noise, and that the detectors are fabricated with low noise.

Photo credit: General Electric Company

Sensor focal plane array of 128 by 128 detector elements. These elements convert light energy into electrical signals. Focal plane arrays are the electro-optical equivalent of film in a camera. Some SDI sensors may require focal planes containing hundreds of thousands of detector elements.

elements have been fabricated. The focal plane array (FPA) for the planned Airborne Optical Adjunct (AOA) experiment will have a 38,400-element three-color FPA.[32] However, none of these detectors was designed to the radiation hardness needed for BMD sensors.

Detector Radiation Hardness.—Ballistic missile defense sensors must withstand radiation from distant nuclear explosions. Current detectors are fabricated from relatively thick bulk materials such as silicon or mercury cadmium telluride (HgCdTe) which are susceptible to radiation damage. Other materials, such as gallium arsenide or germanium, or thinner detector structures would be needed to achieve radiation hardness goals. Impurity band conductor (IBC) detectors, which are only 10 to 12 μm thick, can withstand 10 to 100 times more radiation than common bulk silicon de-

[32]See *Aviation Week and Space Technology*, Nov. 10, 1986, p. 87.

tectors. Arrays with up to 500 IBC elements have been fabricated in the laboratory.

The electronic readout from FPAs must also be resistant to radiation damage. In the past, charge-coupled devices (CCD) were used to read out large detector arrays. To reduce susceptibility to radiation damage, researchers are butt-bonding switching metal oxide semiconductor field effect transistor (MOSFET) readouts to the detectors.

Detector Manufacturing Capacity.—Industry produces about 1 million IR detectors per year. Many of these are small linear arrays of 16 to 180 elements each, used for tactical IR missiles or scanning IR imaging systems. The "Teal Ruby"[33] experiment's bulk-silicon array is the largest built so far. Production would have to increase by one or two orders of magnitude to satisfy the ambitious BMD goals: very large, radiation-hard, low-noise arrays would be required. For example, just one BMD sensor would require several, perhaps up to 10, times the current annual production capacity—and there could be many tens of sensors in a second-phase space-based BMD system. The SDIO has programs underway intended to

[33]Teal Ruby is an experimental satellite designed to detect aircraft from space with an LWIR detector array.

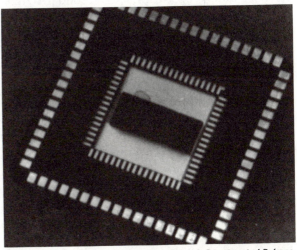

Photo credit: U.S. Department of Defense, Strategic Defense Initiative Organization

Impurity Band Conduction Long-Wave Infrared Detector Array

achieve these improvements in manufacturing capability.

Conversion from laboratory fabrication to full-scale manufacturing of the new IBC detectors—assuming they continue to be the preferred detector—could limit BMD sensor deployment. Industry performance in converting to the manufacture of bulk silicon IR "common module" arrays in the early 1980s was not good. Producing arrays of just 60, 120, or 180 elements once held up the completion of M-1 tanks that use forward looking IR (FLIR) sensors.

Manufacturing yield (the ratio of the number of acceptable arrays to the number manufactured) for IR detectors would have to be improved. The overall yield (including read-out) for the Teal Ruby array was about 2 percent. Since yield was so low, every element had to be individually tested at cryogenic (10° K) temperatures: testing might be the limiting manufacturing process. The SDIO has initiated programs to address this problem in fiscal year 1988.

Signal Processing Improvements.—Projected signal processing rates for BMD sensors would exceed current space-based operational capabilities by factors of a few hundred. Current operational signal processors can handle up tens of millions operations per second (MOPS), while BMD signal processing requirements might exceed 10 billion operations per second, or 10 giga-OPS (GOPS).

Projected on-board memory requirements for BMD sensors vary from 10 million to 100 million bytes of information. Reaching these memory and processing goals by the 1990s seems likely, given the progress in very high speed integrated circuits (VHSIC).

Power consumption of signal processors must be reduced. The AOA experiment will require less than 10 kilowatts (KW) of power to drive a 15 GOP processor, or over 1.5 MOPS/W. Hardened VHSIC technology offers the promise of many times less power consumption (40 MOPS/W) and good radiation resistance.

Active Sensors

How Active Sensors Work.—Active sensors illuminate the target with radiation and monitor reflected energy. In general, active sensors have the advantage of adequate illumination under all conditions: they do not have to rely on radiation from the target or favorable natural lighting conditions. They suffer the disadvantage, under some circumstances, of being susceptible to jamming or spoofing: the opponent can monitor the illumination beam and retransmit a modified beam at the same frequency to overpower or confuse the receiver. At the very least, the illumination beam can alert the enemy that he is under surveillance or attack. This might be a concern for surveillance and tracking of defense suppression weapons such as direct-ascent or orbiting ASATs.

Microwave radar, an active sensor used so successfully in tracking aircraft, might support some phases of BMD, particularly for terminal defense. These ground-based radars might use advanced data processing techniques to generate pseudo-images of RVs to distinguish between RVs and decoys, as described below. Conventional microwave radar has two serious limitations for most space-based BMD functions: limited resolution and large power requirements. Because of the large antennae, large power requirements, and survivability issues, microwave radar is not a prime candidate for BMD space applications.[34] However, the SDIO still believes that microwave radar might be included in future BMD systems.

SDI researchers are also investigating laser radar or "ladar" for applications such as measuring the range to a target and discriminating RVs from decoys. In principle, ladar is equivalent to radar with much shorter (opti-

---

[34]The SDIO had considered developing shorter millimeter wave radar to provide better radar resolution and lower power requirements. With reduced funding, support for millimeter radar has been reduced. Distributed antenna arrays are also being considered to provide space surveillance of aircraft and cruise missiles for the Air Defense Initiative.

cal or infrared) wavelengths. With shorter wavelength, ladars generally would give better resolution with less power and weight. Ladars cannot operate in all weather conditions on earth. They are therefore better suited for space applications.

Imaging Radars.—If an object is moving relative to a radar, then the radar return signal is shifted in frequency, similar to the Doppler frequency shift of a train whistle as it passes by a stationary observer. For objects that rotate, such as spinning satellites or reentry vehicles, pseudo-images can be generated by processing the doppler frequency shifts of radar signals stored over time. This is a process similar to synthetic aperture radar, sometimes called inverse synthetic aperture radar (ISAR).[35]

Consider a conical RV spinning about its axis (figure 4-8). The tip of the cone has no significant motion due to rotation, and little doppler frequency shift. The back edge of the cone has a large motion (proportional to the radius of the cone and the angular velocity of the RV) and a large doppler frequency shift. A plot of range to target versus doppler frequency shift will therefore resemble the shape of the RV for most orientations of radar beam to spinning RV.[36]

The resolution of range/doppler pseudo-images does not depend on radar-beam spot size. The beam floods the target area, so precise beam pointing is unnecessary. Range resolution is inversely proportional to the band-

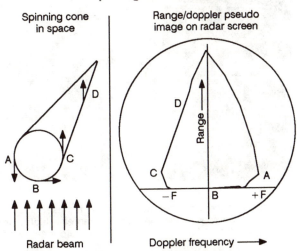

Figure 4-8. — Illustration of an Imaging Radar Viewing a Spinning Conical Target

Point "A" on the base of the cone has the most motion toward the radar, producing the largest doppler frequency shift. The echo from this point would appear at point "A" on a radar-generated plot of range versus doppler frequency shift. Point "B", at about the same range as point "A", is moving perpendicular to the radar beam, and will have no doppler frequency shift; its echo would be plotted as shown. Similarly, point "C" is moving away from the radar, and would have a negative doppler frequency shift. Finally, points along the cone such as point "D" have lower frequency shifts, since they are closer to the spinning axis. The resulting range-doppler plot will therefore resemble the conical target.

width of the transmitted signal. For example, a one gigahertz[37] bandwidth radar signal could have a range resolution capability of 15 cm. Resolution in the cross-track direction (corresponding to the radius of the spinning cone) is limited by the minimum doppler frequency shift that can be detected, radar wavelength (smaller is better), and the rotation rate of the RV (larger is better).[38] For microwave radars, typical doppler frequency shifts are in the tens to hundreds of hertz. Many radar pulses must be stored and analyzed to measure these low frequencies, which requires substantial data processing.

[35]An airborne synthetic aperture radar system generates an image of the ground by measuring the doppler frequency shifts of all return radar signals. Targets directly ahead of the radar aircraft have maximum Doppler frequency shift because the relative velocity between the ground and the aircraft is a maximum. Targets perpendicular to the aircraft flight path have no relative motion toward the aircraft and no Doppler frequency shift. By storing all the radar returns and processing data over time, a pseudo image of the ground is generated.

[36]If an imaging radar were boresighted along the trajectory of an RV, there would be no doppler frequency shift and no image. Conversely, if the radar looked perpendicular to the RV flight path, there would be no information on the length of the RV: any range spread would be due to the radius of the cone, independent of length. For other radar look angles between these extremes, the doppler frequency shift would be proportional to the sine of the look angle, and the range spread would be proportional to the cosine of that angle.

[37]Gigahertz is a unit of frequency equal to one billion cycles per second.

[38]Note that doppler (cross-track) *resolution* of these pseudo images is not equivalent to *positional accuracy*. Object details on the order of a few cm may be resolved in these images, but the cross-track position of the object will not be known to better than the radar beam width, which might be tens of kms wide.

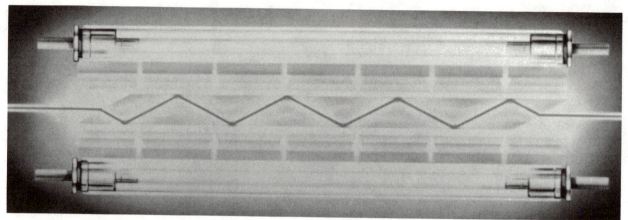

Artist's concept of laser tube assembly for laser radar sensor system. Such laser radars, or "ladars" might be deployed on space-based interceptor carrier vehicles or on space surveillance and tracking system satellites to help identify or track incoming missiles.

Ladar.—The short wavelength and very short pulse-length of a laser might prove very useful for several BMD functions. A laser radar or ladar system would illuminate the target cloud with a pulsed beam of light. An optical receiver would detect the reflected echoes, in direct analogy to a microwave radar. Various types of ladars could supply one-dimensional range to the target (a laser range-finder), or they could generate 2- or 3-dimensional images.

Several modes of imaging operation are possible:

- Scanning beam or "angle/angle" mode: a pulsed laser beam is focused and scanned over the scene. A single optical detector records the time sequence of reflections from each returned laser pulse, and a three dimensional map of target position is generated in computer memory. Ladar resolution would depend on the beam spot size, which could be as small as 3 m at 3,000 km with reasonably sized optics.[39] Very short-wavelength lasers are preferred to minimize spot size. The range resolution would be on the order of 1.5 m with 10-nanosecond long laser pulses, which are commercially available.

- Focal plane array: a passive imager, similar to the IR sensors, records the scene illuminated by a laser. The laser is the "flash lamp".

- Doppler ladar: the optical analog of a microwave Doppler imaging radar might be feasible if lasers with adequate coherence could be built. Doppler resolution of a coherent ladar could be excellent. A 30-cm RV rotating once per second would generate a 3.8 megahertz (million cycles/second—MHz) frequency shift in the ladar return signal, compared to only 60 hertz for an X-band imaging radar. Since the resolution of this pseudo-image would be independent of spot size, there would be no need to operate at short UV or visible wavelengths. This fine image resolution would not, however, yield good positional information. A narrow beam (short wavelength) angle/angle ladar would be required for good angular resolution.

Active Discrimination.—A ladar might be very useful for discriminating between RVs and decoys as they were ejected from a PBV. The PBV would perceptibly change its velocity as each heavy RV was discharged, but not as light decoys were dispensed. A ladar could be designed with the spatial resolution to resolve independently the PBV and the RV or decoy and, in theory, to measure the differen-

---

[39]A 0.5 μm laser with a 60-cm mirror would produce a diffraction-limited spot 3 m in diameter at a distance of 3,000 km.

tial velocities before and after each deployment.[40]

Light decoys might inflate as they left the PBV. A high resolution imaging ladar could in principle observe this inflation and so identify balloon decoys.[41] A precision doppler ladar might also observe small vibration or nutation (wobbling) differences between an RV and a decoy. Light decoys might vibrate at tens to hundreds of kilohertz (kHz), heavier RVs at less than a few kHz. Over tens of seconds, the nose of a spinning RV also nutates a few millimeters: a very high resolution ladar might detect this motion, but long integration times and high data storage rates would be necessary.

Current Status of Active Sensors.—Active sensor technologies have been tested and deployed in some form since the radars of World War II. Considerable development remains, however, before active sensors will be ready for advanced BMD systems.

Phased-array Search Radars.—Ground-based phased-array radars are currently deployed in both the United States and the Soviet Union to detect objects in space and give early warning of missile attack. The "PAVE PAWS" radars now at Otis AFB on Cape Cod and at Beale AFB near Sacramento have two large faces each, with active areas 22 m square, providing 240° coverage. Each face has 1,792 active antenna elements, with provisions to upgrade each face to 31 by 31 m active areas with 5,354 elements. Two additional PAVE PAWS radars are being built in Georgia and Texas.

The United States plans to replace the three existing Ballistic Missile Early Warning System (BMEWS) mechanically scanned radars at Clear, Alaska; Thule, Greenland; and Fylingdales Moor in England with phased array radars. The old Distant Early Warning radars will also be replaced by 52 new phased array North Warning System (NWS) radars. These radars, along with the mothballed phased array radar near Grand Forks, North Dakota, might supply RV target coordinates to an ERIS exoatmospheric interceptor system.[42]

Imaging Radars.—Several radars have been operated in the range-doppler imaging mode since the early 1970s. These ground-based radars are used to image satellites, RVs, and other space objects. MIT's Lincoln Labs operates an L-band and an X-band imaging radar at Millstone Hill in Massachusetts.

Ladars.—Ladar systems have not been placed in operation, but they have been tested. In 1981 MIT Lincoln Laboratories built the "Firepond" CO_2 ladar, which had a 15 kW peak power and 1.4 kW average power. With a one microradian resolution, this ladar could detect targets spaced 3 m apart at a distance of 3,000 km. This ladar has been reactivated for the SDI program. It will be operated in the range-doppler mode to investigate RV imaging in a ground-based field test. Two other lasers are planned. One will have a very short (nanosecond), high peak power pulse to yield good range resolution. The other will use a lower peak power, frequency-chirped pulse. To recover good range resolution, this chirped pulse is compressed electronically in a data processor. This same pulse compression technique has been used successfully to reduce the peak power required in more conventional microwave radars.

---

[40]Consider a PBV with 10 RVs. The PBV velocity would change very little if a light decoy were ejected. Ejecting the first RV, if it weighed 1/15th of the remaining PBV weight, would cause the PBV to slow by 1/15th of the RV-PBV separation velocity. That is, if the two objects were designed to move apart at a 15cm/sec rate, then the PBV would slow down by 1 cm/sec and the RV would speed up by 14 cm/sec after separation. Later RV's would cause the PBV to slow down more, as the ratio of RV to remaining PBV weight increased. The ladar would therefore need a velocity resolution of 1 cm/sec in this example.

[41]One countermeasure to block the observation of decoy inflation (as well as differential velocity detection) would be to inflate the decoys under a long shroud, although there is some concern that the PBV rocket plume might interfere with a shroud. Alternatively, decoys and RVs could be tethered together so that their rotation would confuse the sensor, which could not keep track of each object (see ch. 10.)

[42]SDIO's phase-one Strategic Defense System plans one or more optical sensors for cueing ERIS interceptors. However, Lockheed—the ERIS developer—and others have proposed an "early deployment" version of ERIS that would utilize existing radars. The computing capabilities of these radars would have to be improved to handle hundreds of targets. The systems would be susceptible to electromagnetic pulse, microwave jamming, and blast damage in the event of nuclear war. At this time, phased-array radars are the only sensors available for early deployment of ERIS-like BMD systems.

Work is also proceeding on diode-pumped glass lasers, excimer lasers, and bistatic CO_2 ladars. Glass lasers are typically pumped with flash lamps, resulting in very low efficiency (typically less than 0.2 percent), since the spectrum of the flash lamp does not match the absorption bands of the Nd:glass material. By pumping the Nd:glass laser with an array of incoherent laser diodes, efficiency can be increased significantly and the thermal distortion which normally limits these lasers to very low repetition rates can be controlled.

Excimer lasers have the advantage of generating UV radiation, which demands the smallest mirrors for a given resolution.

Key Issues for Active Sensors.—Current SDI phase-two concepts call for ground-based radars for directing late mid-course and terminal defense. Space-based ladars are suggested for boost-phase ranging, to observe PBV deployment, and for determining accurate target position during mid-course discrimination. Ladars might also be used for air-borne ranging to assist terminal defense. Issues for these active sensors include the following.

Ground-based Radar.—Ground-based radars would have to be large, phased-array devices to focus adequate energy on many targets. Two key issues would be survivability and data processing. Surge fuses at each radiating diode in the array could probably protect large antennas from nuclear burst-generated electromagnetic pulse (EMP). Shielding the structure and building could protect interior electronics. Most EMP energy would be below 150 MHz, so radar radio frequency (RF) circuits at 10 GHz could be safe.

However, these antennas would be susceptible to in-band radiation from dedicated jammers. It might be a challenge to design effective electronic counter-countermeasures to protect these large and critical assets from electronic jamming by Soviet satellites. Some system architects have suggested that these radars be mobile, possibly on railroad cars. Mobility might reduce susceptibility to jamming.

Data processing might also be challenging. Consider an X-band (3-cm wavelength) radar. Its data processor might have to handle 5 million bits per second of incoming data for each of 5,000 antenna dipoles, or a total of 25 billion bits per second for the entire radar.[43] These data must be stored and processed to determine the direction to each target (by phasing the receiving array) and a Fast Fourier Transform (FFT) operation would have to be performed on each range bin to measure doppler frequency shift over many pulses.

Doppler imaging radars might be fooled if RVs (and decoys) were covered with "fronds," —strips painted with irregular patterns of volatile material. Attached at various places on an object, these strips would move about at random in space as the volatile material evaporated. This motion would give different parts of the target different doppler velocities independent of their positions on the RV or decoy cone. Such extraneous frequency shifts might confuse the radar processor, obscuring the image of the RV body.

Ladar Active Discrimination.—Significant advances would be required in ladar technology before it could be utilized to observe PBV deployment of RVs and decoys. Key issues would be resolution, beam steering, and data processing to handle the expected traffic.

Direct angle/angle ladar imaging of PBVs would take very large mirrors.[44] The alternative would be doppler processing to improve cross-track resolution. While microwave syn-

---

[43]This data rate assumes that radar bandwidth is 1 GHz to yield a 15-cm range resolution. The radar tracks each target to within 100-m accuracy before hand-over to an image mode processor, which maintains a sliding range gate 100 m wide about each high-speed target. The radar pulse repetition rate is set by the highest expected doppler frequency shift produced by RV rotation. For clear images of a 20-cm radius RV rotating at 3 hertz, the pulse repetition frequency (PRF) must be 500 hertz or higher. (This imaging doppler radar would be highly ambiguous with respect to RV velocity, which would require MHz type PRFs to measure actual velocity.)

[44]To image a 30-cm diameter RV, a ladar designer would like 10 resolution elements across the object to resolve shape or details, or 3 cm resolution. Thus, an impractically large 60-m mirror would be required for 3 cm resolution at 3,000 km range with a visible laser.

thetic aperture radars have been successfully operated for over 20 years, this process has not been extended to optical wavelengths. Building stable but powerful space-based lasers with the coherence necessary for doppler processing would be a major challenge.

Interactive Sensors

The consensus in the SDI technical community is that passive and active sensors may not be adequate to discriminate between RVs and decoys in the future. The Soviet Union probably has the necessary technology to develop decoys and real RVs with nearly the same infrared and radar signatures. Decoys would not be extraordinarily difficult to fabricate and disperse in space, and they would weigh only a small fraction of an RV. There is a serious question whether, once dispersed, they could be distinguished from real RVs by any passive or active sensor. If not, the offense could overwhelm a space-based or ground-based mid-course defense system with literally hundreds of thousands of false targets.

Mid-course decoy discrimination would become crucial if the Soviets could:

- deny a phase-one boost-phase defense through countermeasures such as moderately fast-burn (e.g., 120- second) boosters, and
- deny significant post-boost kills by moving to faster PBV deployment times or to single warhead missiles.

If an initial U.S. deployment of kinetic energy weapons could no longer destroy many ICBMs in the boost or post-boost phase, and if directed-energy weapons were not yet available, then **mid-course discrimination would become indispensable to a viable BMD system.**

There would be two possibilities for effective mid-course discrimination under these circumstances: ladar discrimination during post-boost decoy dispersal, or interactive discrimination after the RVs and decoys were released. As discussed in the preceding section, ladar detection during decoy deployment would be very challenging. Moreover, simple measurement of RV and PBV recoil velocities might

be thwarted completely if the Soviets could disperse decoys and RVs simultaneously in pairs. Even fine doppler imaging would be foiled if the Soviet PBV could obscure the deployment operation with a shroud. This would leave interactive discrimination as the main approach to keeping BMD viable in the long term.

How Interactive Discriminators Would Work. —In interactive discrimination, a sensor system would perturb each target and then measure its reaction to determine if it were a decoy or an RV. For example, a dust cloud of sufficient density and uniformity could be placed in front of a group of objects. The resulting collisions would slow down light decoys more than heavy RVs. A ladar would monitor the change of velocity of all objects, thereby identifying real RVs.

Two general classes of discriminators have been proposed: kinetic energy and directed energy perturbers.

Kinetic Energy Discriminators.—Two methods have been proposed to project particles in front of an oncoming cloud of decoys and RVs: rocket-born particles and nuclear-explosion-projected particles. A rocket-borne cloud would be limited to late mid-course, unless the rockets were fired from submarines or based in Canada or the Arctic. Presumably one rocket would be necessary for the cylindrical cluster (or "threat tube") of RVs and decoys emanating from each PBV. To slow down decoys measurably, a rocket would have to carry enough mass to cover the full lateral extent of the threat tube with a sufficiently dense cloud. A ladar would have to measure velocity changes in the 10-cm/sec to 1-m/sec range.

Directed-energy Discriminators.—Several forms of directed energy have been proposed for interactive discrimination. They would all have the advantage of long range, extending the discrimination capability back to the beginning of the mid-course if not to the post-boost phase.

The laser is the best developed directed-energy perturber currently available, although further development would be needed to produce lasers with the brightness required for interactive discrimination. Lasers could heat unknown targets (called "thermal tagging"). Alternatively, a short pulse of laser light could change the velocities of targets (called "impulse tagging").

In thermal tagging, a laser of the appropriate wavelength would heat a light-weight decoy more than an RV—assuming they both absorbed laser energy and radiated IR (thermal) energy to the same degree. A separate IR sensor, possibly mounted on SSTS satellites, would then detect the warmer decoy.

Pulsed lasers could shock the unidentified objects. Energy would be deposited in microseconds instead of the milliseconds taken by thermal tagging. A high-power pulse would boil away material perpendicular to the surface of the target. The reaction of ablation products would cause the target to change velocity. A heavier RV would recoil less than a decoy, providing a mass-dependent indicator. A separate ladar would monitor the change of each object's velocity.

The SDIO has chosen the neutral particle beam (NPB) as the most promising interactive discrimination perturbation source. The particle beam source is derived from well-established particle accelerators used for several decades in physics research experiments around the world. A neutral particle beam could be composed of hydrogen atoms,[45] accelerated to velocities about half that of the speed of light. Since the particle beam would be relatively broad, on the order of 2 microradian beam width, it would not require the pointing accuracy of 50-nanoradian-wide laser beams.

These energetic particles would be deposited several cm deep inside an RV.[46] As they were absorbed, these particles would produce gamma rays and neutrons. Neutron or gamma-ray detectors on many satellites—located closer to the targets than the accelerator—might monitor the emissions coming from a massive RV. Light weight decoys, in contrast, would not emit much radiation.

High energy particles must be electrically neutral to propagate through the Earth's variable magnetic field (charged particles would bend in unpredictable paths.) But a particle must be charged to be accelerated. Therefore the NPB would first accelerate negatively charged hydrogen ions. After acceleration to a few hundred MeV (million electron volts) energy, this beam would be aimed toward the target by magnetic steering coils. Once steered, the charged beam would be neutralized by stripping off the extra electron from each particle. Thin foils or gas cells are currently used to neutralize beams in laboratory experiments.

A relativistic (i.e., near-speed-of-light) electron beam could also be used as a discriminator. The detector in this scheme would monitor x-rays from the more massive RV. Such a system might be ground-based, popping up on a rocket to monitor the mid-course phase. The main advantage would be the avoidance of space-based assets for interactive discrimination. However, an e-beam discriminator would need some air to form a laser-initiated channel, so it could only operate at altitudes between 80 to 600 km.

Current Status of Interactive Sensors.—Interactive sensors have not yet been built for any military mission. All the concepts described above have been invented to solve the severe discrimination problem unique to mid-course ballistic missile defense.

Key Issues for Interactive Discrimination.—The overriding issue for interactive discrimination is effectiveness in the face of evolving Soviet countermeasures. There are some common issues for any discriminator and some issues unique to each approach.

Laser Radar.—Any discriminator would require a high resolution laser radar to accurately locate and identify each object in space. One

---

[45] An NPB could also utilize deuterium or tritium, the heavier isotopes of hydrogen. These heavier isotopes would experience less divergence in the beam neutralization process after acceleration. Tritium, the hydrogen isotope with two neutrons, must be produced in a nuclear reactor and is radioactive with a half-life of 12.3 years. Deuterium, the non-radioactive hydrogen isotope with one neutron, would most likely be used.

Another approach calls for cesium instead of hydrogen atoms in a "momentum rich beam." A heavy cesium beam would impart a velocity change to the target, so it is more analogous to a laser impulse tagger than to a hydrogen NPB.

[46] The electron on each hydrogen atom would be stripped off, leaving the proton which penetrates into the target.

Table 4-3.—Key Issues for Interactive Sensors

For all discriminators:
- Laser radar required for accurate target location: (corner cube reflector is inexpensive counter-measure.)
- Rapid retargeting: 3-50 targets/second

For NPB accelerator:
- Voltage and duty cycle must be increased without increasing beam emittance
- Beam expansion
- Beam sensing must be developed
- Beam pointing system must be developed
- Beam propagation in space
- Space charge accumulation
- Accelerator arcing in space
- Weight

For NPB neutron detectors:
- RV detection with nuclear precursor background
- Missed target indicator

For laser thermal tagger:
- Moderate to high power pulsed lasers
- Thermal shroud on RV

For laser impulse tagger:
- Needs ladar imager to tell orientation
- High to very high average power, microsecond-long pulsed lasers
- Thruster-compensated RVs

For dust cloud tagger:
- Dispersal of dust cloud

SOURCE: Office of Technology Assessment, 1988.

possible countermeasure to ladar would be an inexpensive corner-cube reflector on each RV and decoy. This corner cube would essentially swamp the ladar receiver: the beam would be returned on itself and the ladar would be unable to measure target characteristics. A counter-countermeasure would be a bistatic ladar with a laser transmitter on one platform and a light detector on a separate satellite not far away. Reflected energy from a corner cube would travel harmlessly back to the transmitter, thus failing to blind the receiver. Bistatic operation would be feasible, but it would complicate system design, construction, and operation.

Beam Steering.—A directed-energy interactive discriminator would have to steer its beam rapidly from one object to the next. Beam steering requirements are set by the number of expected targets and the number of directed-energy satellites within range of those targets. Typical estimates are that hundreds of thousands of RVs and decoys might survive the

boost phase defense.[47] Assuming that midcourse discrimination of sophisticated decoys must be completed in 15 minutes, then each platform would have to interrogate 3 to 50 targets per second. The directed-energy source would have to be steered accurately from one target to the next in less than 20 to 300 milliseconds. This would be a formidable challenge.

NPB Accelerator.—Neutral particle beam accelerator development faces many key hurdles. Beam energy must be increased by a factor of 20, which should not be difficult. Duty cycle and beam diameter must be increased by a factor of 100 without degrading beam quality or emittance—a more challenging task. An accelerator would have to operate in space without electrical breakdown or arcing that would short out its electrical system. Communications and electronic controls would have to operate even with electrical charge build-up in space. An NPB would have to propagate over long distances in space with little divergence. To point accurately at targets, it would have to be effectively boresighted to an optical system.

These same issues would have to be resolved for an NPB weapon accelerator. A weapon-grade NPB would probably dwell longer on each target to assure destruction of at least the internal electronics, but might otherwise be very similar to one designed for interactive discrimination. A more detailed discussion of NPB accelerator issues appears in the DEW section of chapter 5.

Neutron Detection.—Calculations indicate that large neutron detectors placed on hundreds of separate satellites near the targets could detect the neutron flux from RVs. The offense might intentionally detonate nuclear weapons in space before an attack to saturate these neutron detectors. With sufficiently high particle-beam energy (on the order of 200 MeV),

[47]An interactive discriminator would not have to interrogate all objects in space. Unsophisticated decoys, discarded booster stages and other debris could probably be identified by passive or active sensors. With adequate battle management to keep track of extraneous objects, the process of "bulk filtering" would eliminate these objects from the interactive discriminator's target list.

the energy of some neutrons ejected from an RV would be higher than that expected of neutrons emanating from nuclear detonations. Therefore an energy threshold circuit would eliminate most of the signal from the latter source, allowing identification of the neutrons from RVs.

Another issue is how to confirm that targets had been hit by an NPB, since the neutron detectors would receive no signal from decoys. How would a system distinguish between decoys and RVs which were missed by the beam? One possibility, being tested in the laboratory, would be to monitor each object with a UV sensor on the assumption that the outer surface of the RVs (and the decoys) would emit UV light when struck by the particle beam. This UV sensor simply would confirm that the particle beam had hit a target.

If based on current technology, neutron-detector platform weights would be excessive. Each platform would weigh up to 30 tonnes. System designers hope that lighter detector elements and power supplies can reduce this weight to 5 tonnes per platform by the mid-1990s. If this goal were achieved, then the several hundred detector satellites could be orbited with about 100 launches of the proposed Advanced Launch System.

Laser Thermal Tagger.—Very high power lasers would be required to tag space targets for an interactive discriminator. A laser thermal tagger, like all interactive sensors, would require a separate laser radar to locate targets precisely. For example, cold RVs (and decoys) would have to be tracked by long-wavelength LWIR passive sensors. These sensors could only determine a target's position to within 18 m, assuming a 2-m sensor mirror at 3,000 km.[48] But the interrogating laser beam might have a spot size of only 1 or 2 m. A more accurate laser radar would be required to guide an HF laser beam to the target.

Detecting small temperature rises on several hundred thousand objects would also stress LWIR sensor technology. Monitoring closely spaced targets would demand large LWIR mirrors. For example, to distinguish objects spaced 10 m apart, a sensor 3,000 km away would need a 4-m mirror. Steering this large mirror to, say, 15 targets per second would be another major challenge.

Decoys might be modified to respond to thermal tagging as an RV would. Due to their lower mass, decoy surfaces should became hotter than RV surfaces after laser illumination. However, the outer layer of the decoys could in principle be built to absorb less laser light or to emit more IR heat. These decoys would then reach the same temperature as an RV after exposure to laser light. Or, an RV could simply be covered by an insulating blanket that would decouple the exterior thermal response from the internal RV mass. **It appears that laser thermal tagging would have limited usefulness against a committed adversary.**

Laser-impulse Discriminator.—The energy density required for laser impulse discrimination would be in the range of 7 to 30 times more than for thermal tagging. In addition, the laser pulses would have to be very short, on the order of microseconds instead of milliseconds, which makes the peak laser power extraordinarily high. This high peak power would be difficult to generate and handle, since mirrors and other optical components would be susceptible to damage by the intense pulses. While less powerful than proposed laser weapons, lasers for impulse discrimination would still be a major development.[49]

Laser impulse discrimination might be countered by equipping RVs or decoys to react deceptively. Small thrusters on RVs might cause them to move as a decoy would under a laser impulse. Alternatively, thrusters on relatively sophisticated decoys might counteract the laser impulse.

---

[48]A single target could be located to within less than the 18-m LWIR resolution element by a process called "beam-splitting": the target is assumed to be in the center of the IR signal waveform. If there were two targets or a target and a decoy within the 18-m resolution element, however, then the sensor would falsely indicate one target located between the two objects.

[49]The primary measure of a laser's effectiveness as a weapon is beam "brightness," the average power radiated into a given solid angle. An HF laser impulse tagger would be brighter than any laser built to date, but still a factor of 2 to 200 less bright than that needed for BMD against a responsive Soviet threat.

All interactive discriminators would probably require an imaging ladar to provide adequate resolution both to hit targets with a probe beam and to measure target response accurately. A laser impulse discriminator would bear the additional burden of determining target (and particularly decoy) orientation. The orientation of a conical decoy, for example, could affect its reactive motion in response to the laser pulse.

Dust-cloud Discriminator.—The key issue for a dust cloud discriminator is how to position the cloud accurately in front of the oncoming RV-decoy constellation at the proper time.

If the particles were dispersed too widely, the required amount would become excessive. If clustered too closely, they could miss some decoys. As with any discriminator, a precision ladar would be required to measure velocity changes accurately.

Laser impulse discrimination might be countered by equipping RVs or decoys to react deceptively. Small thrusters on RVs might cause them to move as a decoy would under a laser impulse; alternatively, thrusters on relatively sophisticated decoys might counteract the impulse.

SENSOR TECHNOLOGY CONCLUSIONS

Phase 1

1. **A boost surveillance and tracking satellite (BSTS) could most probably be developed by the mid-1990s.** Short-wave and middle-wave infrared (S/MWIR) sensors, could provide early warning and coarse booster track data sufficient to direct SBI launches.[50]

2. **Space surveillance and tracking system (SSTS) satellites would not be available for tracking individual RVs and decoys before the late 1990s.** The ability to discriminate possible decoys in this time frame is in question. Smaller but similar sensors for a phase-one system might be placed on individual SBI platforms or on ground-based, pop-up probes.

3. **An airborne optical system could probably be available by the mid-1990s to detect and track RVs and decoys with IR sensors (although not to discriminate against a replica decoy above the atmosphere). However, its utility may be limited in performance and mission:**
   - Performance may be limited by the vulnerability and operating cost of its aircraft platform, and IR sensors

might be confused during battle by IR-scattering ice crystals formed at 60 to 80 km altitude by debris reentering the atmosphere.
   - The relatively short range of airborne IR sensors would limit the AOS mission to supplying data on approaching objects for endo-atmospheric interceptor radars, and possibly for exo-atmospheric interceptors a short while before RV reentry. Airborne IR sensors, unless very forward-based, could utilize only a small portion of the time available in mid-course for discrimination and therefore could not take full advantage of the fly-out range of ground-based exoatmospheric interceptors.

   In any case, an Airborne Optical System is not now included in SDIO phase-one deployment plans.

4. **Effective discrimination against more sophisticated decoys and disguised RVs in space is unlikely before the year 2000, if at all.**

Phase 2

5. **By the late 1990s at the earliest, a space surveillance and tracking system (SSTS) might furnish post-boost vehicle (PBV) and reen-**

---

[50]One uncertainty is the protection of the BSTS sensors from future airborne or spaceborne laser jammers which could permanently damage IR detector elements during peacetime.

try vehicle (RV) track data with long-wave infrared (LWIR) above-the-horizon (ATH) sensors suitable for directing SBI launches in the mid-course. New methods would be needed for the manufacture of large quantities of radiation-hardened focal plane arrays. Another issue is the operation of LWIR sensors in the presence of precursor nuclear explosions (including those heaving atmosphere into the ATH field of view) or other intentionally dispersed chemical aerosols. Effective mid-course SBI capability is unlikely before the late 1990s to early 2000s.

6. **There are too many uncertainties in projecting sensor capabilities and the level of Soviet countermeasures to specify a discrimination capability for SSTS.** It appears that Soviet countermeasures (penetration aids and decoys) could keep ahead of passive IR discrimination techniques:

   - Passive IR discrimination could be available by the mid-1990s, but probably would have marginal utility against determined Soviet countermeasures.
   - Active laser radar (ladar) imaging of PBV deployment offers some promise of decoy discrimination, provided that the Soviets did not mask dispersal of decoys. Space-borne imaging ladars probably would not be available until the late 1990s at the earliest.
   - Laser thermal tagging of RVs is unlikely to be practical given the need for complex, agile steering systems and given likely countermeasures such as thermal insulation of RVs and decoys.
   - Laser impulse tagging is even less likely to succeed in this phase because high-power pulsed lasers would be required.

7. **Ground-based radar (GBR) might be available by the late 1990s to direct interceptors to re-entering warheads.** There may be some

questions about its resistance to RF jammers. Signal processors may have difficulty handling large numbers of targets in real-time.

Phase 3

8. Accurate IR sensors, UV ladar, or visible ladar would have to reside on each DEW platform.

9. **Interactive discrimination with neutral particle beams (NPB) appears the most likely candidate to reliably distinguish decoys from RVs, since the particles would penetrate targets, making shielding very difficult.** Before one could judge the efficacy of a total NPB discrimination system, major engineering developments would be required in: weight reduction, space transportation, neutral particle beam control and steering,[51] automated accelerator operation in space, and multi-megawatt space power.

   It is unlikely that a decision on the technical feasibility of NPB discrimination could be made before another decade of laboratory development and major space experiments. Given the magnitude of an NPB/detector satellite constellation, **an effective discrimination system against sophisticated decoys and disguised RVs would not likely be fully deployed and available for BMD use until the 2010 to 2015 period at the earliest.**

10. **Nuclear bomb-projected particles might also form the basis of an effective interactive discriminator,** if reliable space-based ladar systems were also developed and deployed to measure target velocity changes. There are too many uncertainties to project if or when this approach might succeed.

---

[51]Since the particle beams are invisible, novel approaches would be required to sense the direction of the beam so that it could be steered toward the target.

Chapter 5

Ballistic Missile Defense Technology: Weapons, Power, Communications, and Space Transportation

CONTENTS

Ballistic Missile Defense Technology: Weapons, Power, Communications, and Space Transportation

INTRODUCTION

This chapter reviews weapon technologies relevant to ballistic missile defense (BMD). It emphasizes the chemically propelled hit-to-kill weapons most likely to form the basis of any future U.S BMD deployment in this century. The chapter also covers the directed-energy weapons, power systems, and communication systems of most interest for the Strategic Defense Initiative (SDI). Finally, it considers the new space transportation system essential for a space-based defense.

WEAPONS

A weapon system must transfer a lethal dose of energy from weapon to a target. All existing weapons use some combination of kinetic energy (the energy of motion of a bullet, for example), chemical energy, or nuclear energy to disable the target. The SDI research program is exploring two major new types of weapon systems: directed-energy weapons and ultra-high accuracy and high velocity hit-to-kill weapons. Not only have these weapons never been built before, but no weapon of any type has been based in space. Operating many hundreds or thousands of autonomous weapons platforms in space would itself be a major technical challenge.

Directed-energy weapons (DEW) would kill their prey without a projectile. Energy would travel through space via a laser beam or a stream of atomic or sub-atomic particles. Speed is the main virtue. A laser could attack an object 1,000 km away in 3 thousandths of a second, while a high-speed rifle-bullet, for example, would have to be fired 16 minutes before impact with such a distant target. Clearly,

DEW, if they reach the necessary power levels, would revolutionize ballistic missile defense.

DEWs offer the ultimate in delivery speed. But they are not likely to have sufficient deployed power in this century to destroy ballistic missiles, and they certainly could not kill the more durable reentry vehicles (RVs). In hopes of designing a system deployable before the year 2000, the SDI research program has emphasized increased speed and accuracy for the more conventional kinetic-energy weapons (KEW), such as chemically propelled rockets. With speeds in the 4 to 7 km/s range, and with terminal or homing guidance to collide directly with the target, these KEW could kill a significant number of today's ballistic missiles. With sufficient accuracy, they would not require chemical or nuclear explosives.

Although DEWs will not be available for highly effective ballistic missile defense during this century, they could play a significant role in an early 1990s decision on whether to deploy *any* ballistic missile defense system. That is, the deployment decision could hinge on our ability to persuade the Soviets (and ourselves) that defenses would remain viable for the foreseeable future. Kinetic-energy weapons

---

Note: Complete definitions of acronyms and initialisms are listed in Appendix B of this report.

work initially against the 1990s Soviet missile threat. But Soviet responsive countermeasures might soon render those weapons ineffective. Thus, a long-term commitment to a ballistic missile defense system would imply strong confidence that new developments, such as evolving DEW or evolving discrimination capability, could overcome and keep ahead of any reasonable Soviet response.

Strategic Defense Initiative Organization (SDIO) officials argue that perceived future capabilities of DEW might deter the Soviet Union from embarking on a costly defense countermeasures building program; instead, the prospect of offensive capabilities might persuade them to join with the United States in reducing offensive ballistic missiles and moving from an offense-dominated to a defense-dominated regime. To foster this dramatic shift in strategic thinking, the evolving defensive system would have to appear less costly and more effective than offensive countermeasures.

Today, the immaturity of DEW technology makes any current judgments of its cost-effectiveness extremely uncertain. It appears that many years of research and development would be necessary before anyone could state with reasonable confidence whether effective DEW systems could be deployed at lower cost than responsive countermeasures. **Given the current state of the art in DEW systems, a well-informed decision in the mid-1990s to build and deploy highly effective DEW weapons appears unlikely.**[1]

Kinetic-Energy Weapons (KEW)

Today's chemically propelled rockets and sensors could not intercept intercontinental ballistic missiles (ICBMs) or reentry vehicles

[1]The Study Group of the American Physical Society concluded in their analysis of DEW that "even in the best of circumstances, a decade or more of intensive research would be required to provide the technical knowledge needed for an informed decision about the potential effectiveness and survivability of DEW systems. In addition, the important issues of overall system integration and effectiveness depend critically upon information that, to our knowledge, does not yet exist." See American Physical Society, *Science and Technology of Directed Energy Weapons: Report of the American Physical Society Study Group,* April, 1987, p. 2.

(RVs) in space. No currently deployable projectile system has the accuracy or speed to consistently intercept an RV traveling at 7 km/s at ranges of hundreds or thousands of kilometers. The SAFEGUARD anti-ballistic missile (ABM) system built near Grand Forks, North Dakota in the early 1970s, and the existing Soviet Galosh ABM system around Moscow both would compensate for the poor accuracy of their radar guidance systems by exploding nuclear warheads. The radiation from that explosion would increase the lethal radius so that the interceptors, despite their poor accuracy, could disable incoming warheads.

The goal of the SDI, however, is primarily to investigate technology for a non-nuclear defense. This would dictate the development of "smart" projectiles that could "see" their targets or receive external guidance signals, changing course during flight to collide with the targets.

The following sections discuss proposed KEW systems, KEW technologies, the current status of technology, and key issues.

KEW Systems

Four different KEW systems were analyzed by SDI system architects, including space-based interceptors (SBIs, formerly called space-based kinetic kill vehicles or SBKKVs), and three ground-based systems. All four systems would rely on chemically propelled rockets.

Space-Based Interceptors (SBIs).—Each system architect proposed—and the SDIO "phase-one" proposal includes—deploying some type of space-based projectile. These projectiles would ride on pre-positioned platforms in low-Earth orbits, low enough to reach existing ICBM boosters before their engines would burn out, but high enough to improve the likelihood of surviving and to avoid atmospheric drag over a nominal seven-year satellite life. The range of characteristics for proposed SBI systems is summarized in the classified version of this report.

It would take a few thousand carrier satellites in nearly polar orbits at several hundred km altitude to attack effectively a high percentage of the mid-1990s Soviet ICBM threat. There was a wide range in the number of interceptor rockets proposed by system architects, depending on the degree of redundancy deemed necessary for functional survivability, on the number of interceptors assigned to shoot down Soviet direct-ascent anti-satellite weapons (ASATs), and on the leakage rates accepted for the boost-phase defense.

In late 1986, the SDIO and its contractors began to examine options for 1990s deployment which would include constellations of only a few hundred carrier vehicles (CVs) and a few thousand SBIs. This evolved into the phase-one design which, if deployed in the mid to late 1990s, could only attack a modest fraction of the existing Soviet ICBMs in their boost and post-boost phases.

Exo-atmospheric Reentry Interceptor System (ERIS).—The ERIS would be a ground-based rocket with the range to attack RVs in the late midcourse phase. Existing, but upgraded, ra-

dars such as BMEWS, PAVE PAWS, and the PAR radar north of Grand Forks, North Dakota might supply initial track coordinates to ERIS interceptors.[2] (These radars might be the only sensors available for near-term deployments.) Alternatively, new radars or optical sensors would furnish the track data. Upgraded radars would have little discrimination capability (unless the Soviets were to refrain from using penetration aids); moreover, a single high altitude nuclear explosion could degrade or destroy them.

Optical sensors might reside on a fleet of space surveillance and tracking system (SSTS) satellites or on ground-based, pop-up probes based at higher latitudes. Such sensors might supply early enough infrared (IR) track data

---

[2]The range of planned ground-based radars such as the Terminal Imaging Radar (TIR), which could discriminate RVs from decoys, might be too short to aid ERIS long-range interceptors; the TIR was planned for the lower HEDI endoatmospheric system. A longer-range Ground-based Radar (GBR) system has also been proposed. This system may be capable of supporting ERIS interceptors.

How ERIS would work.—The ERIS vehicle would be launched from the ground and its sensors would acquire and track a target at long range. ERIS would then maneuver to intercept the target's path, demolishing it on impact.

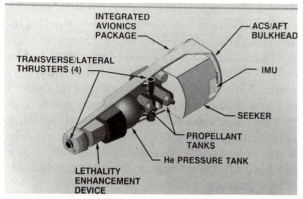

INTEGRATED AVIONICS PACKAGE

ACS/AFT BULKHEAD

TRANSVERSE/LATERAL THRUSTERS (4)

IMU

SEEKER

PROPELLANT TANKS

He PRESSURE TANK

LETHALITY ENHANCEMENT DEVICE

Photo Credit: Lockheed Missiles and Space Company

ERIS kill vehicle concept.—The Integrated Avionics Package (IAP) computer (top left) receives interceptor position data from the on-board Inertial Measurement Unit and target position data from the seeker, or infrared sensor. The seeker acquires and tracks the incoming warhead. The IAP sends guidance commands to the two transverse and two lateral thrusters, which maneuver the vehicle to the impact point. Helium is used to pressurize the fuel tanks and also as a propellant for the attitude control system at the aft bulkhead. The lethality enhancement device would deploy just before impact to provide a larger hit area.

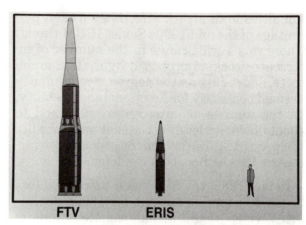

FTV   ERIS

Photo Credit: Lockheed Missiles and Space Company

ERIS Functional Test Validation (FTV) v. baseline ERIS concept.—Sizes of the FTV vehicle and baseline ERIS concepts are compared to a 6-foot-tall man. ERIS is designed as a ground-launched interceptor that would destroy a ballistic missile warhead in space. The FTV vehicle is 33 feet tall, large enough to carry both an observational payload to observe the impact with the warhead and the telemetry to relay information to the ground during the flight tests. The baseline interceptor concept is less than 14 feet tall, more compact because it will not require all the sensors and redundancies that are demanded by flight tests.

to take full advantage of the ERIS fly-out range.[3] If deployed, an airborne optical system (AOS) could give some track data late in midcourse. None of these sensors has been built, although the Airborne Optical Adjunct (AOA), a potential precursor to the AOS airborne system, is under construction and will be test flown in the late 1980s.

An on-board IR homing sensor would guide the interceptor to a collision with the RV in the last few seconds of flight. This homing sensor would derive from the Homing Overlay Experiment (HOE) sensor, which successfully intercepted a simulated Soviet RV over the Pacific on the fourth attempt, in 1984.

No major improvements in rocket technology would be necessary to deploy an ERIS-like system, but cost would be an important factor. The Army's Strategic Defense Command proposes to reduce the size of the launch vehicle in steps. The Army has proposed—

partly to reduce costs—to test this system with a Functional Technical Validation (FTV) rocket in 1990-91. This missile would have approximately twice the height, 10 times the weight, and twice the burn time of the planned ERIS rocket. The planned ERIS rocket system has a target cost of $1 million to $2 million per intercept in large quantities. Research is proceeding with a view to possible deployment by the mid-1990s.

Much development would be necessary to upgrade the experimental HOE kinetic kill vehicle technology for an operational ERIS interceptor. The IR sensors are being radiation-hardened. Since the operational sensor could not be maintained at the cryogenically low temperatures required for the HOE experiment, higher operating-temperature sensors are being developed, with cool-down to occur after alert or during rocket flight.

High Endo-atmospheric Defense Interceptor (HEDI).—The HEDI system would attack RVs that survived earlier defensive layers of ground-based, high-velocity interceptor

---

[3]The ERIS, as presently designed, requires a relatively high target position accuracy at hand-off from the sensor. The BSTS would not be adequate for this.

rockets. HEDI would take advantage of the fact that the atmosphere would slow down light-weight decoys more than the heavier RVs. Since it would operate in the atmosphere, HEDI might attack depressed trajectory submarine-launched ballistic missile (SLBM) warheads that would under-fly boost and midcourse defensive layers—provided it received adequate warning and sensor data.

According to one plan, an AOS would track the RVs initially, after warning from the boost-phase surveillance and tracking system (BSTS) and possible designation by SSTS (if available). The AOS would hand target track information off to the ground-based terminal imaging radar (TIR). The TIR would discriminate RVs from decoys both on shape (via doppler imaging) and on their lower deceleration (compared to decoys) upon entering the atmosphere. Interceptors would attack the RVs at altitudes between 12 and 45 km. The HEDI system thus would combine passive optics (IR signature), atmospheric deceleration, and active radar (shape) to distinguish RVs from decoys.

The penalty for waiting to accumulate these data on target characteristics would be the need for a large, high-acceleration missile. The HEDI would have to wait long enough to provide good atmospheric discrimination, but not so long that a salvage-fused RV would detonate a nuclear explosion close to the ground. To accelerate rapidly, the HEDI 2-stage missile must weigh about five to six times more than the ERIS missile.

The key technology challenge for the HEDI system would be its IR homing sensor. This non-nuclear, hit-to-kill vehicle would have to view the RV for the last few seconds of flight to steer a collision course.[4] But very high acceleration up through the atmosphere would severely heat the sensor window. This heated window would then radiate energy back to the IR sensor, obscuring the RV target. In addition, atmospheric turbulence in front of the window could further distort or deflect the RV image. No sensor has been built before to operate in this environment.

The proposed solution is to use a sapphire window bathed with a stream of cold nitrogen gas. A shroud would protect the window until the last few seconds before impact. Since reentry would heat the RV to temperatures above that of the cooled window, detection would be possible. Recent testing gives grounds for optimism in this area.

Fabrication of the sapphire windows (currently 12 by 33 cm) would be a major effort for the optics industry. These windows must be cut from crystal boules, which take many weeks to grow. At current production rates, it would take 20 years to make 1,000 windows. Plans are to increase the manufacturing capability significantly.

The HEDI sensor suite also uses a Nd:YAG[5] laser for range finding. Building a laser ranger to withstand the high acceleration could be challenging.

As with ERIS, plans call for testing a HEDI Functional Technical Validation missile, which is 2 to 3 times larger than the proposed operational vehicle. The proposed specifications of HEDI are found in the classified version of this report.

Flexible Light-Weight Agile Experiment (FLAGE).—The weapon system expected to evolve from FLAGE research would be the last line of defense, intercepting any RVs which leaked through all the other layers. Its primary mission would be the defense of military targets against short range missiles in a theater war such as in Europe or the Middle East. The FLAGE type of missile would intercept RVs at altitudes up to 15 km. The homing sensor for FLAGE would use an active radar instead of the passive IR sensor proposed for on all other KEW homing projectiles.

---

[4]The HEDI interceptor would probably include an explosively driven "lethality enhancer."

[5]"Nd:YAG" is the designation for a common laser used in research and for military laser range-finders. The "Nd" represents neodymium, the rare element that creates the lasing action, and "YAG" stands for yttrium-aluminum-garnet, the glasslike host material that carries the neodymium atoms.

The FLAGE system was flown six times at the White Sands Missile Range. On June 27, 1986, the FLAGE missile successfully collided with an RV-shaped target drone which was flown into a heavily instrumented flight space. The collision was very close to the planned impact point. Another FLAGE interceptor collided with a Lance missile on May 21, 1987.

The FLAGE program ended in mid-1987 with the Lance intercept. A more ambitious Extended Range Intercept Technology (ERINT) program succeeds it. The ERINT interceptors will have longer range and "a lethality enhancer." FLAGE was a fire-and-forget missile; no information was transmitted from any external sensor to the missile once it was fired. The ERINT missiles are to receive midcourse guidance from ground-based radars. Six test launches are planned at the White Sands Missile Range.

KEW Technology

Three types of KEW propulsion have been proposed for SDI: conventional projectiles powered by chemical energy, faster but less well-developed electromagnetic or "railgun" technology, and nuclear-pumped pellets. All system architects nominated the more mature chemically propelled rockets for near-term BMD deployments.

How Chemical Energy KEWs Work.—There are three different modes of operation proposed for chemically propelled KEWs:

- space-based rockets attacking boosters, post-boost vehicles (PBVs), RVs, and direct-ascent ASATs;
- ground-based rockets attacking RVs in late mid-course outside the atmosphere, and
- ground-based rockets attacking RVs inside the atmosphere.

Two or more rocket stages would accelerate the projectile toward the target. The projectile would be the heart of each system and would entail the most development.

The smart projectile for the space-based mission would need some remarkable features. It would be fired at a point in space up to hundreds of seconds before the actual interception.[6] After separation from the last rocket stage, the projectile would have to establish the correct attitude in space to "see" the target: in general the line-of-sight to the target would not correspond with the projectile flight path. If it had a boresighted sensor that stared straight ahead, then the projectile would have to fly in an attitude at an angle to its flight path to view the target (see figure 5-1).[7]

The projectile would have to receive and execute steering instructions via a secure communications channel from the battle manager. Usually just a few seconds before impact, the projectile would need to acquire the target—either a bright, burning booster or a much dimmer PBV—with an on-board sensor. It would then make final path corrections to effect a collision. Fractions of a second before impact, it might deploy a "lethality enhancement device" —like the spider-web structure used in the Army's Homing Overlay Experiment (HOE)— to increase the size of the projectile and therefore its chance of hitting the target.

The SBI projectile must have these components:

- an inertial guidance system,
- a secure communications system,
- a divert propulsion system,
- an attitude control system,
- a sensor for terminal homing (including vibration isolation),
- a lethality enhancement device (optional?), and
- a computer able to translate signals from the sensor into firing commands to the divert propulsion system in fractions of a second.

The on-board sensors envisaged by most system architects for more advanced "phase-two"

---

[6]A computer in the battle management system would estimate the actual interception aim-point in space by projecting the motion or track of the target using the sensor track files.

[7]For non-accelerating targets, this look angle would not change, even though the target and the projectile were traveling at different velocities. In this "proportional navigation" mode, the projectile orientation would be fixed once the sensor was aimed at the target.

Figure 5-1.—Orientation of SDI to RV

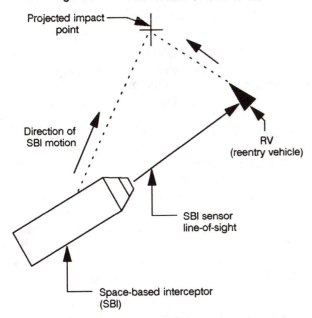

Orientation of the space-based interceptor (SBI) to the reentry vehicle (RV) during the homing phase of the flight. (This drawing shows a sensor bore-sighted with the axis of the SBI, which is common for guided missiles operating in the atmosphere. For space-based interceptors, the sensor could just as well look out the side of the cylindrical projectile.) The SBI sensor would have to be aimed at the RV so that its line-of-sight would not be parallel to the SBI flight path (except for a head-on collision.) For a non-accelerating RV, the angle from the sensor line-of-sight to the SBI flight path would be fixed throughout the flight. Since targets such as ICBM boosters and post-boost vehicles do change acceleration during flight, then this look angle and hence the orientation of the SBI would have to be changed during the SBI flight.

SOURCE: Office of Technology Assessment, 1988.

space-based interceptors may be particularly challenging because they would perform several functions. They would track not only the ICBM during the boost phase, but also the PBV, RVs, and direct-ascent ASAT weapons sent up to destroy the BMD platforms. Each SBI would, ideally, kill all four types of targets.

In the boost phase, a short-wave infrared (SWIR) or medium-wave infrared (MWIR) sensor with existing or reasonably extended technology could track a hot missile plume. An SBI would still have to hit the relatively cool missile body rather than the hot exhaust plume. Three approaches have been suggested for detecting the cooler missile body: computer al-

gorithm, separate long-wave infrared (LWIR) sensor, or laser designation.

A computer algorithm would steer the SBI ahead of the plume centroid by a prescribed distance that would depend on the look angle of the SBI relative to the booster and on the booster type. Predicting the separation between the plume centroid and the booster body under all conditions might be difficult or even impractical if that separation varied from one booster to the next.

A separate LWIR sensor channel might acquire and track the cold booster body.[8] One designer proposed a single detector array, sensitive across the IR band, in combination with a spectral filter. This filter would move mechanically to convert the sensor from MWIR to LWIR capability at the appropriate time. Finally, in some designs a separate laser on the weapon platform or on an SSTS sensor would illuminate the booster. In this case a narrow-band filter on the interceptor's sensor would reject plume radiation, allowing the SBI to home in on laser light reflected from the booster body.

In the post-boost and mid-course phases of the attack, the SBI would have to track hot or warm PBVs and cold RVs. Therefore either SBIs would need to have much more sophisticated LWIR sensors, or they would need something like laser designators to enhance the target signature. This laser illumination need not be continuous, except possibly during the last few seconds before impact. But intermittent illumination would place another burden on the battle manager: it would have to keep track of all SBIs in flight and all SBI targets, then instruct the laser designator at the right time to illuminate the right target.

An SBI lethality enhancer might, for example, consist of a spring-loaded web which ex-

---

[8]There is also a possibility that an SWIR or MWIR sensor could acquire a cold booster body. At 4.3 μm, for example, the atmosphere is opaque due to the CO_2 absorption, and the upper atmosphere at a temperature of 220° K would be colder than a booster tank at 300° K. As an SBI approached a booster, the latter would appear to a 4.3 μm sensor as a large, warm target against the background of the cool upper atmosphere.

panded to a few meters in diameter or an explosively propelled load of pellets driven radially outward. Weight would limit the practical diameter of expansion. System designers would have to trade off the costs of increased homing accuracy with the weight penalty of increased lethality diameter.

Ground-based KEW capabilities would resemble those of space-based interceptors. Exoatmospheric projectiles that intercept the RVs outside the Earth's atmosphere would use LWIR homing sensors to track cold RVs, or they would employ other optical sensors to track laser-illuminated targets. These interceptors would be command-guided to the vicinity of the collision by some combination of ground-based radars, airborne LWIR sensors (AOS) or space-borne LWIR sensors (SSTS, BSTS, or rocket-borne probes). Long-wave infrared homing sensors in the projectile would have to be protected during launch through the atmosphere to prevent damage or overheating.

Current Status of Chemically Propelled Rockets.—No interceptor rockets with BMD-level performance have ever been fired from space-based platforms. Operational IR heat-seeking interceptor missiles such as the air-to-air Sidewinder and the air-to-ground Maverick are fired from aircraft, but both the range and the final velocity of this class of missiles are well below BMD levels.

The SDIO's Delta 180 flight test included the collision of two stages from a Delta rocket after the primary task of collecting missile plume data was completed. However, these two stages were not interceptor rockets, were not fired from an orbiting platform, did not have the range nor velocity necessary for BMD, and were highly cooperative, with the target vehicle orienting a four-foot reflector toward the homing vehicle to enhance the signal for the radar homing system. Note that this test used radar homing, whereas all SBI designs call for IR homing or laser-designator homing. This experiment did test the tracking algorithms for an accelerating target, although the target acceleration for this nearly

head-on collision was not as stressing as it would be for expected BMD/SBI flight trajectories.[9]

Engineers have achieved very good progress in reducing the size and weight of components for the proposed space-based interceptors. They have developed individual ring laser gyroscopes weighing only 85 g as part of an inertial measuring unit. They have reduced the weight of divert propulsion engines about 9 kg to 1.3 kg. Gas pressure regulators to control these motors have been reduced from 1.4 kg to .09 kg each. The smaller attitude control engines and valves have been reduced from 800 g each to 100 g each. Progress has also been made on all other components of a SBI system, although these components have not as yet been integrated into a working prototype SBI system.

Ground-based interceptor rockets are one of the best developed BMD technologies. The Spartan and Sprint interceptor missiles were operational for a few months in the mid 1970s. Indeed parts of these missiles have been recommissioned for upcoming tests of SDI ground-based weapons such as the endo-atmospheric HEDI. The production costs for these missiles would have to be reduced substantially to make their use in large strategic defense systems affordable, but no major improvements in rocket technology are needed for ground-based interceptors, other than a 30 percent improvement in speed for the HEDI missile. As discussed in chapter 4, however, major sensor development would be necessary for these interceptors.

Key Issues for Chemical Rockets.—Chemical rocket development faces four key issues, all related to space-based deployment and all derived from the requirement to design and make very fast SBIs.

Constellation Mass. —The overriding issue for SBIs is mass. The SBIs must be so fast

---

[9]Previous tests of IR guided projectiles such as the Homing Overlay Experiment against a simulated RV and the F-16 launched ASAT test against a satellite, shot down nonaccelerating targets.

that a reasonably small number of battle stations could cover the entire Earth. But, for a given payload, faster rockets consume much more fuel—the fuel mass increases roughly exponentially with the desired velocity. The designer must compromise between many battle stations with light rockets or fewer battle stations with heavier rockets.[10]

These trade-offs are illustrated in figure 5-2, which assumes a boost-phase-only defense with three hypothetical rocket designs: a state-of-the-art rocket based on current technology; a "realistic" design based on improvements in rocket technology that seem plausible by the mid-1990s; and an "optimistic" design that assumes major improvements in all areas of rocket development. The key parameters assumed for SBI rocket technology appear in the classified version of this report. In all cases analyzed, OTA assumed the rockets to be "ideal": the mass ratio of each stage is the same, which produces the lightest possible rocket.[11] The first chart in figure 5-2a shows that rocket mass increases exponentially with increasing velocity, limiting practical SBI velocities to the 5 to 8 km/s range for rockets weighing on the order of 100 kg or less.

For analytic purposes, OTA has considered constellations of SBIs that would be necessary to intercept virtually 100 percent of postulated numbers of ICBMs. *It should be noted that since the system architecture analyses of 1986, SDIO has not seriously considered deploying SBIs that would attempt to intercept anywhere near 100 percent of Soviet ICBMs and PBVs.*[12] This OTA analysis is intended only

to give a feel for the parameters and trade-offs involved in a system with SBIs.

Deployment of a system of "state-of-the-art" SBIs intended to provide 100 percent coverage of Soviet ICBMs would entail 11.7 million kg of CVs; waiting for the development of the "realistic" SBI would reduce the mass to orbit by a factor of two.

Figure 5-2b shows the number of SBI carrier platforms and figure 5-2c shows the number of SBIs for a 100 percent-boost-phase defense as a function of SBI velocity. The last chart (figure 5-2d) shows the total constellation mass as a function of velocity. The number of CVs was calculated initially to optimize coverage of existing Soviet missile fields: the orbits of the CVs were inclined so that the CVs passed to the north of the missile fields by a distance equal to the SBI fly-out range.[13] Each CV therefore stayed within range of the ICBM fields for a maximum period during each orbit.

The "optimal" number of CVs resulting from this calculation was so low as to endanger system survivability (see ch. 11), calling for up to 100 SBIs per carrier to cover the existing Soviet ICBM threat: such concentrations would provide lucrative targets for the offense's ASATs. To increase survivability, the number of CVs was therefore increased by a factor of 3 for the data in figure 5-2. Some polar orbits were added to cover the SLBM threat from northern waters.

The number of SBIs was calculated initially to provide one SBI within range of each of 1,400 Soviet ICBMs sometime during the boost phase. The booster burn time was taken as similar to that of existing Soviet missiles, with a reasonable interval allotted for cloud-break, initial acquisition, tracking, and weapons launch.

One SBI per booster would not do for a robust (approaching 100 percent coverage) boost-phase defense. A substantial number of SBIs

---

[10]Projectile mass might not be as critical for ground-based as for space-based KEW projectiles, since there would be no space transportation cost. However, the projectile mass should still be minimized to reduce the over-all rocket size and cost, and to permit higher accelerations and final velocities.

[11]The mass fraction for a rocket stage is defined as the ratio of the propellant mass to the total stage mass (propellant plus rocket structure). The mass fraction does not include the payload mass. For the calculations reported here, an ideal rocket is assumed: it has equal mass ratios for each stage, where mass ratio is defined as the initial stage weight divided by the stage weight after burn-out (both including the payload; it can be shown that the rocket mass is minimized for a given burnout velocity if each stage has the same mass ratio.)

[12]As indicated in chapters 1, 2, and 3, SDIO argues that the deterrent utility of defenses far more modest than those needed for "assured survival" would make them worthwhile.

[13]The locations of Soviet missile fields are estimated from maps appearing in U.S. Department of Defense, *Soviet Military Power, 1987* (Washington, D.C.: Department of Defense, 1987), p. 23. See adaptation of this map in chapter 2 of this OTA report.

Figure 5-2a.—Space-Based Interceptor Mass v. Velocity

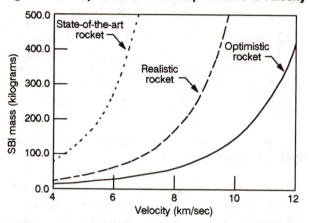

The SBI mass versus SBI velocity. These data assume 100% coverage of the current Soviet threat of 1,400 ICBMs. It should be noted that the SDIO currently proposes a substantially lower level of coverage for SBIs. Therefore, the absolute numbers in the OTA calculations are not congruent with SDIO plans. Rather, the graphs provided here are intended to show the relationships among the various factors considered. It should also be noted that numerous assumptions underlying the OTA analyses are unstated in this unclassified report, but are available in the classified version.

SOURCE: Office of Technology Assessment, 1988.

Figure 5-2b.—Number of Satellites v. SBI Velocity

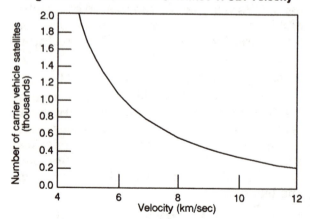

The number of SBI carrier satellites v. SBI velocity.

SOURCE: Office of Technology Assessment, 1988.

Figure 5-2c.—Number of Space-Based Interceptors v. Velocity (inclined orbits + SLBM polar orbits)

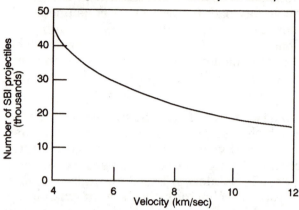

The number of space-based interceptors (SBIs) required to provide one SBI within range of each of 1,400 existing Soviet ICBMs before booster burnout.

SOURCE: Office of Technology Assessment, 1988.

Figure 5-2d.—Constellation Mass v. SBI Velocity

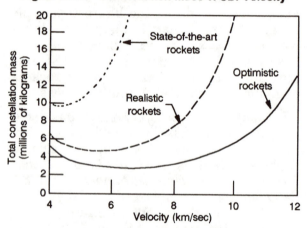

The total constellation mass in orbit (SBIs and carrier vehicles, excluding sensor satellites) v. SBI velocity. The minimum constellation mass for the "realistic" SBI to be in position to attack all Soviet boosters would be about 5.3 million kg. Faster SBIs would permit fewer carrier vehicles and fewer SBIs, but the extra propellant on faster SBIs would result in a heavier constellation. For reference, the Space Shuttle can lift about 14,000 kg into polar orbit, a 5.3 million kg constellation would require about 380 Shuttle launches, or about 130 launches of the proposed "Advanced Launch System" (ALS), assuming it could lift 40,000 kg into near-polar orbit at suitable altitudes.

SOURCE: Office of Technology Assessment, 1988.

would fail over the years just due to electronic and other component failures. The number of SBIs in figure 5-2 was increased by a plausible factor to account for this natural peacetime attrition. In addition, during battle, some SBIs would miss their targets, and presumably Soviet defense suppression attacks would eliminate other CVs and draw off other SBIs for self-defense.

Given the above assumptions, figure 5-2 represents the SBI constellation for nearly 100 percent coverage of the existing Soviet ICBM fleet in the boost phase, with modest survivability initially provided by substantial SBI redundancy, degrading to no redundant SBIs as "natural" attrition set in.

Note that for each type of rocket there is an optimum velocity that minimizes the total mass that would have to be launched into space; lower velocity increases the number of satellites and SBIs, while higher velocity increases the fuel mass. In OTA's analysis, the minimum mass which would have to be launched into orbit for the "realistic" rocket is 5.3 million kg (or 11.7 million lb); the mass for a constellation of "optimistic" SBIs would be 3.4 million kg.

The data for figure 5-2 all assume booster burn times similar to those of current Soviet liquid-fueled boosters. Faster-burning rockets would reduce the effective range of SBIs and would therefore increase the needed number of carrier satellites. The same SBI parameters are shown in figures 5-3a and b with an assumption of ICBM booster burn time toward the low end of current times. The minimum constellation mass has increased to 29 million and 16 million kg, respectively, for the "realistic" and "optimistic" rocket designs.

Several studies of "fast-burn boosters" concluded that reducing burn-time would impose a mass penalty, so the Soviets would have to off-load RVs (or decoys) to reduce burn time significantly. But these same studies showed that there is no significant mass penalty for burn times as low as 120 s. About 10-20 percent of the payload would have to be off-loaded for burn times in the 70 to 90 s range.

Figure 5-3a.—Number of Projectiles v. SBI Velocity
(160 second burn-time)

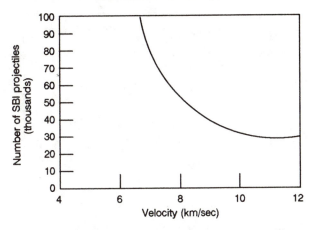

The number of space-based interceptors v. SBI velocity for reduced booster burntime (within currently applied technology).

SOURCE: Office of Technology Assessment, 1988.

Figure 5-3b.—SBI Constellation Mass v. SBI Velocity
(160 second burn-time)

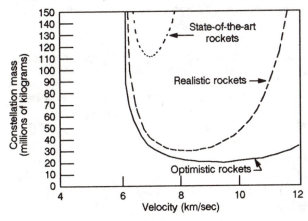

The total constellation mass (carrier vehicles and SBIs) versus SBI velocity for reduced booster burn times, assuming one SBI within range of each of 1,400 boosters before burnout.

SOURCE: Office of Technology Assessment, 1988.

If the Soviet Union could reduce the burn time of its missiles below that of any currently deployed ICBMs, then the total SBI constellation mass necessary for boost-phase intercept would increase dramatically. The minimum constellation mass to place one SBI within range of each ICBM during its boost phase is shown in figure 5-4 as a function of

Figure 5-4.—Total SBI Constellation Mass in Orbit v. Booster Burn Time

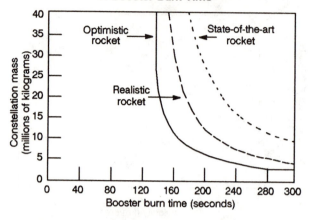

The effect of Soviet booster burn time on SBI constellation mass. If we consider 40 million kg as a maximum conceivable upper bound on constellation mass (corresponding to 2,800 Shuttle flights or 1,000 launches of the proposed ALS system), then booster times of 120 to 150 seconds would severely degrade a 100%-boost-phase defense with chemically propelled rockets. The ability of smaller constellations of SBIs to achieve lesser goals would be analogously degraded by the faster burn times.

All assumptions are the same as for the previous figures, except for the burn-out altitude, which varies with burn-time.

SOURCE: Office of Technology Assessment, 1988.

booster burn time for the three canonical rocket designs.

The masses described above for a boost-phase-only defense are clearly excessive, particularly for a responsive Soviet threat. Adding other defensive layers would reduce the burden on boost-phase defense. The next layer of defense would attack PBVs, preferably early in their flight before they could unload any RVs.

A PBV or "bus" carrying up to 10 or more RVs would be more difficult to track and hit than a missile. A PBV has propulsion engines that emit some IR energy, but this energy will be about 1,000 times weaker than that from a rocket plume.[14] A PBV is also smaller and less fragile than a booster tank. In short, a PBV is harder to detect and hit with an SBI. However, a PBV is still bigger and brighter than

---

[14]The first stage of an ICBM might radiate 1 million W/sr, the second stage 100,000 W/sr, while a PBV may emit only 100 W/sr. On the other hand, the RV radiates only 5 W/sr, so the PBV is a better target than an RV.

---

an RV; sensors might acquire the PBV if its initial trajectory (before its first maneuver) can be estimated by projecting the booster track.

The effectiveness of a combined boost and post-boost defense in terms of the percentage of RVs killed is estimated in figure 5-5 for the "realistic" SBI rocket. The calculation assumes that 1,400 missiles resembling today's large, heavy ICBMs are spread over the existing Soviet missile fields.

The net effect of attacking PBVs is to reduce the number of SBIs needed to kill a given number of RVs. For example, to destroy 85 percent of the Soviet RVs carried by ICBMs, a boost-only defense system would require about 26,000 SBIs in orbit. Adding PBV interceptions reduces the number of SBIs needed to about 17,000.

A defensive system must meet the expected Soviet threat at the actual time of deployment, not today's threat. For example, the Soviet Union has already tested the mobile, solid-fueled SS-24 missile, which can carry 10 war-

Figure 5-5.—Boost and Post-Boost Kill Effectiveness (1,400 ICBMs v. "Realistic" SBIs)

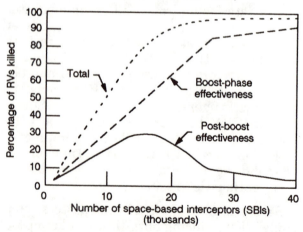

Percentage of reentry vehicles (RVs) killed as a function of the number of space-based interceptors (SBIs) deployed in space. This calculation assumes a threat of 1,400 ICBMs spread over the Soviet missile fields. The SBIs have a plausible single-shot probability of killing a booster and a slightly smaller chance of killing a PBV; a substantial fraction of the SBIs are used for self-defense (or are not functional at the time of attack).

SOURCE: Office of Technology Assessment, 1988.

heads. There is no reason to doubt that the Soviets could deploy this kind of missile in quantity by the mid-1990s. Such a fleet would particularly stress a space-based defense if deployed at one or a few sites, since more SBIs would be needed in the area of deployment concentration.

The effects on the combined boost and post-boost defense of clustering 500 shorter-burn-time, multiple-warhead missiles at three existing SS-18 sites are shown in figure 5-6a. It would take about 23,000 SBIs to stop 85 percent of these 5,000 warheads. If the assumed 500 ICBMs were concentrated at one site (but still with 10 km separation to prevent "pin-down" by nuclear bursts), then 30,000 SBIs would be needed (see fig. 5-6b).[15]

Finally, the Soviets might deploy 200 (or more) current-technology, single-warhead missiles at one site, as shown in figure 5-7. In this case, no reasonable number of SBIs could intercept 85 percent of these 200 extra warheads (50,000 SBIs in orbit would kill 70 percent). Twice as many RVs are destroyed in the post-boost period as the boost-phase. Once this concentrated deployment was in place, the defense would have to add about 185 extra SBIs and their associated CVs to achieve a 50 percent probability of destroying each new ICBM deployed.

SBI Projectile Mass.—The constellation masses shown above assume that the mass of the smart SBI projectile (including lateral divert propulsion, fuel, guidance, sensor, communications, and any lethality enhancer) can be reduced to optimistic levels. Current technology for the various components would result in an SBI with a relatively high mass. Thus mass reduction is essential to achieve the results outlined above; total constellation mass would scale almost directly with the achievable SBI mass.

[15]Concentrating 500 missiles at one site would have disadvantages for an offensive attack: timing would be complicated to achieve simultaneous attacks on widely separated U.S. targets, and Soviet planners may be reluctant to place so many of their offensive forces in one area, even if the missiles are separated enough to prevent one U.S. nuclear explosion from destroying more than one Soviet missile.

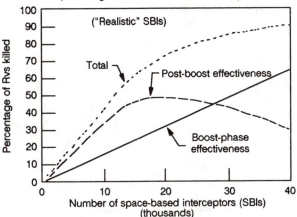

Figure 5-6a.—Boost and Post-Boost Kill Effectiveness
(500 single-RV ICBMs at three sites)

The percentage of RVs from modestly short-burn ICBMs killed as a function of the number of SBIs deployed in space. This curve corresponds to 500 such ICBMs deployed at 3 existing SS-18 sites. All SBI parameters are the same as in previous figures.

SOURCE: Office of Technology Assessment, 1988.

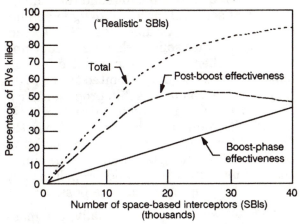

Figure 5-6b.—Boost and Post-Boost Kill Effectiveness
(500 single-RIV ICBMs at one site)

This curve assumes that all 500 shorter-burn ICBMs are deployed at one site (but still with 10 km separation to prevent pin-down). All other parameters are the same as figure 5-6a.

SOURCE: Office of Technology Assessment, 1988.

Rocket Specific Impulse.—Similarly, the specific impulse of the rocket propellant would have to be improved from current levels. The specific impulse, expressed in seconds, measures the ability of a rocket propellant to change mass into thrust. It is defined as the ratio of thrust (lb) divided by fuel flow rate (lb/s).

Figure 5-7.— Boost and Post-Boost Kill Effectiveness
(200 "medium-burn-booster" ICBMs at one site)

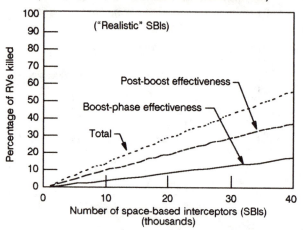

Percentage of single-warhead ICBM RVs killed as a function of number of SBIs in space. The 200 single-warhead ICBMs are deployed at one site with 10 km separation. All SBI parameters are as in previous figures.

SOURCE: Office of Technology Assessment, 1988.

The specific impulse of current propellants varies from 240 to 270 s for solid fuel and up to 390 s at sea level for liquid oxygen and liquid hydrogen fuel. Assuming that BMD weapons would utilize solid fuels for stability and reliability, then the specific impulse for current technology would be limited to the 270-s range.[16] One common solid propellant, hydroxyl-terminated polybutadiene (HTPB) loaded with aluminum, has an impulse in the 260-to-265-s range. This can be increased to 280 s by substituting beryllium for the aluminum. Manufacturers of solid propellant say that further improvements are possible.

Rocket Mass Fraction.—Finally, the mass fraction—the ratio of the fuel mass to the stage total mass (fuel plus structure but excluding payload)—would have to be raised to meet SDI objectives. Large mass fractions can be achieved for very big rockets having 95 percent of their mass in fuel. It would be more difficult to reduce the percentage mass of structure and propulsion motor components for very small SBI rockets.

The mass fraction can be increased by reducing the mass of the rocket shell. New lightweight, strong materials such as carbon graphite fiber reinforced composite materials or judicious use of titanium (for strength) and aluminum (for minimum mass) may permit increased mass fractions for future rockets.

How Electromagnetic Launchers (EML) Work. —Electromagnetic launchers or "railguns" use electromagnetic forces instead of direct chemical energy to accelerate projectiles along a pair of rails to very high velocities. The goal is to reach higher projectile velocities than practical rockets can. This would extend the range of KEW, expanding their ability to attack faster-burn boosters before burn-out. Whereas advanced chemically propelled rockets of reasonable mass (say, less than 300 kg) could accelerate projectiles to at most 9 to 10 km/s, future EML launchers might accelerate small projectiles (1 to 2 kg) up to 15 to 25 km/s. SDIO has set a goal of reaching about 15 km/s.

In principle, chemical rockets could reach these velocities simply by adding more propellant. The efficiency of converting fuel energy into kinetic energy of the moving projectile decreases with increasing velocity, however: the rocket must accelerate extra fuel mass that is later burned. A projectile on an ideal, staged rocket could be accelerated to 15 km/s, but only 17 percent of the fuel energy would be converted into kinetic energy of the projectile, down from 26 percent efficiency for a 12 km/s projectile. Since a railgun accelerates only the projectile, it could theoretically have higher energy efficiency, which would translate into less mass needed in orbit.

In practice, however, a railgun system would not likely weigh less than its chemical rocket counterpart at velocities below about 12 km/s, since railgun system efficiency would probably be on the order of 25 percent at this velocity.[17]

---

[16]The SBI divert propulsion system in the final projectile stage would probably use liquid fuel, and some have suggested that the second stage also use liquid fuel.

[17]This assumes 50 percent efficiency for converting fuel (thermal) energy into electricity, 90 percent efficiency in the pulse forming network, and 55 percent rail efficiency in converting electrical pulses into projectile kinetic energy. The SDIO has a goal of reaching 40 percent overall EML system efficiency, but this would require the development of very high temperature (2,000 to 2,500° K) nuclear reactor driven turbines. The total system mass might still exceed that of a comparable chemical rocket system.

Therefore a railgun system would have to carry as much or more fuel than its chemical rocket equivalent—in addition to a massive rocket-engine generator system, an electrical pulse-forming network to produce the proper electrical current pulses, and the rail itself.

The conventional "railgun" (see figure 5-8) contains a moving projectile constrained by two conducting but electrically insulated rails. A large energy source drives electrical current down one rail, through the back end of the moving projectile, and back through the other rail. This closed circuit of current forms a strong magnetic field, and this field reacts with the current flowing through the projectile to produce a constant outward force. The projectile therefore experiences constant acceleration as it passes down the rail.

The final velocity of the projectile is proportional to the current in the rail and the square root of the rail length; it is inversely propor-tional to the square root of the projectile mass. High velocity calls for very high currents (millions of amperes), long rails (hundreds of m), and very light projectiles (1 to 2 kg).

For the BMD mission, the projectile must be "smart". That is, it must have all of the components of the chemically propelled SBIs: a sensor, inertial guidance, communications, divert propulsion, a computer, and possibly a lethality enhancement device. The EML projectile must be lighter, and it must withstand accelerations hundreds of thousands times greater than gravity, compared to 10 to 20 "g's" for chemically propelled SBIs.

Researchers at Sandia National Laboratory have proposed another type of EML launcher which would employ a series of coils to propel the projectile. Their "reconnection gun" would avoid passing a large current through the projectile, eliminating the "arcs and sparks" of the conventional railgun. The term "reconnection" derives from the action of the moving projectile: it interrupts the magnetic fields of adjacent coils, and then these fields "reconnect" behind the projectile, accelerating it in the process.

Current Status of EMLs.—Several commercial and government laboratories have built and tested experimental railguns over the last few decades. These railguns have fired very small plastic projectiles weighing from 1 to 2,500 g, accelerating them to speeds from 2 to 11 km/s. In general, only the very light projectiles reached the 10 km/s speeds.

One "figure of merit," or index, for railgun performance is the kinetic energy supplied to the projectile. For BMD applications, SDIO originally set a goal of a 4 kg projectile accelerated to 25 km/s, which would have acquired 1,250 MJ of energy. SDIO officials now state that their goal is a 1 kg projectile at 15 km/s, which would acquire 113 MJ of kinetic energy. The highest kinetic energy achieved to date was 2.8 MJ (317 g accelerated to 4.2 km/s), or about 50 to 400 times less than BMD levels.

Finally, there have been no experiments with actual "smart" projectiles. All projectiles have been inert plastic solids. Some (non-operating)

Figure 5-8.—Schematic of an Electromagnetic Launcher (EML) or "Railgun"

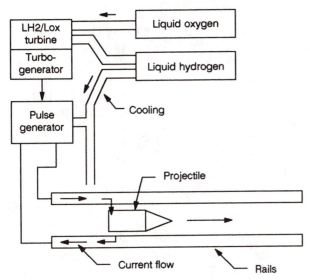

Schematic of an electromagnetic launcher (EML) or "Railgun." In operation, a strong pulse of electrical current forms a circuit with the conducting rails and the projectile. This current loop generates a magnetic field. The interaction of this field with the current passing through the moving projectile produces a constant outward force on the projectile, accelerating it to high velocities.

SOURCE: Office of Technology Assessment, 1988.

Electromagnetic launcher.—This experimental electromagnetic launcher at Maxwell Laboratories, Inc., San Diego, CA, became operational late in 1985.

Table 5-1.—Key Issues for Electromagnetic Launchers (EML)

- Low-mass (2 kg or less), high acceleration (several hundred thousand g) projectile development.
- High repetition rate rails (several shots per second for hundreds of seconds).
- High repetition rate switches with high current (several million A versus 750,000 A)
- Pulse power conditioners (500 MJ, 5 to 20 ms pulses versus 10 MJ, 100 ms pulses)
- Efficiency
- Mass
- Heat dissipation

SOURCE: Office of Technology Assessment, 1988.

EML Projectile.—If based on current technology for sensors, inertial guidance, communications, and divert propulsion systems, the lightest "smart" projectile would weigh over 10 kg. The total mass must shrink by at least a factor of 5, and the projectile must withstand over 100,000 g's of acceleration. If the projectile could only tolerate 100,000 g's, then the railgun would have to be 112 m long to impart a 15 km/s velocity to the projectile. Higher acceleration tolerance would allow shorter railguns. (200,000 g's would allow a 56-m long gun, etc.)

The SDIO has consolidated the development of light-weight projectiles for all kinetic energy programs into the "Light-weight Exo-atmospheric Projectile" (LEAP) program. Although researchers first saw a need for light-weight projectiles for railguns, the primary initial users of LEAP technology are to be the chemical rocket KEW programs (SBI, ERIS, HEDI). The phase-one LEAP projectile would weigh about 5 kg according to current designs (see figure 5-9), if all component developments met their goals. This projectile would weigh too much for any railgun, and it will therefore not be tested at high acceleration. This technology might evolve into a 2-kg projectile by the early 1990s. In any case, there are no plans now to build a gun big enough to test even the phase-two 2 kilogram projectile.

High Repetition Rate.—A railgun would have to fire frequently during an attack, engaging several targets per second. The penalty for low repetition rates would be additional railguns in the space-based constellation to cover

electronic components, including focal plane arrays, have been carried on these plastic bullets to check for mechanical damage. Results have been encouraging.

Key Issues for EMLs.—Much more research must precede an estimate of the potential of EML technology for any BMD application. The key issues are summarized in table 5-1. There is uncertainty at this time whether all these issues can be favorably resolved.

Figure 5-9.—Lightweight Homing Projectile

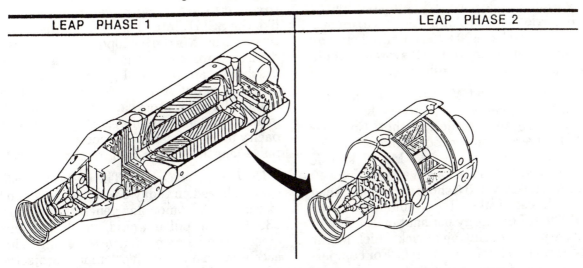

Illustration of planned projectiles for the Lightweight Exoatmospheric Projectile (LEAP) program. This program is developing projectile technology for both the rocket propelled and electromagnetic launcher (railgun) programs. However, the phase 1 projectile at 5 kg and even the more conceptual phase 2 projectile with a mass projection of 2 kg are too heavy for any existing or planned railguns. There are no plans to test either projectile at the 100,000s of g acceleration necessary for railgun operation. These projectiles will benefit the SBI, ERIS, and HEDI programs.

SOURCE: Office of Technology Assessment, 1988.

the threat. Most railguns to date have been fired just once: the rails eroded and had to be replaced after one projectile. Newer systems can fire ten shots per day, and at least one experiment has fired a burst of pellets at a rate of 10/s. Researchers at the University of Texas plan to fire a burst of ten projectiles in 1/6 of a second, or a rate of 60/s.

Key issues for high repetition-rate guns are rail erosion,[18] heat management, and high repetition-rate switches to handle the million-ampere current levels several times per second. Conventional high repetition-rate switches can

[18]New rail designs have shown promise of minimum erosion in laboratory tests; it remains to be proven that rails would survive at weapons-level speeds and repetition rates.

handle up to 500 A today, although one special variable resistance switch tested by the Army carried 750,000 A. An Air Force test successfully switched 800,000 A, limited only by the power supply used. EML systems would have to switch 1 to 5 million A.

EML Power.—An EML would consume high average electrical power and very high peak power during each projectile shot. Consider first the average power requirements: a 1 kg projectile would acquire 112 MJ of kinetic energy if accelerated to 15 km/s. Assuming 40 percent efficiency and 5 shots per second, then the EML electrical system would have to deliver 280 MJ of energy per shot or 1.4 GW of average power during an attack which might last for several hundred seconds. For comparison, a modern nuclear fission power plant delivers 1 to 2 GW of continuous power.

The SP-100 nuclear power system being discussed for possible space application would produce only 100 to 300 kW of power. The only apparent near-term potential solution to providing 2.5 GW of power for hundreds of seconds would be to use something like the Space Shuttle Main Engine (SSME) coupled to a turbogenerator. Assuming 50 percent electrical conversion efficiency, then one could convert the SSME 10 GW of flow energy into 5 GW of average electrical power while the engines were burning.

High average power would not suffice. The electrical energy would have to be further concentrated in time to supply very short bursts of current to the railgun. For example, a 112-m long railgun with 100,000-g acceleration would propel a projectile down its length in about 15 milliseconds (ms) to a final velocity of 15 km/s. The peak power during the shot would be 50 GW.[19] And the EML system designer would like to shorten the 112-m railgun length and increase acceleration, which would mean further shortening the pulse length and increasing peak power.

Several techniques are under consideration to convert the average power from something like the SSME into short pulses. One laboratory approach is the homopolar generator: this device stores current in a rotating machine much like an electrical generator and then switches it out in one large pulse. Existing homopolar generators can supply up to 10 MJ in about 100 ms; therefore, energy storage capacity must increase by a factor of 50 and the pulse length shorten by a factor of 5 to 20.

EML Mass to Orbit.—The mass of an EML system based on today's technology would be excessive. A homopolar generator to supply 280 MJ per pulse would weigh 70 tonnes alone.[20] The rails would have to be long to limit acceleration on sensitive "smart" projectiles, which would have to be very strong (massive) to resist the outward forces from the high rail currents. The platform would have to include an SSME-type burst power generator, a thermal management system to dispose of the energy deposited in the rails, divert propulsion to steer the railgun toward each target, and the usual satellite communications and control functions.

Given the early stage of EML research, estimates of total platform mass could be in error by a factor of 10. At this time, a total mass of about 100 tonnes would seem likely, meaning that each EML would have to be launched in several parts, even if the United States developed an Advanced Launch System (ALS) that could carry about 40 tonnes maximum per flight to high inclination orbits. It is conceivable that, in the farther term, superconductive electrical circuits could significantly reduce the mass of an EML. Lighter compulsators (see below) might also reduce EML mass.

Nuclear-Driven Particles.—A nuclear explosion is a potent source of peak power and energy. If even a small fraction of the energy in a nuclear explosion could be converted into kinetic energy of moving particles, then an extremely powerful nuclear shotgun could be im-

---

[19]For a frame of reference, consider that the total power available from the U.S. power grid is several hundred gigawatts.

[20]Assuming today's energy density for homopolar generators of 4 kJ/kg.

agined. These particles could be used for interactive discrimination as described above, since the particles would slow down light decoys more than heavy RVs. With more power, nuclear-driven particles could conceivably destroy targets. This concept is discussed in more detail in the classified version of this report.

Directed-Energy Weapons

Directed-energy weapons (DEW) offer the promise of nearly instantaneous destruction of targets hundreds or thousands of km away. While a KEW system would have to predict target positions several minutes in the future and wait for a high speed projectile to reach the intended target, the DEW could—in principle—fire, observe a kill, and even order a repeat attack in less than a second.

DEW Systems

Although no DEW are planned for phase-one BMD deployment, both ground-based and space-based DEW systems are possible in the next century.[21] Candidate DEW systems include:

- free electron lasers (FEL) (ground-based or space-based),
- chemical lasers (space-based),
- excimer lasers (ground-based),
- x-ray laser (pop-up or space-based), or
- neutral particle beam (space-based).

The FEL is the primary SDIO candidate for ground-based deployment (with the excimer laser as a back-up). The hydrogen-fluoride (HF) laser and the neutral particle beam weapon are the primary candidates for space-based DEWs, although a space-based FEL or other chemical laser concepts might also be possible.

Ground-Based Free Electron Laser (GBFEL). —A GBFEL system would include several ground-based lasers, "rubber mirror" beam directors to correct for atmospheric distortions and to direct the beams to several relay mirrors in high-Earth orbit, and tens to hundreds of "battle-mirrors" in lower Earth orbit to focus the beams on target. It would take several laser sites to assure clear weather at one site all the time. Several lasers per site would provide enough beams for the battle. Ideally these lasers should be at high altitudes to avoid most of the weather and atmospheric turbulence. But the FEL, as currently envisioned, requires very long ground path lengths for beam expansion and large quantities of power.

The logical location for relay mirrors would be geosynchronous orbit, so that the ground-based beam director would have a relatively fixed aim point. The effects of thermal blooming[22] may best be avoided, however, by placing the relay mirrors in lower orbit: the motion of the laser beam through the upper atmosphere as it follows the moving relay mirror would spread the thermal energy over a large area.[23]

Adaptive optics would correct for atmospheric turbulence. The optical system would sense turbulence in real time and continuously change the shape of the beam-director mirror to cancel wave-front errors introduced by the air. A beacon would be placed just far enough in front of the relay satellite that the satellite would move to the position occupied by the beacon in the time it took for light to travel to the ground and back. A sensor on the ground would detect the distortions in the test beam of light from the beacon, then feed the results to the "rubber mirror" actuators. With its wave front so adjusted, the laser beam would pass through the air relatively undistorted.

---

[21]SDIO asserts that some versions of DEW could be deployed late in this century. It is examining designs for "entry level" systems with limited capabilities.

[22]Thermal blooming occurs when a high-power laser beam passes through the atmosphere, heating the air which disturbs the transmission of subsequent beam energy. See the section below on key DEW issues for details.

[23]For example, a 10-m diameter laser beam which tracked a relay mirror at 1,000 km altitude would pass through a clean, unheated patch of air at 10 km altitude after 140 ms. If thermal blooming resulted from relatively long-term heating over a few seconds, then scanning across the sky could ameliorate its effects. While beam energy at altitudes below 10 km would take longer than 140 ms to move to unheated patches of the atmosphere, lower altitude blooming could be more readily corrected by the atmospheric turbulence compensation systems proposed for ground based lasers: atmospheric compensation works best for "thin lens" aberrations close to the laser beam adaptive mirror on the ground.

This concept is discussed further below, under the heading of "Key DEW Issues."

Table 5-2 compares the characteristics of current research FELs with those needed for BMD operations, as derived from elementary considerations in the American Physical Society study.[24] The key figure of merit is beam brightness, defined as the average laser output power (watts) divided by the square of the beam's angular divergence. Brightness is a measure of the ability of the laser beam to concentrate energy on the target (see figure 5-10). Another important figure of merit is the retarget time—the time needed to switch from one target to another.

Existing FELs operate in a pulsed mode: the energy is bunched into very short segments, as illustrated in figure 5-11 for the radio frequency linear accelerator (RF linac) and for the induction linear accelerator, two types of accelerators proposed for the FEL. The power at the peak of each pulse is much higher than the average power. In the proposed induction linac FEL, peak power might exceed average power by 60,000 times. But it is the average power that primarily determines weapons effectiveness.[25]

The RF linac experiments to date have produced 10 MW of peak power at 10 μm wave-

---

[24]American Physical Society, op. cit., footnote 1, chapters 3 and 5.

[25]Short pulses of energy may foster coupling of energy into a target, however, so the average power required from a pulsed laser could, in principle, be less than the average power of a continuous wave (CW) laser. This will be the subject of further SDI research.

Table 5-2.—Characteristics of a Ground-Based FEL Weapons System

	Current status		Operational requirements against a fully responsive Soviet threat[a]
Free Electron Laser	RF	Induction	
Number of laser sites	—	—	5-8
Wavelength (μm)	9-35	8,800	.8 to 1.3
Average power (MW)	.006	.000014	100 to 1,000
Peak power (MW)	10	1,000[b]	
Beam diameter (m)	(4)[c]	(4)	10 to 30
Brightness (W/sr)	3.6×10^{14}	1×10^6	several $\times 10^{22}$
Peak brightness (W/sr)	6.3×10^{17}	4.9×10^{13}	[d]
Beam director:			
Diameter (m)	(4)		10^5
Number of actuators	(10^3)		10^3 to 10^4
Frequency response (Hz)	10^3		hundreds
Relay mirrors:			
Number of mirrors	—		3-5?
Diameter (m)	—		10 or more
Altitude (km)	—		tens of thousands
Steering rate (retargets/s)	—		4-10
Battle-mirrors:			
Number of mirrors:	—		30-150
Diameter (m)	(4)		10
Altitude (km)	—		1,000-4,000
Steering rate (retargets/s)	—		2-5

[a]Operational requirements are taken from American Physical Society, Science and Technology of Directed-Energy Weapons: Report to the American Physical Society of the Study Group, April 1987. SDIO disagrees with some of the numbers, but their disagreements are classified and may be found in the classified version of this report. Further, SDIO has identified BMD missions other than dealing with a fully responsive Soviet threat. An "entry-level" system (with a brightness on the order of 10^{20}), might be developed earlier than the one with the above characteristics and would have less stressing requirements.
[b]Segments of a 3-meter active mirror have been built, and a 4-meter, 7-segment mirror is under construction. Parentheses in this table indicate that the mirror technology exists, but the mirrors have not yet been integrated with the laser.
[c]A weapons system would require the average power levels listed above. The FEL is a pulsed laser—the power of each pulse is much higher than the average power when the pulses are both on and off. Depending on how targets and pulses interact, these short pulses might be lethal even with lower average power.
[d]Peak brightness, like peak power, is not the relevant measure of weapons lethality.
[e]The American Physical Society, op. cit., footnote a, estimated that brightnesses on the order of 10^{22} W/sr might be necessary to counter a responsive threat. A 10-meter diameter mirror would be required for the lower power (100MW) FEL module to reach 10^{22} W/sr brightness. The more probable approach would be to combine the beams from ten 10-meter mirrors in a coherent array.

SOURCE: Office of Technology Assessment, American Physical Society Study Group, and Strategic Defense Initiative Organization, 1987 and 1988.

Figure 5-10. — Illustration of the Relationships Between Laser Parameters and Power Density Projected on a Target

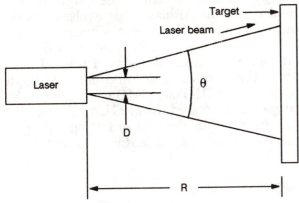

Laser output power = P (watts)
Beam diameter = D (meters)
Divergence angle = θ (radians)
    For a diffraction-limited beam,

$$\theta \approx \frac{\lambda}{D} \quad (\lambda = \text{wavelength})$$

Brightness = B

$$B = \frac{P}{\theta^2}$$

Power density on target = I (watts/square cm)

$$I = \frac{B}{R^2}$$

Illustration of the relationships between laser parameters and power density projected on a target. The key figure of merit for any laser is its brightness. Brightness measures the ability of the laser to concentrate power on a distant target. High brightness requires high laser power and low angular divergence. Low angular divergence in turn requires short wavelength and a large beam diameter. The power density on target is equal to the laser brightness divided by the square of the distance to that target.

SOURCE: Office of Technology Assessment, 1988.

Figure 5-11. — FEL Waveforms

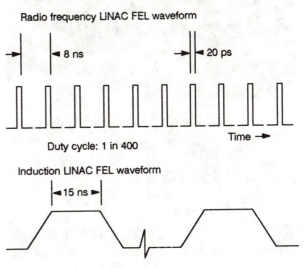

Duty cycle: Much lower than radio frequency LINAC

Existing laser waveforms from the radio frequency linear accelerator (RF linac) free electron laser (FEL) and the induction linear accelerator FEL. The laser light is emitted in very short pulses. The peak power during these short pulses would have to be extremely high to transmit high average power to the targets. This peak intensity, particularly for the induction linac FEL, would stress mirror coatings and could induce other nonlinear losses such as Raman scattering in the atmosphere. Therefore, a weapon-grade induction-linac FEL would have to have higher repetition rates, perhaps on the order of 10 kilohertz.

SOURCE: Office of Technology Assessment, 1988.

length, but only 6 kW of average power—which would translate into a brightness 100,000,000 times less than the level needed for a BMD weapon against hardened Soviet boosters.[26] This 6-kW average power was averaged over a 100-microsecond long "macropulse" in a given second.

[26]This brightness calculation assumes that the beam would be expanded to fill a state-of-the-art 4-m diameter mirror and was diffraction-limited.

It should be noted, however, that these experiments were not designed for maximum average power. Low repetition rates were used primarily for economic reasons. SDIO scientists say that scaling up the number of macropulses from 1/s to 5,000/s is not a serious problem. If correct, this would mean that 30-MW average power could be produced with technology not radically different from today's. In addition, a ground-based weapon would use a wavelength an order of magnitude smaller. The brightness scales as the inverse of the wavelength squared. For a given mirror diameter, then, if a similar power output could be produced at a smaller wavelength, and the high repetition rate were achieved, the brightness would only need to be increased by a factor of about 200 for 30 MW at 1 μm. Accomplish-

Photo credit: U.S. Department of Defense

Model of ALPHA experimental chemical laser.—This experimental chemical laser and its large vacuum chamber have been constructed by TRW at a test site near San Juan Capistrano, CA. The cylindrical configuration of the laser design may be most suitable for basing in space.

ing both modifications would entail significant development work.

Space-based Chemical Lasers.—Placing high-power lasers directly on satellites would eliminate the needs for atmospheric compensation, redundant lasers to avoid inclement weather, and relay mirrors in high orbits; it would also reduce beam brightness requirements by a factor of 4 to 10 (depending on the wavelength and atmospheric factors) since the atmosphere would not attenuate the beam.[27] These advantages are offset by the engineering challenge of operating many tens or hundreds of lasers autonomously in space and by the possible higher vulnerability of lasers relative to battle-mirrors.

The laser should operate at short wavelength (to keep the mirror sizes small) and should be energy efficient (to reduce the weight of fuel needed in orbit). Although its wavelength band (near 2.8 μm) is rather long, the hydrogen fluoride (HF) laser is the most mature and most efficient laser available today. Table 5-3 compares the characteristics of a potential high performance HF laser BMD system with the current mid-infrared chemical laser (MIRACL) (using deuterium fluoride, or DF) operating at the White Sands Missile Range in New Mexico.[28]

DEW Technology

How DEW Work.—Directed energy weapons would change stationary, stored energy from a primary fuel source into a traveling beam of energy that could be directed and focused on a target. Several stages of energy conversion may be necessary. The challenge is to build an affordable, survivable, and reliable machine that can generate the necessary beam of energy. Lasers can be driven by electrical energy, chemical energy, or nuclear energy.

Free Electron Lasers.—Through 1987, the SDIO chose the FEL research program to receive the most DEW emphasis (recently, SDIO has returned to favoring research in space-based chemical lasers). The FEL uses a relativistic[29] electron beam from an accelerator to amplify a light beam in a vacuum. The key advantage of the FEL is the lack of a physical gain medium: all other lasers amplify light in a solid, liquid, or gas. This gain medium must be stimulated with energy to produce an excited population inversion of atoms or molecules. The fundamental limitation with these lasers is the need to remove waste heat before it affects the optical transparency of the medium. The FEL achieves its gain while pass-

---

[27]One defense contractor estimated that a space-based chemical laser system, including space transportation, would cost about 10 times less than the proposed ground-based free electron laser weapon system.

[28]The SDIO is also considering lower-performance, "entry level," space-based chemical lasers for more limited BMD missions.

[29]A beam of particles is deemed "relativistic" when it is accelerated to speeds comparable to a fraction of the speed of light and acquires so much energy that its mass begins to increase measurably relative to its rest mass.

Table 5-3.—Characteristics of an HF Laser Weapons System

	Current status	Estimated operational requirements[a]
Number of laser satellites	—	50-150
Altitude (km)		800-4,000
Beam diameter (m)	1.5[b]	10
Power (MW)	greater than 1	hundreds (single beam)
Brightness (W/sr)	several $\times 10^{17}$[c]	several $\times 10^{21}$
Phased array alternative:		
Number of beams		7
Beam diameter (m)		10
Total power (MW):		100 (14 MW per beam)

[a]These numbers derived from first principles, and from American Physical Society, *Science and Technology of Directed-Energy Weapons: Report of the American Physical Society Study Group,* April 1987, which contains estimates of booster hardness for a fully responsive threat. The SDIO neither confirms nor denies these estimates. Current SDIO estimates may be found in the classified version of this report. In addition, SDIO has identified earlier entry-level systems with less stressing missions and less stressing requirements with brightnesses on the order of 10^{20} W/sr.

[b]The LAMP mirror, not yet integrated with a high-power laser, has a diameter of 4 m.

[c]Assuming perfect beam quality for a multi-megawatt system with the characteristics of the MIRACL laser.

SOURCE: Office of Technology Assessment, American Physical Society Study Group, and Strategic Defense Initiative Organization, 1987 and 1988.

ing through an electron beam plasma, so much of the "waste heat" exits the active region along with the electron beam at nearly the speed of light.

Two types of electron beam accelerator are currently under investigation in the SDIO program: the radio frequency linear accelerator (RF linac) and the induction linac.[30]

In the RF linac, electrical energy from the primary source is fed to radio-frequency generators that produce an RF field inside the accelerator cavity. This field in turn accelerates low energy electrons emitted by a special source in the front end of the accelerator. The accelerator raises this electron beam to higher and higher energy levels (and hence higher velocity) and they eventually reach speeds approaching that of light. Simultaneously, the electrons bunch into small packets in space, corresponding to the peaks of the RF wave.

This relativistic beam of electron packets is inserted into an optical cavity. There the beam passes through a periodic magnetic field (called a "wiggler" magnet) that causes the electrons

to oscillate in space perpendicular to the beam axis. As a result of this transverse motion, weak light waves called synchrotron radiation are generated. Some of this light travels along with the electron packets through the wiggler magnets. Under carefully controlled conditions, the electron beam gives up some of its energy to the light beam. The light beam is then reflected by mirrors at the end of the optical cavity and returns to the wiggler magnet synchronously with the next batch of electrons. The light beam picks up more energy from each pass, and eventually reaches high power levels. This type of FEL is an optical "oscillator": it produces its own coherent light beam starting from the spontaneous emission from the synchrotron radiation.

As more energy is extracted from the electron beam, the electrons slow down. These slower electrons are then no longer synchronized with the light wave and the periodic magnet, so the optical gain (amplification) saturates. To increase extraction efficiency, the wiggler magnet is "tapered": the spacing of the magnets or the magnetic field strength is varied so that the electrons continue in phase with the light wave and continue to amplify the beam as energy is extracted.

For high-power weapon applications, the power from an oscillator might be too weak:

---

[30]Other types of accelerators are possible for a free electron laser, such as the electrostatic accelerator FEL under investigation at the University of California at Santa Barbara, but the RF linac and induction linac have been singled out as the primary candidates for initial SDI experiments.

the limit for an RF linac FEL oscillator is near 20 MW. In this case additional single-pass amplifiers can boost the beam energy. This system is called a master oscillator power amplifier (MOPA) laser.

In the second type of FEL, the induction linac, large electrical coils accelerate narrow pulses of electrons. The high energy electrons interact with an optical beam as in the RF linac FEL, but the optical beam as currently planned would be too intense to reflect off mirrors and recirculate to pick up energy in multiple passes as in the RF oscillator. Rather, all of the energy transfer from the electron beam to the optical beam would occur on a single pass. This would entail very high gain, which demands very high density electron beams and very intense laser light coming into the amplifier. The induction linac FEL therefore depends on an auxiliary laser to initiate the optical gain process; this limits the tunability of the induction linac FEL to the wavelengths of existing conventional lasers of moderately high power.

The process of converting electron energy into light energy can theoretically approach 100 percent efficiency, although it may take very expensive, heavy, and fragile equipment.[31] Nevertheless, the FEL could achieve very high power levels, and, unlike other lasers, the RF linac FEL can be tuned to different wavelengths by changing the physical spacing or field strength of the wiggler magnets or the energy of the electron beam.[32] Tunability is desirable for ground-based lasers, which must avoid atmospheric absorption bands (wavelengths of light absorbed by the air) if they are to reach into space.

Chemical (HF) Lasers.—The HF laser derives its primary energy from a chemical reaction: deuterium and nitrogen trifluoride gases react in a device resembling a rocket engine. Hydrogen gas mixes with the combustion products. Chemical energy raises the resulting HF molecules to an excited state, from which they relax later by each emitting a photon of light energy in one of several wavelength lines near 2.8 μm in the MWIR. A pair of opposing mirrors causes an intense beam of IR energy to build up as each pass through the excited HF gas causes more photons to radiate in step with the previously generated light wave.[33] Some additional electrical energy runs pumps and control circuits.

Excimer Laser.—In an excimer[34] laser, electrical energy, usually in the form of an electron beam, excites a rare gas halide[35] such as krypton fluoride or xenon chloride.[36] These gases then emit in the ultraviolet (UV) region of the spectrum, with wavelengths in the range from .2 to .36 μm. This very short wavelength permits smaller optical elements for a given brightness. However, the optical finish on those UV optics would have to be of proportionately higher quality.

Ultraviolet light is also desirable for space applications, since its high energy generally causes more damage to the surfaces of targets than does that of longer-wavelength visible or IR light. One drawback is that internal mirrors resistant to UV radiation damage are more difficult to make. Another is that UV cannot readily penetrate the atmosphere. These obstacles, combined with their relative immaturity and low efficiency, have relegated high power excimers to a back-up role to the FEL for the ground-based BMD laser.

---

[31]Total system efficiency would probably be about 20 percent-25 percent at best, assuming a reasonably optimistic 50 percent-60 percent efficiency to convert chemical to electrical energy using a rocket-driven turbine, and 40 percent efficiency to generate RF power.

[32]The wavelength of the FEL is proportional to the wiggler magnet spacing and inversely proportional to the square of the electron beam energy. Higher beam energies are necessary for the short wavelengths needed for BMD.

[33]This process of repeated radiation in step is called "stimulated emission": the traveling wave of light stimulates the excited molecule to radiate with the same phase and direction as the stimulating energy. The resulting beam of light is "coherent": it can be focused to a very small spot. The term "laser" is derived from the phrase "Light Amplification by Stimulated Electromagnetic Radiation."

[34]Excimer is short for "excited state dimer"; the excitation of these rare gas halides produces molecules that only exist in the excited state, unlike other lasing media which decay to a ground state after emitting a photon of light.

[35]A "halide" is a compound of two elements, one of which is a halogen: fluorine, chlorine, iodine, or bromine.

[36]Krypton fluoride produces a wavelength too short to penetrate the atmosphere; for ground-based applications, xenon chloride would be of interest.

Passing a laser beam through a Raman gas cell can improve its quality. This cell, typically filled with hydrogen gas, can simultaneously shift the laser frequency to longer wavelengths (for better atmospheric propagation), combine several beams, lengthen the pulse (to avoid high peak power), and smooth out spatial variations in the incoming beams. A low-power, high quality "seed" beam is injected into the Raman cell at the desired frequency. One or more pump beams from excimer lasers supply most of the power. In the gas cell, Raman scattering transfers energy from the pump beams to the seed. This process has been demonstrated in the laboratory with efficiencies up to 80 percent.

X-ray Laser.—A nuclear explosion generates the beam of an x-ray laser weapon. Since this type of laser self-destructs, it would have to generate multiple beams to destroy multiple targets at once. It has been proposed that x-ray lasers would be based in the "pop-up" mode; their launch rockets would wait near the Soviet land mass and fire only after a full-scale ICBM launch had been detected. Since the x-rays could not penetrate deeply into the atmosphere unless self-focused, the earliest application for the x-ray laser would likely be as an ASAT weapon.

Neutral Particle Beam (NPB) Weapon.—The NPB weapon, like a free electron laser, would use a particle accelerator (see figure 5-12). This accelerator, similar to those employed in high energy physics experiments, would move charged hydrogen (or deuterium or tritium) ions to high velocities. Magnetic steering coils would aim the beam of ions toward a target. As the beam left the device, a screen would strip the extra electrons off the ions, resulting in a neutral or uncharged beam of atoms.[37]

Unlike laser beams, which deposit their energy on the surface of the target, a neutral particle beam would penetrate most targets, causing internal damage. For example, a 100-MeV particle beam would penetrate up to 4

Figure 5-12.—Schematic of a Neutral Particle Beam Weapon

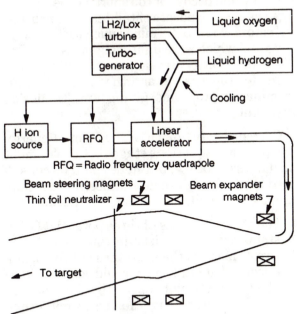

Schematic of a neutral particle beam weapon. Primary power might be generated by firing a rocket engine, similar to the Shuttle main engine, coupled to an electrical generator. Alternately, the hydrogen and oxygen could be combined in a fuel cell to produce electricity. The resulting electrical current would drive the accelerator that would produce a beam of negatively charged hydrogen ions. This negatively charged beam would be expanded and directed toward the target by magnets. Just before leaving the device, the extra electron on each hydrogen ion would be stripped off, leaving a neutral particle beam that could travel unperturbed through the earth's erratic magnetic field.

SOURCE: Office of Technology Assessment, 1988.

cm into solid aluminum and a 200-MeV beam would deposit energy 13 cm deep.[38] These penetrating particles could damage sensitive circuits, trigger the chemical high explosives in nuclear warheads, and—at high enough incident energy levels—melt metal components. Shielding against neutral particle beams would be difficult, imposing a large weight penalty.

As mentioned in chapter 4, the NPB may be usable first as an interactive discriminator. The beam of energetic hydrogen atoms would dislodge neutrons from massive RVs (the dis-

---

[37]A charged beam could not be aimed reliably, since it would be deflected by the Earth's erratic magnetic field, so the beam must be uncharged or neutral.

[38]See W. Barkas and M. Berger, *Tables of Energy Losses and Ranges of Heavy Charged Particles*, (Washington, DC: NASA, 1964).

criminator NPB would presumably dwell on each RV and decoy for too short a time to damage the RV). Separate satellites with neutron detectors would determine which targets were RVs and which were light-weight decoys. The NPB technology development would be the same for the weapon and the interactive discrimination programs, giving it multi-mission capability.

Current Status of DEW.—Directed energy weapons are at various stages of development as discussed below, but none could be considered ready for full-scale engineering development or deployment in the next decade.[39]

The characteristics of three potential DEW systems are summarized in table 5-4. A key figure of merit is the brightness of the beam. Precisely what brightness would destroy different targets is still under investigation: the SDI research program is measuring target lethality for different wavelengths and for different classes of targets. The brightness levels of table 5-4 are derived from physical first principles and assume that the Soviets could convert their missiles to hardened, solid-fueled boosters by the time DEWs could be deployed.[40]

---

[39]SDIO has recently been considering "entry-level" options that it currently considers feasible for phase-two deployment.

[40]SDIO is considering "entry level" DEWs that would have much lower brightness and might be effective against today's more vulnerable boosters. A synergistic mix of KEW-DEW boost-phase intercept capability and DEW discrimination is being considered by SDIO as possible parts of a phase-two system.

The Accelerator Test Stand (ATS) neutral particle beam experimental accelerator at Los Alamos National Laboratory is the weapon candidate closest to lethal operating conditions: its brightness would need to rise by about a factor of 10,000 to assure destruction of electronics inside an RV at typical battle ranges (thousands of km). However, in this kill mode, it may be hard to determine whether the electronics actually had been destroyed. Another factor of 10 to 100 might be needed to produce visible structural damage.

The MIRACL DF chemical laser operating at White Sands has greater than 1 megawatt output power, but its relatively long wavelength, the challenge of unattended space operation, and the uncertainty of scaling this laser to the power levels necessary for ballistic missile defense would make a deployment decision now premature. The brightness of an HF or DF laser would have to be increased by a factor of 10,000 to 100,000 over current levels to be useful against responsively hardened Soviet boosters. However, an "entry-level" system that might be useful against current boosters would entail an increase in brightness of only several hundred to several thousand times.

To test some aspects of a space-based HF laser, TRW is installing its "Alpha" laser in a large space-simulation chamber near San Juan Capistrano, California. The Alpha laser uses a cylindrical geometry (MIRACL uses lin-

Table 5-4.—Characteristics of Directed Energy Weapons Against a Fully Responsive Soviet Threat[a]

	FEL—ground-based	HF—space-based	NPB—space-based
Primary energy source	Electric	Chemical	Electric
Wavelength or energy	0.8-1.3 μm	2.7 μm	100-400 MeV
Required brightness (W/sr)	Several $\times$ 10^{22}	Several $\times$ 10^{21}	Several $\times$ 10^{19} (for electronics kill)
Current brightness (W/sr)	Several $\times$ 10^{14} (considering unintegrated components)	Several $\times$ 10^{17}[b] (potential for about 10^{18} if unintegrated components considered)	10^{15}-10^{16} (considering unintegrated components)
Minimum penetration altitude (km)	About 30	About 30	130-170

[a]The numbers in this table are obtained from the American Physical Society, *Science and Technology of Directed-Energy Weapons: Report of the American Physical Society Study Group*, April 1987, and apply to an advanced BMD system against a responsive threat. The estimates are neither confirmed nor denied by SDIO. SDIO has identified other BMD missions for which lower "entry-level" systems with lower specifications (on the order of 10^{20} W/sr) would be adequate.
[b]Assuming perfect beam quality for a system with the characteristics of the MIRACL laser.

SOURCE: Office of Technology Assessment, American Physical Society Study Group, and Strategic Defense Initiative Organization, 1987 and 1988.

ear flow) with the supersonic gas flowing outward from a central 1.1-m diameter cylinder formed by stacking rings of carefully machined nozzles. The laser beam will take the form of an annulus passing just outside the radially directed nozzles. A complex aspheric mirror system will keep the laser beam within this narrow ring. The goal of this program is to demonstrate multi-megawatt, near-diffraction limited operation in 1988.

The brightness of a 4-m diameter (the size of the Large Aperture Mirror Program mirror), perfect, diffraction-limited beam[41] from, for example, a 1-MW laser, would be over 10^{18} watts/steradian (W/sr). The Alpha laser was designed to be scaled to significantly higher levels by stacking additional amplifier segments. It would take a coherent combination of many such lasers to make a weapon able to engage a fully responsive missile threat.

Chemical lasers to meet a responsive Soviet missile threat would need brightnesses of 10^{21}-10^{22} W/sr. The level needed would depend on the target dwell and retarget times. These times, in turn, depend on the laser constellation size and geometry, booster burn time and hardness, and number of targets which must be illuminated per unit time. If the Soviets were to increase the number of ICBMs in a particular launch area or decrease booster burn times, then the laser brightness needed would increase.

The brightness of a ground-based FEL would have to increase by a factor of 4 to 10 to account for energy losses as the beam passed through the atmosphere and travelled to and from relay mirrors in space. Several free electron lasers have been built. None has operated within a factor of 100 million (10^8) of the lethal brightness levels needed for a fully-responsive BMD system. Part of the reason is the low repetition rate of the pulses in experimental machines. For example, one experiment ran with the accelerator operated at a rate of one electron beam pulse every two seconds. Future accelerators will probably increase this rate to thousands of pulses per second. This will increase average brightnesses accordingly, although, as previously discussed, several more factors of 10 improvement would be needed.

Lawrence Livermore National Laboratory is conducting experiments with an FEL based on an induction linear accelerator (linac). Boeing Aerospace is constructing an RF linac FEL, based on technology developed by Boeing and Los Alamos National Laboratory.

Initial experiments on the Livermore FEL in 1985 produced microwave beams at 8.6 mm wavelength with peak powers of 100 MW. More recently, the peak power risen to 1.8 GW (1.8×10^9 W),[42] although this intensity lasts for only 15 nanoseconds (15×10^{-9} s); the average power at the repetition rates of one shot every 2 seconds was only 14 W. Scaling to shorter wavelengths demands higher quality and very high-energy electron beams. Livermore Laboratory achieved FEL lasing at 10 μm in the far IR with its "Paladin" laser experiment in late 1986. Boeing and a TRW/Stanford University collaboration have operated 0.5 μm visible lasers, but at low average power levels.

The Boeing RF linac FEL has the advantage of multiple optical passes through the wiggler of the optical oscillator. This means that high gain is not necessary, as it is with single-pass induction linacs.[43] The RF linac also has more tolerance of variations in electron beam quality or emittance. The emittance of the RF linac electron beam could grow (i.e., deteriorate) by almost a factor of 10 without deleterious effects. In contrast, the induction linac electron beam cannot increase in emittance by more than a factor of two without degrading optical beam brightness.[44] However, there has been more uncertainty as to whether RF linacs could be scaled to the high current levels needed for BMD. Induction linacs, on the other hand,

---

[41]See American Physical Society, op. cit., footnote 1, p. 179.

[42]Andrew M. Sessler and Douglas Vaughan, "Free-Electron Lasers," *American Scientist*, vol. 75, January-February, 1987, p. 34.

[43]The RF linac might require single-pass amplifiers in addition to their multi-pass oscillators (MOPA configuration) to achieve weapons-class power levels.

[44]Private communication, John M.J. Madey, 1987.

have inherently high-current capability. Recently, the two FEL concepts have appeared on the whole to compete closely with one another.

Excimer lasers have been utilized for lower power research and some commercial applications. The UV energy from an excimer laser is generally more damaging than visible or IR energy. However, UV light can also damage mirrors and other optical components within the laser system, making high-power operation much more difficult. Scaling to higher power is possible, but SDIO has judged the excimer program less likely to succeed, and has cut it back. The Air Force ASAT program is funding continued excimer laser research jointly with SDIO.

Los Alamos National Laboratory researchers have conducted NPB-related experiments on their ATS. They have produced a current level of 0.1 A at 5 MeV. Rocket-borne tests of parts of a NPB system were planned for the late 1980s. The SDIO had planned a series of full space tests to begin in the early 1990s, including a NPB accelerator with a target satellite and a neutron detector satellite as part of the interactive discrimination experimental program. Recently, scheduling of these tests has been delayed due to funding constraints.

Key DEW Issues.—With such a wide gap between operational requirements and the current status of DEW, many key technical issues remain. DEW research over the next 10 to 20 years could resolve some issues judged crucial today, but could also uncover other, unforeseen, roadblocks. Some of the current issues of concern (large mirrors, pointing and tracking, and lethality measurements) are generic to all laser systems, while others are specific to particular weapon systems.

Large Mirrors.—All laser systems (except the x-ray laser) need very large mirrors to focus the beam to a small spot at the target.[45]

---

[45]Spot size is inversely proportional to mirror diameter. Laser brightness, the primary indicator of weapon lethality, increases as the square of mirror diameter. Thus doubling the mirror size from 2 meters to 4 meters would increase laser brightness by a factor of 4.

This is true for both ground-based lasers with multiple relay mirrors in space and for space-based lasers with the mirror adjacent to the laser. In either case, the size of the last mirror (closest to the target) and its distance from the target determine the size of the laser spot focused on that target. To achieve the brightness levels of 10^{21} to 10^{22} W/sr for BMD against a fully responsive threat, laser mirrors would have to be at least 4 m (assuming mirrors were ganged into coherent arrays), and preferably 10 to 20 m, in diameter.

The largest monolithic telescope mirrors today are about 5 m in diameter (Mt. Palomar), and the largest mirror built for space application is the Hubble Space Telescope at 2.4 m. The Hubble or Palomar mirror technologies would not simply be scaled up for SDI applications. The current trend both in astronomy and in military applications is to divide large mirrors into smaller segments. Electro-mechanical actuators within the mirror segments adjust their optical surfaces so that they behave as a single large mirror.

Even for these segments, direct scaling of old mirror manufacturing techniques using large blocks of glass for the substrate is not appropriate: these mirrors must weigh very little. They must be polished to their prescribed surface figure within a small fraction of the wavelengths they are designed to reflect. Brightness and precision make opposite demands: usually, a thick and relatively heavy substrate is necessary to keep good surface figure. SDIO has developed new technologies to reduce substrate weight substantially.

Two segments of a 3-segment, 3-m mirror (HALO) have been built. The 7-segment, 4-m mirror (LAMP) is now assembled and currently being tested. One segment of a 10-m mirror is to be built by 1991, but there are no current plans to assemble a complete 10-m mirror. Recently, the SDIO has begun tests of the lightweight LAMP mirror, designed for space-based lasers.

Durable, high-reflectivity mirror coatings are essential to prevent high laser power from damaging the mirrors. The largest mirror that has been coated with a multi-layer dielectric coating to withstand high energy-density levels is 1.8 m in diameter. Multi-layer dielectric coatings are generally optimized to produce maximum reflectivity at the operating wavelength. Their reflectivity at other wavelengths is low (and transmission is high), meaning that off-wavelength radiation from another (enemy) laser could penetrate and damage them.[46] These coatings may also be susceptible to high-energy particle damage in space, either natural or man-made.

Finally, the optical industry must develop manufacturing techniques, infrastructure, and equipment to supply the hundreds of large mirrors for BMD DEW deployment. The SDI research program has targeted mirror fabrication as a key issue, and progress has been good in the last few years. Techniques have been developed to fabricate light-weight, segmented mirrors with hollow-cored substrates and actuators to move each segment to correct for surface figure errors.

These active mirrors could correct both for large-scale manufacturing errors and for operational changes such as distortions due to thermal warping. They could even correct for broad phase errors in the laser beam. The price would be added complexity. A complex electro-mechanical-optical servo system would replace a simpler static mirror. And, to make the necessary corrections, another complex wave-front detection system would measure the phase distortions of the laser beam in real time.

With reliable active mirrors, it might be possible to coherently combine the output energy from two or more lasers. The brightness of "N" lasers could theoretically be increased to "N²" times that of a single laser with this coherent addition. (See section below on chemical lasers for more details.)

Pointing, Tracking and Retargeting Issues. —A DEW beam must rapidly switch from one target to the next during a battle. Assuming that each DEW battle-station within range of Soviet ICBMs would have to engage 2 ICBMs per second,[47] then the beam would have to slew between targets in 0.3 s to allow 0.2 s of actual laser dwell time. In addition, the mirror would have to move constantly to keep the beam on the target: the target would move 1.4 km during 0.2 s exposure, and the beam would have to stay within a 20- to 30-cm diameter spot on the moving target.

Large 10- to 30-meter mirrors could move continuously to track the general motion of a threat cloud, but jumping several degrees to aim at a new target in 0.3 s would be rather difficult.[48] One solution would be to steer a smaller, lighter-weight secondary mirror in the optics train, leaving the big primary mirror stationary. This approach would yield only limited motion, since the beam would eventually walk off the primary mirror; in addition, the smaller secondary mirror would be exposed to a higher laser intensity, making thermal damage more difficult to avoid.

Alternatively, small-angle adjustments could be made with the individual mirror segments that would constitute the primary mirrors. These mirror segments would probably have mechanical actuators to correct for gross beam distortions and thermal gradient-induced mirror warpage. Again, moving individual mirror segments would produce only limited angular motion of the total beam.[49]

---

[46]Dielectric coatings are nominally transmissive off the main wavelength band, but there are always defects and absorbing centers that absorb energy passing through, often causing damage and blow-off. At best the transmitted energy would be deposited in the substrate, which would then have to be designed to handle the high power density of offensive lasers.

[47]Of a laser battle-station fleet of 120, perhaps 10 to 12 would be within range of the missile fields. Assuming that average Soviet booster burn times were in the range of 130 seconds by the time a DEW system could be deployed, and allowing 30 seconds for cloud break and initial track determination, then each DEW platform in the battle space would have to engage an average of about 130 ICBMs in 100 seconds. This required targeting rate of about 1.3 per second could be increased by factors of 2 to 5 or more if the Soviet Union decided to deploy more ICBMs, and if they concentrated those extra ICBMs at one or a few sites. For this discussion, a figure of 2 per second is taken.

[48]Slewing requirements can be minimized by using appropriate algorithms.

[49]Alternate concepts are being investigated to allow retargeting at large angles with steerable secondary mirrors.

The mirror servo system would have to accomplish these rapid steering motions without introducing excessive vibration or jitter to the beam. To appreciate the magnitude of the steering problem, consider that a vibration that displaced one edge of a 10-m mirror by 1 micrometer (1 μm—40 millionths of an inch or twice the wavelength of visible light) would cause the laser to move one full spot diameter on the target.[50] This small vibration would cut the effective laser brightness in half. Allowable jitter is therefore in the 20 nanoradian, or one part in 50 million, range. Since any servo system would undoubtedly exceed these jitter limits immediately after switching to a new target, there would be a resettling time before effective target heating could begin. This resettling time would further decrease the allowable beam steering time, say from 0.3 s to 0.2 or 0.1 s.

Non-inertial methods of steering laser beams are under investigation. For example, a beam of light passing through a liquid bath which contains a periodic acoustical wave is diffracted at an angle determined by the acoustical frequency. By electronically changing the acoustical frequency in the fluid, the laser beam could be scanned in one direction without any moving parts. Two such acousto-optic modulators in series could produce a full two-dimensional scanning capability.

Alternatively, the laser beam could be reflected off an optical grating that diffracted it at an angle that depended on its wavelength. If the laser wavelength could be changed with time, then the beam could be scanned in one direction. Most of these non-inertial scanning techniques could not operate at weapons level laser power without damage. Others place constraints on the laser, such as limiting tunability.

Approximate beam steering and retargeting levels are summarized in table 5-5. These parameters would vary with specific weapons design, system architecture, and assumed threats. In general, demands on beam steer-

Table 5-5.—Possible Beam Steering and Retargeting Requirements for Boost-Phase Engagement

Retargeting rate	2 targets/second
Retarget time	0.1 to 0.2 seconds
Jitter resettling time	0.1 to 0.2 seconds
Average laser dwell time	0.2 seconds
Laser angular beamwidth[a]	120 nanoradians
Allowable beam jitter	20 nanoradians

[a]The diffraction-limited beam spread for a 1 μm laser with a 10 m diameter mirror is 120 nr.

SOURCE: Office of Technology Assessment, 1988.

ing speed and precision would increase if the DEW range were extended (by deploying fewer than the 120 battle stations assumed here, for example), or if the Soviets increased the offensive threat above 1,400 ICBMs with average burn time of 130 s assumed above.

Beam steering and retargeting needs for post-boost and midcourse battle phases could be more stressing if boost-phase leakage were high and discrimination were not reasonably effective. In general there would be more time for midcourse kills, and more DEW platforms would engage targets, but the hard-shelled RVs would withstand much more laser irradiation and hence impose longer dwell times. Lasers do not appear likely candidates for midcourse interception of RVs.

A neutral particle beam weapon (NPB) would not have to dwell longer on RVs than on boosters or PBVs, since energetic particles would penetrate the RV. Without midcourse discrimination, the NPB system might have to kill from 50,000 to 1,000,000 objects surviving the boost phase, and a weapon platform would have to kill an average of 3 to 50 targets per second. At the other extreme, with effective discrimination, each NPB platform in the battle might have to engage only one RV or heavy decoy every 20 s.[51]

Atmospheric Turbulence and Compensation for Thermal Blooming.—One current DEW candidate is the ground-based free electron la-

---

[50]This assumes a 20-cm spot diameter on a target 1,000 km away, or an angular motion of 200 nanoradians.

[51]Assume 6,000 RVs, 6,000 heavy decoys, and 10 percent leakage from the boost phase defense. If the discrimination system reliably eliminated all light decoys and debris, then, with 30 of the 120 DEW platforms in the midcourse battle, each platform would engage, on the average, one target every 22.5 seconds.

ser. The beam from this laser would be directed to a mirror in space that would reflect the beam to "fighting mirrors" closer to the targets. The laser beam would be distorted in passing through the atmosphere, for the same reason that stars "twinkle." If not corrected, atmospheric distortion would scramble the beam, making it impossible to focus with sufficient intensity to destroy ICBM boosters.

Techniques have been developed to measure this distortion of the optical wave front and to modify the phase of low power laser beams to nearly cancel the effects of the turbulent atmosphere. To correct distortion, the mirror is manufactured with a flexible outer skin or with separate mirror segments. Mechanical actuators behind the mirror surface move it to produce phase distortions that complement phase errors introduced by the atmosphere. This "rubber mirror" must continuously adjust to cancel the effects of atmospheric turbulence, which varies with time at frequencies up to at least 140 hertz (cycles per second).

To measure atmospheric distortion, a test beam of light must be transmitted through the same patch of atmosphere as the high power laser beam. For the BMD application, this test beam would be projected from a point near the relay mirror in space, or a reflector near that relay mirror would return a test beam from the ground to the wave-front sensing system. Signals derived from the wave-front sensor computer in response to the test beam would drive the mirror actuators to correct the high-power laser beam.

The wave-front sensor must generate a coherent reference beam to compare with the distorted beam, as in an interferometer. One technique, called shearing interferometry, causes two slightly displaced versions of the incoming distorted image to interfere. A computer then deduces the character of the distorted wave front by interpreting the resulting interference fringes,

Another wave-front sensor system under investigation filters part of the incoming reference beam to produce a smooth, undistorted wave front. This clean wave front can then be combined with the distorted wave front, producing interference fringes that more clearly represent the atmospheric distortion. Unfortunately the energy levels in the filtered wave front are too low, so an operational system might need image intensifiers.

Atmospheric compensation of low power beams has been demonstrated in the laboratory and in tests during late 1985 at the Air Force Maui Optical Station (AMOS) in Hawaii. In this test, an argon laser beam was transmitted through the atmosphere to a sounding rocket in flight. A reflector on the sounding rocket returned the test signal. Wave-front errors generated on Maui drove a "rubber mirror" to compensate for the turbulence experienced by a second Argon laser beam aimed at the rocket. A set of detectors spaced along the sounding rocket showed that this laser beam was corrected to within a factor of two of the diffraction limit.

Successful atmospheric compensation will entail resolution of two key issues: thermal blooming and fabrication of large, multi-element mirrors. As a high-power laser beam heats the air in its path, it will create additional turbulence, or "thermal blooming," which will distort the beam. At some level, this type of distributed distortion cannot be corrected. For example, if thermal blooming causes the laser beam to diverge at a large distance from the last mirror, then the test beam returning from the relay satellite would also spread over a large area and would not all be collected by the wave-front sensor. Under these conditions, complete compensation would not be possible.

Laboratory tests of thermal blooming were planned at MIT's Lincoln Labs and field-testing was planned for early 1989 using the high-power MIRACL laser at the White Sands Missile Range. The latter series of tests is on hold due to lack of funding.

The mirror for a BMD FEL would need 1,000 to 10,000 actuators for effective atmospheric compensation.[52] Experiments to date have used cooled mirrors with a relatively small

---

[52]American Physical Society, op. cit., footnote 1, p. 190.

number of elements, and Itek is currently building a large uncooled mirror with many more.

Nonlinear optical techniques may offer an alternative to the active-mirror correction of atmospheric turbulence. Laboratory experiments at low power have already demonstrated beam cleanup by stimulated Brillouin scattering, for example. In this technique, a beam of light with a wave front distorted by the atmosphere enters a gas cell. The beam passes partially through this gas and is reflected back with complementary phase distortion. This complementary or "conjugate" phase exactly cancels the phase distortions introduced by the atmosphere. The key is to amplify the phase conjugate beam without introducing additional phase errors. If perfected, this approach would eliminate moving mirror elements.

Target Lethality.—One term in the DEW effectiveness equation is the susceptibility of current and future targets to laser and neutral particle beams. Current U.S. missile bodies have been subjected to HF laser beams in ground-based tests, and various materials are being tested for durability under exposure to high-power laser light.[53] Laser damage varies with spot size, wavelength, pulse length, polarization, angle of incidence, and a large range of target surface parameters, making lethality test programs complex.[54] FEL beams with a series of very short but intense pulses may produce an entirely different effect than continuous HF chemical laser beams.

Measuring the lethality of low-power neutral particle beam weapons intended to disrupt electronics could be more complicated. Damage thresholds would depend on the electronics package construction. However, current plans call for particle beam energy density which would destroy virtually any electronic sys-

tem.[55] The kill assessment issue for NPB weapons would then become one of hit assessment: the system would have to verify that the particle beam hit the target.

FEL.—The two types of FEL systems (induction linac and RF linac) face different sets of key issues (table 5-6). The induction linac FEL has the potential of very high power, but all of the laser gain must occur on one pass through the amplifier as currently designed. (Almost all other lasers achieve their amplification by passing the beam back and forth between two mirrors, adding up incremental energy on each pass.)

To achieve BMD-relevant power levels on one pass, the FEL beam diameter must be very small, on the order of a millimeter (mm). Furthermore, the beam must be amplified over a very long path, on the order of 100 m. But a millimeter-diameter beam would naturally expand by diffraction over this long path length,[56] so the induction linac must utilize the electron beam to guide and constrain the light beam while it is in the wiggler magnet amplifier, much like a fiber optic cable. This optical guiding by an electron beam has been demon-

---

[55]That is, the NPB would be designed to deliver 50 J/gm at the target, whereas 10 J/gm destroys most electronics (see American Physical Society, op. cit., footnote 1, p. 306. This would assure electronics kill unless massive shielding were placed around key components.

[56]A 1-mm beam of unconstrained 1-μm light would expand to 120 mm after traveling 100 m.

Table 5-6.—Key Issues for Free Electron Lasers (FEL)

For induction linear accelerator driven FELs:
—Electron beam guiding of the optical beam
—Generation of stable, high current, low-emittance e-beams
—Scaling to short wavelengths near 1 μm
—Raman scattering losses in the atmosphere

For radio frequency accelerator-driven FELs:
—Scaling to 100 MW power levels
—Efficiency
—Mirror damage due to high intercavity power
—Cavity alignment

For any FEL:
—Long cavity or wiggler path lengths
—Sideband instabilities (harmonic generation)
—Synchrotron/betatron instabilites (lower efficiency)

SOURCE: Office of Technology Assessment, 1988.

---

[53]In one highly publicized test at the White Sands Missile Range, a strapped-down Titan missile casing, pressurized with nitrogen to 60 pounds per square inch pressure to simulate flight conditions, blew apart after exposure to the megawatt-class MIRACL laser.

[54]Computer models have been developed to help predict target lethality, and these models will be refined and correlated with ongoing lethality measurements.

strated, but not under weapon-like FEL conditions.

Two other disadvantages derive from this narrow, intense beam of light produced by the induction linac FEL. First, the beam is so intense that it would damage any realizable mirror surface. The current plan is to allow the beam to expand by diffraction after leaving the FEL, traveling up to several km in an evacuated tunnel before striking the director mirror which would send the beam to the relay mirror in space.

A second disadvantage of such intense pulses of light is that they would react with the nitrogen in the atmosphere by a process called "stimulated Raman scattering." Above a threshold power density, the light would be converted to a different frequency which spreads out of the beam, missing the intended target.[57] Again, this effect could be ameliorated by enclosing the beam in an evacuated tube, allowing it to expand until the power density were low enough for transmission through the atmosphere to the space relay. On the return path to the target, however, the beam would have to be focused down to damage the target.

The experimental induction linac at Livermore currently uses a (conventional, non-FEL) laser-initiated channel to guide the electron beam before it is accelerated. This beam has drifted several millimeters laterally during the FEL pulse in initial experiments, severely limiting FEL lasing performance because the electron beam does not remain collinear with the FEL laser beam.

The RF linac FEL, as currently configured, has shorter pulse lengths (20 picoseconds v. 15 nanoseconds for the induction linac FEL) but much higher pulse repetition rates (125 MHz v. 0.5 MHz[58]), giving it higher duty cycle and lower peak intensity for a given output average power level. It is uncertain whether the RF linac can be scaled up to produce power levels which seem probable for the induction linac. By adding a set of power amplifiers in series, it might be possible to reach the power needed for a lethal laser weapon with an RF linac FEL.

The RF linac generates very high power levels inside the optical cavity. Mirror damage is therefore an issue, as is the problem of extracting energy out of the cavity at these high power levels. Cavity alignment is also critical: the mirrors must be automatically aligned to maintain path-lengths within micrometers over many tens of meters during high-power operation.

The RF linac currently has low efficiency. In 1986, Los Alamos National Laboratory and a TRW-Stanford team demonstrated an energy recovery technique whereby much of the unused energy in an electron beam was recovered after the beam passed through a wiggler-amplifier. In principle, this energy could be coupled back to the RF generator to improve efficiency in an operational system. At the higher optical energy levels envisaged for the amplifiers, the RF linac amplifier should achieve 20 percent to 25 percent conversion efficiency, making energy recovery less advantageous.

An FEL would tend to be fragile. Accelerators are notorious for demanding careful alignment and control, taking hours of manual alignment before operation. Major engineering developments in automatic sensing and control would be necessary before an FEL could become an operational weapon. Los Alamos is working to automate its ATS particle beam accelerator; FEL systems would have to incorporate similar automation, with the added complexity of optical, as well as accelerator, alignment.

An FEL may suffer from electron beam (e-beam) instabilities. For example, unwanted longitudinal e-beam excursions could create "sideband instabilities," in which part of the optical energy would be diverted to sideband frequencies. Laser light at these extraneous frequen-

---

[57]The Raman threshold for stimulated gain in nitrogen gas at one μm light is about 1.8 MW/cm^2. Above this power density, the atmosphere becomes a single-pass nitrogen laser: much of the beam energy is converted to different (Stokes and anti-Stokes) wavelengths which diverge and cannot be focused on the target.

[58]The induction linac at Livermore could be operated up to 1 kHz for up to 10 pulses. An operational linac FEL would have a repetition rate as high as tens of kilohertz.

cies could damage optical components designed to handle high power only at the main lasing frequency. Such sideband frequencies have been observed in FEL experiments. Lateral motion of the e-beam, called "synchrotron/betatron instabilities" could reduce FEL efficiency, although calculations indicate that this should not be a problem.

Chemical Laser Issues.—The chemical HF laser has some disadvantages relative to the FEL. Its longer wavelength (2.8-μm range) would demand larger mirrors to focus the beam on target. In general, targets would reflect a higher percentage of IR light than visible or, particularly, UV light. Hence, for a given mirror size, an HF laser would have to generate 7 to 10 times more power than an FEL laser operating at one μm, or 80 to 200 times more power than a UV laser, to produce the same power density at the target.

Chemical laser experts do not believe that an individual HF laser could be built at reasonable cost to reach the 10^{21} to 10^{22} W/sr brightness levels needed for BMD against a responsive threat, since the optical gain volume is limited in one dimension by gas flow kinetics, and by optical homogeneity in the other directions. However, by combining the outputs from many HF lasers, it might be possible to produce BMD-capable HF arrays (table 5-7).

These beams must be added coherently: the output from each laser must have the same frequency and the same phase.[59] Controlling the phase of a laser beam is conceptually easy, but difficult in practice—particularly at high power and over very large apertures. Since an uncontrolled HF laser generates several different frequencies in the 2.6 to 2.9 μm band, the laser array would have to operate on one spectral line, or one consistent group of lines.

Three coherent coupling techniques have been demonstrated in the laboratory:

1. Coupled Resonators—the optical cavities of several lasers are optically coupled, so they all oscillate in phase;
2. Injection Locked Oscillators—one low power oscillator output light beam is injected into the optical cavity of each laser;
3. Master Oscillator/Power Amplifier (MOPA)—each laser is a single-pass power amplifier fed by the same master oscillator in parallel.

In one experiment, 6 CO_2 lasers were joined in the coupled resonator mode. With incoherent addition, the output would have been 6 times brighter than that of a single laser; with perfect coupling, the output would have been 36 times brighter. The experiment actually produced 23.4 times greater brightness. Experiments are under way to couple two 1-kW, HF/DF lasers (with the coupled resonator approach) and to demonstrate MOPA operation of two HF laser amplifiers.[60]

Neutral Particle Beam.—Although accelerator technology is well established for ground-based physics experiments, much research, development, and testing are prerequisite to a judgment of the efficacy of a space-based particle beam weapon *system*. Key issues are presented in table 5-8.

Table 5-7.—Key Issues for the HF Chemical Laser

Coherent beam combination: (many HF laser beams would have to be combined to achieve necessary power levels)

Required beam brightness against a responsive threat . . .	several $\times\ 10^{21}$ W/sr[a]
Reasonable HF Laser brightness for a single large unit (10 MW power and 10-m mirror)	8.6×10^{19}
Coherent Array of seven 10 MW/10-m HF lasers	4.2×10^{21}

[a]The American Physical Society, *Science and Technology of Directed-Energy Weapons: Report of the American Physical Society Study Group*, April 1987, p. 55, estimated hardness for a responsive threat to be well in excess of 10 kJ/cm². Given a range of 2,000 km and a dwell time of 0.2 s, the denoted brightness is appropriate.

SOURCE: Office of Technology Assessment, 1988.

[59]If added coherently, the beam brightness of "N" lasers would be "N²" times the brightness of one laser. If the "N" lasers were not coherent, then the brightness of the combination would be the sum or "N" times the brightness of one laser.

[60]Actually, the MOPA experiment will utilize one amplifier with three separate optical cavities: one for the master oscillator and two for the amplifiers. (Source: SDI Laser Technology Office, Air Force Weapons Laboratory, unclassified briefing to OTA on Oct. 7, 1986.)

Photo Credit: U.S. Department of Defense,
Strategic Defense Initiative Organization

Artist's conception of a phased array of lasers.—Since it may be impractical to build a single module space-based chemical laser of a size useful for ballistic missile defense, scientists and engineers are exploring the possibility of using several smaller laser modules that would be phase-locked to provide a single coherent beam. This technique could increase the attainable power density on a target by a factor of N^2 (instead of N for incoherent addition), where N is the number of modules.

Table 5-8.—Neutral Particle Beam Issues

- Major issues:
  —Beam divergence: 50 times improvement required
  —Weight reduction (50 to 100 tonnes projected)
  —Kill assessment (or hit assessment)
- Other issues:
  —Beam sensing and pointing
  —Duty factor: 100 times improvement required
  —Ion beam neutralization (50% efficient)
  —Space charge accumulation
  —ASAT potential

SOURCE: Office of Technology Assessment, 1988.

The NPB ATS now at Los Alamos generates the necessary current (100 mA) for a NPB weapon, but at 20 to 40 times lower voltage, about 100 times lower duty cycle, and with about 50 times more beam divergence than

would be needed for a space-based weapon. A continuous ion source with the necessary current levels has been operated at the Culham Laboratory in the United Kingdom with 30-s pulses, but not as yet coupled to an accelerator.

Researchers have planned a series of ground-based and space-based experiments to develop beams meeting NPB weapons specifications. It is possible that these experiments would encounter unknown phenomena such as beam instabilities or unexpected sources of increased beam divergence, but there are no known physics limitations that would preclude weapons applications.

High energy density at the accelerator would not be sufficient for a weapon. The beam would have to be parallel (or well-collimated, or have "low emittance" in accelerator parlance), to minimize beam spreading and maximize energy transmitted to the target. In general, higher energy beams have lower emittance, but some of the techniques used to increase beam current might increase emittance, possibly to the point where increased current would decrease energy coupled to the distant target. With high emittance, the NPB would be a short-range weapon, and more NPB weapons would be necessary to cover the battle space.

The divergence of existing, centimeter-diameter particle beams is on the order of tens of microradians; this divergence would have to be reduced by expanding the particle beam diameter up to the meter range.[61] This large beam would have to be steered toward the target with meter-size magnets. Full-scale magnetic optics have not been built or tested. However, one-third scale optics have been built by Los Alamos National Laboratory and successfully tested at Argonne National Laboratory on a 50 MeV beam line.

The weight of the NPB system would have to be reduced substantially for space-based operation. The RF power supply alone for a

[61]In theory, beam divergence decreases as the beam size is increased. In practice, the magnets needed to increase the beam diameter might add irregularities in transverse ion motion, which could contribute to increased beam divergence; not all of the theoretical gain in beam divergence would be achieved.

weapon-class NPB would weigh 160,000 kg (160 tonnes) if based on existing RF radar technology.[62] Using solid-state transistors and reducing the weight of other components might reduce RF weight about 22 tonnes.[63] One study concluded that a total NPB platform weight of 100 tonnes is "probably achievable."[64] Los Alamos scientists have estimated that the NPB platform weight for an "entry level," 100-MeV, NPB system could be 50 tonnes. Someday, if high-temperature, high-current superconductors became available, NPB weights might be reduced substantially.

Thermal management on a NPB satellite would be challenging. A NPB weapon might produce 40 MW of waste heat.[65] One proposal is to use liquid hydrogen to dispose of this heat. About 44 tonnes of hydrogen could cool the NPB for 500 s.[66] The expulsion of hydrogen gas would have to be controlled, since even a minute quantity of gas diffused in front of the weapon could ionize the beam, which would then be diverted by the Earth's magnetic field. Since the hydrogen gas would presumably have to be exhausted out opposing sides of the spacecraft to avoid net thrust, it might be difficult to keep minute quantities of gas out of the beam.

A state-of-the-art ion accelerator (the Ramped Gradient Drift Tube Linac) can raise beam energy about 4 MeV per meter of accelerator length. At this gradient rate, a 200-MeV beam would have to be over 50 m long. This accelerator could be folded, but extra bending magnets would increase weight and could reduce beam quality. The gradient could be increased, but if the ion beam energy were increased in a shorter length, then there would be more heating in the accelerator walls. This implies another system trade-off: reducing length in an attempt to cut weight might eventually reduce efficiency, which would dictate heavier RF power elements and more coolant. Again, future superconductors might ameliorate this problem.

The beam would have to be steered to intercept the target. A NPB would have two advantages over laser beams: the convenience of electronic steering and a lesser need for steering accuracy. Magnetic coils could steer negatively charged hydrogen ions before the extra electrons were stripped off. However, the angular motion of electronic steering would be limited: the entire accelerator would have to maneuver mechanically to aim the beam in the general direction of the target cluster. Like laser weapons, a NPB must have an agile optical sensor system to track targets. However, the divergence of the NPB is larger than most laser beams (microradians versus 20 to 50 nanoradians), so the beam steering need not be as precise.

On the other hand, a hydrogen beam could not be observed directly. The particle beam direction is detected in the laboratory by placing two wires in the beam. The first wire casts a shadow on the second wire placed downstream. By measuring the current induced in this downstream wire as the upstream wire is moved, the beam direction can be estimated to something like 6 microradian accuracy.

New techniques would be needed to sense the beam direction automatically with sufficient accuracy. One approach utilizes the fact that about 7 percent of the hydrogen atoms passing through a beam neutralization foil emerge in a "metastable" excited state: the electrons of these atoms acquire and maintain extra energy. Passing a laser through the beam can make these excited atoms emit light. The

[62]The vacuum-tube (klystron) RF power supply for the PAVE PAWS radar system weighs approximately 2 g/W of power. A NPB weapon would emit an average power of 20 MW (2×10^7 watts), assuming 200 MeV beams at a current of 0.1 A. Assuming an overall efficiency of 25 percent (50 percent accelerator efficiency and 50 percent beam neutralization efficiency), the power supply would have to generate 80 MW average power, and would weigh 160 tonnes.

[63]This assumes that the RF power is generated with 1-kW, commercial quality power transistors (80,000 transistors would be required for the hypothetical 80 MW supply). These transistors can only be operated at 1 percent duty factor. New cooling technology would have to be developed to operate at the 100 percent duty factor required for a NPB weapon. (See American Physical Society, op. cit., footnote 1, pp. 149 and 361.) The overall efficiency of these power supplies would be 40 percent.

[64]Ibid., p. 152.

[65]Assuming a 200-mA, 100-MeV beam, 50 percent neutralization efficiency, and 50 percent power generation efficiency.

[66]Assuming heat of vaporization only (450 J/g), and no temperature rise in the hydrogen. If the gas temperature were allowed to rise by 100° K, then the hydrogen mass could be reduced to about 14 tonnes.

magnitude of this fluorescence depends on the angle between the particle beam and the laser beam. Thus the NPB direction can be deduced and the beam boresighted to an appropriate optical tracking system. Laboratory tests have demonstrated 250 microradian accuracy, compared to the 1-microradian accuracy necessary.[67] More recent tests at Argonne at 50 MeV have yielded better results.

The current technique to neutralize the hydrogen ions is to pass them through a thin foil or a gas cell. This process strips off, at most, 50 percent of the electrons, cutting the efficiency of the system in half and thus increasing its weight. A gas cell is not practical for space applications. A stripping foil must be extraordinarily thin (about .03 to .1 μm, or ten times less than the wavelength of visible light). In the proposed NPB weapon, a thin foil 1 m in diameter would have to cover the output beam. Clearly such a foil could not be self-supporting, but Los Alamos scientists have tested foils up to 25 cm in diameter that are supported on a fine wire grid. This grid obscures about 10 percent of the beam, but has survived initial tests in beams with average power close to operational levels.

Another beam neutralization concept is to use a powerful laser to remove the electrons—a technique that some assert may yield 90 percent efficiency. However, the laser stripping process would call for a 25 MW Nd:YAG laser (near weapon-level power itself), and it would eliminate the excited state hydrogen atoms needed for the laser beam sensing technique.[68]

Charged hydrogen ions that escaped neutralization might play havoc with an NPB satellite. The accumulation of charge might severely degrade weapon system performance in unforeseen ways, although NPB scientists are confident that this would not be an issue.[69] The Beam Experiment Aboard Rocket (BEAR) experiment with an ion source and the planned Integrated Space Experiment (ISE) should answer any remaining doubts about space-charge accumulation.

Arcing or electrical breakdown that could short out highly charged components may also be a problem in space. Dust or metal particles generated in ground-based accelerators fall harmlessly to the ground. In space, floating particles could cause arcing by forming a conducting path between charged components.

Existing accelerators demand many hours of careful manual alignment before an experiment. Neutral particle beam weapons would have to operate automatically in space. Current plans call for the ATS accelerator at Los Alamos to be automated soon.

Kill assessment might be difficult for weak particle beam weapons. Damage deep inside the target might completely negate its function with no visible sign. The choices would be either to forgo kill confirmation or to increase NPB energy levels until observable damage were caused, possibly the triggering of the high-energy explosive on the RV. The current plan is to forgo kill confirmation per se, but to increase the NPB power level to assure electronic destruction. Sensors would determine that the particle beam had hit each target. Experiments are planned to assess whether UV light emissions would indicate that a particle beam had struck the surface of a target.

The planned (and now indefinitely postponed) ISE illustrates a point made in chapter 11 of this report: many BMD weapons would have ASAT capabilities long before they could destroy ballistic missiles or RVs. The ISE accelerator, if successful, would have ASAT lethality at close range, although for a limited duty cycle. Beam divergence might limit range, but it could probably destroy the electronics in existing satellites within 500 to 1,000 km.[70] Even though not aiming a beam

[67]See American Physical Society, op. cit., footnote 1, p. 172.

[68]See American Physical Society, op. cit., footnote 1, p. 148.

[69]One suggested that the neutralizing foil be thicker so that two electrons are stripped from some hydrogen ions, forming positive hydrogen ions (protons) to help neutralize the charge in the vicinity of the spacecraft.

[70]This experiment could have nearly BMD-level lethality, possibly raising issues with respect to the ABM Treaty. However, it would not have the necessary beam sensing and pointing or the computer software and hardware for a BMD weapon; SDIO considers the experiment to be treaty compliant.

at other than a target satellite, this experiment conceivably might disrupt nearby satellite electronics. Although this may not be serious (calculations indicate that it should not), there is enough uncertainty to cause ISE planners to ask whether they should wait until the Space Shuttle had landed before turning on the ISE.

X-ray Laser.—The nuclear bomb-driven x-ray laser is the least mature DEW technology.

To date this program has consisted of theoretical and design work at Livermore National Laboratory and several feasibility demonstration experiments at the underground Nevada nuclear weapons test site. Actual x-ray generation technology may or may not reach suitable levels in the years ahead; currently the methods to convert this technology into a viable weapons system remain paper concepts.

POWER AND POWER CONDITIONING

The average electrical power consumed by some proposed BMD spacecraft during battle might be factors up to 100,000 over current satellite power levels. Most existing satellites are powered by large solar arrays that would be vulnerable to defense suppression attack. To provide sufficient *survivable* power for space applications, most BMD satellites would require either nuclear reactors, rocket engines coupled to electrical generators, or advanced fuel cells.

In addition to high average power, some proposed weapon satellites would demand high peak power: energy from the prime source, either a nuclear reactor or a rocket-driven turbo-alternator, would have to be stored and compressed into a train of very high current pulses. For example, a railgun might expend 500 MJ of energy in a 5-millisecond (ms) pulse, or 100 GW of peak power. This is about 1,000 times more than current pulse power supplies can deliver.

The following sections outline satellite power demands and the technologies that might satisfy them. While space systems would call for the primary advances, ground-based FELs would also depend on advances in pulsed-power supply technology. Some of the technology developed for space-borne neutral particle beam systems, such as RF power sources, might be applicable to FELs.

Space Power Requirements

Estimates of power needs of space-based BMD systems are summarized in table 5-9. Since most of these systems have not been designed, these estimates could change significantly: the table only indicates a possible range of power levels. Power is estimated for three modes of operation: base-level for general satellite housekeeping and continuous surveillance operations lasting many years; alert-level in response to a crisis, possibly leading to war;

Table 5-9.—Estimated Power Requirements for Space Assets
(average power in kilowatts)

Mode of operation	Base	Alert	Burst (battle)
BSTS	4-10	4-10	4-10
SSTS (IR)	5-15	5-15	15-50
Ladar	15-20	15-20	50-100
Ladar imager	15-20	15-20	100-500
Laser illumination	5-10	5-10	50-100
Doppler ladar	15-20	15-20	300-600
SBI carrier	2-30	4-50	10-100
Chemical laser	50-100	100-150	100-200
Fighting mirror	10-50	10-50	20-100
NPB/SBFEL	20-120	1,000-10,000	100,000-500,000
EML (railgun)	20-120	1,000-10,000	200,000-5,000,000

SOURCE: Space Defense Initiative Organization, 1988.

and burst-mode for actual battle, which may last hundreds of seconds.

In addition to average-power and survivability perquisites, a space-based power system would have to be designed to avoid deleterious effects of:

- thrust from power-generating rockets upsetting aiming,
- torque due to rotating components,
- rocket effluent disrupting optics and beam propagation,
- vibration on sensors and beam steering,
- thermal gradients, and
- radiation from nuclear reactors.

Power systems would also have to operate reliably for long periods unattended in space.

Space Power Generation Technology

There are three generic sources of electrical power in space: solar energy, chemical energy, and nuclear energy.

Solar Energy

Solar panels have supplied power for most satellites. The sun produces about 1.3 kW of power on every square meter of solar array surface. An array of crystalline silicon cells converts the sun's energy into direct electrical current through the photovoltaic effect, with an efficiency of about 10 percent. Thus a 1-m^2 panel of cells would produce about 130 watts of electricity, assuming that the panel were oriented perpendicular to the sun's rays. A 20-kW array, typical for a BMD sensor, would then have about 150 m^2—roughly, a 12-m by 12-m array. The Skylab solar array, the largest operated to date, produced about 8 kW. NASA has built, but not yet flown in space, a 25-kW experimental solar array designed to supply space station power.

The major disadvantage of solar arrays is that their large size makes them vulnerable to attack. Crystalline silicon photovoltaic cells are also vulnerable to natural and man-made radiation. One approach to reduce both vulnerabilities to some degree would be to concentrate the sun's rays with a focusing optical collec-

tor. The collector would still be vulnerable, but if the system efficiency could be improved, then the area of the collector would be smaller than equivalent ordinary solar cell arrays.

There are two other ways to convert the energy from solar collectors into electricity. One is to use solar thermal energy to drive a conventional thermodynamic heat engine. The other is to focus sunlight on more radiation-resistant and higher-efficiency photovoltaic cells such as gallium arsenide. Depending on the temperature of the working fluid in a thermodynamic heat engine cycle, efficiencies of 20 percent to 30 percent might be achieved. Gallium arsenide cells have shown up to 24 percent efficiency in the laboratory, so 20 percent efficiency in space may be reasonable. Thus, either technology could cut the required collector area in half compared to conventional solar cells, or 75 m^2 per 20-kW output. Neither approach has been tested in space, but NASA is pursuing both for future space applications.

Nuclear Energy

Nuclear energy has also been used in space. There are two types of nuclear energy sources: radioactive isotope generators that convert heat from radioactive decay to electricity, and nuclear fission reactors. Both have flown in space, but the radioactive isotope generator is more common.

Both radioactive decay and a controlled fission reaction produce heat as the intermediate energy form. This heat can be converted into electricity by static or dynamic means. A static power source produces electricity directly from heat without any moving parts, using either thermoelectric or thermionic converters. These converters generate direct current between two terminals as long as heat is supplied to the device. The efficiency and total practical power levels are low, but for applications of less than 500 W, the advantage of no moving parts makes a radioisotope thermoelectric generator (RTG) a primary candidate for small spacecraft.

To produce more than 500 W, a radioisotope source could be coupled to a dynamic heat engine. One dynamic isotope power system (DIPS) with 2 to 5 kW output has been ground-tested. This system weighs 215 kg. However, the U.S. production capacity for radioactive isotopes would limit the number of satellites that could be powered by DIPS.

BMD satellites needing more than 5 to 10 kW of power might carry a more powerful nuclear fission reactor. Static thermoelectric converters would still convert the heat to electricity. This is the approach proposed for the SP-100 space power program, the goal of which is to develop elements of a system to provide power over the range of 10 to 1,000 kW. The Departments of Defense and Energy and NASA are producing a reference design incorporating these elements to produce a 100-kW test reactor.[71] This is the major focus for the next generation of space power systems.

The SP-100 reactor, as currently designed, would use 360 kg of highly enriched uranium nitride fuel with liquid lithium cooling operating at 1,350° K. This heat would be conducted to 200,000 to 300,000 individual thermoelectric elements which would produce 100 kW of electricity. The overall efficiency of the system would be about 4 percent, which would entail the disposal of 2.4 MW of waste heat. Large fins heated to 800° K would radiate this heat into space.

The SP-100 program faces numerous challenges. In addition to being the hottest running reactor ever built, the SP-100 would be the first space system to:

- use uranium nitride fuel,
- be cooled by liquid lithium,
- use strong refractory metals to contain the primary coolant,
- have to start up with its coolant frozen,
- have two independent control mechanisms (for safety), and
- use electronic semiconductors under such intense heat and radiation stress.[72]

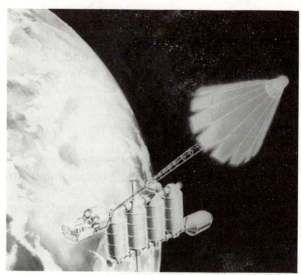

Photo Credit: U.S. Department of Defense

Artist's concept of a space-based nuclear power source.—The painting depicts a 100-kilowatt nuclear power source scheduled for demonstration in space in the 1990s. It is known as SP-100 and is a joint effort of the Defense Advanced Research Projects Agency, the Department of Energy, and the National Aeronautics and Space Administration.

The estimated mass of the SP-100 is 3,000 kg, or a specific mass of 30 kg/kW. Original plans called for building a ground-test prototype SP-100 based on the 100-kW design by 1991, with a flight test several years later. Subsequently a 300-kW design was considered which would have pushed initial hardware toward 1993, but current schedules are fluid due to uncertain funding.

To produce power levels in excess of a few hundred kW, one would have to take the next step in the evolution of space nuclear power systems: a nuclear reactor coupled through a dynamic heat engine to an electrical generator. In principle, large reactors in space could generate hundreds of MW, satisfying the most stressing BMD average power demands.

A "multimegawatt," or MMW, project has begun to study some of the fundamental issues raised by large reactors, including daunting engineering challenges such as high temperature waste heat disposal in space, safety in launch, operation, and decommissioning. These large nuclear systems might have to be

[71]Original SDIO plans called for designing a 300 KW system, but as of this writing the goal has been reduced to 100 KW.

[72]See Eliot Marshall, "DOE's Way-out Reactors," *Science*, 231:1359, March 21, 1986.

operated "open-cycle," requiring much "fuel" in the form of cooling gas to dispose of excess heat. At this writing the MMW project is in the conceptual phase with no well-defined research program. Multi-megawatt nuclear reactors in space would have to be considered a 20-to-30 year project.

In summary, space nuclear power systems would require extensive development to achieve reliable space operation at the 100-300 kW level by the mid-to-late 1990s. Given current engineering and budget uncertainties, development of megawatt-class nuclear power systems for space cannot be projected until well into the 21st century.

Chemical Energy

Satellites frequently employ chemical energy in the form of batteries, fuel cells, and turbogenerators. Batteries would be too heavy for most BMD applications, except possibly for pop-up systems with very short engagement times. Fuel cells, which derive their power by combining, e.g., hydrogen and oxygen, are under active consideration for driving the accelerators of NPB weapons.

For the short bursts of MMW power needed by some BMD weapons, an electrical generator driven by a rocket engine (e.g., burning liquid hydrogen and liquid oxygen) might be the only available technology in the foreseeable future. The Space Shuttle main engine (SSME) develops about 10 GW of flow power, which could generate 5 GW of electrical energy if it could be coupled to a turboalternator. Alternatively, rocket exhaust could, in principle, be converted to electricity by magnetohydrodynamics (MHD).

The engineering challenges of using rocket engines to produce electrical power on board a BMD satellite are posed not only by the generator itself, but by its effects on other components such as sensors, electronics, and weapons. Two counter-rotating and counter-thrusting rockets would probably be essential to cancel torque and thrust. Even then, sensors and weapons-aiming devices would have to be isolated from vibration. Similarly, the effluent from the rocket engines must not interfere with sensors or weapon beam propagation, and electrical noise must not interfere with communication or data processing electronics.

It might be necessary to place rocket engines and power generators on separate platforms hundreds or a few thousands of meters away to achieve the necessary isolation, transmitting power by cable or microwaves. This method, however, would raise vulnerability issues, presenting to the adversary an additional target and a vulnerable umbilical cord.

Power Conditioning

Power conditioning is matching the electrical characteristics of a power source with those required by the load. A generator might produce a continuous flow of electrical current, but a load, such as railgun firing, would require a series of very high-current pulses. Power conditioning equipment would convert the continuous flow into pulses.

In some cases the projected power conditioning device requirements exceed existing capabilities by two or three orders of magnitude, even for ground-based experiments. In many areas, no space-qualified hardware exists at any power level. Pulsed power technology development efforts are underway in capacitive and inductive energy storage, closing and opening switches, transformers, RF sources, AC-DC converters, and ultra high-voltage techniques and components.

Particle accelerators that drive the FEL and the NPB use RF power. Railgun requirements would present the greatest challenge: very short (millisecond) pulses of current several times a second. Many electrical components would have to be developed to produce the proper current pulses for a railgun.

A homopolar generator combined with an inductor and opening switch is now the primary candidate for the generation of very short pulses. A homopolar generator is a rotating machine that stores kinetic energy in a rotating armature. At the time of railgun firing, brushes would fall unto the armature, extracting much of its energy in a fraction of a second. This would result in a sudden jerk in the torque of the generator, which would disturb a spacecraft unless compensated by a balanced homopolar generator rotating in the opposite direction.

The brushes would also wear out, which raises questions about the durability of a rail-gun with high repetition rates. Very fast switches would be essential. These switches would have to be light enough to move rapidly, but heavy enough to handle the extraordinarily high currents.

Researchers at the University of Texas have investigated one advanced modification to the homopolar generator. They have replaced brushes and switches with inductive switches in a ''compulsator,'' a generator which produces a string of pulses. By replacing non-current carrying iron with graphite-epoxy composites, these compulsators could be much lighter than the homopolar generators.

While space applications drive power development requirements, emerging ground-based defensive systems would also stress existing power sources. Ground-based BMD elements might require diesel and turbine driven electric generators and MHD generators for mobile applications. A fixed-site system such as the FEL might draw on the commercial utility grid, dedicated power plants, or superconducting magnetic energy storage (SMES). The electrical utility grid could meet peacetime housekeeping power needs and could keep a storage system charged, but, due to its extreme vulnerability to precursor attack, could not be relied on to supply power during a battle. Therefore, a site-secure MMW power system would probably be necessary.

Superconducting magnetic energy storage is a prime candidate for ground-based energy storage; an SMES system would be a large, underground superconducting coil with continuous current flow. The science of SMES is well established, but engineering development remains.

Recent discoveries of high-temperature superconductors could have an impact on future power supplies and pulse conditioning systems. Given the likely initial cost of manufacturing exotic superconducting materials and the probable limits on total current, their first applications will probably be in smaller devices such as electronics, computers, and sensor systems. But if:

- scientists could synthesize high temperature superconducting materials able to carry very large currents; and
- engineers could develop techniques to manufacture those materials on a large scale suitable for large magnetic coils, RF power generators, accelerator cavity walls, the rails of electromagnetic launchers, etc.;

then superconductors could substantially reduce the power demand. Efficiency of the power source and power conditioning networks could also be improved. High temperature superconductors would be particularly attractive in space, where relatively cold temperatures can be maintained by radiation cooling.

COMMUNICATION TECHNOLOGY

Communication would be the nervous system of any BMD system. A phase-one defense would include hundreds of space-based components, separated by thousands of kilometers, for boost and post-boost interception. A second-phase BMD system would include many tens of sensors in high orbits and hundreds to several thousands of weapons platforms in low-Earth orbits.

Three fundamental communication paths would link these space assets: ground to space, space to space, and space to ground. Ground command centers would at least initiate the battle; they would also receive updates on equipment status and sensor data in peacetime and as the battle developed.

The attributes of an effective communication system would include:

- adequate bandwidth and range,
- reliability,
- tolerance of component damage,
- security from interception or take-over,
- tolerance of nuclear effects, and
- jam- or spoof-resistance.

The bandwidths, or frequency space available, from links in the millimeter-wave bands would be adequate for most near-term BMD functions. The most demanding element would be the boost surveillance and tracking system (BSTS) satellite, with perhaps a 1-million-bit-per-second data rate. Second-phase elements such as a space surveillance and tracking system (SSTS) sensor satellite might operate at much higher rates, up to 20 million bits per second, while battle management might take 50 or more million bits per second of information flow. Various additional data for synchronization signals would have to be communicated. Transmission bandwidths might have to be very large—perhaps 1-10 gigahertz (GHz) —to reduce the chances of jamming.

The communication system must be durable and survivable even if some nodes fail due to natural or enemy action. Redundant links in a coupled network might assure that messages and data got through even if some satellites were destroyed. Tying together a vast BMD space network would be challenging, especially given that the satellites in low-Earth orbit would constantly change relative positions.

One key issue for BMD communications is jamming by a determined adversary. Successfully disrupting communications would completely negate a BMD system that relied on sensors and command and control nodes separated from weapons platforms by tens of thousands of km. Jammers could be developed, deployed, and even operated in peacetime with little risk of stimulating hostile counteraction.

Space-to-ground communication links would be particularly vulnerable. Ground-based, ship-based or airborne high-power jammers might block the flow of information to satellites. In wartime, nuclear explosions could disrupt the propagation of RF waves. Ground-based receivers would also be susceptible to direct attack. Even space-based communications would be susceptible to jamming.

Recently there have been two primary SDI candidates for BMD communication links in space: laser links and 60-GHz links. A 60-GHz system once seemed to promise a more jam-resistant channel for space-to-space communications, since the atmosphere would absorb enough 60-GHz energy to reduce the threat of ground-based jammers. Recent analyses, however, indicate that space- and air-based jammers may limit the effectiveness of 60-GHz links.

60-GHz Communication Links

The operating frequencies of space communication systems have been steadily increasing. For example, the Milstar communications satellite will use the extremely high frequency (EHF) band with a 44-GHz ground-to-space uplink and a 20-GHz downlink. These high frequencies allow very wide bandwidth (1 GHz in the case of Milstar) for high data transmission rates, but also for more secure communications through wide-band-modulation and frequency-hopping anti-jamming techniques.

For space-to-space links, BMD designers are considering even higher frequencies—around 60 GHz. This band includes many oxygen absorption lines. It would be very difficult for ground-based jammers to interfere with 60-GHz communications between, for example, a BSTS early warning satellite and SBI CVs: oxygen in the atmosphere would absorb the jamming energy.

Pre-positioned jammer satellites, or possibly rocket-borne jammers launched with an attack, might still interfere with 60-GHz channels. The main beam of radiation from a 60-GHz transmitter is relatively narrow, making it difficult for an adversary to blind the system from the main lobe: the enemy jammer transmitter would have to be located very close to the BMD satellite broadcasting its message. But a 60-GHz receiver would also pick up some energy from the "sidelobes" and even some from the opposite side of the receiver (the "backlobes"). While a receiver may be 10,000 to 100,000 times less sensitive to energy from these sidelobes than from the main lobe, it must be extremely sensitive to pick up signals from a low-Earth orbit satellite tens of thousands of km away.

At high-Earth orbit, a near-by jammer with only a few hundred watts of power could overwhelm a much more powerful 60-GHz system on a sensor satellite. This neighbor might masquerade as an ordinary communications satellite in peacetime. In wartime, it could aim its antenna at the BSTS and jam the channel. The countermeasure would be to station the BSTS out of standard communications satellite orbits.

Laser Communication Links

The low-power diode laser offers the possibility of extremely wideband, highly directional, and, therefore, very jam-proof communications. The MIT Lincoln Laboratory has designed a 220 megabit-per-second (Mbs) communication link that would need just 30 milliwatts of laser power from a gallium aluminum arsenide (GaAlAs) light emitting diode (LED) to reach across the diameter of the geosynchronous orbit (about 84,000 km). The receiver, using heterodyne detection,[73] could pull

in a signal of just 10 picowatts (10^{-11} W) power. A 20-cm mirror on the transmitter would direct the laser beam to an intended receiver.

The high directionality of narrow laser beams also complicates operation. A wide-angle antenna could flood the receiver area with signal, even sending the same message to many receivers in the area at one time. A narrow laser beam must be carefully aimed at each satellite. This would require mechanical mirrors or other beam-steering optics, as well as software to keep track of all friendly satellites and to guide the optical beam to the right satellite. The lifetime of a laser source and an agile optical system may be relatively short for the first few generations of laser communication systems.

A laser communication system, as presently designed, would require up to eight minutes to establish a heterodyne link between a transmitter and a receiver. Plans call for reducing this acquisition time to one minute. With a very narrow laser beam, even minute motions of the transmitter platform could cause a momentary loss of coupling, forcing a delay to reacquire the signal.

While laser links might provide jam-proof communications between space-based assets of a BMD system, laser communications to the ground would have to overcome weather limitations. One approach would use multiple receivers dispersed to assure one or more clear weather sites at all times. Alternatively, one could envisage an airborne relay station, particularly in time of crisis.

---

[73]The common "heterodyne" radio receiver includes a local oscillator which generates a frequency that is combined or "mixed" with the incoming radio signal. This process of "mixing" the local oscillator signal with the received signal improves the ability to detect a weak signal buried in noise, and reduces

interference. A laser heterodyne receiver would include its own laser source, which would be "mixed" at the surface of a light detector with the weak light signal from a distant laser transmitter.

SPACE TRANSPORTATION

Reasonable extensions of current U.S. space transportation capability might launch the tens of sensor satellites envisaged by some BMD architectures, but entirely new space

launch capabilities would be necessary to lift several hundred to over one thousand carrier vehicles and their cargoes of thousands to tens of thousands of kinetic kill missiles into space in a reasonable period of time. Therefore space launch capability would have to evolve along with phase-one and phase-two weapon systems to assure the United States—and to persuade the Soviet Union—that a defense-dominated world would be feasible and enduring.

Space Transportation Requirements

Space-based interceptors and their carrier satellites would dominate initial space deployment weights. Assuming that a phase-one deployment would include a few hundred CVs and a few thousand SBIs based on the "state-of-the-art" rockets described above, then total launch weight requirements might be in the range of 1 million to 2 million kg.

The range of weights estimated by SDI system architects for a more advanced phase varied from 7.2 to 18.6 million kg. The large range of weight estimates reflects differences in architectures, and particularly differences in survivability measures. Several contractors indicated that survivability measures—such as shielding, decoys, proliferation, and fuel for maneuvering—would increase weight by a factor of about three. One could infer that the heavier designs might be more survivable.

Additional space transportation would be required over time for servicing, refueling, or replacement of failed components. One unresolved issue is how best to maintain this fleet of orbiting battle stations: by originally including redundant components such as interceptor missiles on each satellite, by complete replacement of defective satellites, by on-orbit servicing, or by some combination of the above. One contractor estimated, for example, that it would take 35 interceptor missiles on each battle station to assure 20 live missiles after 10 years, with the attrition due entirely to natural component failures.

Soviet countermeasures might drive up weight requirements substantially in later years. Increased Soviet ICBM deployments might be countered with more SBI platforms. Defense suppression threats such as direct-ascent ASATs might be countered in part by proliferation of SBI battle stations or by other heavy countermeasures. Advanced decoys dispersed during the post-boost phase of missile flight might require some type of interactive discrimination system in space. Reduced Soviet booster burn times would eventually impel a shift to DEW. Deploying these countermeasures would necessitate additional space transportation capability. Directed-energy weapon components in particular would probably be very heavy. The range of SDI system architects' estimates for some far-term systems was from 40 million to 80 million kg.

Space Transportation Alternatives

There seem to be two fundamental options for lifting the postulated BMD hardware into space: use derivatives of existing space transportation systems; or design, test, and build a new generation space transportation system. The first option might be very costly; the second might postpone substantial space-based BMD deployment into the 21st century.

Some BMD advocates outside the SDIO have suggested that existing United States space launch systems might be adequate for an initial space-based BMD deployment in the early 1990s. But the existing United States space launch capability is limited in vehicle inventory, payload capacity per launch, cost, launch rate, and launching facilities. As shown in table 5-10, today's total inventory of U.S. rockets could lift about 0.27 million kg into low-Earth orbit (180 km) at the inclination angle of the launch site (28.5° for the Kennedy Space Center in Florida).[74]

The bulk of early SBI deployments would have to be launched into near-polar orbits from Vandenberg AFB, which would now only be possible for the 6 remaining Titan 34D vehicles with a combined lift capacity of 75,000 kg.

---

[74]Missile launch capacity is usually specified in terms of the payload which can be lifted into direct East-West flight at an altitude of 180 km, which produces an orbit inclined at the latitude of the launch point. Extra propellant is required to lift the payload to higher inclinations or to higher altitudes. Proposed BMD weapons systems would require higher inclinations (70° to 85°) and higher altitudes (600 to 1,000 km), which translates into lower payload capacity.

This would correspond to about 6 percent of the initial phase-one BMD space deployment requirements. Some have suggested refurbishing Titan-IIs, which have been retired from the ICBM fleet. If all 69 Titan-IIs were refurbished, then the United States could lift another 130,000 kg into polar orbit, or another 11 percent of the near-term BMD needs.

The rate of missile launch might also be limited by the existing space transportation infrastructure. Launching one Shuttle now takes a minimum of 580 hours at the Kennedy Space Center (and might take about 800 hours at Vandenberg AFB[75]), limiting potential launches to one per month or less from each complex. After the Shuttle accident, NASA estimated that 12 to 16 flights per year would be reasonable. Clearly 16 launches per year would not be sufficient for BMD deployment.[76]

Several aerospace companies have proposed building launch vehicles with increased lift capacity to meet SDI, DoD, and civilian space transportation demands. Many of these vehicles would be derived from various Shuttle or

Titan predecessors, such as the Titan-4, included in table 5-10. Twenty-three Titan-4s will be built by 1988, but these have only marginally increased lift capacity. A major increase in lift capacity to the 40,000 to 50,000 kg range would be required for an effective space-based BMD system. Even for a phase-one system, far more would be needed by the mid-1990s. Both SDIO and Air Force officials have called for a new space transportation system that is not a derivative of existing technology.

Four aerospace companies analyzed various space transportation options under joint Air Force/NASA/SDIO direction. The Space Transportation Architecture Study (STAS) compared manned v. unmanned vehicles, horizontal v. vertical take-off, single v. 2-stage rockets, and various combinations of reusable v. expendable components.[77] The Air Force, after reviewing the initial STAS work, appears to be leaning toward a decision that the BMD deployment should use an unmanned, expendable, 2-stage heavy-lift launch vehicle (now called the ALS or advanced launch system).[78]

---

[75]Completion of the Vandenberg Shuttle launch site SLC-6 has been postponed until 1992.

[76]Assuming 16 Shuttle launches per year with 9,000 kg payload to low polar orbit, it would take between 8 to 12 years to deploy a phase-one BMD system and 48 to 125 years to deploy a phase-two system weighing 7 to 18 million kilograms.

[77]The Space Transportation Architecture Study (STAS) was a joint Air Force/NASA/SDIO study on future space transportation systems. The Air Force Systems Division contracted with Rockwell and Boeing, while NASA employed General Dynamics and Martin Marietta to analyze U.S. civilian and military space requirements and possible alternatives to satisfy them.

[78]The name HLLV (heavy lift launch vehicle) was changed to ALS in April 1987.

Table 5-10.—Current U.S. Space Launch Inventory[a]

	Inventory quantity	Payload per vehicle (thousands of kg)		
		LEO (180 km)	Polar (180 km)	Geo
Shuttle	3	25	15	Centaur-G:4.5 IUS: 2.3
Titan 34D	6	15.3	12.5	IUS: 1.8
Titan-4[b]	(23)	17.7	14.5	Centaur-G:4.6 IUS: 2.4
Titan II-SLV	(13)[c]	3.6	1.9	
Delta	8	2.9		
Delta (MLV)	(7)	4		1.5
Atlas	13	6		
Scout	21	.26		
(ALS)[d]	?	(50-70)	(40-55)	

[a]Parentheses indicate future systems.
[b]The Titan-4 or the Complementary Expendable Launch Vehicle (CELV) is the latest in the line of Titan missile configurations; 23 have been ordered.
[c]The Titan II-SLVs are being refurbished from the ICBM inventory. The first Titan-II may be available by 1989. An additional 56 Titan II could be refurbished from the retired ICBM fleet.
[d]The Advanced Launch System is proposed to deploy the bulk of the BMD space components.

SOURCE: Office of Technology Assessment, 1988.

An interim STAS study suggested that such a vehicle would have to evolve to a partially reusable system to meet SDIO cost reduction goals. The STAS contractors projected that development of a heavy-lift unmanned vehicle would require about 12 years, although at least one aerospace company estimates that an ALS could be developed in 6 years. If the original 12-year estimate is correct, significant space deployment of a BMD system could not begin until the turn of the century even if the weapon systems were ready earlier. If the 6-year estimate were correct, then initial deployment could begin by 1994.

To deploy space-based assets earlier, SDIO has suggested a two-tier level program: build part of an ALS by the mid-1990s, but design this system to evolve into the long-range system by the year 2000. The initial system would include some of the advanced features of the heavy-lift launch vehicle concepts outlined by STAS, but would not have a fly-back booster and would not meet the SDIO cost goals of $300 to $600 per kilogram. The interim goal would be to reduce the current costs of $3,000-$6,000 per kilogram to $1,000-$2,000. Building a space transportation system while trying to meet these two goals simultaneously could be risky. Compromises might be required either to meet the early deployment date or to meet the long-term cost and launch rate goals.

The estimated launch rate for a fully developed ALS vehicle is about once per month per launch complex.[79] Assuming a 40,000-kg payload to useful BMD orbits, then between 30 and 45 successful flights would be required for a phase-one BMD deployment and from 180 to 460 flights for a much larger second phase. Allocating 5 years to deploy the latter system, the United States would need to build three to eight new launch facilities.[80]

Photo credit: U.S. Department of Defense, Strategic Defense Initiative Organization

Advanced launch system (ALS).—Large-scale deployment of space-based interceptors (SBI) or other weapons in space will require a dramatic expansion of U.S. space-launch capabilities. Various proposals, including a Shuttle-derived, unmanned launch vehicle such as this have been under consideration by the Air Force, NASA, and the SDIO.

Figure 5-13 presents one very optimistic scenario which might lead to space launch facilities adequate for proposed second-phase BMD

---

[79]The current maximum launch rate for Titans is three per year from each pad, which might be increased to five per year. Further increases are unlikely because the Titans are assembled on-site. This is one of the reasons an entirely new space launch system would be needed to meet the SDI launch rates.

[80]The United States now has four launch pads for Titan-class boosters, two on the east coast and two on the west coast. One west coast pad is being modified to handle the CELV. Since

SBIs would have to be launched from Vandenberg to reach near-polar orbits, all early deployments would have to be from one pad. The estimated time to build a new launch pad complex is 7 to 10 years.

Figure 5-13a.—Annual Space Launch Capacity
(near polar orbits at 800 km)

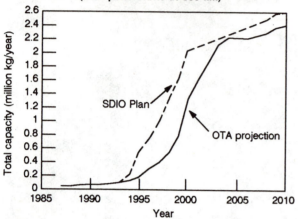

This is one possible scenario to achieve the 2 million kg per year space launch capability into near-polar orbits required for an intermediate ballistic missile defense system. This system could conceivably reach this goal by the year 2003, assuming that three new launch pads were built at Vandenberg AFB, and the proposed Heavy Lift Launch Vehicle (HLLV)/Advanced Launch System (ALS) could be developed, flight tested, and ready for initial service with 30,000 kg lift capacity by 1994. This would be 5 years ahead of the schedule initially suggested by the Space Transportation Architecture Study (STAS). The HLLV is further assumed to evolve into a 44,000 kg capability by the year 2000, without any engineering delays. The SDIO launch goals as of early 1987 are shown for comparison.

SOURCE: Office of Technology Assessment, 1988.

Table 5-11.—Space Transportation

Vehicle capacity to 800 km, high inclination: (thousands of kilograms)	
CELV (Titan-4)	11.5
Titan 34D	10
Early HLLV	30 (1995-2000)
Final HLLV	44 (2000+)

Launch pads:	4-East: (34D/CEL)	SLC-6 (HLLV)	New (HLLV)	New (HLLV)	New (HLLV)	Total annual launch capacity (M kg)
Year:						
1985	3					0.03
1986	3					0.03
1987	3					0.03
1988	3					0.03
1989	4					0.05
1990	4					0.05
1991	5					0.06
1992	5					0.06
1993	6					0.07
1994	6	1				0.10
1995	7	2				0.14
1996	7	6				0.26
1997	8	8	1			0.36
1998	8	10	2	2		0.51
1999	8	12	4	4	2	0.75
2000	8	12	6	6	4	1.32
2001	8	12	8	8	6	1.59
2002	8	12	10	10	8	1.85
2003	8	12	12	12	10	2.12
2004	8	12	12	12	12	2.20
2005	8	12	12	12	12	2.20
2006	8	12	12	12	12	2.20
2007	8	12	13	12	12	2.25
2008	8	12	13	13	12	2.29
2009	8	12	14	13	13	2.38
2010	8	12	14	14	13	2.42

Tabular data for figure 3-13a.

SOURCE: Office of Technology Assessment, 1988.

systems by 2000-2005. This scenario assumes that the SDIO two-level space transportation development approach would be successful: an interim ALS vehicle, with a 30,000 kg capability to near-polar orbits, would be available by 1994; a more advanced ALS would come on line in 2000 with 44,000 kg capacity. Three new launch pads would be built (although there is no room for three new pads at Vandenberg AFB, the only existing site in the contiguous United States with near-polar orbit capability).

Assuming approval to proceed with the new launch system in 1988, the first flights of the new ALS would begin in 1994, using the refurbished SLC-6 launch pad at Vandenberg, built originally for the Space Shuttle. The three new pads would become operational in 1997, 1998, and 1999. Flights would be phased in at each site, increasing up to 12 flights per year per pad. With these assumptions, the SDIO goal

of 2 to 2.5 million kg per year could be achieved by 2003.

If the United States were to operate 10 launch facilities, each with one ALS launch per month, then it would take about 10 years to orbit the 50 million kg estimated for a far-term, third-phase system.[81] If political or strategic considerations (such as transition stability) would not allow as long as 10 years to deploy, then the United States would have perhaps three choices:

1. develop another new vehicle with lift capacity above 50,000 kg to 800-km, high inclination orbits;
2. build and operate more than ten ALS launch facilities simultaneously; or

[81]The 50 million kg assumes the low end of the 40 to 80 million kg estimated above for phase three with space-based lasers. A successful ground-based laser system could reduce this estimate by about 15 million kg, or 25 to 65 million kg for a total phase-three constellation.

3. improve launch operations to reduce turn-around time below 30 days per pad.

The country would have to expand booster manufacturing capacity to meet this demand for up to 120 launches per year. Historically, Titan production lines completed up to 20 missiles per year, and Martin Marietta has estimated that it could easily produce 14 of the Titan class per year with existing facilities.[82]

Space Transportation Cost Reduction

Identifying 42 technologies related to space transportation, the STAS listed several where research might lead to reduced operating costs (it emphasized the first three as offering especially high leverage for cost reduction):

- lightweight materials,
- expert systems and automated programming to cut software costs,
- better organization,
- reducing dry weights substantially,
- better ground facilities,
- higher performance engines,
- fault-tolerant avionics,
- reusability of major components, and
- better mating of spacecraft to launch vehicle for reduced ground costs.

[82]This would include 5 CELVs, 6 Titan IIs, and 3 Titan 34Ds.

The operating (as opposed to life-cycle) costs of space transportation are currently estimated at $3,300 to $6,000 per kilogram of payload to low-Earth orbit, and $22,000 to $60,000 per kilogram to geosynchronous orbit. At that rate, it would cost $24 billion to $200 billion to launch a phase-two BMD system, and $140 billion to $450 billion for a responsive phase-three deployment, based on the constellation weights estimated by various SDIO system architects. The SDIO has set a goal of reducing launch operating costs by a factor of 10.

Operating costs are estimated at about one third of the total *life-cycle* costs of a space transportation system. Based on current operating costs, total life-cycle costs for transporting a phase-two BMD system into space might be $72 billion to $600 billion; for phase three, the costs might range from $420 billion to $1.35 trillion. Reaching the goal of reducing operating costs by a factor of 10 would reduce life-cycle costs for space transportation by only 30 percent. Assuming that this percentage would be valid for a new space transportation system, and assuming a 10 to 1 reduction in operating costs only, then the total life-cycle costs for space transportation might be $50 billion to $420 billion for a phase-two deployment and $290 billion to $900 billion for a phase-three deployment. **Clearly the other kinds of costs for space transportation would have to be reduced along with the operating costs.**

CONCLUSIONS

Weapon Technology Conclusions

Phase One

Kinetic Energy Weapons.—KEWs (or else the kinds of nuclear-armed missiles developed for BMD in the 1960s) would most likely be the only BMD weapons available for deployment in this century and possibly the first decade of the 21st century. Several varieties of non-nuclear, hit-to-kill KEW form the backbone of most near- and intermediate-term SDI architecture proposals. Considering the steady evolution of rockets and "smart weapon" homing sensors

used in previous military systems, it seems likely that these KEWs could have a high probability of being able to destroy individual targets typical of the current Soviet ICBM force by the early to mid-1990s. The key unresolved issue is whether a robust, survivable, integrated system could be designed, built, tested, and deployed to intercept—in the face of likely countermeasures—a sizeable fraction of evolving Soviet nuclear weapons.

Space-Based Interceptors.—SBIs deployed in the mid to late 1990s could probably destroy some Soviet ICBMs in their boost phase. The key issue is whether the weight of the SBI projectiles could be reduced before Soviet booster burn times could be shortened, given that existing SS-24 and SS-25 boosters would already stress projected SBI constellations. The probability of post-boost vehicle (PBV) kills is lower due to the smaller PBV size and IR signal, but SBIs might still achieve some success against current PBVs by the mid to late 1990s.

Exo-atmospheric Reentry Interceptor System.—The ERIS, which has evolved from previous missiles, could probably be built by the early to mid-1990s to attack objects in late midcourse. The key unknown is the method of tracking and discriminating RVs from decoys. Existing radar sensors are highly vulnerable, the SSTS space-based IR sensor probably would not be available until the late 1990s to early 2000s, and the AOS airborne sensor would have limited endurance and range. This would leave either new radars or some type of pop-up, rocket-borne IR probe, which have apparently received little development effort until recently. Given the uncertainty in sensors suitable for the ERIS system, its role would probably be confined to very late midcourse interceptions and it might have limited BMD effectiveness until the late 1990s.

Phase Two

High Endo-atmospheric Defense Interceptor.—The HEDI could probably be brought to operational status as soon as the mid-1990s. To overcome the unique HEDI window heating problem, the HEDI on-board homing IR sensor needs more development than its ERIS cousin. But the HEDI system does not depend on long-range sensors to achieve its mission within the atmosphere. The HEDI could probably provide some local area defense of hardened targets by the mid-1990s against non-MaRVed RVs.[83] HEDI performance against MaRVed RVs appears questionable.

SBIs against Reentry Vehicles.—The probability that SBIs would kill RVs in the mid-course is low until the next century, given the difficulty in detecting and tracking many small, cool RVs in the presence of decoys, and given uncertainties in the SSTS sensor and battle management programs.

Phase Three

Directed-Energy Weapons.—It is unlikely that any DEW system could be highly effective before 2010 to 2015 at the earliest. No directed energy weapon is within a factor of 10,000 of the brightness necessary to destroy responsively designed Soviet nuclear weapons. (OTA has not had the opportunity to review recent SDIO suggestions for "entry level" DEWs of more modest capability. SDIO contends that effective space-based lasers of one to two orders of magnitude less than that needed for a responsive threat could be developed much sooner.) At least another decade of research would likely be needed to support a decision whether any DEW could form the basis for an affordable and highly effective ballistic missile defense. Further, it is likely to take at least another decade to manufacture, test, and launch the large number of satellite battle stations necessary for highly effective BMD. Thus, barring dramatic changes in weapon and space launch development and procurement practices, a highly effective DEW system is unlikely before 2010 to 2015 at the earliest.

Neutral Particle Beam.—The NPB, under development initially as an interactive discriminator, is the most promising mid-course DEW.[84] Shielding RVs against penetrating particle beams, as opposed to lasers, appears prohibitive for energies above 200-MeV. Although laboratory neutral particle beams are still about 10,000 times less bright than that needed for sure electronics kills of RVs in space, the necessary scaling in power and reduction in beam divergence appears feasible, if challenging.

---

[83]"MaRV" refers to maneuvering reentry vehicles, or RVs which can change their course after reentering the atmosphere to improve accuracy or to avoid defensive interceptors.

[84]The NPB would have virtually no boost phase capability against advanced "responsive" boosters since particle beams cannot penetrate below about 150 kilometers altitude.

However, as discussed in chapter 4 under the topic of NPB interactive discrimination, it is unlikely that engineering issues could be resolved before the late 1990s, which would most likely postpone deployment and effective system operation to at least 2010-2015.

Free Electron Laser.—The free electron laser (FEL) is one of the more promising BMD DEW weapon candidates. The FEL is in the research phase, with several outstanding physics issues and many engineering issues to be resolved. Even if powerful lasers could be built, the high power optics to rapidly and accurately steer laser beams from one target to the next could limit system performance. Although the basic system concept for an FEL weapon is well developed, it is too early to predict BMD performance with any certainty.

Chemical Laser.—There are too many uncertainties to project BMD performance for the chemically pumped hydrogen fluoride (HF) laser. The HF laser has been demonstrated at relatively high power levels on the ground, although still 100,000 times less bright than that needed for BMD against a responsive threat. Scaling to weapons-level brightness would require coherent combination of large laser beams, which remains a fundamental issue. This, coupled with the relatively long wavelength (2.8 micron region), make the HF laser less attractive for advanced BMD than the FEL.

Electromagnetic Launcher.—There are too many uncertainties in the EML or railgun program to project any significant BMD capabilities at this time.

Space Power Conclusions

Phase One

Power Requirements.—Nuclear power would be required for most BMD spacecraft, both to provide the necessary power levels for station-keeping, and to avoid the vulnerability of large solar panels or solar collectors.

Dynamic Isotope Power System.—The DIPS, which has been ground-tested in the 2 to 5 kW range, should be adequate and available by the mid to late 1990s, in time for early BSTS-type sensors.

Phase Two

Nuclear Reactors.—Adequate space power may not be available for SSTS or weapon platforms with ladars before the year 2000. For BMD satellites that require much more than 10 kW of power the SP-100 nuclear reactor/thermoelectric technology would have to be developed. This is a high-risk technology, with space-qualified hardware not expected before the late 1990s to early 2000s.

Phase Three

Chemical Power.—Chemically driven energy sources (liquid oxygen and liquid hydrogen driving turbogenerators or fuel cells) could probably be available for burst powers of MW up to GW to drive weapons for hundreds of seconds by 2000-2005.

Power for Electromagnetic Launchers.—High-current pulse generators for electromagnetic launchers (EML) would require extensive development and engineering, and would most likely delay any EML deployments well into the 21st century.

High-Temperature Superconductors.—Research on high-temperature superconductors suggests exciting possibilities in terms of reducing the space power requirements and improving power generation and conditioning efficiencies. At this stage of laboratory discovery, however, it is too early to predict whether or when practical, high current superconductors could affect BMD systems.

Space Communications Conclusion

Laser communications may be needed for space-to-space and ground-to-space links to overcome the vulnerability of 60-GHz links to jamming from nearby satellites. Wide-band laser communications should be feasible by the mid-1990s, but the engineering for an agile beam steering system would be challenging.

Space Transportation Conclusions

Phase One

Mid-1990s Deployments.—Extrapolating reasonable extensions of existing space transportation facilities suggests that a limited-effectiveness, phase-one BMD system begun in the mid-1990s could not be fully deployed in fewer than 8 years.[85] Assuming that the hardware could be built to start deployment in 1994, the system would not be fully deployed until 2002. A more ambitious launcher-development program and a high degree of success in bringing payload weights down might shorten that period.

Phase Two

New Space Transportation System.—A fully new space transportation system would be required to lift the space assets of a "phase-two" BMD system. This system would have to include a vehicle with heavier lift capability (40,000 to 50,000 kg v. 5,000 kg for the Titan-4), faster launch rates (12 per year v. 3 per year per pad), and more launch pads (4 v. 1).

Optimistic Assumptions.—Even under very optimistic assumptions,[86] **the new space transportation system would be unlikely to reach the necessary annual lift requirements for a large-scale, second-phase BMD until 2000-2005, with full phase-two deployment completed in the 2008-2014 period.**

Phase Three

Ultimate DEW Systems.—**It might take 20 to 35 years of continuous launches to fully deploy far-term, phase-three BMD space assets designed to counter with very high effectiveness an advanced, "responsive," Soviet missile threat.** This estimate assumes deployment of the proposed ALS space transportation system and the kind of advanced space-based laser constellation suggested by SDI system architects. A set of ground-based laser installations could reduce the space launch deployment time estimate to 12-25 years.

---

[85]This assumes that two launch pads at Vandenberg AFB, 4-East and the SLC-6 pad intended for the Shuttle, are modified to handle the new Titan-4 complementary expendable launch vehicle (CELV), and the launch rates are increased from three Titans per year per pad up to six per year.

[86]This assumes that the SDIO bifurcated goal is met: a revolutionary space transportation system with 10 times lower cost is developed in 12 years, while a near-term component of that system yields a working vehicle of reduced capability by 1994.

System Development, Deployment, and Support

CONTENTS

Box

Figures

Tables

System Development, Deployment, and Support

INTRODUCTION

The preceding chapters review the status of key ballistic missile defense (BMD) technologies, describing the progress made and the additional advances still needed to meet various BMD goals. These technologies would have to work together in an integrated system. The United States would have to develop the infrastructure to fabricate, test, deploy, operate, and maintain that system, and modify it in response to Soviet countermeasures. In the case of space-based elements, now considered essential for a highly effective defense, the United States would have to design, test, and build a new space transportation system. Anything but the fastest development of this transportation system could delay all but the most modest space-based BMD deployment to well into the 21st century.

This chapter explores the steps involved in moving from the current research and development phase to operational status. These steps include:

- architecture definition,
- system development,
- system testing,
- fabrication,
- deployment, and
- operation and maintenance.

Given the complexity of a global BMD system and the immaturity of many technologies, this chapter can only outline and give some indication of the multitude of challenges that would face engineers and manufacturers if a decision were made to proceed to full-scale engineering development (FSED) and then to deployment. From the beginning, the development and deployment of dependable computer software would be a key issue; the subject of software is deferred until chapter 9.

ARCHITECTURE DEFINITION

The first step toward deployment would be to complete the detailed system design or architecture. As noted in chapter 3, five defense contractors have competed with different BMD system designs. The Strategic Defense Initiative Organization (SDIO) has conducted additional analyses outside the main architecture contracting framework. A single system architect is to be chosen in 1988. This architect is to define the actual BMD system in detail, providing information for a decision on whether to proceed to the next step: full-scale engineering development. The SDIO has proposed an early 1990s decision on FSED but its schedules are slipping as a result of funding levels that are below its earlier expectations.

In the meantime, common elements in the existing architecture studies can be used to guide the research program.[1] All of the space- and ground-based architecture designs included space-based infrared (IR) sensors and space-based interceptors (SBIs). All assumed

---

[1] Each architect defined three architectures: a combination space and ground-based system, a ground-only system, and a theater defense system. In addition, most architects have considered various time-phased options. For this discussion we are considering primarily the combined space- and ground-based architectures.

Note: Complete definitions of acronyms and initialisms are listed in Appendix B of this report.

some type of ground-based exo-atmospheric reentry interceptor system (ERIS). All saw a critical need for midcourse interactive discrimination, although this task might be too difficult for a near-term, phase-one deployment.

The "concept validation" program approved by the Secretary of Defense in September 1987, included work on SBIs, ERIS, and associated sensors and battle management technology.

SYSTEM DEVELOPMENT

The system engineer must combine various components and sub-systems defined by the architecture into a working system. A typical BMD system as envisioned by system architecture contractors for intermediate-term ("phase-two") deployment might have included 30,000 major sub-systems of nine different types (for suggested major components of a phase-two system, see table 1-2 in ch. 1). The sub-systems would be tied together by a communications network. These sub-systems would have to work together under the direction of battle management computers.[2]

For each of these components, the system engineer would have to consider the following issues:

- **Mass** is particularly critical for SBIs: they would have to be light to reduce space transportation costs and to achieve the necessary velocity during battle.
- Total **volume** may be limited by the space transportation system. All space sub-systems would have to conform to the launch vehicle internal dimensions, preferably with minimum wasted payload space.
- For early deployment (late 1990s), the choices for space base-load **power** would be limited to solar (which is vulnerable), or nuclear, which would have to be developed and space-qualified in the power ranges needed for BMD. Far-term directed-energy weapons could be driven by liquid oxygen/liquid hydrogen turbogenerators or fuel cells for a few hundred seconds. The weight of power supplies might dominate future systems.

- **Heat** rejected by the various devices would have to be minimized and properly managed, since cooling systems take up weight and power.
- Almost all sub-systems would have to be **produced in large quantities** compared to previous space systems. These components would have to be capable of mass production, as compared to the one-of-a-kind laboratory fabrication used in many of the SDIO technology demonstration projects. The United States has never mass-produced any satellites.
- All components would have to withstand severe **radiation** environments, including nearby nuclear explosions. This would be particularly stressing on electronic components such as IR detectors. The detectors and most electronics used for demonstration experiments would not be suitable for BMD deployment.
- These systems would have to **endure** and operate on call after sitting dormant (except possibly for periodic tests) for years. The current goal is at least 5-year life for first-phase deployment, with 7 years desirable. Limited lifetimes would further burden the space transportation system with replacement or repair missions.
- Many systems might have to **operate within seconds or minutes** after warning, although there might be an alert status lasting for days or weeks. Trade-offs between long alert times and fuel consumption might be necessary.
- All space-based systems would have to **operate automatically**, compared to the careful "hand tweaking" common in experiments. In particular, there would be little or no opportunity for the routine

---

[2]As discussed in ch. 7, this battle management function would likely be distributed among many computers on different satellites for survivability.

maintenance common to all terrestrial military systems.

- Various sub-systems and components would have to **work together**. For example, radiation from a nuclear power supply must not degrade the operation of sensitive IR sensors or electronics. Similarly, fumes from a propulsion system must not fog the optics of critical sensors, and vibration from power sources must not degrade weapons pointing accuracy.
- If components are prone to failure, they should be **easily replaceable or adjustable**. For space-based systems, a key issue would be whether to replace entire satellites when they failed, or to attempt periodic manual or robotic repair.
- All systems and components should **survive both natural and man-made environments**. Survivability measures such as decoys, redundancy, shielding, maneuverability, electronic jamming, and shootback would add mass to space-based components. One system architect estimated that survivability measures would account for 70 percent of on-orbit mass for SBI systems.
- The communications channels would have to be **secure** against interception, manipulation, and jamming.
- The systems should be **safe** in manufacture, assembly, transport, and operation.

SDIO is funding research in all of these areas. Optimists believe these characteristics may be achievable; pessimists question whether the break necessary from past practice and experience is possible; others say it is too early in the research program to judge whether the United States could achieve all of these attributes in a working system.

SYSTEM TESTING

Testing of both hardware and software is essential to any engineering project. Components are tested and modified to overcome deficiencies. Sub-systems are tested and modified. Finally, prototypes of the complete system are built and tested under full operating conditions whenever possible. These system tests invariably reveal faults in the original design, faults which must be corrected before production begins.

A ballistic missile defense system could not be tested in a full battle condition. Instead, the systems engineer would have to rely on some combination of computer simulations and operation under simulated conditions. The anti-ballistic missile (ABM) treaty prohibits space-based tests in an ABM mode which would be necessary to establish even minimal confidence in SBIs.

In place of complete system testing, the SDIO is developing the National Test Bed. This test bed (see ch. 8) is to tie together many communication nodes and computers via satellite, simulating some of the complexity of BMD. Some types of hardware (such as sensors) would also be coupled into this test system as they became available, "talking" to the computers as they would in a real battle. The cost of simulation will be high, but this is the only way to give leaders some degree of confidence in system operation. One of the key judgments the President and Congress will have to make about the SDI program will be the level of confidence to be placed in a global system that has never been tested in a full operational mode.

Testing so far under the SDIO program has been limited to the component or sub-system level, usually under simplified or artificial conditions. These experiments have yielded valuable information necessary for the ongoing research and development effort; the United States should not, however, confuse a demonstration test with operational readiness (see box 6-A).

Box 6-A.—SDIO Demonstration Experiments[1]

Homing Overlay Experiment: The HOE demonstrated on the fourth test (June 10, 1984) that an experimental IR homing vehicle can acquire and collide with a simulated reentry vehicle in flight. The RV was launched aboard a test ICBM from Vandenberg AFB in California. After detection by radars on Kwajalein, a rocket carrying the experimental ground-launched interceptor was fired from a nearby island toward the oncoming RV. The IR sensor on the interceptor then acquired the RV and guided the interceptor to a direct hit high above the Pacific.

While this was an encouraging and successful experiment, it does not mean that the United States could deploy operational exoatmospheric interceptors tomorrow. The HOE experiment used parts of an existing missile, too large and expensive for an affordable BMD system. The IR sensor was cooled for many hours prior to the test; an operational system could not be maintained at such cold temperatures. The detectors were not hardened against nuclear radiation; new types of detectors would be required for the operational system. The simulated RV fired from Vandenberg AFB in California radiated about 10 times more IR energy than that expected from today's Soviet RV, and future RVs could have even lower IR signatures with thermal shrouds. There was only one RV, and the experimenters knew when and where it would be fired; the real issue for exoatmospheric interception is decoy discrimination—separating one RV out of a cloud of hundreds or thousands of other objects, including tethered balloons. Opinions differ on how difficult this would be.

Delta 180: The Delta 180 mission (Sept. 5, 1986) launched a Delta missile into space; the two upper stages of this missile were both placed in orbit. Each contained sensors later used to measure radiation from the other and from another missile launched from White Sands, New Mexico during one orbit. One stage also contained a radar sensor used to guide the two stages into a collision course at the end of the experiment.

The Delta 180 was a very successful measurement program, providing useful information about radiation from rocket exhaust plumes, both at close range in space and from the ground-launched Aries rocket. Some radiation patterns confirmed expectations, but there were some surprises which could improve our ability to detect and track future missile plumes. Tracking algorithms were also tested in the final interception with the target stage accelerating, which is more difficult than for targets with constant velocity. The entire Delta 180 mission took only 18 months from start to finish, requiring extraordinary management and dedicated performance by defense contractors.

However, this measurements program should not be confused with a demonstration of the near operational readiness of space-based interceptors. This interception had little resemblance to the BMD problem—and could not have without violating the ABM treaty. The relative velocities and ranges of the two stages were far less than those required for BMD. The target stage had a large radar reflector (over 1 square meter). The size and mass of the interceptor stage (over 2,000 kg compared to a goal of less than 200 kg for SBIs) would eliminate any possibility of achieving the velocities required of a SBI to kill an ICBM. All planned SBIs discussed to date would require an IR sensor for final homing, while Delta 180 used a Phoenix air-to-air missile radar. Finally, the near head-on aspect of the final kill would not be typical for a BMD mission, and did not stress the divert capability of the interceptor.

FLAGE: Six of nine planned tests of the "flexible, light-weight agile guided experiment"(FLAGE) short-range terminal interceptor missile have been completed. On the second test, the radar-guided homing interceptor passed very close to the target, again indicating that hit-to-kill interceptors are feasible under appropriate conditions.

In the FLAGE tests, the target vehicle was flown into a highly instrumented volume of air above the White Sands Missile Range. Although artificial, this controlled environment is appropriate for an experiment, which should collect as much data as possible. The successful interception

[1]These comments on the SDI validation experiments should not be construed as criticism of SDIO management. These are all sound experiments properly designed to collect bits of information necessary on the path to developing a working system. At this time we have no major element of a non-nuclear ballistic missile defense system which has been tested in a system mode with equipment suitable for actual operation.

does not imply that the United States could build a FLAGE interceptor system today that would be effective against uncooperative targets in all types of weather. A FLAGE-derived interceptor would not be suitable for defending soft targets such as cities.

MIRACL Laser Test: The MIRACL DF laser at White Sands was aimed at a strapped-down Titan rocket casing. The booster casing was stressed with high pressure nitrogen to simulate the stresses expected in flight. The laser beam heated the skin of the tank, which then exploded in a few seconds as the shell weakened.

This experiment essentially tested target lethality: how much IR energy is required to weaken a Titan tank until it ruptures? The laser beam was about 100,000 times less bright than one required to destroy a responsive Soviet booster from a distance of 1,000 km or more. It was *not* a test of a directed-energy weapon *system*. The key issues for any DEW are target acquisition and tracking, beam pointing over very large distances, and particularly the questions of retargeting and beam jitter: could one keep the laser beam focused on one spot on the booster body while the booster and the DEW platform travel through space at many kilometers per second? Other more complex experiments would be required to answer these crucial questions. Real confidence in any DEW would require space-based testing under dynamic conditions.

FABRICATION

Once a system had been developed and tested to the degree possible, it would have to be manufactured. The manufacturing tools and facilities to fabricate much of the specialized equipment needed for BMD are not yet available. In some cases, expansion or modification of existing manufacturing facilities might be adequate. In other cases, entirely new manufacturing techniques would have to be developed and skilled workers trained. The SDI research program is addressing some key manufacturing issues, such as mirror and focal plane array (FPA) fabrication techniques.

Some of the key manufacturing challenges are summarized in table 6-1, along with an estimated comparison of current manufacturing capacity with second-phase BMD needs. These comparisons are not always valid, however. For example, current (FPA) manufacturing capacity is for non-radiation hardened arrays with less than 180 detector elements. Ballistic missile defense sensors must survive in a radiation environment, so new types of detectors are being developed, along with all new manufacturing techniques.

The items in table 6-1 represent only phase-two BMD deployments, excluding items such as interactive discrimination apparatus and

Table 6-1.—Examples of Current v. Required Manufacturing Capacity for Proposed BMD Systems

	Current capacity	Required capacity for Phase-II BMD
Large area mirrors (square meters per year)	1-2	100-2,000
Focal plane arrays (number of elements made per year)	10^6	10^7-10^9
Sapphire windows (for HEDI; number per year) .	50	600-1,000
Precision guided missiles (per year)	100s	1,000-5,000
Satellites (per year)	10s	300-500
Space-launch rockets	10s	100s

SOURCE: Office of Technology Assessment, 1988.

directed-energy weapons (DEW).[3] Building hundreds of space-qualified neutral particle beam accelerators or high power lasers with their rapid pointing and retargeting mechanisms would certainly stress manufacturing capability.

Any manufacturing process must minimize cost and delivery time while maintaining high quality. These three virtues have added significance for BMD.

---

[3]Note, however, that recently the SDIO has suggested the possibility of including such elements in phase two.

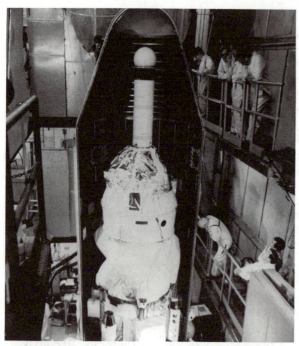

Photo credit: U.S. Department of Defense

Delta 180 payload—The payload of the Delta 180 experiment, atop a Delta booster, is shown during shroud installation on Pad 17 at Cape Canaveral. Multiple boxes carrying optical sensors are mounted on the side of the rocket's second-stage truss at bottom. The mast on top of the third stage is a Phoenix missile sensor, which helped guide an intercept between the two vehicles to obtain rocket motor plume data at short distances.

Photo credit: U.S. Department of Defense

Lethal test of high-velocity projectiles.—Electromagnetic launchers might hurl small homing projectiles at distant missile stages or warheads. In this test of the effects of high-velocity impact, a small (unguided) plastic projectile hit a cast aluminum block at 7 km/s. This was a test of lethality, not of a weapon: the projectile was not launched from an electromagnetic launcher.

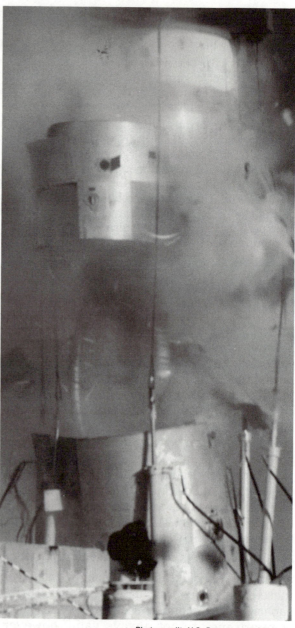

Photo credit: U.S. Department of Defense

Laser lethality test.—In September 1986 this test at White Sands Missile Range, N.M., investigated the possible effects of a laser beam on a rocket booster. The test vehicle was the second stage of a Titan I booster missile body. External loads were applied to the booster to simulate flight conditions typical of current operational Soviet missile systems. The test vehicle contained no liquid propellant or explosives. It was irradiated with a high-energy laser beam for several seconds before being destroyed. The laser used, the Mid-Infrared Advanced Chemical Laser, generates a beam energy greater than 1 MW/sr. It is a test laser, not developed for deployment in space.

Cost

The projected costs for a BMD system will strongly affect a national decision on whether to proceed with production or deployment. In addition to total costs, the incremental costs of BMD would have to be less (some think substantially less) than the perceived incremental cost of Soviet countermeasures. Thus the unit costs of a deployed SBI might have to be less than 1/370th to 1/12th the cost of a Soviet booster.[4] On the other hand, the leverage provided by a successful "adaptive preferential defense" might improve this cost-exchange ratio (see ch. 1).

The allowable costs for a ground-based exoatmospheric interceptor would depend on the system architecture. With low leakage from the boost phase and good discrimination, each interceptor would have to engage only a small percentage of the attacking Soviet reentry vehicles (RVs), and the interceptor could be relatively expensive. If discrimination were poor, which might be the case in a phase-one deployment, then the interceptor might be competing with cheap decoys. The defense would not be cost-effective at the margin if every exoatmospheric interceptor had to cost less than 10 light-weight decoys, or even less than 10 heavy decoys.[5]

Time

The time to manufacture components for BMD might be crucial in several respects.

Ideally the system should be deployed quickly to avoid transition instabilities, although system architects differ on this point. Components could be produced and stockpiled until deployment began.[6] To the degree that space transportation would pace deployment, production times would not be critical.

But the United States would also be locked in a race with Soviet countermeasures. If the United States could not produce and deploy enough SBIs before the Soviets had reduced a substantial number of their booster burn times below 140 seconds, then BMD boost-phase system effectiveness would drop significantly, perhaps to zero. The SBIs might force the Soviets to faster post-boost vehicle (PBV) dispersals, which could reduce the number of RVs. At some point, however, there would be no sense in deploying SBIs (and particularly SBIs which did not have any midcourse capability against RVs) until DEW were developed. (See also ch. 5 and the key-issues section at the end of this chapter for more analysis of SBI effectiveness against boosters with moderately fast burn times.)

On the other hand, if the United States could produce and deploy an SBI system in a few years, and if it could build and deploy a credible DEW system as the Soviet Union converted to faster-burning boosters and fast-dispersing PBVs, then BMD effectiveness might continue.

Production time involves not only the production rate, but the time to design, build, and debug the manufacturing facilities, including necessary training of production workers. Since many new technologies are contemplated, there might be relatively long periods before routine production could begin.

Quality

Quality control would be essential, particularly for space-based deployment. Repair or even replacement of failed assets in space

---

[4]The 12-to-1 cost ratio assumes that 8 percent of the SBIs would be within range of the Soviet missile fields and that one SBI is fired at each booster or PBV. There are no extra SBIs for redundancy or shoot-back against Soviet ASATs. In this case the United States would have to add about 12 SBIs (and another carrier satellite) for each new Soviet booster. The 370-to-1 cost ratio comes from a concentrated basing of new Soviet boosters in a relatively small area, say 150 km by 150 km. In this case the United States would have to deploy 370 extra SBIs and their associated satellites for each new Soviet booster to achieve an 85 percent probability of destroying that extra RV.

[5]If the boost phase defense let through 10 percent of the boosters, and each booster carried 10 warheads, 10 heavy decoys, and 100 light decoys, then the exo-atmospheric interceptor system would have to engage one warhead, one heavy decoy, and 10 light decoys for each booster launched. With perfect discrimination, one deployed interceptor would have to cost less than one loaded booster. Without any discrimination, one interceptor would have to cost 1/12th of the booster.

[6]See U.S. Congress, Office of Technology Assessment, *Ballistic Missile Defense Technologies*, OTA-ISC-254 (Washington, D.C.: U.S. Government Printing Office), p. 119.

might severely stress space transportation, particularly if space launch facilities were completely occupied over a period of 5 to 10 years just to lift the initial BMD equipment into place.

DEPLOYMENT

Given that some boost-phase defense capability would be key to a highly effective BMD system, and given that the United States currently has very little space launch capability, deployment of space-based assets would most likely limit the operational starting date for BMD. As shown in the space transportation section of chapter 5, the United States would have to build a new space launch system to lift into orbit the necessary number of SBIs and their supporting satellites. The timing of the development and availability of a new space launch system is unclear, but it is doubtful that it would be possible to launch significant numbers of SBIs before the mid to late 1990s.

Several years of continuous space launch activities from several launch pads would then be necessary to deploy enough SBIs to provide one shot against each missile or PBV in today's fleet of Soviet intercontinental ballistic missiles (ICBMs). The SDIO, however, does not propose deploying that many SBIs in a first-phase system. It argues that lesser capabilities would still have worthwhile deterrent value. (See section below on scheduling and deployment issues for discussion of the effect of deployment rates on SBI system effectiveness.)

OPERATION AND MAINTENANCE

Once deployed, the BMD system would have to be kept in operating order. Ground-based elements such as ERIS could be periodically tested, disassembled, and repaired as needed. For space-based assets, both testing and repair would be difficult unless built into the initial design. Methods would be needed to determine if the sensor or the guidance system on a dormant SBI would operate in a war. Computer systems would have to be exercised to make sure radiation in space had not altered a key software bit that might subsequently inhibit successful operation. The status of dormant space assets would have to be monitored carefully and frequently.

Once defective space systems were diagnosed, they would have to be replaced or repaired. The system architecture would have to incorporate some combination of redundancy or on-orbit repair or replacement to maintain the total system. The space transportation system would have to be sized to handle this load.

Space-based assets might also need to be modified in response to Soviet countermeasures. SBI sensors initially designed for tracking only booster plumes with short or medium-wave IR sensors might become worthless against faster-burning boosters. Should a second-phase system add LWIR sensors to previously deployed SBIs to give them midcourse kill capability? Trade-off studies would determine whether it would be more cost-effective to replace components on obsolete satellites or simply to add entirely new satellites.

EXAMPLE BMD SUB-SYSTEM: SSTS

To appreciate some of the complexity of a BMD system, consider just one of the systems in table 1-2: a moderately sophisticated Space Surveillance and Tracking System (SSTS). The potential sub-systems of an SSTS are shown in table 6-2. Almost every subsystem on this list would require development to meet the probable BMD specifications.

At the next level down, just one sub-system from the SSTS, a three-color LWIR sensor, would include the components listed in table 6-3. Again, most of these components must be developed to meet BMD specifications. An analysis of the other SSTS sub-systems and the other major sub-systems in the three phases of SDI would reveal literally hundreds of sizeable development programs which would have to come together to form the complete system.

Table 6-2.—SSTS Sub-Systems

	Development required
Propulsion (for station-keeping)	Low
Communications (space-to-space)	High
Communications (space-to-ground)	High
Power source	High
Three-color LWIR sensor(s)	High
SWIR/MWIR sensor(s)	Medium
Laser ranger/designator	High
Star tracker(s)	Medium
Computer and memory	Medium
Waste heat rejection	Medium
Support structure	Low

SOURCE: Office of Technology Assessment, 1988.

Table 6-3.—Three-Color LWIR Sensor Components

	Development required
Primary mirror	High
Secondary mirror	High
Cryo-cooler	Medium
Three-color focal plane array (FPA)	High
Signal processor	High
Three-axis gimbal	Medium
Servo control system	Medium
Thermal control system	Low
Sun shield	Low
Support structures	Low

SOURCE: Office of Technology Assessment, 1988.

KEY SYSTEM ISSUES

Building and deploying a system on the scale of proposed BMD architectures would stress the U.S. engineering and manufacturing infrastructure on many fronts. However, three critical systems issues are unique to ballistic missile defense with space-based components: the lack of realistic system testing, the necessity for automated, computer-controlled operation, and the difficulties of scheduling and space deployment.

System Testing

The inability to test fully a global BMD system (both hardware and software) would cast doubt on its operational effectiveness. The administration and Congress will have to decide on the deployment of a system whose performance would have to be predicted largely by computer simulations. The National Test Bed and future component tests would improve the verisimilitude of those simulations, but they could not encompass all of the complexity of the real world. Some issues such as sensor operation against a nuclear explosion background in space could not be tested even at the component level without abandoning the Limited Test Ban Treaty. Except in computer simulations, the system could not be tested, short of war, with even 10 percent of the possible wartime threat.

It is true that all military systems are subject to uncertainty when they first go into battle. A fighter aircraft, despite the best flight test program, can never be tested with all the variables that will arise in a real battle. An aircraft-carrier battle group could never anticipate all possible situations in some future battle with a capable adversary, and might be susceptible to unforeseen vulnerabilities. The U.S. carrier battle groups have never fought against an enemy with modern "smart weapons." There is uncertainty in the performance predictions of these conventional military systems.

A global BMD system would have even more complex, untestable sub-system interactions. Even full interception tests, using SBIs fired against ICBMs launched from Vandenberg AFB, could involve at best a salvo launch of a few missiles. This would not substitute for the launching of a thousand missiles by the Soviet Union at a time of their choosing, preceded by anti-satellite weapon (ASAT) attacks and nuclear precursor explosions. Individual components such as sensors, data processors, and communication equipment could be tested by themselves to full operational capacity in the laboratory or in simulated space chambers, and some effects of nuclear explosions could be tested at the Nevada test site. In any case, the complete BMD system could not be tested as an integrated unit against a real threat. Neither, on the other hand, could the Soviet offensive ballistic missile force.

Automatic Operation

Automation has made dramatic changes in factories and some military weapons systems. Robotics is firmly established in many manufacturing situations, and will grow in the future. However, space-based BMD systems would cross into new engineering domains of automatic operation on several counts:

- continuous unattended stand-by operation for years,
- a continuously changing constellation of components which would have to operate together as a unit, and
- operation under adverse conditions against an opponent determined to defeat the system.

None of these limitations is encountered in automated factories.

Automatic fire control systems are common in today's weapons. Human intervention is always possible, however, to repair and maintain the system. The United States has never operated a weapon system in space. Both the United States and the Soviet Union have operated sensor systems in space for surveillance and early warning of ballistic missile attack. The challenge would be to integrate more sophisticated early warning satellites with actual weapon platforms thousands of kilometers away.

Sensor satellites currently in orbit operate autonomously, with directions from a few ground-based mission control nodes. Once the battle began, BMD systems might require the autonomous operation of 30 to 40 sensors working in conjunction with hundreds or thousands of SBI carrier satellites. Sensors and carrier satellites would be moving in different orbits, so that the particular weapons platforms and sensors making up a "battle group" (in one possible battle management architecture) would be constantly changing with time. (See ch. 7 on wartime operation.) These battle groups would have to be connected by secure communication links. Higher system effectiveness would entail tighter coordination.

Automatic operation would be further challenged by Soviet defense suppression tactics. The system would ideally adapt to lost or noisy communication links and continue to manage the battle on the basis of degraded information. (See ch. 9 for a fuller discussion of BMD software dependability.)

Scheduling and Deployment: An Illustrative Scenario

If an administration and Congress were to decide that our national security would be improved by deploying some type of BMD, a major issue would be when to begin deployment. Early deployment (e.g., 1995-2000) of a phase-one system would risk "locking in" immature BMD technology that might be less effective against the projected threat. Waiting for more advanced technology would give the Soviet Union more time to prepare countermeasures, increasing the risk that the defense effectiveness would remain low. Early deployment would strain space transportation facilities, and the long deployment time would preclude a fast transition from offense- to defense-dominated status. But a decision to wait for later deployment could, some fear, indefinitely postpone any deployment at all.

Ballistic missile defense system effectiveness would depend not only on the U.S. deployment schedule, but also on the timing of Soviet countermeasures. The longer it took to deploy a defense, the more time the Soviets would have to respond by improving their offensive forces. To illustrate the interplay between defensive and offensive deployments over time, OTA constructed a plausible scenario for the 1994-2010 period, then estimated the effectiveness of an SBI system as a function of time. For the defense, we assume that:

- SBI deployment would be limited only by the capacity of future United States space transportation systems. That is, the United States could produce and operate in space as many SBIs as it could launch. *Note that it is emphatically not the SDIO proposal to deploy this many SBIs.*
- The SDIO two-track space transportation scenario succeeds in building a heavy lift expendable launch vehicle by 1994 with 30,000 kg lift to near polar orbits, and this same technology simultaneously evolves into an economical, partially reusable vehicle with 44,000 kg capacity by the year 2000.
- Three new launch pad complexes would be built at Vandenberg AFB and launch rates would be increased from 3 per year per pad up to 12 per pad per year, bringing the total lift capacity to near polar orbits to 2.2 million kg per year by 2004.
- Three different classes of SBIs might be available with varying masses and velocities: a "state-of-the-art," a "realistic," and an "optimistic" interceptor. (Specification of the characteristics of each are in the classified version of this report.)
- The SBIs would be replaced at the end of a useful life of 5 to 10 years, which limits the number of SBIs in orbit unless the space transportation system capacity continues to grow with time.

For the Soviet offensive response, OTA assumed:

- a gradual decrease in the burn-time of Soviet ICBM boosters and in the RV and decoy dispersal time of its PBVs through the introduction of one new class of 10-warhead missiles every five years;
- that these new missiles would be clustered at three existing SS-18 missile sites, which would cover an area of 500,000 square km;
- retirement of old Soviet missiles as the latest models were introduced, keeping the total RV count at 10,000 (case 1), or an increase of their ICBM's by 100 per year after the year 2000 (case 2);
- no other Soviet countermeasures, except a significant Soviet ASAT capability, implied by our reserving a substantial fraction of U.S. SBIs for self-defense or to account for inoperable SBIs that fail over time.

While these assumptions are technically plausible, they are not based on any Department of Defense or intelligence community estimates of what the Soviets could or would do.

Table 6-4.—Assumed Distribution of Soviet ICBMs for 1990-2010

All ICBMs are assumed to carry 10 warheads. Please note that the mix of forces here reflects neither Department of Defense nor intelligence community estimates of what the Soviets actually may do. Instead, this table merely lays out a purely hypothetical sequence of a phasing-in of faster-burning ICBMs at 5-year intervals beginning in 1990. Older missiles are retired as new ones are deployed, keeping the total RV count fixed at a hypothetical number of 10,000. The slow-burn boosters are distributed over existing Soviet missile fields, while the other four classes are assumed concentrated at three existing sites.

ICBM type	Number of ICBMs				
	SBB	MBB-1	MBB-2	FBB-1	FBB-2
Year:					
1991	500	500	—	—	—
1992	500	500	—	—	—
1993	500	500	—	—	—
1994	500	500	—	—	—
1995	500	500	—	—	—
1996	400	500	100	—	—
1997	300	500	200	—	—
1998	200	500	300	—	—
1999	100	500	400	—	—
2000	—	500	500	—	—
2001	—	400	500	100	—
2002	—	300	500	200	—
2003	—	200	500	300	—
2004	—	100	500	400	—
2005	—	—	500	500	—
2006	—	—	400	500	100
2007	—	—	300	500	200
2008	—	—	200	500	300
2009	—	—	100	500	400
2010	—	—	—	500	500

Legend:
SBB: Slow-Burn Booster
MBB-1: Medium-Burn Booster—First Generation
MBB-2: Medium-Burn Booster—Second Generation
FBB-1: Fast-Burn Booster—First Generation
FBB-2: Fast-Burn Booster—Second Generation

SOURCE: Office of Technology Assessment, 1988.

Space Transportation Limits on Deployment

As indicated in chapter 5, a new space transportation system would be needed to launch the space-based assets of a highly effective BMD system. Even a more modest system, such as that proposed by SDIO for the first phase, would call for considerable new space transportation capacity. The SDIO has identified two potentially conflicting space transportation goals: reducing launch costs by a factor of 10 and beginning some launches in the mid-1990s. Derivatives of existing Shuttle/Titan launch systems are not likely to lead to

major cost reductions; an entirely new system would be needed. But a revolutionary new space transportation system would not likely be ready before the year 2000.

To achieve both the cost and schedule goals, SDIO has proposed a dual-track formula: a new space transportation system would be developed with a goal of a tenfold cost reduction by 2000 or so, but parts of this new system would be available by the mid-1990s for early deployments, probably with reduced lift capacity and higher cost. This approach might create design compromises. Either cost reductions might have to be postponed to meet the schedule, or the schedule might have to be slipped to meet the eventual cost goals: a space transportation system designed to meet just one of these goals might look quite different from the hybrid. In this scenario, however, we assume that both goals could be achieved simultaneously.

The United States now has one pad capable of launching more than 10,000 kg to the high inclination orbits and altitudes of several hundreds of kilometers to be occupied by the SBI constellation.[7] The Shuttle pad at Vandenberg Air Force Base could be modified by 1992 to launch the Titan-4 (CELV) vehicle with a capacity of about 14,500 kg to SBI orbits. In the past, building new launch pads has taken from 7 to 10 years and there is some question whether there is adequate space at Vandenberg to add even a few more pads and their necessary assembly facilities. (The Air Force has been examining the possibility of launching rockets from an off-shore oil rig.) Survivability of launch facilities would also be questionable if all U.S. polar-orbit pads were located at one coastal site. In this scenario, we assume that these difficulties are overcome.

Launch rates have been in the range of three to five per year from one pad. This rate is

---

[7]The 4-East pad at Vandenberg Air Force Base in California is equipped to launch the Titan 34D and Titan-4 (CELV) vehicles into polar or high inclination orbits. The 4-West pad at Vandenberg can handle the Titan-2 vehicle, which has less than 2,000 kg capacity. Two pads at Kennedy Space Center (#40 and #41) can launch Titan 34Ds and Titan-4s, but not into near-polar orbits. There are no Delta launch facilities at Vandenberg.

limited by the necessity to assemble the launch vehicles at the site. Studies are underway to determine if these launch rates could be increased to 6 per year, with some experts suggesting that rates up to 8 per year might be feasible in the future for the Titan class vehicles, and 12 per year per pad for the new vehicle.

SBI Characteristics

OTA analyzed three classes of SBIs, corresponding to assumed improvements in SBI technology as discussed in chapter 5. The "state-of-the-art" rocket would probably be the best technology available for a first-phase deployment in the mid-1990s. For the most part, this SBI would use components that have been demonstrated in the laboratory (as of 1988), but not as yet assembled into a working system. The "realistic" SBI represents a plausible level of technology after more component research and development, and might be available by the mid to late 1990s; the overall rocket mass assumption of well under 100 kg would be particularly challenging. The "optimistic" SBI assumes improvements in all areas of development, and would be much less likely, but possible. Other assumptions about SBI redundancy factors and kill probabilities are the same as those applied earlier in chapter 5 of this report.

Given the optimistic space launch projections from chapter 5 and the different assumptions for SBI masses, one can estimate the total number of SBIs that might be placed in orbit as a function of time, as shown in figure 6-1. The lifetimes of SBIs in space would be critical, since defunct interceptors would have to be replaced, taking space transportation capacity away from the tasks of increasing SBI deployments or other BMD assets. It might turn out, however, that on-orbit repair could reduce the numbers of spares and replacements needed. As shown in figure 6-1, the number of state-of-the-art rockets would reach a plateau by about 2006 if better SBIs could not be developed: a space transportation system sized to put the original constellation in place would operate full-time just to replace these

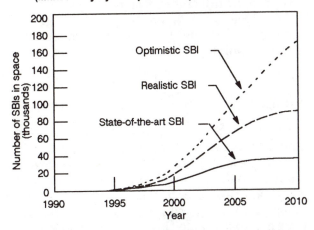

Figure 6-1.— Number of Space-Based Interceptors Launched Into Space
(limited only by the space transportation system)

Maximum number of SBIs that could be launched into orbit based on the assumed space transportation revolution described in chapter 5. This chart assumes that all space launch capability is devoted to SBIs and their associated carrier vehicles. The net mass per SBI, including the pro-rated share of the carrier vehicle mass, would be 334, 179, and 129 kilograms for "state-of-the-art," "realistic," and "optimistic" SBIs, with life-times of 5, 7, and 10 years.

SOURCE: Office of Technology Assessment, 1988.

SBIs and maintain the constellation in a steady-state constellation.

For the lighter and faster "optimistic" SBIs, the assumed transportation system could lift up to 160,000 SBIs into orbit by the year 2010. This assumes that no other space assets would be launched into near polar orbits during the entire 1994-2010 period. Thus any later deployments of interactive discrimination systems or directed-energy weapons would reduce the possible number of SBIs in orbit. In any case, it is obvious that the United States would not try to manufacture, lift into space, and manage a constellation of 160,000 SBIs.

The "optimistic" SBI effectiveness curves which follow are therefore unrealistic; they are shown only to indicate upper bounds on SBI boost and post-boost effectiveness. They suggest that while SBIs might be considered for a system intended to enhance deterrence, they would not, by themselves, be suitable for a system intended to assure very RV low leakage rates. They also suggest that, barring substantial offensive force reductions, the initial effectiveness of an SBI system might be eroded by appropriate countermeasures. In that case, directed-energy weapons might have to be brought on line just to maintain previous defense capability.

Assumed Soviet Offensive Countermeasures

As the U.S. space transportation system (and hence the number of possible SBIs in space) grew, Soviet ICBM and submarine-launched ballistic missile SLBM forces would most likely also change with time. One central question for evaluating BMD effectiveness is whether reasonable Soviet countermeasures could keep ahead of possible U.S. BMD deployments. Here, OTA analyzed the effects of just three Soviet countermeasures: reduced booster burn and PBV dispersal times and clustering of new missiles at three existing missile sites. These analyses assumed that the Soviet Union reduced its booster burn and PBV times gradually over the next two decades, introducing a new class of weapon each 5 years with moderately improved performance. Three cases were assumed: optimistic (relatively long booster burn times), base case, and pessimistic threats. Even the "pessimistic" threat case assumes a 90-second burn-time by 2006, still more than the 60- to 80-second burn-times deemed feasible for the next century by some rocket experts. Thus these threat assumptions are all conservative compared to what may be technically feasible.

SBI Boost and Post-Boost Effectiveness

We next calculated the maximum possible number of RVs that could be destroyed each year by SBIs in either the boost or the post-boost phase, simply by calculating how many SBIs would be within range of the booster or the post-boost vehicle at the time each RV was deployed.

We assumed uniform, serial RV deployment over the PBV dispersal time. Each SBI at-

tacked the booster first if it was within range, then the PBV at the earliest possible time. Two shots were taken if more than one SBI could reach a booster or PBV. Perfect battle management was assumed: the battle manager knew exactly where all boosters and SBIs would be at burnout, and assigned SBIs to their highest value targets without error. These calculations assumed that a substantial fraction of SBIs are used for self-defense (or are inoperable)—an on orbit repair system, however, might reduce the extra numbers needed. Other assumptions were that each SBI had a reasonably high single-shot kill probability against the boosters and and a slightly smaller one against the PBV.

The resulting system effectiveness (the number of RVs leaking through the boost and post-boost SBI defense) is plotted as a function of time in figure 6-2 for the three canonical SBIs

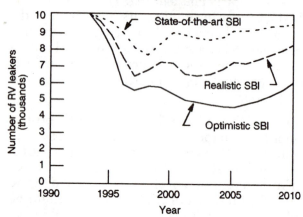

Figure 6-2.—Number of Warheads Leaking Through Boost and Post-Boost Defenses

BMD system effectiveness in terms of the number of RVs (out of a hypothetical attack of 1,000 missiles with 10,000 RVs) which would leak through a boost and post-boost defense, limited only by the ability of the U.S. space transportation system to lift space-based interceptors (SBIs) into orbit (figure 6-1 indicates the number of SBIs available each year for each type of SBI). The SBIs have a reasonable probability of destroying a booster and a slightly smaller probability of killing a PBV; a substantial percentage of the SBIs are used for self-defense or are otherwise inoperative. The Soviet threat has a constant 10,000 warhead level, but with decreases in booster burn-times and PBV dispersal times as described in the text.

SOURCE: Office of Technology Assessment, 1988.

of chapter 5, assuming OTA's hypothetical Soviet threat. In the very near term, the United States could only deploy the "state-of-the-art" SBI. According to these simplified calculations, this type of defense could at best destroy 2,500 RVs out of the OTA-postulated 1,000-missile, 10,000-RV threat by 1998 when the United States would have orbited 4,100 SBIs; 7,500 RVs (and their associated decoys) would pass through to the later defensive layers.

Performance would degrade over time with quicker dispersal of Soviet RVs. If the United States could develop the lighter and faster "optimistic" SBIs, then the defense could reach 50 percent effectiveness by 2001, but this would imply the deployment of 40,000 SBIs by then. Furthermore, to maintain this approximate level of effectiveness with 5,000 warheads leaking through to the midcourse, the United States would have to continue deploying these SBIs, reaching levels of 160,000 SBIs by 2010. Even then, the Soviet penetration to the midcourse would have increased slightly to 6,000 warheads.

The most likely "realistic" SBI would result in a minimum leakage of 6,000 warheads to midcourse. To come close to maintaining this leakage, the United States would have to continue devoting all space launch capability to the SBI system; by 2010 there would be 90,000 SBIs in orbit and 8,000 warheads would survive to midcourse. Again, such figures illustrate that SBIs should not be expected to stop high percentages of Soviet missiles in a massive attack. Nor is it reasonable to expect them to sustain initial boost- and post-boost phase capabilities against a "responsive" Soviet missile threat of the future. The SDIO does not support either expectation.

The sensitivity of SBI effectiveness to the Soviet threat is shown in figure 6-3, assuming the "realistic" SBI rocket parameters in all cases. With the "optimistic threat" scenario, the SBI BMD system could achieve 50 percent effectiveness by 2005, assuming that the United States had deployed 70,000 SBIs. Again, this constellation would have to be increased to 90,000 by the year 2010, and even then the Soviet RVs leaking through could

Figure 6-3.—Number of Warheads Leaking Through Boost and Post-Boost Defenses

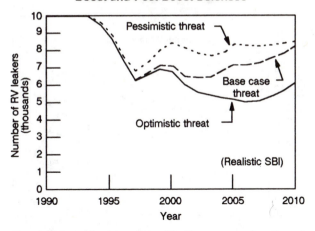

Boost and post-boost system effectiveness as a function of time for three different Soviet threat models described above. "Realistic" SBIs were used in all cases.

SOURCE: Office of Technology Assessment, 1988.

number 6,000 warheads and be increasing. These numbers suggest that directed-energy weapons would be needed, sooner or later, to achieve and sustain high kill levels against advanced Soviet boosters and PBVs.

The previous two figures assume that the Soviets retire old missiles as new ones are deployed, keeping the total at 10,000 warheads available. In the absence of arms control treaties, they could keep old missiles in place, and continue to add faster-burning boosters. The BMD effectiveness for this situation is shown in figure 6-4, assuming that all initial medium-burn boosters are retained, and that 100 of the faster-burning boosters (FBB) are added each year after 2000. Under the most optimistic (for the defense) conditions, the Soviets could maintain 6,000 warheads surviving into mid-course.

Assuming penetration aids to be available by the 2000-2005 time period, these 6,000 warheads and their associated decoys would make passive midcourse discrimination and RV kills very difficult. The leakage against SBIs in all cases would increase with time, most likely reaching the 10,000 warhead level by 2010, despite the presence of up to 160,000 SBIs in space.[8]

---

[8]For analytic purposes, we have ignored the questions of maintenance and battle management of so many interceptors.

Figure 6-4a.—Number of Warheads Leaking Through Boost and Post-Boost

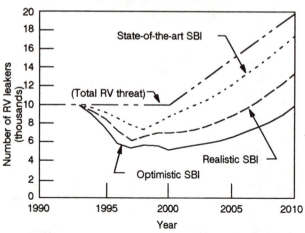

Boost and post-boost effectiveness limited only by space transportation capability, assuming that the Soviet threat increases in quality (shorter deployment times) and quantity (after 2000). Effectiveness shown for three different types of space-based interceptors against the "base case" Soviet threat.

SOURCE: Office of Technology Assessment, 1988.

Figure 6-4b.—Number of Warheads Leaking Through Boost and Post-Boost Defenses

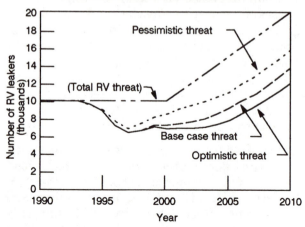

Boost and post-boost effectiveness against three different Soviet threats, all assuming "realistic" space-based interceptors.

SOURCE: Office of Technology Assessment, 1988.

SYSTEM CONCLUSIONS

Testing

1. **If the United States abandoned or achieved modification of the ABM Treaty, it could test a limited constellation of SBIs against a few ICBM's launched from Vandenberg AFB. But this would not replicate the conditions of a massive, surprise launch of hundreds or thousands of ICBMs, ASATs, and nuclear precursors from the Soviet Union.**

2. **A BMD system could not be tested against the real threat of up to thousands of ICBMs combined with defense suppression and nuclear precursors. However, neither could such a coordinated offensive attack be fully tested.**

3. **Key elements, such as IR sensors, could not be realistically tested against a background disrupted by nuclear explosions without abrogating the Limited Test Ban Treaty.**

Automation

4. **No technical barriers appear to preclude automatic operation of a space-based BMD system, but the task of operating an automatic, constantly changing constellation of sensors and weapons platforms in the face of defense suppression tactics would be a major challenge with little or no analogous experience from any other automated systems.**

Scheduling and Deployment

Phase One

5. **A near-term deployment (1995-2000) of state-of-the-art SBIs might stop up to 2,500 of an assumed constant 10,000 Soviet warhead threat in the boost and post-boost phases— if the United States devoted all of its space launch capability to lifting SBIs into orbit.**

This assumes that the burn times and post-boost vehicle dispersal times of future Soviet ICBM's decrease over time in a reasonable manner. Of course, fewer SBIs could kill similar percentages of boosters if a smaller attack were assumed. The SDIO argues that defenses that are far from perfect still offer significant enhancement of deterrence (see chs. 1, 2, and 3).

Phase 2

6. **An intermediate-term or "phase-two" deployment of more advanced SBIs might kill up to 5,000 of the hypothesized fixed number of 10,000 Soviet RVs in the boost and post-boost phases, but only by orbiting from 90,000 to 160,000 SBIs.** Therefore, the United States would be unlikely to rely on SBIs for continued boost-phase interception of advanced Soviet missiles.

7. **Given the assumptions of OTA analyses, under the most optimistic conditions the Soviet Union could maintain an RV leakage into midcourse at or above the 6,000 warhead level by increasing the number of ICBMs deployed by 100 per year after the year 2000.** Under any of the assumed conditions, the Soviet Union could increase the rate of warhead penetration against

SBIs and into midcourse after 2005, reaching the pre-BMD levels of 10,000 leaking warheads by 2010. Therefore, SBIs should not be expected to achieve the strategic goal of "assured survival" against nuclear attack by a Soviet missile force unconstrained by arms reductions and limitations.

Phase 3

8. **A highly effective BMD system would require either very effective midcourse discrimination or a very effective directed-energy weapon (DEW) system, and preferably both,** since an SBI system, as limited by the most optimistic space transportation system, could never assure that fewer than 5,000 Soviet warheads and their associated decoys would leak through to the midcourse,

9. As concluded in chapter 5, it is unlikely that the United States could determine the feasibility of DEW systems by the late 1990s, and deployment probably could not begin until 2005-2010 at the earliest. **It therefore appears likely that the Soviet Union, unless constrained by offensive arms control agreements, would be able to maintain leakage rates of a few thousand nuclear warheads until at least the period 2005-2010.**

System Integration
and Battle Management

CONTENTS

System Integration and Battle Management

INTRODUCTION

Chapter 6 discusses developing, deploying, and maintaining a ballistic missile defense (BMD) system. Once deployed, BMD components would have to work together to form a fighting system. Maintaining such integration would require regular, routine support. This chapter looks at integrated operation of the system. Although some system capabilities could be used during peacetime, e.g., for surveillance, fully integrated use would only be required during battle.[1] Accordingly, most of this chapter is concerned with battle management, i.e., how the system would be managed to fight effectively.

A major assumption in the discussion that follows is that the system is sufficiently well-integrated during peacetime that it can be moved promptly to a full fighting status. As examples, the communications network that permits battle managers to exchange information would have to be working and the battle managers would need timely data on the number, kinds, and locations of resources available to them. Peacetime activities needed to keep the system integrated, such as sending updates of resource-availability data and new versions of software to battle managers, would have to be performed routinely. Operational readiness, testing and evaluation, and repair or replacement of failing system components would also have to be routine.

---

[1]Peacetime simulations of battles would also require considerable integration, but would probably omit operations such as use of interactive discriminators and firing and controlling weapons.

BATTLE MANAGEMENT

The battle management portion of a BMD system would combine the data provided by sensors and the capabilities offered by weapons into a defensive system. The battle management computers would provide computational and decisionmaking capability. The battle management software would be the glue bonding the components together into a fighting system. Battle management includes strategy, tactics, resource allocation algorithms, and status reporting.

Battle management computing may be distributed among many different platforms or consolidated on just a few. In either case, the battle management functions would remain the same, although the capabilities needed in supporting functions, such as communications,

---

Note: Complete definitions of acronyms and initialisms are listed in Appendix B of this report.

might vary. This chapter describes the conduct of a battle from the battle management viewpoint, from alert through the actual battle sequence. *The scenario is only meant to be illustrative, not comprehensive. Its purpose is to convey a sense of the complexity of the battle management task, not to provide an actual battle management system design.*

In peacetime, the system might be in a quiescent mode, conserving fuel and other resources, with some components shielded from space. As the probability of a battle increased, the system might move through a series of alert levels, during which sensors such as the Boost Surveillance and Tracking System (BSTS) and Space Surveillance and Tracking System (SSTS) would be fully opened to space and weapons would be prepared for battle, including warm-up and status checks. At the highest alert level, the system would be fully prepared to fight a battle.

The battle may be partitioned into different phases, each distinguished by a different set of offensive actions. The phases are boost, post-boost, mid-course, and terminal. For an individual reentry vehicle (RV) or decoy, the phases occur in the sequence given. Different RVs and decoys may be in different phases concurrent-ly, requiring the defense to fight in different phases at the same time. In addition, the BMD system might have to defend itself against defense suppression attacks during any phase. For a description of the phases of ballistic missile flight, see chapter 3, table 3-6.

CONDUCT OF THE BATTLE

Our battle scenario assumes, for simplicity, a system with a second-phase architecture as described in chapter 3. We assume that it is in an alert stage from which it could be moved directly to fully automated battle management.[2] The battle would commence with the launch of Soviet intercontinental ballistic missiles (ICBMs). We assume a mix of ICBMs, some of which would burn out above the atmosphere, and some of which would burn out in the atmosphere. The ICBMs release post-boost vehicles (PBVs) carrying both RVs and decoys. The PBVs would maneuver to dispense their payloads, inserting each RV and decoy into a pre-planned trajectory. RVs and decoys would then coast until they started to reenter the atmosphere. RVs would continue on to their targets, accompanied partway by those decoys designed to simulate reentry.

Besides launching ICBMs, the Soviets might employ a variety of defense-suppression measures. For example, they might launch direct-ascent anti-satellite weapons (ASATs) at BMD system satellites. Such a weapon might carry one or more warheads and decoys. The defense suppression attack might begin before an ICBM launch.

The following sections describe briefly the functions that a BMD system would have to perform during the battle. Requirements for recovering from damage and failures occurring during battle are given simplified treatment later. Table 7-1 gives a more detailed description, with examples, of the defensive functions, organized by function and by missile flight phase.

Battle Management Functions

In all phases of a battle the defensive system would have to track targets, assign weapons to destroy targets, aim, fire, and control those weapons, and assess the damage they do. It would also continually report on system status to human commanders, transmit information among computer battle managers within a battle phase, and from the battle managers in one phase (e.g., boost) to the battle managers in another phase (e.g., terminal). Additional functions, unique to each phase, are described in the following sections.

Each of these functions would involve making many decisions in short spaces of time using data obtained from a variety of sources. For example, aiming a weapon at a target might be based on tracking data obtained from a BSTS combined with data from a laser range finder located on satellite battle station, and would require the prediction of an intercept point for the target and weapon.

Boost Phase

The task of detecting booster launches would be unique to the boost phase as would be predicting the approximate trajectories of PBVs from those boosters penetrating the boost-phase defense. Trajectory prediction would needed so that space-based interceptors (SBIs)

---

[2]Although the assumption that there would be sufficient prior warning to an attack that a BMD system could be moved to an alert stage makes the scenario easier to describe, the system's designers could not depend on such an assumption to be true. There would have to be some provision to go from peacetime to battle in seconds in the event that no warning is received or that such warnings are ignored.

Table 7-1.—Ballistic Missile Defense Battle Management Functions

The components of any ballistic missile defense (BMD) system would have to be tied together in a battle management network. The table below lists the kinds of functions such a battle management system would have to perform, assuming a second- phase architecture of the type shown in Table 3-5. Computers would have to perform most of the functions. The BMD system architecture would specify locations and interrelationships among the computers. The system might be more or less centralized, more or less hierarchical. The elements of the system need to be tied together in a communications network. Chapter 8 of this report further discusses battle management communications and computation requirements.

Because different system components often perform the same functions in different ways, the table gives hypothetical examples of how the functions are accomplished in different battle phases. *The "hypothetical examples' are just that: this table does not purport to outline a complete BMD architecture.*

The table is organized into 6 sections. The first 5 sections correspond to the boost, post-boost, mid-course, terminal, and self-defense parts of a BMD battle. The sixth outlines a battle of BMD system self-defense against anti-satellite weapons. The functions and their descriptions are the same for each section of the table; what varies is the way the functions are accomplished. Thus, to find out how objects might be tracked as part of the acquisition and discrimination function during the terminal phase, one reads the hypothetical example in the section of the table devoted to the terminal phase.

Boost Phase

Function	Description	Hypothetical Boost Phase Example
Acquire and discriminate objects	Sense objects of interest	Short and mid-wavelength infrared telescopes on BSTS detect hot exhaust plumes from launch of boosters
	Distinguish between targets to attack and decoys or debris	BSTS starts track files to distinguish moving ICBMs from stationary background and cloud clutter
	Track objects	SSTS sensors start to observe and record paths of identified objects
	Associate and Correlate objects sensed by different means or from different platforms	Battle management computers compare information gathered on two separate SSTS platforms and give same identification number to the same observed objects
Assess Situation	Estimate whether enemy is attacking, and if so with how many of what kinds of weapons with what battle tactics	BSTS detects ICBM launches, notes numbers and locations of launch sites, and determines types of missiles
	Assess which of own BMD forces are available for battle	Battle management computers determine which space based space-based interceptor (SBI) carrier vehicles (CVs) are in range of launched ICBM boosters, and will be in range of Post-Boost Vehicles (PBVs) when they are released from ICBMs.
Decide Course of Action	Authorize firing when ready, based on direction from higher authority if available, or as pre-authorized if not	If 3 or more ICBMs are launched within 1 minute, space battle management computers are programmed to command launch of space-based SBIs when the 4th ICBM is detected
	Determine strategy and battle plan	Determine plan for which kinds of ICBMs from which locations and which PBVs to attack first based on trajectories, CV positions, predicted RV impact points, and predicted times of PBV separation from missile
Select Targets & Direct Weapons	Choose which targets to strike	Select the booster or PBV whose trajectory will place it closest to the fly-out range of a particular CV
	Assign weapons	Battle management computer decides that SBIs no. 7888 and 7930 should attack target booster no. 754, and commands CVs to flight-check SBIs.
	Prepare engagement instructions	Battle management computers send flight plans and target track information to CVs.
	Assess kill: decide which targets have been destroyed	Remove a booster from the active target list
Employ Weapons	Control weapon	Feed target information to SBI guidance package
	Enable weapon	
	Prepare weapon	Conduct flight check of SBI

Table 7-1.—Ballistic Missile Defense Battle Management Functions—continued

| | Launch weapon | Open launch tube, eject and orient SBI, ignite SBI rocket motor |
| | Fly-out and kill | Battle manager transmits guidance update to SBI based on SSTS tracking data; SBI homes in on target booster or PBV |

Post-Boost Phase

Function	Description	Hypothetical Post Boost Phase Example
Acquire and discriminate objects	Sense objects of interest	Infrared telescope on SSTS detects PBV after it separates from missile, and RVs and decoys after separation from PBV
	Distinguish between targets to attack and decoys or debris	From differences in IR signatures and other data, such as PBV recoils, sensor systems on SSTS distinguishes among PBVs, expended boosters, RVs, and decoys
	Track objects	SSTS sensors continue to observe and record paths of identified objects
	Associate and correlate objects sensed by different means or from different platforms	Computers on two separate SSTS platforms compare information gathered by each and give same identification number to the same observed objects
Assess Situation	Estimate whether enemy is attacking, and if so with how many of what kinds of weapons with what battle tactics	
	Assess which of own BMD forces are available for battle	Battle management computers determine whichs CVs are in range of targetable PBVs and RVs
Decide Course of Action	Authorize firing when ready	
	Determine Strategy and Battle Plan	Battle management computers determine plan for attacking targetable PBVs that have survived earlier SBI intercepts and when to start attacking RVs that have been deployed from PBVs
Select Targets & Direct Weapons	Choose which targets to strike	Battle management computers target the PBVs that will first be in range of SBIs
	Assign weapons	Battle management computer decides that space-based SBI no. 12,543 should attack PBV no. 328 and commands CVs to flight check SBIs
	Prepare engagement instructions	Battle management computers send flight plans and target track information to CVs
	Assess kill: decide which targets have been destroyed	Remove a PBV from the active target list
Employ Weapons	Control weapon	Feed target information to SBI guidance package
	Enable weapon	
	Prepare weapon	Conduct flight check of SBI
	Launch weapon	Open launch tube, eject and orient SBI, and fire SBI rocket motor
	Fly-out and kill	Battle manager transmits guidance update to SBI; SBI homes in on target PBV or RV

Mid-Course Phase

Function	Description	Hypothetical Mid-course Example
Acquire and discriminate objects	Sense objects of interest	Infrared telescope on SSTS detects RVs and decoys
	Distinguish between targets to attack and decoys or debris	From differences in motion after passage through dust cloud, laser range-finding radar on SSTS identifies target RVs v. decoys
	Track objects	SSTS sensors continue to observe and record paths of identified objects

Table 7-1.—Ballistic Missile Defense Battle Management Functions—continued

Function	Description	Example
	Associate and correlate objects sensed by different means or from different platforms	Computers on two separate SSTS platforms compare information gathered by each and give same identification number to the same observed objects
Assess Situation	Estimate whether enemy is attacking, and if so with how many of what kinds of weapons with what battle tactics	
	Assess which of own BMD forces are available for battle	Computers determine which ERIS interceptors are in range of RVs
Decide Course of Action	Authorize firing when ready	
	Determine Strategy and Battle Plan	Determine plan for which RVs to attack first
Select Targets & Direct Weapons	Choose which targets to strike	Select the RVs within shortest flight time of a particular ERIS site
	Assign weapons	Battle management computer decides that ERIS interceptor no. 3001 should attack target RV no. 10,005 and commands fire control computer to flight check the interceptor
	Prepare engagement instructions	Battle management computer sends flight plan and target track information to ERIS fire control computer
	Assess kill: Decide which targets have been destroyed	Remove an RV in mid-course from the active target list
Employ Weapons	Control weapon	Feed target information to ERIS guidance package
	Enable weapon	Turn on ERIS warhead sensor
	Prepare weapon	Cool down ERIS homing sensor
	Launch weapon	Fire ERIS rocket motor
	Fly-out and kill	Battle manager transmits guidance updates to ERIS; ERIS homes in on target RV

Terminal Phase

Function	Description	Hypothetical Terminal Phase Example
Acquire and discriminate objects	Sense objects of interest	Infrared telescope on AOS detects RVs and decoys based on data received from SSTS; AOS passes data to TIR
	Distinguish between targets to attack and decoys or debris	From differences in motion after passage through the upper atmosphere, ground-based radar identifies target RVs v. decoys
	Track objects	Ground-based radars continue to observe and record paths of identified objects
	Associate and correlate objects sensed by different means or from different platforms	Ground-based battle management computer compares track information handed-off by space-based battle management computer with ground-based radar data and gives same identification number to the same observed objects
Assess Situation	Estimate whether enemy is attacking, and if so with how many of what kinds of weapons with what battle tactics	
	Assess which of own BMD forces are available for battle	Computers determine which HEDIs are in range of incoming RVs
Decide Course of Action	Authorize firing when ready	
	Determine Strategy and Battle Plan	Choose plan for which RVs to attack first
Select Targets & Direct Weapons	Choose which targets to strike	Select the RVs nearest to a target and that can be reached by a HEDI
	Assign weapons	Decide that HEDI no. 1897 should attack target RV no. 257
	Prepare engagement instructions	Ready flight plan and target tracking information for HEDI
	Assess kill: Decide which targets have been destroyed	Remove an RV in terminal from the active target list

Employ Weapons	Control weapon	Feed target information to HEDI guidance package
	Enable weapon	Turn on HEDI warhead sensor
	Prepare weapon	Cool down HEDI homing sensor
	Launch weapon	Fire HEDI rocket motor
	Fly-out and kill	Battle manager transmits guidance update to HEDI; HEDI homes in on target RV

BMD System Self-Defense

Function	Description	Hypothetical Self-Defense Example
Acquire and discriminate objects	Sense objects of interest	Infrared telescope on SSTS detects direct ascent ASAT
	Distinguish between targets to attack and decoys or debris	
	Track objects	SSTS sensors continue to observe and record paths of identified objects
	Associate and correlate objects sensed by different means or from different platforms	Computers on two separate SSTS platforms compare information gathered by each and give same identification number to the same observed objects
Assess Situation	Estimate whether enemy is attacking, and if so with how many of what kinds of weapons with what battle tactics	
	Assess which of own BMD forces are available for battle	Computers determine target of ASAT and which CVs may be used to defend against approaching ASAT
Decide Course of Action	Authorize firing when ready	
	Determine Strategy and Battle Plan	Choose plan for which ASATs to attack first
Select Targets & Direct Weapons	Choose which targets to strike	Select the ASAT nearest to a particular CV
	Assign weapons	Battle management computer decides that SBI no. 1024 should attack target ASAT no. 128, and commands CVs to flight check SBIs
	Prepare engagement instructions	Battle management computers send flight plans and target track information to CVs
	Assess kill: decide which targets have been destroyed	Remove an ASAT from the active target list
Employ Weapons	Control weapon	Feed target information to SBI guidance package
	Enable weapon	
	Prepare weapon	Conduct flight check of SBI
	Launch weapon	Open launch tube, eject and orient SBI, and fire SBI rocket motor
	Fly-out and kill	Battle manager transmits guidance update to SBI; SBI homes in on target ASAT

NOTE: The first two columns of this table draw heavily from work of Albert W. Small and P. Kathleen Groveston, *Strategic Defense Battle Operations Framework*, (Bedford, MA: The MITRE Corp., July 1985). The hypothetical examples are supplied by OTA.

could be launched in time to intercept the PBVs before they dispensed their payloads.

Post-Boost Phase

Tasks unique to the post-boost phase would be noting the separation of PBV from missile and observing the PBV as it dispensed its payload. To have a chance to destroy most PBVs, the interceptors would have to have been launched during boost phase, perhaps before PBV separation. To intercept the PBVs, the system would have to guide the SBIs launched earlier. For PBVs that survived to dispense their payloads, the system might start discriminating between RVs and decoys, perhaps by trying to observe differences in PBV recoil during the dispensing process.

Mid-Course Phase

The primary problem for the defensive system during mid-course would be to discriminate real warheads from decoys. The number of decoys may be in the hundreds of thousands, or even greater. Decoys and warheads may appear very similar to optical, infrared, radar, and other sensors, both passive and active.[3]

Terminal Phase

During terminal phase, the defensive system would have to discriminate RVs from decoys using data handed off from earlier phases and using the atmosphere and radar signatures as discriminators.

Table 7-1 shows the different functions a BMD system would have to perform during battle, and how different components would participate in different phases of the battle. The table assumes a second-phase architecture, such as described in table 3-6. It also shows the functions that would serve to defend the system against defense suppression threats.

Interactions Among the Phases

A BMD system would not be a single, monolithic entity. Instead, it would comprise many different elements, some of which would participate in only one or two phases of the battle. In most system architectures, battle management would be conducted by different battle managers during the different phases. Furthermore, some battle managers might be fighting one phase of the battle while others are fighting a different phase. Boost, post-boost, and mid-course managers would be located in space, while terminal phase managers would likely be on the ground. For the system to function most effectively, information, such as tracks and status of RVs and decoys, would have to be communicated from battle managers in earlier phases to battle managers in later phases.

Interactions for Tracking Purposes

Establishing, distributing, and correlating track information is a good example of a problem involving interaction among different system elements and cooperation among battle managers. Detecting, identifying, and noting the current position of a target would not be sufficient for guiding a BMD weapon system. The target would move between the time that the sensor records its position and the time the weapon is fired. An SBI traveling at, say, 8 km/sec, would take 250 seconds to reach an RV target if the SBI were fired at a range of 2,000 km from the impact point. During those 250 seconds, the RV would move 1750 km. Just as the hunter must lead the duck in flight as he fires his shotgun, the BMD system would have to aim its SBI well ahead of the speeding RV.[4]

The BMD system would therefore have to keep track of each target's motion and predict where the target would be at later times. The sensors would have to generate a "track file," i.e., a history of each target's motion through space. Given the target's past history in terms of position, velocity, and acceleration *in three dimensions*, a computer could then predict its future position. This prediction could then be used to aim and fire the weapon system. After the SBI was fired, the sensors would have to continue to track the target (and possibly the SBI), the track files would have to be updated, and mid-course guidance corrections sent to keep the SBI on a collision course. Mid-course corrections would be mandatory if the target acceleration changed after the SBI was fired, as would occur with multi-stage missiles.

For directed-energy weapons or interactive sensor systems, the delay from the time that energy is emitted by the target until it reaches the sensor, and then from the firing of the weapon until the arrival of the kill energy traveling at the speed of light, would be very short, but not zero. At 2,000 km range, for example, 13 milliseconds would elapse from the last sensor reading until the time a laser beam could reach the target. The RV would move about 91 meters in this time, so some predictive ca-

---

[3]Chapters 4 and 10 discuss the issues of discrimination during mid-course in more detail.

[4]However, the RV would be moving on a ballistic or free-fall flight with no external acceleration other than the force of gravity. Therefore, predicting its future path or trajectory would be possible provided that the sensor generated two or more accurate three dimensional target positions. Predicting the future path of an accelerating, multi-stage missile would be much more difficult. RVs that could maneuver would worsen the difficulties.

pability would be required.[5] In addition, the observable characteristics of the target would change drastically during the tracking operation. The sensor systems would begin tracking the hot booster plume. For boost phase kills, the sensors would have to acquire and track the cold booster body, or rely on calculations of the missile body position relative to the booster plume for all booster/sensor orientations. After the last booster stage had burned out, the battle management computers would have to continue the track file on the surviving post-boost vehicles (PBV), even though tracking data might be derived from other types of sensors. Finally, as individual RV's and decoys were deployed, the track files would have to proliferate, taking the last PBV track projection as the recently deployed RV track file, until it could be verified and updated by long wavelength infrared sensors.

The data handling problem would be compounded by RV's that survived the boost and post-boost defensive attacks. The surviving RV's would usually pass out of the field of view of the initial sensor. The track file obtained from one sensor's data would then have to be correlated with the data from another sensor.[6] Track data would be passed to the appropriate weapons platform at each stage of the battle. Eventually the track files of surviving targets should be passed on to the ground-based terminal defensive systems to aid in the final kill attempts. Information on decoys and other rocket or killed target debris should also be

_____

[5]In general it would take additional time for the sensor signal processor to analyze the sensor data and for the track file to be updated after the last signal was received; the actual elapsed time between observation and the order to fire the weapon might be 5 to 10 seconds, so the target might move as much as 70 km even for a directed-energy weapon.

[6]If battle managers, sensors, and weapons were organized into autonomous battle groups, then each battle manager would have to hand off and receive track data as targets passed through the field of view of sensors in its group, or it would have to perform all of its own target acquisition and discrimination. If there were a single battle manager to handle all tracking and correlation, it would have to maintain track files on all targets. Such an organization would tie system survivability to survivability of the central battle manager. Finally, if battle groups were to use fixed battle management platforms, but different sensors and weapons as the battle continued, then the battle managers would have to correlate tracks from different sensors as the sensors moved in and out of its group.

transmitted, to avoid attacking too many false targets.

System Performance and Interaction

The ability to correlate data well from different sensors (required to get accurate three-dimensional track histories) could have a strong effect on system performance, as could the ability to correlate track files exchanged among battle managers both within and between phases. Poor performance in the early phases would mean many RVs leaking into later phases, with possible overload of resources assigned to mid-course and terminal phases.

Distinctions Among the Phases

In all phases the defensive system would have to perform many similar functions, such as tracking; weapons assignment; aiming, firing and controlling weapons; and reporting status. Sensors and weapons would vary considerably from one phase to another, however. For example, boost, post-boost, and mid-course tracking would be done primarily by space-based infrared sensors such as those incorporated in the BSTS and SSTS systems. Terminal phase tracking would be done by a combination of airborne infrared sensors and ground-based radars. The software and hardware used to perform the sensing, discrimination, and tracking functions in different phases would likely be quite different; aiming, firing, and controlling weapons might be similar.

Some phases would require unique functions. A good example is interactive discrimination of RVs from decoys for mid-course defense. Candidates for such discrimination, such as neutral particle beam systems, would likely be controlled by unique computer software and hardware adapted to the task.

Reconfiguration

In addition to fighting the battle, the system would also have to be able to reconfigure itself during and after the battle, to compensate for damage done to it, in preparation for further or continued engagements. In the post-

Photo credit: U.S. Air Force

Command Post of the North American Aerospace Defense (NORAD) Cheyenne Mountain Complex near Colorado Springs, Colorado. In case of war, computerized information on an incoming bomber or missile attack on the United States would be analyzed here and passed on to other civilian and military officials. If the United States had a boost-phase ballistic missile defense system, the time available for human decisionmaking on whether to use the system might be measured in seconds.

battle case, this might be done with human assistance.

Opportunities for Human Intervention

Tracking and discriminating objects, aiming and firing weapons, and managing the battle would require computers. During peacetime, humans could monitor surveillance data after it had been processed and displayed in a form suitable for human interpretation. Human decisionmakers could deduce from the events monitored, among other things, whether and when the defensive system should be placed in alert status, ready to cope with a battle. Once the battle started, however, the response time and data processing requirements would severely limit the opportunities for human intervention. There are four possible human intervention points under consideration in currently suggested BMD architectures:

- the decision to move the system from peacetime status to alert status,
- the decision to release weapons,
- the decision to switch to a back-up for one or more of the algorithms (see box 7-A) used by the battle management computers, and
- selection from a pre-specified set of tactics for terminal phase, made as a result of observations of earlier phases of the battle.

Transition to Alert Status

Humans could decide to move from one level of alert to another in hours or minutes, as compared to fractions of seconds for computers

Box 7-A.—Algorithms

Methods for solving problems by the use of computers are often expressed as algorithms. As described by John Shore,

> An algorithm is a precise description of a method for solving a particular problem using operations or actions from a well-understood repertoire.[1]

More technical definitions often require that the description contain a finite number of steps, each of which can be performed in a finite amount of time, and that there be specific inputs and outputs. As explained by computer scientist Donald Knuth,

> The modern meaning of algorithm is quite similar to that of recipe, process, method, technique, procedure, routine, . . .[2]

Carrying out the steps of an algorithm is known as "executing it." If one thinks of a recipe for baking a cake as an algorithm, then executing the algorithm consists of following the recipe to produce the cake. The following is a simplified example of an algorithm that might be used in the early stages of the design of a BMD system. The purpose of the algorithm is to detect the launch of boosters. We assume that the system uses a sensor on a satellite that can scan the Soviet Union. The sensor is composed of a number of different elements, each of which is sensitive to the radiation emitted by a booster. The Soviet Union is divided into regions, and each detector element periodically scans sequentially across a number of regions.

1. For each detector element, record all detected radiation sources greater than the threshold for a booster as the detector scans across the Soviet Union. Record the time of occurrence of each detection as well as the intensity of the source.
2. For each source recorded, identify its region of origin.
3. Compare the occurrences of sources in the current scan with occurrences from the previous two scans. Count all events consisting of occurrences of sources in the same region for three consecutive scans. Flag each such event as a launch.
4. If data have been saved from more than 2 consecutive scans, discard the data from the oldest scan and save the data from the current scan.
5. If no launches were observed, go back to step 1, otherwise continue with step 4.
6. If launches were observed, notify the system operator.

While this description is simplified, e.g., omitting consideration of booster movement across regions, it is an algorithm because the operations needed to perform each step could be completely specified; furthermore, it could be implemented as a computer program.

Although the number of steps used in describing an algorithm must be finite, the definition does not require that the algorithm terminate when executed. Many algorithms are designed to be non-terminating, such as the following simplified description of how a radar processing system might operate:

1. Send out radar pulse.
2. Wait a pre-calculated interval for a return pulse.
3. If there was a return pulse calculate the distance to the object.
4. Go back to step 1.

Despite not terminating, this algorithm still produces useful results. Some algorithms terminate under certain conditions, but do not terminate and produce no results under other conditions. Conditions under which algorithms do not produce the desired results are known as *error* or *exception* conditions and the occurrence of such conditions as *undesired events*. For the following simplified algorithm, which tracks a target based on radar returns, the failure of the radar pointing mechanism is an undesired event that causes the algorithm to continue endlessly, producing no useful result.

1. Retrieve the last known target location, velocity, and acceleration.
2. Calculate the estimated current target location.

[1]John Shore, *The Sachertorte Algorithm and Other Antidotes to Computer Anxiety* (New York, NY: Viking Press, 1985), p. 131.
[2]Donald E. Knuth, *The Art of Computer Programming, Vol. 1: Fundamental Algorithms* (Reading, MA: Addison Wesley, 1974), p. 4.

---

3. Point the radar at the estimated current target location and attempt object detection.

4. If the radar locates no object at the estimated range to the target, revise the estimated target location and return to step 3. Otherwise, continue with step 5.

5. If the radar locates an object at the estimated range to the target, update the target location, velocity, and acceleration.

A real version of such a tracking algorithm would have to take into account the possibility that the radar might fail in any of several different ways, or that earlier estimates of target position might be grossly wrong.

---

during battle. The humans' decisions could be based on data gathered from sources both within and outside the BMD system. The computerized battle-time decisions would be based on data acquired by the system's sensors.

Weapons Release

Once a human had permitted the transition to the highest level of alert, the system would function automatically, responding to threats as it perceived them.[7] It would be possible to build human intervention points for the release of weapons into the battle management process. In the first-phase and second-phase systems described in chapter 3, the first weapons to be released would be the SBIs. The period from the time that a missile launch was first perceived by BMD sensors until SBIs would have to be launched to intercept a missile still in its boost phase would be quite short—a few minutes at most. Accordingly, if humans were to control the release of weapons, they would have to monitor the defense system's operation continuously once it had moved to the highest alert status.

Since it may be necessary to release hundreds or thousands of SBIs within minutes, a human operator would not be able to authorize release of individual SBIs. Because of the rapid reaction times needed, continual human intervention in the weapons release process would likely degrade system effectiveness unacceptably. It might be feasible to intervene when previously unused weapon systems were

brought into the battle. As an example, if neutral particle beam (NPB) weapons had not been used before enemy missiles reached midcourse, then a human might be called on to authorize their use during the mid-course part of the battle. Even such occasional intervention might degrade performance somewhat.

Switching to Back-ups

During the course of the battle it might be possible for a human observer to determine that a BMD system was malfunctioning. For a human to notice, the malfunction would probably have to be gross, such as a failure to fire interceptors or firing interceptors in obviously wrong directions. If the problem lay in the algorithms used by the battle management computers, and if the system were designed in such a way that back-up algorithms were available to the computers, then the human might command the battle management computers to switch to a particular back-up algorithm.[8]

Human intervention of this type is rarely used in existing systems because the human cannot interpret the situation correctly in the available time, and because it is difficult to design the software to switch algorithms successfully in mid-computation. In most systems, the gain is not worth the added software complexity. The potential gain for BMD from such intervention would be that in the cases where

---

[7]The AEGIS ship defense system, often cited as performing many of the same functions as a BMD system, reacts completely automatically to incoming threats when in the highest level of alert mode. For some threats, AEGIS must react within 15 seconds from the time a threat is detected.

[8]Switching to a back-up algorithm should not be confused with situations where a computer uses built-in diagnostics to determine the occurrence of a hardware malfunction and then automatically switches operation to a redundant component. Such diagnostics and hardware redundancy for automatic switching are now used in some critical applications, such as airline transaction systems, telephone switching systems, and battle management systems such as AEGIS.

the system had been badly spoofed by the enemy, and the human operator quickly recognized the symptoms, cause, and needed corrective action, recovery might be possible in time to continue the battle. The risk would be that the operator would misjudge the situation, or that the complications involved in providing the appropriate interface to the operator, both in additional software, hardware, and communications capability, would make the system less reliable.

Selection of Tactics

Because the boost, post-boost, and midcourse phases of a BMD battle would last 20-30 minutes, a human commander might be able to evaluate the results of those phases in time to affect the tactics used during the terminal phase. To do so, he would have to be presented with status reports during the battle. Based on his analysis of the battle, and on choices of previously-determined tactics presented to him by an automated battle manager, he could choose the terminal phase tactics to be used. Again, because of the time-scales and data volumes involved, he would probably not be able to alter his choice once the terminal phase began.

Increasing degrees of human intervention would require increasing complexity in the interface between humans and the battle management system. A sophisticated interface between human and computer would be needed, allowing the human to observe status and issue commands, and, when appropriate, receive acknowledgements. Such an interface would add complexity to the software. Furthermore,

the human operator(s) would probably have to have authority to release weapons, as there might not be time to consult with higher authorities.

Common to all BMD system designs that require human intervention at any stage is the need to provide secure, rapid communications between the human and the battle management computers. If part of the system were in space, then most likely there would be a need for space-to-ground communications.[9]

For all of the preceding reasons, it seems likely that a BMD system would operate almost completely automatically once moved to an alert status in preparation for battle.

The preceding analysis illustrates the difficult trade-offs involved in designing a battle management system. In considering the interface between humans and the system, the designer must trade off communications security against the need for human intervention against system structure against complication of the computing tasks. He must also balance system performance against all other considerations, deciding whether the system could perform better and more dependably with the aid of a human than without, and whether any extra complication in the human-computer interfaces would be worth whatever capability and trustworthiness might be added by the human.

---

[9]Even if a human operator were space-based, he might need to communicate with higher authority on the ground. Such communications would probably not require as rapid data communication rates as battle-management-to-operator communications.

SUPPORTING FUNCTIONS

Table 7-1 shows the primary battle management functions, but does not include several supporting functions. Most important of these are communications and recovery from damage and from failures. Both of these functions are needed in all phases, with communications playing its traditionally crucial role in battle management and with recovery invoked as

needed. Both communications and recovery procedures would be completely automated during a battle. Because of the short decision times involved during boost, post-boost, and terminal phases, recovery would have to be extremely rapid; delays would result in RVs moving on to the next phase or reaching their targets. Long delays in recovery could also reduce the opportunities for a battle manager fighting in one phase to pass information along to battle managers fighting in the next phase.

Communications

Automated communications links between sensors and battle management computers, between different battle management computers, between battle management computers and weapons, and between battle management computers and humans, would all be needed for effective battle management. Data would be continually transmitted over a battle management communications network during all battle phases.

Recovery From Damage and Failures

Present in all phases would be the need to recognize and recover from system failures and from damage to system resources. Individual system components would have to monitor and report their own status continually. They would have to try to recover from local failures, whether internally generated—perhaps by a software error—or externally generated—perhaps by a detonation of a nearby nuclear antisatellite weapon causing radiation damage in a computer chip.

Some instances of system damage and failure, such as destruction of several adjacent battle management platforms or communications controllers, would require recovery based on "global information," i.e., information about the status of the entire BMD system and the entire battle. Examples are knowing how to reroute communications around damaged nodes in the communications network, or knowing which battle management computers were in position, both physically and in terms of resources available, to take over the functions of a disabled battle manager.

COMPLEXITY OF BATTLE MANAGEMENT

Conduct of a successful BMD battle would be similar to the conduct of a large conventional battle in that it would require the orchestration of many different kinds of components under precise timing constraints. The problem may be ameliorated somewhat by preplanning some of the orchestration. The difference is that in a BMD battle the time constraints would be tighter, the battle space would be larger, the fighting would largely be automated, the components would be previously untested in battle, and there would be little chance to employ human ingenuity to counter unanticipated threats or strategies.

The only kind of BMD system for which the U.S. has battle management software development experience and an understanding of the attendant problems is a terminal defense system, such as SAFEGUARD. Some consider even this experience as suspect, since SAFEGUARD and other systems like it were never used in a real battle. Adding a boost-phase defense would add complexity to the system and require the inclusion of technologies hitherto untried in battle. It would also be the first time that software was used to control highly automated space-based weapons.

Adding a mid-course defense would probably increase the software complexity past that of any existing systems. The burden of effectively integrating information from different sensors, controlling different weapons, coordinating interactive discrimination to distinguish among hundreds of thousands of potential targets, and selecting effective strategy and tactics—all while trying to defend against active countermeasures—would fall on the software. (Software issues are discussed in detail in ch. 9.)

Approaches to reducing complexity center on "divide and conquer" strategies applied to architecture definition, aided by simulations of the effectiveness of different battle management architectures. Those who favor such approaches believe that the system could be designed and built in small, relatively independent pieces that could each be adequately tested, and that could be jointly subjected to peacetime tests. As an example, each interceptor carrier vehicle might contain a battle manager, designed to fight independently of other battle managers. They argue that the system could be easily expanded by adding more pieces, e.g., more CVs each with its own battle manager. Since the pieces would tend to be independent, the reliability of the system would be more strongly related to the reliability of an individual piece, rather than to the joint reliability of all pieces, i.e., knowing that individual pieces were reliable would suggest that the whole system was reliable. Also, the failure of a single piece might not be as cata- strophic as in an architecture where the pieces were highly interdependent.

Those who doubt the effectiveness of such a strategy in the face of the complexity induced by BMD requirements argue that making the pieces independent would require making them very complex. They further note that historically no approach has led to the development of a weapon system whose software worked correctly the first time it was used in battle. The greater complexity of BMD software over existing weapon systems leads them to believe that a BMD system would have little chance of doing so.

BATTLE MANAGEMENT ARCHITECTURE

A *battle management architecture* is a specification of the battle management functions to be performed by different system components and the relationships among those components. Components may be software, such as a set of computer programs that would allocate weapons to targets, or hardware, such as the computer(s) used to execute those programs. (See also ch. 3.)

A significant architectural trade-off concerns the degree of coupling among battle managers (see box 7-B). Some proposed architectures use a very loosely coupled system with little communication among battle managers, similar to the "almost perfect" architecture described in the Fletcher Report.[10] Such architectures tend to locate battle managers on board carrier vehicles. Others use a more tightly coupled system with track and other data exchanged among battle managers for coordination purposes. They often locate battle managers on separate platforms.

---

[10]James C. Fletcher, Study Chairman and B. McMillan, Panel Chairman, *Report of the Study on Eliminating the Threat Posed by Nuclear Ballistic Missiles: Volume V, Battle Management, Communications, and Data Processing,* (Washington, DC: Department of Defense, Defensive Technologies Study Team, Oct. 1983), p. 19.

Box 7-B.—Centralization, Distribution, and Coupling

A centralized system concentrates computing resources in one location and may consist of several processors that share the same memory and are housed together physically. Such a system is known as a multiprocessor. The processors are able to communicate with each other at very high data rates, and are said to be *tightly coupled*. As the processors are physically moved apart, acquire their own, separate memories, and as the data communication rates among them decrease, they acquire the characteristics of a distributed system, also called decentralized, and are said to be *loosely coupled*.

An important factor in understanding the degree of coupling is the criterion used to partition the battle space into segments so that each battle management computer has responsibility for a segment. Indeed, criteria for segmentation are one way of distinguishing among architectures. Segments might be geographically determined and of fixed location, or might be determined by the clustering of targets as they move through space, or might be determined by the location of battle managers, CVs, sensors, and other system resources during a battle.

Although the Eastport Group[11] recommended that BMD battle managers be hierarchically structured, the Fletcher Report[12] suggested that a logical battle management structure that was almost perfect would not be hierarchical, but would consist of a single battle manager replicated a number of different times, with each copy physically located on a different platform. The Fletcher report also noted that such an architecture might be very costly, that there might be equally effective and cheaper alternatives, and that it was important to look at technical issues that distinguished among those alternatives. An example given was the effectiveness of algorithms that allocated weapons to targets based only

on local data. **As yet, few detailed studies of such technical issues appear to have been made.**

The Eastport Group recommended the development of a decentralized, hierarchical battle management architecture.[13] Architectures currently under consideration for BMD systems are consistent with that recommendation. In a typical such architecture, each battle manager would report as necessary to battle managers at higher levels, and would receive commands from them. There might be 3 layers of battle managers; the lowest layer would be local battle managers, which perform the fighting functions. The next layer would be regional

---

[11]Eastport Study Group Report, "Report to the Director, Strategic Defense Initiative Organization, 1985."

[12]Fletcher Report, op. cit., footnote 10, pp. 9-21.

[13]The Eastport Study Group is the name used to refer to the SDIO Panel on Computing in Support of Battle Management. It was appointed "to devise an appropriate computational/communication response to the SDI battle management computing problem and make recommendations for a research and technology development program to implement the response." Its report was issued in December 1985.

Box 7-C.—Hierarchies and System Design

Designers of systems find it useful to impose a structure on the design. For complex systems, several different structures may be used, each allowing the designer to concentrate on a different concern. In systems where many components are involved, such as complex software systems, large communications systems, and complex weapons systems, the structures used are often hierarchical. Each hierarchy may be specified by identifying the participating components and a relationship among them. The military command structure is an example of a hierarchy. The components are individuals of different rank, and the relationship is "obeys the commands of," e.g., a lieutenant obeys the commands of a captain.

Many proposed SDI battle management architectures use some variation of the relationship "resource contentions are resolved by." Thus, local battle managers' resource contentions are resolved by regional battle managers. However, another important battle management hierarchy is "communicates track data to." This latter hierarchy is important in determining communications needs for the BMD system, and is sometimes confused with the former.

A *tree* is a special form of hierarchy in which a component at one level is only related to one component at the next higher level. The military chain of command is an example. A lieutenant is only commanded by one captain, although a captain may have several lieutenants under his command. The Eastport Group considered battle management architectures that were structured as trees to be the most promising for SDI.[1]

Structures may describe relationships among entities in a design, independent of physical relationships among system components. Such structures are sometimes known as *logical structures*.[2]

---

[1]The Eastport Study Group is the name used to refer to the SDIO Panel on Computing in Support of Battle Management. It was appointed "to devise an appropriate computational/communication response to the SDI battle management computing problem and make recommendations for a research and technology development program to implement the response." Its report was issued in December 1985.

[2]See, for example, *Report of the Study on Eliminating the Threat Posed by Nuclear Ballistic Missiles*, James C. Fletcher, Study Chairman, Volume V, *Battle Management, Communications, and Data Processing*, (Washington, DC: Department of Defense, Defensive Technologies Study Team, October 1983), p. 18.

battle managers, which would resolve contentions for resources among local battle managers, as battle managers, sensors, and weapons moved, and which would assign responsibility for targets passing between battle spaces. At the top would be a global battle manager that would establish strategy for the regional and local battle managers and that which would provide the interface between humans and the system. The battle space would be partitioned into segments such that each battle manager in the lowest layer of the hierarchy had responsibility for a segment. As battle managers and targets moved through the battle space, information concerning them, such as type of target, location of target, and trajectory of target, would have to be moved from one computer to another.

Some recent proposals have suggested fewer layers in the battle management hierarchy. In such architectures, the hierarchy of automated battle managers is flat, i.e., there are no regional battle managers, and the top layer is a human commander. Such organizations have been designed so that battle managers may act almost independently of each other.

The volume of data to be communicated among the battle management computers would depend on the degree of coordination among the battle managers required by the battle management architecture. (See chapter 8 for estimates of communication requirements.) The determining factor is the amount of target tracking information that would have to be exchanged. Since there might be hundreds of thousands of objects to be tracked during mid-course, architectures that required tracks of all objects to be exchanged among battle managers would place a heavier load on communications than those that required no object tracks to be exchanged. The price paid for exchanging less information, however, would be the traditional one: the ability to coordinate the actions of different battle managers would be hampered and the overall efficiency of battle management might be decreased.

The efficiency-volume trade-off may be seen by considering the transition from one phase of the battle to the next. As an example, the terminal-phase battle managers would have the best chance to destroy targets if they received target-tracking information from the mid-course battle managers. Without such information they would have to acquire, track, and discriminate among targets before pointing and firing weapons. With such information they would only have to continue tracking targets and point and fire weapons. In such a situation, one might suggest combining the mid-course and terminal-phase battle managers into one set of programs on one computer as opposed to a more distributed system with information transmitted among battle managers. Unfortunately, this organization would probably complicate the battle management task, since there would be somewhat different functions to be performed in the different phases, and since the way functions would be implemented in different phases would be different.[14]

The Eastport Group believed that a hierarchical battle management organization would simplify the computing job of each battle manager and would allow the battle managers to act without frequent interchange of information.[15] The concerns of each battle manager could then be simplified more than in a nonhierarchical organization, battle managers could be added to the system as needed, and the system would still survive if a few lower level battle managers were lost.

---

[14]Since different weapons would be used in the terminal phase as compared to the mid-course, pointing and controlling the weapons would be done differently. Similarly, different sensors may be used to discriminate between targets and decoys, requiring the allocation of resources with different characteristics and therefore a different resource allocation algorithm.

[15]Some earlier proposed architectures required the battle managers to be tightly coupled, exchanging considerable information with each other frequently. The Eastport Study Group rejected such an architecture because of the computing and communications burden it would place on the battle managers, and because of the complexity it would induce in the battle management software.

Decentralizing battle management means that the battle management task would be physically distributed among different computers. Decentralization would permit other battle managers to continue fighting even if a local battle manager were disabled. However, if the degree of coupling were high, the loss of data from the disabled battle manager might result in reduced effectiveness of the others. Without a specific design and a way of effectively testing architectures, it is difficult to verify claims about their merits and deficiencies. Such tests would have to be based on simulations and on whatever peacetime tests could be conducted.[16] However, the apparent disadvantages of a decentralized, hierarchical system would be:

- contentions for resources would have to be resolved at upper levels of the hierarchy, possibly adding complexity to the computational problem as a whole,
- the actions of battle managers would be based mainly on local data, perhaps resulting in inefficiencies, e.g., adjacent battle managers might both shoot at some of the same targets, thereby wasting shots, un-

---

[16]The proposed National Test Bed, might provide some of the simulation capabilities needed for architecture evaluation.

less sophisticated battle management algorithms to compensate for the information loss could be developed,

- if strategic and tactical decisionmaking were concentrated at one level in the hierarchy, disabling some or all of that level could greatly reduce system performance. Such damage would be easier to accomplish if there were relatively few battle managers at that level, as might be true at the higher levels of the hierarchy.

The Eastport group believed that the advantages of a hierarchical, decentralized system far outweighed the disadvantages. Evaluation of advantages and disadvantages must await a design specific enough to be tested, and an effective test method.

No matter the choice of structure for battle management, some technology would be strained and software dependability would be a key issue. Centralization would appear particularly to stress computational performance and survivability. Decentralization would appear to require more sophisticated software at the local battle manager level and would increase the weapons supply needed. All architectures would require secure communication, whether to exchange track data, or to receive sensor data, or to communicate with the ground.

CONCLUSIONS

Ballistic missile defense battle management would be an extremely complex process. The number of objects, volume of space, and speed at which decisions would have to be made during a battle preclude most human participation. Aside from authorizing the system to move to alert status, prepared to fight automatically, at best the human's role would be to authorize the initial release of weapons and to change to back-up, previously-prepared, strategy or tactics. **Decisions about which weapons to use, when to use them, and against which targets to use them would all be automated.** Inclusion of human intervention points would likely add

complexity to an already complex system and to compromise system performance in some situations. On the other hand, if an attacker had successfully foiled the primary defensive strategy, human intervention might allow recovery from defeat.

Battle management architectures as yet proposed are not specific enough for their claimed advantages and disadvantages to be effectively evaluated. Such evaluation must await both better architecture specifications and the development of an effective evaluation technique, perhaps based on simulation.

196

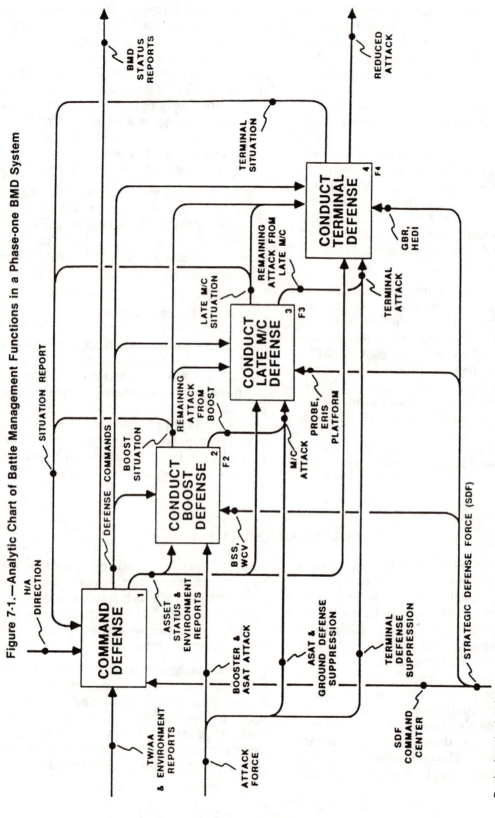

Figure 7-1.—Analytic Chart of Battle Management Functions in a Phase-one BMD System

Designing the battle management sub-system (including command, control, and communications) for a BMD system will require precise specification of all the necessary channels of communication and points of decision. "Pipeline" charts like this help analysts conceptualize battle management complexities. Later, computer programs must be engineered to carry out the functions identified by the analysts.

SOURCE: Strategic Defense Initiative Organization, 1987.

Chapter 8
Computing Technology

CONTENTS

Boxes

Tables

Computing Technology

INTRODUCTION

This chapter discusses the demands that ballistic missile defense (BMD) systems would place on computing technology, and the trade-offs that would have to be considered in satisfying those demands. Initial sections discuss why BMD would need computers and how it would use them for battle management, weapons control, sensor data processing, communications, and simulation. Later sections describe the technology used to build computers and the requirements that the Strategic Defense Initiative (SDI) imposes on that technology. The chapter concludes with key issues posed by SDI computing needs. Any description of computing technology must be accompanied by a discussion of software and software technology issues; these can be found in chapter 9 and appendix A.

The Need for Automation

The rapid response times and volume of data to be processed would require the use of computers in every major BMD component and during every phase of battle. Humans could not make decisions fast enough to direct the battle. The launch of thousands of intercontinental ballistic missiles (ICBMs), some employing fast-burn rocket boosters, might permit less than 60 seconds to detect, track, aim, and fire weapons at the first boosters to clear the atmosphere. During mid-course it might be necessary to account for a million objects and to discriminate among hundreds of thousands of decoys and thousands of reentry vehicles (RVs). In the terminal stage, RVs in the atmosphere would have to be quickly located, tracked, and destroyed by interceptor missiles.

Mutual occupation of space by two defensive systems of comparable capabilities might require considerably faster reaction times than

Note: Complete definitions of acronyms and initialisms are listed in Appendix B of this report.

those needed to meet a ballistic missile attack alone. Countering an attack by space-borne directed-energy weapons would require response times of seconds or less to avoid the loss of critical defensive capabilities. The critical part of such a battle could well be over before humans realized that it was taking place.

Although automated decision-making is a focus of concern for the use of computers in BMD, computers would also serve many other purposes. Table 8-1 shows many of the places where computers would be used.

Integrating Sensors, Weapons, and Computers

An automated BMD system would require some degree of coordination among different computers, but there would be many places where computers would act independently of each other. Table 8-1 shows many such cases, e.g., computers incorporated into sensor systems, such as radars, to perform signal processing on data perceived by the sensor. In each case the computer may be specially designed for its job and is physically a part of the system of which it is a component.

As an example, an imaging radar would build up an image of an object such as an RV by analyzing the returns from the object over a period of seconds. The radar would process each return individually and store the results. With sufficient individual returns, the radar could analyze them to form an image of the object. A single computer incorporated into the radar would perform the processing, storage, and analysis. From the viewpoint of an external observer, such as a battle management computer residing on a different platform, the radar is a black box that produces an image of an RV. The external observer need know nothing about the computer inside the

Table 8-1.—Computers in a Ballistic Missile Defense System

Component	Purpose of Computers
First- and Second-Phase Systems:	
Battle Management Computers[a]	Coordinate track data (e.g, maintain a track data base and correlate data from multiple sensors); maintain status of and control defense assets; select strategy; select targets; command firing of weapons; assess situation.
Boost Phase Surveillance and Tracking Satellite (BSTS)	Process signals to transform IR sensor data into digital data representing potential booster tracks; process images to recognize missile launches and to produce crudely-resolved booster tracks; communicate with battle management computers; maintain satellite platform: guidance, station keeping, defensive maneuvering; housekeeping.
Space Surveillance and Tracking Satellite (SSTS)	Process signals to transform IR, laser range-finder, and radar sensor data into digital data representing potential tracks; process images and data for fine-tracking of launched boosters, post-boost vehicles, RVs and decoys and to discriminate RVs from decoys; point sensors; communicate with other elements of the BMD system; guidance, station keeping, defensive maneuvering, housekeeping (maintain mechanical and electronic systems).
Laser Thermal Tagger	Point the laser beam; communicate with other elements of the BMD system; maintain satellite platform: guidance, station keeping, defensive maneuvering; housekeeping.
Carrier Vehicle (CV) for Space-based Interceptors (SBI)	Monitor status of SBIs; control launching of SBIs; communicate with battle manager; maintain satellite platform: guidance, station keeping, defensive maneuvering; housekeeping.
Space-based Interceptor (SBI)	Guide flight based on commands received from battle manager; Track target and guide missile home to target; communicate with battle manager; housekeeping.
Airborne Optical System (AOS)	Process signals to transform IR data into digital data representing potential tracks; process images and data for fine-tracking of post-boost vehicles, RVs and decoys and, if possible, discriminating RVs from decoys; point sensors; communicate with other elements of the BMD system; control of airborne platform; housekeeping.
Exo-atmospheric Interceptor System (ERIS)	Guide flight; process signals and images from on-board sensor for terminal guidance and target tracking; communicate with battle manager and SSTS, AOS, and probe sensors; housekeeping.
Ground-based Terminal Imaging Radar	Process signals and images to convert radar returns to target tracks; process images and data to discriminate between decoys and RVs; control radar beam; communicate with battle managers and other elements of BMD system; housekeeping.
High Endo-atmospheric Interceptors (HEDI)	Guide missile flight based on commands received from battle manager; process signals and images from on-board sensor for terminal guidance and target tracking; communicating with battle manager; housekeeping.
Third Phase, Add:	
Ground-based Laser, Space-based Mirrors	Manage laser beam generation; Control corrections to beam and mirrors for atmospheric turbulence; steer mirrors; communicate with battle manager; housekeeping.
Space-based Neutral Particle Beam (NPB)	Manage particle beam generation; steer the accelerator; track potential targets; communicate with battle manager and neutron detector; maintain satellite platform: guidance, station keeping, defensive maneuvering, housekeeping.
Radiation Detector Satellites	Discriminate between targets and decoys based on sensor inputs; communicate with battle manager and/or SSTS; maintain satellite platform: guidance, station keeping, defensive maneuvering; housekeeping.

[a]May be carried on sensor platforms, weapon platforms, or separate platforms; ground-based units may be mobile.

SOURCE: Office of Technology Assessment, 1988.

radar, or how it operates, but only the form and content of its output.

Customizing the Computer for the Application

The above "black box" design strategy is based on sound engineering principles and tends to simplify the battle management architecture, but it still involves some difficult trade-offs. One such trade-off is that between developing special-purpose computers for different sensors and weapons versus utilizing commercially available hardware. Utilizing commercially available computers may simplify the job of software development. There would be people available who have experience with existing hardware. In addition, support tools for software development on available computers already exist. As a result, software developed for commercially available computers would probably be more reliable, more efficient, and less expensive than software developed for new computers built specifically for BMD. Furthermore, software development would not have to wait for development of the hardware, reducing the risk of not meeting schedules.

On the other hand, hardware specially built for BMD is likely to be more efficient and better suited to the job, possibly offsetting efficiency losses in software. Moreover, maintainability, reliability of the hardware, and life-cycle cost would have to be taken into account. Software experts at OTA's SDI Software Workshop suggested that hardware customization v. software reliability and cost was an important trade-off that should be resolved in favor of simplifying software development. However, some SDI computing might require the use of novel hardware designs, even though this might require designing new and complex software from scratch.

Communications and Computer Networks

Battle management requires communications among the battle managers, sensors, and weapons forming a BMD system and between the battle managers and the human operators of the system. Space-to-space, space-to-ground, and ground-to-space communications would be required. As in traditional battle management, information must be sent in useful form, on time, and securely to the place where it is needed. Also as in traditional battle management, information transmitted among battle managers concerns the location of targets and weapons, the status of resources, and decisions that have been made. Distinct from traditional battle management, information transmitted in a BMD system would all be digitally encoded and the transmissions controlled by computers. As noted in chapter 7, the rate and volume of data to be transmitted depend on the battle management architecture.

Estimates of Communications Requirements

The Fletcher Report estimated that the peak data rate needed by any communications channel in a BMD system would be about 10^7 bits per second (bps).[1] This estimate assumed that an entire track file would have to be transmitted, that the file would contain 30,000 tracks, and that each track could be represented in 200 bits. Except for the number of tracks in a track file, the estimate is based on conservative assumptions. Furthermore, it scales linearly with the number of tracks, i.e., a track file containing 300,000 tracks would require a peak rate of about 10^8 bps.

In more recent work, analysts have made more specific assumptions about architectures and have been able to produce more refined, but still rough, estimates. For example, one study of boost-phase communications uses a highly distributed architecture consisting of sensor satellites and satellite battle groups composed of battle management computers, sensors for booster tracking, and space-based interceptor (SBI) carrier satellites. Additional assumptions were made about numbers of targets tracked per sensor in the battle, number

[1]James C. Fletcher, Study Chairman and B. McMillan, Panel Chairman, *Report of the Study on Eliminating the Threat Posed by Nuclear Ballistic Missiles: Volume V, Battle Management, Communications, and Data Processing*, (Washington, DC: Department of Defense, Defensive Technologies Study Team, Oct. 1983), p. 19.

of bits per target track, non-uniform message traffic density, number of relays per message, varying message types (examples are track data, status information, and engagement data), and number of seconds per frame. The result was a peak link data rate for boost phase within the transmission rates of current technology.[2]

The Fletcher Report noted, and OTA concurs, that:

> The technology exists today to transmit 10^7 to 10^8 bits/sec over data links of the length and kind needed for a BMD system. Therefore, even with 300,000 objects in the track file, existing communication technology could handle the expected data rates. Cost and complexity will vary with the rate designed for, but the Panel concludes that communication rates, per se, will not be a limiting factor in the design of a BMD system.[3]

Communications Networks

Regardless of volume, communications would have to be secure and reliable. It would have to survive attempts by an enemy to intercept, jam, or spoof communications, at best rendering the system ineffective, at worst taking control of it for his own purposes. It would also have to survive physical damage incurred in a battle or defense suppression attack. Understanding the threats requires understanding how communications would function in a BMD system.

Current communications technology, including that proposed for BMD systems, involves establishing a network of computers, each acting as a communications node, that transmit data to each other. One example of an existing network that is widely distributed geographically is the ARPA network, initially developed by the Defense Advanced Research Projects Agency (DARPA) as an experimental network. Another example is the AT&T long distance telephone network. Both differ considerably from a space-based battle communications network, which would have:

1. more nodes and more available direct connections between nodes;
2. different delays between nodes (perhaps 5 milliseconds for the example distributed space-based network described earlier as compared to more than 25 milliseconds for the ARPA network);
3. more stringent security requirements;
4. a need to re-establish links every few minutes; and, probably
5. long repair times for individual nodes.

Nonetheless, the problems are sufficiently similar that the terrestrial networks are useful examples. Each node in the network communicates with several other nodes. Users of the network communicate by submitting messages to the network.[4] The computers controlling and comprising the network route the message from one node to another until it reaches its destination.

Some of the major issues that must be resolved in designing a communications network are:

- the physical arrangement of the nodes and the interconnections among the nodes;
- the unit of data transmission, which may be a complete message or part of a message;
- the algorithm used to decide what route through the network each unit of data transmission will take;
- the algorithm used to encode units of data transmission so that they may be reliably transmitted;
- the algorithm used by nodes for interchanging data so that the start and end of each data transmission may be determined; and
- the methods used to ensure that data communications are secure and cannot be jammed, spoofed, or otherwise rendered unreliable.

---

[2]Personal communication, Ira Richer, The Mitre Corp.
[3]The Fletcher Report, *op. cit.*, footnote 1, p. 40.

[4]In the AT&T network, messages are sent across the network to establish a circuit to be used for a long distance call when a subscriber dials a long distance number. Generally, once a circuit is established, it is dedicated to a call, and communications on it may be sent in non-message form as analogue signals or may be encoded digitally into messages.

Since most of these issues are resolved in software, the solutions chosen have a strong effect on the complexity of the software and the reliability of the battle management system as a whole. The more critical of these issues are discussed in the following sections. **In almost every case, the trade-off is that adding sophistication to the algorithm(s) used to solve the problem results in software that is more complicated and more difficult to debug.**

Network Topology

The arrangement of interconnections among nodes is known as the "network topology." In attempts to improve the efficiency and reliability of networks, numerous topologies have been tried. As an example, until recently the AT&T long distance telephone switching system used a hierarchical topology to establish a circuit to be used for a long distance call.[5] Nodes were organized into levels. Messages requesting the circuit were sent from a lower level to a higher level, then across the higher level and back down to a lower level. If all messages must pass through one or two nodes, then under heavy loads those nodes may form bottlenecks that decrease network performance. If the nodes break down under the traffic load, the network cannot not function at all. As a result, most networks employ algorithms that decide what route each message will take through the network. The route may vary according to the prevailing load conditions and the health of the nodes in the network.

Routing in Networks

In geographically distributed networks with many nodes, the routing algorithm is a sophisticated computer program. Frequently, network performance degrades as a result of incorrect assumptions or errors in the design and implementation of the routing algorithm. Finding and correcting the reason for degraded performance requires knowledge of the network status, including traffic loads at nodes and health of nodes. Since traffic load in particular varies second-by-second, debugging network routing software is a difficult and time-consuming job.

One can only have confidence in relatively bug-free operation by permitting the network to function under operational conditions long enough to observe its performance under varying loads. Stress situations, e.g. especially heavy traffic conditions, tend to cause problems. In operation such conditions are relatively infrequent; they are also hard to reproduce for debugging purposes. Nevertheless, for a dedicated network such as a BMD communications system, it may be easier to simulate heavily loaded conditions than for a commercial network.

Either software failures, such as an error in a routing algorithm, or hardware failures may cause catastrophic network failure. In December, 1986, the east coast portion of the ARPA network was disconnected from the rest of the network because a transmission cable was accidentally cut. Although the ARPA network had evolved over more than 15 years, an opportunity for a single-point catastrophic failure remained in the design.

Sometimes the interaction of a hardware failure and the characteristics of a particular routing algorithm can cause failure. In 1971 normal operations of the ARPA network came to a halt because a single node in the network transmitted faulty routing information to other nodes. Transmission of the faulty data was the result of a computer memory failure in the bad node. Based on the erroneous data, the routing algorithm used by all nodes caused all messages to be routed through the faulty node. The routing algorithm was later revised to prevent the situation from recurring, i.e., the software was rewritten to compensate for certain kinds of hardware failures.[6]

---

[5]To help alleviate bottlenecks in the system, AT&T is now moving toward a non-hierarchical system where nodes can communicate directly with each other rather than going through a hierarchy. Note that decisions to change the structure of the long distance system are made as the result of observing its behavior over extensive periods of use by millions of subscribers.

[6]For a more complete description of this problem, see J. McQuillan, G. Falk, and I. Richer, "A Review of the Development and Performance of the ARPANET Routing Algorithm,"

(continued on next page)

Message Transmission

Information to be sent over a digital communications network, such as used in BMD systems, is organized into messages. In some networks, known as "packet-switched" networks, for transmission purposes the messages are organized into blocks of data "packets."[7] In a packet-switched network the user submits his message to the network unaware of how the message will be organized for transmission. The software that controls the network must incorporate a method for extracting messages from packets when the packets reach their destinations.

Security of Communications

Secure network communications require that the routing algorithm be correct, that nodes cannot be fooled into sending messages to the wrong recipient, and that the physical communications links are secure from unauthorized interceptions. Since a network by its nature involves access to many computer systems, it affords potential saboteurs a chance to access many different computers. Both the ARPA network and the AT&T telephone network have been fooled on many occasions into permitting unauthorized access to the network and, in the case of the ARPA network, to computers on the network. The managers of both networks continually try to improve their protection against such access, but no workable foolproof protection techniques have been found.[8] As noted by Lawrence Castro, Chief of the Office of Research and Development at the National Computer Security Center,

Current computer networking technology has concentrated on providing services in a benign environment, and the security threats to these networks have been largely ignored. While literature abounds with examples of hackers wreaking havoc through access to public networks and the computers connected to them, hackers have exploited only a fraction of the vulnerabilities that exist. Techniques need to be developed that will prevent both passive exploitation (eavesdropping) and active exploitation (alteration of messages or message routing.)[9]

Gaining unauthorized access to a BMD communications network would at least require communications technology as sophisticated as that used in the design and implementation of the network. Furthermore, an enemy would have to penetrate the security of the data links, which would likely be encrypted. Since network communications would be used for coordination among battle managers, and would probably involve transmission of target and health data,[10] the worst result of compromise of the network would be that the enemy could control the system for his own uses. Disruption of communications could result in disuse or misdirection of weapons and sensors, causing the BMD system to fail completely in its mission. To achieve such disruption, it would not be necessary for a saboteur to gain control of a battle management computer, but only to feed it false data. Less subtle ways to achieve the same means might be to destroy sufficient

(continued from previous page)

IEEE Trans. on Communications, vol. COM-26, No 12, December 1978.

The reader should keep in mind that the ARPANET was designed as an experimental network, and not as a high reliability network intended for commercial use.

[7]Depending on the situation, several messages may be combined into one packet, or one message may be split across several packets. In either case, the benefit of packet switching is that network resources may be shared, leading to more efficient routing of messages and more efficient use of the network. The disadvantage is that the job of the routing algorithm may be complicated, and routing may become more difficult to debug.

[8]Access to a network is frequently separated from access to the computers using the network. Entrance to the ARPA network is through computers dedicated to that job, known as ter-

minal access computers (TACs). Until recently, such access was available to anyone who had the telephone number of a TAC. Several so-called hackers have made use of TAC facilities to gain entrance to Department of Defense computer systems connected to the ARPA network, and they have been successfully prosecuted for doing so. Partly as a result of such unauthorized use of TACs, password protection has been added to TAC access procedures. The telephone companies wage constant war against people who attempt to use their long distance networks without paying.

[9]Lawrence Castro, "The National Computer Security Center's R&D Program," *Journal of Electronic Defense*, vol. 10, No. 1, January 1987.

[10]The health of a resource, such as a sensor satellite or weapon satellite, is how well the resource is able to perform its mission and what reserves are available to it. Example measures of satellite health are battery power and efficiency of solar cells. For a BMD satellite, such as a carrier vehicle for SBIs, additional data specific to the function of the satellite, such as number of SBIs remaining, would be included.

communications nodes that routing algorithms become overstressed and fail, or to destroy sufficient nodes that battle managers can no longer communicate with each other. The former attack requires that the enemy have some knowledge of the routing algorithms used; the latter may require considerable expenditure of physical resources such as anti-satellite missiles.

Even passive observation of a BMD communications network could reveal enough about the battle management and communications algorithms used by the network to permit an enemy to devise means of circumventing those algorithms and thereby rendering the defense partially or totally ineffective. To prevent an enemy gaining such knowledge by observation of communications, encryption of communication links and techniques for disguising potentially revealing changes in mes-

sage traffic would have to be incorporated a network design.

Although encryption and other technology could make passive exploitation quite difficult, a saboteur could perhaps gain access to the communications software and hardware. Analysis of the sabotage questions, however, beyond the scope of this study.

Achieving secure, reliable, adequate communications requires the conjunction of at least two technologies. The technology for physical communications, such as laser communications, needs to provide a medium that is difficult to intercept or jam and that can meet the required transmission bandwidth. The network technology must provide adequate, secure service for routing messages to their destinations.

SIMULATIONS AND THE NATIONAL TEST BED

Preceding sections have discussed the role of computers during battle. Computing technology would also play a key role in preparation for battle and in maintaining battle-readiness. Computer simulations (box 8-A) would be needed:

- to anticipate threats against the system,
- to model different ways in which the system might work,
- to provide a realistic environment in which system components may be tested during their development, and
- to test the functioning of the system as a whole, both before and after deployment.

Simulations and Systems Development

Simulators are useful during all stages of the development of complicated systems.

- During the early stages of the development of a system, simulators may predict the behavior of different system designs. An example is simulators that predict

stresses on parts of a bridge for different bridge designs.
- During the middle stages of development, simulators may test individual components of a system by simulating those parts not yet built or not yet connected together. An example is a simulator that reproduces the behavior of the different parts of an aircraft before the aircraft's systems are integrated. A radar simulator can feed data to the radar data processor before the radar itself has been finished.
- During testing, a simulator can be used to reproduce the environment in which the system will operate. Avionics computers and their software are tested before installation by connecting them to an environmental simulator that reproduces the flight behavior of the aircraft's systems to which the computers will be connected when installed in the airplane.
- After deployment, simulators test the readiness of systems by mimicking the environment—including stress conditions

---

Box 8-A.—Simulations

A simulation is a system that mimics the behavior of another system. The difference between the simulation and the system being mimicked (called the target), is that the simulation does not accurately reproduce all of the behavior of the target. Behavior not accurately reproduced is either unimportant to the users of the simulation, unknown to the builders of the simulation, or too expensive to reproduce. Many simulators operate by solving a set of mathematical equations that predict the behavior of the target system under the desired conditions. This process is known as modelling the behavior of the target, and such a simulator is often called a model. Others may do no more than supply a previously determined sequence of values on demand or at fixed time intervals.

Airplane flight simulators are good examples of simulators. Flight simulators used for pilot training reproduce flight conditions well enough to help train pilots how to fly, but not to grant them licenses. No one would trust a pilot all of whose flight time was logged on a simulator. Flight simulators are just not sufficiently accurate reproductions of flight conditions to ensure that the pilot knows what it feels like to fly a real plane. However, a pilot who already has a license may use a simulator to qualify for another aircraft in the same class as his license, e.g., a pilot qualified for a DC-10 could qualify to fly a Boeing 747 based only on simulated flights.

Constructing an accurate simulation requires that the target behavior be well understood and that there be some method for comparing the behavior of the simulator with the behavior of the target. In cases where the physical target behavior is unavailable for comparison, simulator behavior may be compared to other simulators modeled on the same target, or to predictions made by mathematical models of the target. (In cases where the simulator itself is a model, a different model may be used for comparison. If a different model is unknown another simulator already known to be reliable, or hand calculations, may be used.) A simulator that models the trajectory of a missile in flight can be checked against actual missiles and the equations of motion that are known to govern such trajectories. A simulator that models the behavior of the Sun can only be compared to observed solar behavior, and may be quite inaccurate when used to predict behavior under previously unknown conditions.

—for which it is critical that the system operate correctly. Such simulators are often build into the system and contain means of monitoring its behavior during the simulation. The design of the SAFEGUARD anti-ballistic missile system of the early 1970s incorporated a simulator called the system exerciser" to permit simulated operation of SAFEGUARD during development and after deployment.

Current Battle Simulation Technology

As faster, deadlier, and more expensive weapons, such as guided missiles, have been added to arsenals, the demand on simulation technology to analyze their effects has increased. For example, in the early 1970s, single engagement simulations modeled such events as defending against a single missile attacking a single ship. Such simulations can now be run 30 times slower than real time, i.e., 30 seconds of processor time devoted to running the simulation corresponds to 1 second in an actual engagement. However, the demand is now to develop simulators that can model many missiles against many ships.

Work at the U.S. Army's Strategic Defense Command (USASDC) Advanced Research Center (ARC) is representative of current BMD simulation technology. In late 1986, ARC researchers completed a set of mid-course BMD battle simulations. The simulations employed 6 Digital Equipment Corporation VAX 11/780 computers coupled by means of shared memories. Four of the computers could simulate battle managers, one simulated surveillance sensors (all of the same type) and weapons (ground-launched homing interceptors of the Exoatmospheric Reentry vehicle Interceptor

System), and one simulated 32 other engaged platforms.[11]

The ARC researchers ran three battle management design cases:

1. 36 battle managers that communicated among each other, known as the *distributed* case;
2. a single centralized battle manager; and
3. 36 autonomous battle managers that did not communicate with each other, known as the *autonomous* case.

The centralized and distributed cases assumed 236 and 237 interceptors respectively, and the autonomous case assumed 660. The maximum threat simulated was 1,000 objects, which required 7 hours to run. The centralized and distributed cases took 3 and 4 hours respectively to run against a threat of 216 RVs. The simulation took 15 months to develop, and included about 150,000 lines of code, much of it in the Pascal programming language. (Code for the battle managers was replicated for some simulations; the replication is not included in the 150,000 lines.)

Perhaps the largest stumbling block in running larger scale and more realistic simulations for the ARC is the lack of computing power. SDIO expects the EV88 experiment sequence, running through fiscal year 1990, to conduct larger scale simulations involving the ARC, the Airborne Optical Adjunct, prototype space-based BMD components, and the National Test Bed. This series of experiments will require considerably more computing power than is now in place at the ARC.

Simulation experts agree that computing power is currently the major limitation in performing large scale simulations. However, other factors complicate the situation. Where equipment or environments are not well-understood or include many random variables, the accuracy of simulations is difficult to verify. This is the case, for example, in simulations of sea conditions surrounding missile v. ship engagements.

Some military simulation experts noted to OTA staff that every time they performed simulated threat assessments without prior access to the real equipment being modeled, the behavior of the real equipment surprised them. They strongly emphasized that it was only when a simulation could be compared to an actual experiment that the verisimilitude of the simulation could be checked.[12] The implication for BMD is that actual Soviet decoys and missiles would have to be examined and observed in operation to simulate their workings accurately. Similarly, the battle environment, including nuclear effects—where appropriate— and enemy tactics, would have to be well understood to conduct a battle simulation properly.

The National Test Bed

The SDIO is sponsoring the development of a National Test Bed (NTB)—a network of computers and a set of simulations to execute on those computers. A threat model is to simulate the launch of Soviet missiles and display their trajectories after launch. Another model would simulate a complete BMD battle to exercise a deployed BMD system.

The NTB would be utilized in all phases of the development and deployment of a BMD system. It should permit experimentation with various system and battle management architectures, battle management strategies, and implementations of architectures. It would be the principal means of testing BMD system components and subsystems as well as the entire BMD system, thereby providing the basis for their reliability.

Preliminary design work studies for the estimated $1 billion NTB were completed in December 1986.[13] Initially, the NTB is to be a network of computers, each simulating a different aspect of a BMD engagement. The number of computers linked for any particular engage-

---

[11]Depending on the architecture being simulated, the other platforms were either battle managers or sensors.

[12]Experience cited here is drawn from discussions with scientists from the Naval Research Laboratory's Tactical Electronic Warfare Division about simulations of Naval warfare.

[13]Major James Price, SDIO's assistant NTB director, described the NTB as a $1 billion program through 1992 in an interview reported in Defense Electronics in February, 1987.

ment would vary depending on the completeness and depth of detail required. Initial capabilities would not permit simulation of a full battle involving hundreds of thousands of objects.

A major use of the NTB would be to conduct experiments with different BMD technologies and strategies. The currently visualized NTB would link sensors, weapons, or battle managers to simulations that reproduce the data they would handle during a battle. The object could then be tested under varying conditions. The results of such experiments would be quite sensitive to the verisimilitude of the simulations. Accordingly, it is important that there be a way to verify the accuracy of the simulations used in NTB tests and experiments.

Computers in Support of BMD System Development

A BMD system to counter the Soviet ballistic missile threat might be the most complicated system ever built. It would involve the use of many different technologies, the automated interplay of thousands of different computers, sensors, and weapons, and the development of more software than has been used in any single previous project. Accordingly, managing the development of such a system would require considerable computer support to track progress, to identify problems, and to maintain the status of components under development, in test, and deployed.

Computers would also be used to design, generate, and test system hardware and software. Engineers and managers are likely to be geographically dispersed and would need to transfer information from one computer to another. The interaction among people would only be effective if there were a means for effective interaction among the computer systems that they use. Previous sections of this chapter have concentrated on the role of computers in the operation and testing of a BMD system. But it is clear that effective computing technology would be needed not just in a strategic battle, but long before system deployment and throughout the lifetime of the system.

Computing Technology Trade-offs

Chapter 7 and the preceding sections have portrayed some of the trade-offs involved in using computers for ballistic missile defense. The following list summarizes those trade-offs.

- *Processing power required v. volume of data communications among battle managers.* Sharing information among battle managers relieves them of some of the tasks that they might otherwise have to perform, and decreases the processing load on each of the battle managers, but increases the data communications rate requirements and also requires that communications be secure and reliable.
- *Performance v. volume of data communications.* Sharing data among battle managers allows the system to operate more efficiently, but, as in the previous trade-off, greater dependence on communications requires greater communications capacity, reliability, and security.
- *Performance v. degree of automation.* Permitting human intervention during a battle degrades performance under some conditions, but may permit recovery from failures caused by the inability of an automated system to recover from unanticipated and undesired events.
- *Processing power required v. battle management organization.* A distributed organization would require less processing power from each computer but more communications than centralized battle management, which requires placing a considerable concentration of processing power in one computer system.
- *Software complexity v. battle management organization.* A hierarchical battle management architecture simplifies the software design but may leave the system less survivable because of the possibility of command layers being disabled. A decentralized battle management structure would increase the complexity of the communications software and might require more weapon resources, but might result in a more survivable system.
- *Software expense and reliability v. hardware customization.* Customizing hard-

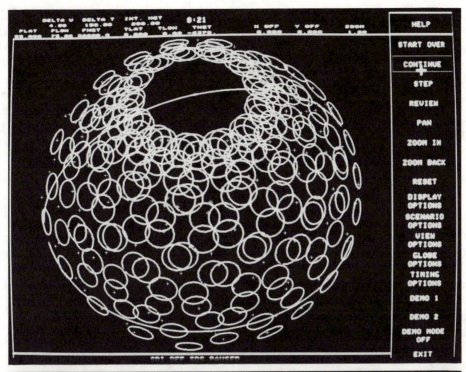

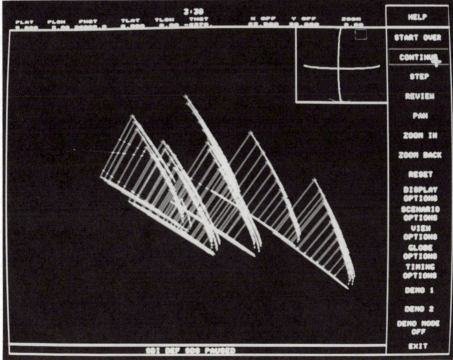

Photo credit: Electronic Systems Division, U.S. Air Force Systems Command.

Computer simulations are to play a key role in the development and testing of SDI systems. The photographs here are of video displays screens generated by a ballistic missile defense battle simulation program developed at the MITRE Corporation. The circles in the scene above depict areas of coverage for a system of space-based interceptors. The scene below indicates the tracks of ICBM boosters a few minutes after launch.

ware to perform efficiently at specific tasks could improve hardware capabilities, but might result in longer software development schedules and decreased software reliability because of lack of experience with and lack of development tools for the hardware.

These trade-offs represent important architectural issues that strongly affect the computing technology needed for BMD. For most of them, the SDI system architects have not yet explored the alternatives in sufficient detail to be able to quantify choices. As a result, there are still only crude estimates of the speeds and sizes of the computers needed, and the rates at which data would have to be communicated among the elements of a BMD system.

PROCESSOR TECHNOLOGY

Table 8-1 shows many of the places where computers would be used in the fighting components of a BMD system and the jobs they would perform. Rough estimates of the required memory capacities and speeds are in included in the classified version of this report.[14] Estimates of computer performance requirements for various BMD *functions* are shown in table 8-2.

Processing requirements are highly dependent on the system and battle management architectures, and on the threat. Without detailed architectural specifications and a precise specification of the algorithms to be used, estimates of speed and memory requirements accurate to better than a factor of 10 probably cannot be made.

Because of the variety of jobs they would perform, BMD computers would vary considerably in speed and memory capacity. Special purpose computers would probably execute some computing tasks, such as signal processing. General-purpose computers faster than any now existing would probably be needed for computationally stressful tasks such as discrimination of RVs and decoys in mid-course. All space-based computers would have to be radiation-hardened beyond the limits of existing computers.[15]

In addition to their use in the fighting components of the system, computers would also be used:

1. in simulators;
2. to help design, test, exercise, and train people in the use of the system; and
3. to assist in supporting the system throughout its lifetime.

Capabilities of Existing Computers

The processing power of a computer is determined by the operating speed of its components and the way they are interconnected (see box 8-B). Processing and memory components are built from semiconductor chips, whose speed is limited by the number and arrangement of circuits that can be placed on a chip. Developments in chip design and production technology, including advances from large scale integrated circuits (LSI) to very large scale integrated circuits (VLSI), have increased processor speeds for general purpose computers by a factor of three to four approximately every 2 years for about the past 10 years. Much of this progress has been the result of refinements in chip design and production. As a result, some existing supercomputers, such as the Cray XMP series or Cray 2, may be close to satisfying most SDI data processing needs, except that such machines are not packaged in a suitable form.

---

[14]For many of the system elements shown in table 8-1, estimates for processing speed and size are not available. The most computationally intensive tasks are probably signal processing for the IR and optical sensors incorporated into BSTS, SSTS, and AOS, especially for the mid-term and far-term architectures.

[15]Radiation hardening to within an order of magnitude of SDI requirements for some critical components of computer systems

---

has been demonstrated. A complete computer system that is space qualified and radiation-hardened to within an order of magnitude of SDI requirements for space-borne computers has yet to be built.

Table 8-2.—Computing Performance Requirements

SDS functions	Present state of the art	DEM/VAL objective	First increment SDS requirement	Follow on SDS requirement	Risk reduction programs
Space based					
General purpose processing hardware					
• Command defense	• Throughput: 1 MIPS (space qualified)	• Throughput: 500 MIPS • Memory: 500 MBYTES • Architecture: heterogeneous • Technology: VHSIC (CMOS), GaAs, SOI • MTBF: 10 years	• Throughput: 10-50 MIPS • Memory: 1000 MBYTES • Architecture: heterogeneous • Technology: VHSIC (CMOS), GaAs, SOI • MTBF: 10 years	• Throughput: 50-150 MIPS • Memory: 1000 MBYTES • Architecture: heterogeneous • Technology: VHSIC (CMOS), GaAs, SOI • MTBF: 20 years	• VHSIC • DARPA strategic computing • SDI BMC³ • MCC
• Maintain positive control					
• Assess situation					
• Select and implement mode					
• Coordinate with others and higher authority					
• Maintain readiness					
• Reconfigure and reconstitute					
• Engagement management					
• Weapon guide and home					
• Assess kill					
• Data distribution					
Special purpose computing hardware					
• Sense and bulk filter	• Throughput: 350 MFLOPS (space qualified)	• Throughput: 2000 MFLOPS • Memory: 500 MBYTES • Architecture: heterogeneous • Technology: VHSIC (CMOS), GaAs, SOI • MTBF: 10 years	• Throughput: 500 MFLOPS • Memory: 1000 MBYTES • Architecture: heterogeneous • Technology: VHSIC (CMOS), GaAs, SOI • MTBF: 10 years	• Throughput: 1-10 MFLOPS • Memory: 1000 MBYTES • Architecture: heterogeneous • Technology: VHSIC (CMOS), GaAs, SOI • MTBF: 20 years	• DARPA • SDI BMC³ • SDI sensors • Commercial
• Track					
• Type and discriminate					
• Data distribution					
Common hardware characteristics	• Space qualified • Hardness (unshielded) Total dose: 10^4 rad Upset: 10^{-9}/sec Survive: 10^9 rad/sec Neutrons/cm²: 10^{18}	• Space qualified • Hardness (unshielded) Total dose: 3×10^7 rads Upset: 10^{-11}/sec Survive: 10^{11} rads/sec Neutrons/cm²: TBD Shielded: none • Fault tolerant • Secure • Ada, COMMON LISP, C • SA/PDL	• Space qualified • Hardness (unshielded) Total dose: 3×10^7 rads Upset: 10^{-11}/sec Survive: 10^{11} rads/sec Neutrons/cm²: TBD Shielded: $5\times$JCS • Fault tolerant • Secure	• Space qualified • Hardness (unshielded) Total dose: 3×10^7 rads Upset: 10^{-11}/sec Survive: 10^{11} rads/sec Neutrons/cm²: TBD Shielded: $10\times$JCS • Fault tolerant • Secure	• DARPA • SDI BMC³ • SDI sensors
Software	• FORTRAN, JOVIAL	• Size Element: 0.5 MSLOC Total: 1.5-3 MSLOC • Fault-tolerant • Secure • Ada, COMMON LISP, C	• Size Element: 1 MSLOC Total: 5 MSLOC • Fault-tolerant • Secure • Ada, COMMON LISP, C	• Size Element: 2 MSLOC Total: 5-10 MSLOC • Fault-tolerant • Secure • Ada, COMMON LISP, C	• AdaJPO • SPC • SEI • SDI BMC³ • DARPA • STARS
• All above					
Ground based					
General purpose processing hardware					
• Command defense	• Throughput: 30-100 MIPS • Technology: bipolar LSI	• Throughput: 500 MIPS • Memory: 500 MBYTES • Architecture: heterogeneous • Technology: VHSIC (CMOS) • MTBF: 1 year	• Throughput: 10-50 MIPS • Memory: 1000 MBYTES • Architecture: heterogeneous • Technology: VHSIC (CMOS) • MTBF: 1 year	• Throughput: 10-50 MIPS • Memory: 1000 MBYTES • Architecture: heterogeneous • Technology: VHSIC (CMOs), GaAs, SOI • MTBF: 1 year	• VHSIC • DARPA strategic computing • SDI BMC³ • MCC
• Maintain positive control					
• Assess situation					
• Select and implement mode					
• Coordinate with others and higher authority					

Table 8-2.—Computing Performance Requirements—continued

SDS functions	Present state of the art	DEM/VAL objective	First increment SDS requirement	Follow on SDS requirement	Risk reduction programs
• Maintain readiness • Reconfigure and reconstitute • Engagement management • Weapon guide and home • Assess kill • Data distribution					
Special purpose computing hardware					
• Sense and bulk filter • Track • Type and discriminate • Data distribution	• Throughput: 100-1000 MFLOPS vector processing	• Throughput: 2000 MFLOPS • Memory: 500 MBYTES • Architecture: heterogeneous • Technology: VHSIC (CMOs) • MTBF: 1 year	• Throughput: 1-3 GFLOPS • Memory: 1000 MBYTES • Architecture: heterogeneous • Technology: VHSIC (CMOS) • MTBF: 1 year	• Throughput: 1-10 GFLOPS • Memory: 1000 MBYTES • Architecture: heterogeneous • Technology: VHSIC II (CMOs), GaAs, SOI • MTBF: 1 year	• DARPA • SDI BM/C³ • SDI sensors • Commercial
Common hardware characteristics			• Fault tolerant • Redundant • Performance monitor • Fault location • Hardness 3 PSI plus associated effects	• Fault tolerant • Redundant • Performance monitor • Fault location • Hardness 5 PSI plus associated effects	• DARPA • SDI BM/C³ • SDI sensors
Software • All above • Readiness, test, health and status report	• FORTRAN, JOVIAL	• Size Element: 0.5 MSLOC Total: 1.5-3 MSLOC • Fault-tolerant • Secure • Ada, COMMON LISP, C • SA/PDL	• Size Element: 1.6 MSLOC Total: 3 MSLOC • Fault-tolerant • Secure • Ada, COMMON LISP, C	• Size Element: 2.3 MSLOC Total: 5 MSLOC • Fault-tolerant • Secure • Ada, COMMON LISP, C	• Ada JPO • SPC • SEI • SDI BM/C³ • DARPA • STARS

SOURCE: Strategic Defense Initiative Organization, U.S. Department of Defense, 1987.

Box 8-B.—MIPS, MOPS, and MEGAFLOPS

The processing power of a computer is often expressed as the rate at which it can execute instructions, measured in instructions per seconds, or ips. A computer that can execute a million instructions per second is a 1 mips machine. Although mips give a crude measure of the speed of a computer, there is too much variability in the time it takes to execute different instructions on the same machine and in the instructions used by different machines for mips to be a true comparative measure of processing power.

Complex instructions may take four or five times longer to execute than simple instructions on the same machine. A complex instruction on one machine may have the same effect in two-thirds the time as three simple instructions on a different machine. To simulate operating conditions, a mix of different instructions are often used in measuring computer performance. Such measurements are sometimes characterized as operations per second, or ops, rather than ips. A computer that can execute a million operations per second is called a 1 mops machine. BMD signal processing needs have been estimated to be as much as 50 billion ops (50 gigops).

One class of instructions, known as *floating point* instructions, are important in numerical calculations involving numbers that vary over a wide range, but are very costly in terms of execution time. A common option on computers is an additional processor, sometimes known as a floating point accelerator, specialized to perform floating point operations. The speed of computers designed to perform numerical floating point operations efficiently is usually measured in floating point operations per second, or flops. A computer that can execute a million floating point instructions per second is a 1 megaflops machine.

To compensate for differences in instruction sets and instruction effects on different computers, standard mixes of instructions are used to compare the performance of different computers. For applications involving widely-ranging numerical calculations, such as track correlation, floating point instructions are included in the mix. The variation in machine performance between machines may be a factor of three or four, depending on the mix, the machines involved, and other factors.

For purposes of estimating processing power needs for SDI BMD, the requirements are not yet known to better than a factor of about 10, which dominates differences in performance on different instruction mixes. Accordingly, estimates in this report will generally be given in terms of mips or mops.

If progress can be continued at the same rate as in recent years, sufficiently powerful processors to meet the most stressing requirements of SDI BMD should be available in about 10 years. An obstacle to satisfying BMD processing power requirements is that the processors with the largest requirements are those that would have to be space-based and therefore radiation hardened. Special development programs would be needed to produce adequate space qualification and radiation hardening for the new processors.

New Computer Architectures

Current chip production technology may soon reach physical limitations, such as the number of off-chip connectors and the size of the features used to construct circuits on the chip. Increases in processor speeds may then have to await new chip production technology or new ways of building processors, e.g., optical techniques. An alternative to increasing computer speeds without improving component speeds is to find better ways of interconnecting components, i.e. better computer *architectures*, and better ways of partitioning computing tasks among computers. Computers constructed by interconnecting many small computers in ingenious ways, such as the Hypercube computers developed at Cal Tech and later produced by Intel as the iPSC machine, are just now appearing on the market.[16]

---
[16] C.L. Seitz, "The Cosmic Cube," *Communications of the ACM*, January 1985.

The iPSC is estimated to run at 100 mips and 8 mflops, but is well-suited only for scientific computing tasks that can be organized to take advantage of the iPSC's architecture. Whether or not such architectures will be useful for the most computationally-intensive BMD tasks will depend on what algorithms are used.

Novel computer architectures, despite their potential processing power, have the drawback that the software technology base needed to capitalize on their potential must be developed. New software is needed to run programs on new computers, to help users decompose their problems to utilize the machine's potential, and to convert existing software to execute on the machine. As an example, to meet Department of Defense (DoD) standards, a computer such as the iPSC would need a compiler for Ada™ (the DoD's standard programming language for weapon systems) and an operating system compatible with Ada™. Although advances in computing hardware have come rapidly, software development is notoriously slow and costly.

Space Qualification and Radiation Hardening

Space-qualified general purpose computers lag ground-based computers in processing power by a factor of 20 or more. The fastest space-qualified—but not radiation-hardened— processors today achieve processing rates of about 1 mips.[17] Adequate radiation hardening of the computers imposes a more significant penalty in cost than in processing speed. The most promising technology for meeting both speed and radiation hardening requirements currently uses gallium arsenide (GaAs) rather than silicon in the manufacture of chips. Although GaAs is more radiation resistant, high defect densities reduce manufacturing yields, making chip production costlier. The higher defect densities also impose smaller chip sizes and fewer electronic circuits per chip. The con-

sequent lower overall level of integration may require processors to have more components and be less reliable. Researchers in chip production say that current problems with manufacturing yields and circuit densities are temporary and will be solved. As Milutinovic states,

> . . . many problems related to materials are considered temporary in nature, and one prediction states that the steady-state cost will be about one order of magnitude greater for GaAs than for silicon.[18]

Space-based computers must be able to withstand long-term cumulative doses of radiation and neutron flux, short bursts of a few highly-energetic particles (known as transient events), and electromagnetic pulses (EMP) resulting from nuclear detonations. Although shielding may protect semiconductors against all three phenomena, it incurs a corresponding weight penalty. Gallium arsenide is a promising material for semiconductors because it is more resistant to cumulative radiation and neutron flux damage than silicon. Resistance of GaAs to transient events is dependent on the particular chip design.

It may be possible to harden space-based computers to survive the radiation of a nuclear weapons battle environment. But it is important to consider the effects of such an environment on *software* as well as on hardware. A transient radiation-caused upset might interrupt the current operation of computer hardware, leading either to a resetting of the processor or to the changing of a bit in memory or in the internal circuitry of the processor. The processor may continue to function, but the state of the computation may be altered, causing an error in software processing, i.e., a system failure.

Consider as an analogy the effects of a single digit error on the computation of an entry for an income tax form. The error may be so small as to be hardly noticeable, and it may even make no difference because the tax scales

---

[17] The Sperry 1637 and Delco MAGIC V avionics processors achieve a rate of about 1 mips, but neither are radiation-hardened nor have they been used in space applications. The Rockwell IDF 224 and Delco MAGIC 362S space-qualified processors achieve a rate of about 600 kops for instruction mixes that do not include floating point operations.

[18] Veljko Milutinovic, "GaAs Microprocessor Technology," *Computer*, October 1986, pp. 10-13.

are incremental, not continuous. On the other hand, a larger error in a single digit may have a considerable effect on the amount of tax paid. In either case, the error may propagate through later entries on the form until it is noticed and corrected. Unless the taxpayer checks his entries for reasonableness, he may not find the error. The IRS may find the error by duplicating the taxpayer's calculations, or by performing consistency and reasonableness checks.

The effects of transient events on computing accuracy are difficult to predict. Designing software to cope with such events is a formidable problem, requiring one to forecast all possible symptoms of upsets and provide error-recovery measures for them.[19] It is also difficult to simulate the occurrence of transient events realistically enough to test the software design. There is little experience with software-intensive systems operating under conditions likely to produce transient events.

---

[19]The design problem may be simplified somewhat by grouping possible symptoms into classes so that all events in a particular class may be handled in the same way. Grouping events into classes and devising the appropriate response for each class is a very difficult design problem.

CONCLUSIONS

A BMD system to counter the Soviet ballistic missile threat might be the most complicated artifact ever built. It would involve the application of many different technologies; the automated interplay of thousands of different computers, sensors, and weapons; and the development of more software than has been used in any single previous project. An advanced BMD system would require computers in every fighting element of the system and in many supporting roles.

The degree of automation demanded entails not only advances in software technology (addressed in chapter 9) but also advances in secure computer networking, processing power, and radiation hardening of electronics. The extent and importance of simulations—in developing, exercising, and otherwise maintaining the system, as well as in training people in its use—would require an advance in simulation technology.

Because several difficult architectural trade-offs have not yet been sufficiently addressed, the scope of the advances needed cannot be well predicted. Until an architectural description is available that clearly specifies battle management structure and allocates battle management functions both physically and within that structure, better predictions will not be possible.

Further discussion of the computing technology issues involved in producing an automated BMD system follows.

Reliable, Secure Communications

Common to all BMD systems that require human intervention at any stage is the need to provide secure, rapid communications between the human and the battle management computers. If part of the system is in space, then most likely there would be a need for space-to-ground communications. Battle management requires communications among the battle managers, the sensors, and the weapons forming a BMD system. The computers forming the communications network would digitally encode and control all the transmissions.

Achieving secure, reliable, adequate communications would call for simultaneous advances in at least two technologies. First, hardware technology, such as laser communications, needs to provide a medium that is difficult to intercept or jam and that can meet the required transmission bandwidth. Second, network technology must provide adequate, secure, survivable service for routing messages to their destinations. When damaged, the network must be able to reconfigure itself without significantly disrupting communications. Such performance would take sophisticated network control software—probably beyond the current state of the art. Proposed solutions to these problems are either untried or have only been tried in ground-based laboratory situations.

Simulations

Simulations would play a key role in all phases of a BMD system's life cycle. The SDIO is building a National Test Bed (NTB) to facilitate the development and use of BMD simulation technology. A full-scale NTB should permit experimentation with different system and battle management architectures, different battle management strategies, and different implementations of architectures. It would be the principal means of testing and predicting component, subsystem, and system reliability. Initially, the NTB would be a link among computers, each simulating a different aspect of a BMD engagement. The number of computers linked for any particular engagement would vary with the completeness and depth of detail required. Initial capabilities would not permit simulation of a full battle involving hundreds of thousands of objects. **Battle simulations on a scale needed to represent a full battle realistically have not been previously attempted. It would be crucial, but very difficult, to find a way of verifying the accuracy of such simulations, when and if they are developed.**

Technology and Architectural Trade-offs

Many difficult trade-offs have yet to be adequately addressed in the design of a BMD system to meet SDI requirements. Novel design ideas or advances in computing technology may decrease the importance of some of these trade-offs. However, no architecture has yet been specified sufficiently to permit clear trade-off studies. Issues that should be addressed include:

- simplifying software at the cost of adding computational burden to the hardware,

- simplifying battle management software by structuring it hierarchically at the expense of survivability,
- increasing survivability by decentralizing battle management at the expense of increasing communications complexity,
- customizing hardware for specific applications at the expense of increased software development cost and decreased software reliability,
- simplifying the problem of communications security at the cost of decreasing the possibilities for human intervention during battle,
- increasing the amount of human control during battle at the expense of fighting efficiency, and
- improving fighting efficiency at the cost of increasing the complexity and volume of communications (and, thereby, the risk of catastrophic communications failure).

None of these trade-offs is easy to make and few can be quantified. Compounding the difficulty is that many of the system elements— e.g., the Boost-phase Surveillance and Tracking System and Space Surveillance and Tracking System sensors, SBIs and associated CVs, high-powered lasers, and neutral particle beams—are still in the research or development stages. Moreover, no previous system has ever required the automated handling of many different devices and different kinds of devices as would an SDI missile defense. Nonetheless, tentative conclusions on some trade-offs have been reached. Most trade-offs could be properly explored by use of an appropriate simulation, such as might be provided by a full-scale National Test Bed.

Computational Requirements

Processing requirements are highly dependent on the system design, the battle management architectures, and the threat. Because detailed architectural and algorithmic specifications for an SDI BMD system are not yet available, estimates of speed and memory requirements accurate to better than a factor of 10 probably cannot be made. However, progress in processing speed has been rapid historically. If it continues at the same pace, it should yield sufficiently powerful processors to meet SDI needs within 10 years or less. Such processors might still have to be space qualified and radiation hardened.

An additional problem in providing radiation-hardened computing hardware is the lack of experience in building software tolerant of radiation-induced faults. There is little experience with complex, large-scale software systems that must operate efficiently despite the occurrence of radiation-induced transient effects in the hardware.

Chapter 9
Software

CONTENTS

Software

INTRODUCTION

The performance of a ballistic missile defense (BMD) system would strongly depend on the performance of its computers. Chapter 8 describes the pervasiveness of computers in the operation of a BMD system, and as well as in its development, testing, and maintenance.[1] Sequences of instructions called *software* would direct the actions of the computers, both in peacetime and in battle. As shown in table 8-1, software is responsible both for the actions of individual components of the system (e.g., a radar), and for coordinating the actions of the system as a whole. As coordinator, software maybe thought of as the glue that binds the system together. As the system manager, software assesses the situation based on data gathered by sensors and reports from system components, determines battle strategy and tactics, and allocates resources to tasks (e.g., the weapons to be fired at targets.)

The role of software as battle manager is crucial to the success of a BMD system. If software in a particular *component* failed—even if the failure occurred in all components of the same type simultaneously—other components of different types might compensate. But if the *battle management* software failed catastrophically, there would be no way to compensate. Furthermore, the battle management software may expected to compensate for systemic failures, both because of its role as manager and because software is perceived to be more flexible than hardware. Consequently, the battle management software would have to be the most dependable kind. Thus it is the focus of most of the SDI software debate.

The BMD Software Debate

The envisaged BMD system would be complex and large, would have to satisfy unique requirements, and would have to work the first time it is used in battle. Many computer scientists, and software engineers in particular, have declared themselves unwilling to try to build trustworthy software for such a system. They claim that past experience combined with the nature of software and the software development process makes the SDI task infeasible. David Parnas has summarized their major arguments.[2] Other computer scientists, however, have stated that their belief that the software needed for a Strategic Defense Initiative (SDI) BMD could be built with today's software engineering technology. Frederick Brooks, for example, has said:

> I see no reason why we could not build the kind of software system that SDI requires with the software engineering technology that we have today.[3]

Those willing to proceed believe that an appropriate system architecture and heavy use of simulations would make the task tractable. Their arguments are summarized in a study prepared for the Strategic Defense Initiative Organization (SDIO) by a group known as The Eastport Group.[4] The critical role played by the software in BMD makes it important to understand both positions.

---

[1]Table 8-1 illustrates many of the ways in which computers would be used in a deployed BMD system.

Note: Complete definitions of acronyms and initialisms are listed in Appendix B of this report.

---

[2]David L. Parnas, "Software Aspects of Strategic Defense Systems," *American Scientist,* 73:432-40, September-October 1985.

[3]From a statement by Dr. Frederick P. Brooks at the Hearings before the Subcommittee On Strategic and Theater Nuclear Forces of the Committee On Armed Services, United States Senate, S. Hrg. 99-933, p. 54.

[4]Eastport Study Group, "A Report to the Director, Strategic Defense Initiative Organization," 1985.

The Role of Software in BMD

Software for BMD would be expected to:

- be the agent of system evolution, permitting changes in system operation through reprogramming of existing computers;
- perform the most complex tasks in the system, such as battle management;
- be responsible for recovery from failures, whether they are hardware or software failures; and
- respond to threats, both anticipated and unanticipated, against the system.

A BMD system would not be trustworthy and reliable unless both hardware and software were trustworthy and reliable. Because of rapid progress in hardware technology in recent years, and because of differences in their natures, hardware reliability is not as hotly-debated an issue as software reliability. As Brooks puts it in his discussion of current software engineering technology:

> Not only are there no silver bullets now in view, the very nature of software makes it unlikely that there will be any—no inventions that will do for software productivity, reliability, and simplicity what electronics, transistors, and large-scale integration did for computer hardware. We cannot expect ever to see twofold gains every two years.

> First, one must observe that the anomaly is not that software progress is so slow, but that computer hardware progress is so fast. No other technology since civilization began has seen six orders of magnitude in performance-price gain in 30 years.[5]

Software Complexity

The software engineer called upon to produce large, complex software systems is partly a victim of his medium. Software is inherently flexible. There are no obvious physical constraints on its design (e.g., power, weight, or number of parts) so software engineers undertake tasks of complexity that no hardware engineer

would. Brooks summarizes the situation as follows:

> Software entities are more complex for their size than perhaps any other human construct because no two parts are alike . . . In this respect, software systems differ profoundly from computers, buildings, or automobiles, where repeated elements abound.

> Digital computers are themselves more complex than most things people build: They have very large numbers of states. This makes conceiving, describing, and testing them hard. Software systems have orders-of-magnitude more states than computers do.[6]

Software Issues

Of course, complex systems *are* successfully built and used. However, given the current state of the art in software engineering, complex systems are not trusted to be reasonably free of catastrophic failures *before* a period of extensive use. During that period, errors causing such failures may be found and corrected. A central issue in the debate over BMD software is whether it can be produced so that it can be trusted to work properly the first time it is used, despite the probable presence of errors that might cause catastrophic failures. A critical point in the debate over this issue is how one would judge whether or not the software was trustworthy. If evaluations of trustworthiness were to rely on the results of simulations of battles, then a second critical point is how closely and accurately actual BMD battles could be simulated.

A second central issue in the software debate is whether a BMD system imposes unique requirements on software. Critical points surrounding this issue are:

- whether there are existing similar systems that could serve as models for the development of BMD software;
- whether requirements would be sufficiently well understood in advance of use so that trustworthy software could be designed;

[5]Frederick P. Brooks, Jr., "No Silver Bullet, Essence and Accidents of Software Engineering," *IEEE Computer* vol. 20, No. 4, April 1987, p. 10.

[6]Ibid.

- whether all potential threats against a BMD system could be anticipated, and, if not; and
- whether the software could be designed to handle unanticipated threats during the course of a battle.

Adding fuel to the debate over whether software could meet BMD requirements is the slow progress in software technology in recent years when compared to hardware technology.

An obstacle to settling this issue is the current uncertainty over the purposes of a BMD system. Software requirements would depend on the threat and countermeasures to be faced, the expected strategies of both the offense and the defense; and the technology to be used in the system, e.g., kinetic-energy v. directed-energy weapons. A system intended to defend the population would have different requirements than one intended to defend only critical military targets. A system to be deployed in phases would oblige the software developers to know the changes in requirements and architecture to be expected between each phase before they designed the software for the initial phase.

Among the developers of large, complex systems who attended OTA's workshop on SDI software, there was unanimous agreement that software development should not be started until there was a clear statement of the requirements of the system.[7] All system requirements would not have to be known in detail before software development could be started. But if the requirements for a system component could not be written, neither could the specifications for the software that was part of that component.

Catastrophic Failure

Both critics and supporters of the feasibility of building software to meet SDI requirements agree that large, complex software systems, such as an SDI BMD system would need, would contain errors. They disagree on whether the software could be produced so that it would not fail catastrophically. Several different meanings of catastrophic failure have been used. It is sometimes related to whether or not a BMD system would deter the Soviets from launching ICBMs at the United States:

> Ballistic missile defense must . . . be credible enough in its projected wartime performance during peacetime operations and testing to ensure that it would never be attacked.[8]

It can also be taken to mean that

> The system has failed catastrophically if the U.S. bases its defense on the assumption that the system will function effectively in battle and then a major flaw is discovered so that we are defenseless.[9]

This chapter assumes a technical definition: a catastrophic failure is a decline in system performance to 10 percent or less of expected performance. A BMD system designed to destroy 10,000 warheads would be considered to have failed catastrophically if it stopped only 1,000 of the 10,000. The figure 10 percent is an arbitrary one; it has been adopted as illustrative of a worst-case failure.

Generic Software Issues

Much of the debate concerning BMD software is about software problems common to all complex, critical software systems.[10] A good example is whether software can be designed to recover from failures automatically. BMD proponents argue that producing trustworthy BMD software would not call for general solutions to such problems. They feel that the specificity of the application permits special-case solutions that would work well enough for BMD. Opponents argue that BMD software would demand better solutions for such problems as failure-recovery than any system

[7]Attendees at the workshop, held Jan. 8, 1987 in Washington, DC, included software developers who participated in the development of SAFEGUARD, Site Defense, telephone switching systems, digital communications networks, Ada compilers, and operating systems.

[8]Charles A. Zraket, "Uncertainties in Building a Strategic Defense," Science 235:1600-1606, March 1987.

[9]David L. Parnas, personal communication, 1987.

[10]As described, for example, in David L. Parnas, "Software Aspects of Strategic Defense Systems," op. cit., footnote 2.

previously built. They say that approaches proposed for SDI have been tried in the past and have not been shown to be effective.

This chapter is primarily concerned with arguments over the generic issues. First, there are as yet no clear statements of BMD software requirements, whether for battle management or particular BMD system components, let alone proposed software designs or proposed solutions for BMD for any of the generic problems. Application-specific analysis must await those requirements, designs, and solutions.

Second, there seems to be agreement that BMD software would be more complex than any previously built. The first conclusion of volume V of the Fletcher report was:

Specifying, generating, testing, and maintaining the software for a battle management system will be a task that far exceeds in complexity and difficulty any that has yet been accomplished in the production of civil or military software systems.[11]

Third, tasks for BMD software differ in important ways from the tasks performed in today's weapons systems and command, control, and communications systems. It is true that many BMD software tasks would resemble those for current systems: e.g., target tracking, weapons release and guidance, situation assessment, and communications control in real time. The differences from current systems are that a BMD system would:

- permit less opportunity for human intervention,
- have to handle more objects in its battle space,
- have to manage a larger battle space,
- use different weapons and sensor technology,
- contain vastly more elements,
- have more serious consequences of failure,

- have to operate in a nuclear environment,
- be under active attack by the enemy, and
- be useless if it failed catastrophically during its first battle.

Accordingly, the debate over generic software issues is an appropriate one for BMD software.

The purpose of this chapter is to examine the key issues in the debate over the feasibility of meeting BMD software requirements. This chapter:

1. discusses why there is such a debate and includes a definition of key terms, such as "catastrophic failure" and "trustworthiness";
2. analyzes properties often claimed to be important for BMD software—e.g., trustworthiness, reliability, correctness, low error incidence, fault tolerance, security, and safety, (including a discussion of the meaning of "reliability" as applied to software and why there is no single, simple measure of software dependability);
3. identifies the major factors that affect software dependability; and
4. characterize the demands placed on BMD software and the BMD software development process in terms of the factors affecting dependability.

The remainder of this chapter begins with a brief discussion of Department of Defense (DoD) software experience, the nature of software, traditional reliability measures, and the pitfalls inherent in applying such measures to software. Following sections deal with properties such as trustworthiness, correctness, fault tolerance, security, and safety, and with the factors that lead people to have confidence that systems have such properties. (The available technology for incorporating these properties into software is analyzed in app. A.) The chapter then presents an analysis of Strategic Defense Initiative BMD requirements from the viewpoint of those factors. The chapter concludes with: a discussion of why BMD software development is a difficult job—perhaps uniquely so; why we are unlikely to have more than a subjective judgment of how trustwor-

[11]James C. Fletcher, Study Chairman and Brockway McMillan, Panel Chairman, *Report of the Study on Eliminating the Threat Posed by Nuclear Ballistic Missiles, Volume V: Battle Management, Communications, and Data Processing* (Washington, DC: Department of Defense, Defensive Technologies Study Team, October 1983).

thy the software is, once produced; and a summary of the key software issues.

The Software Crisis

Since the mid-1970s DoD officials have increasingly recognized the difficulties in producing command, control, and information processing software for weapon systems.[12] As Ronald Enfield says:

> In the 1970s, the world's largest customer for computers—the U.S. Department of Defense—changed its focus from hardware to software as a major obstacle to progress in developing advanced weapons. Reliable software is also a crucial component of complex systems such as nuclear power plants, automatic tellers, and many other technologies that touch our lives in critical ways. Yet, as the software for these systems has grown increasingly complicated, it has become more prone to error.[13]

The complex of problems associated with trying to produce software that operated properly, on time, within budget, and maintainably over its lifetime was dubbed "the software crisis." DoD has found that the software crisis is sometimes forcing the military to wait for software to be debugged before it can use new systems. Progress in alleviating this crisis has been slow, and the same problems would apply to producing software for BMD. Both the Fletcher and Eastport Group reports agreed that software development for BMD would be a difficult, if not the most difficult, problem in BMD development. The Eastport Group noted that:

> Software technology is developing against inflexible limits in the complexity and reliability that can be achieved.[14]

To understand why DoD and other developers of large, complex software systems have been experiencing a software crisis, it is first necessary to understand the nature of software and the demands made on it.

The Nature of Software

Digital computers are among our most flexible tools because the tasks they do can be changed by changing the sequences of instructions that direct them. Such instruction sequences are called *programs*, or *software* and are stored in the computer's memory. Flexibility is attained by loading different programs into the memory at different times.[15] Each make and model of computer has a unique set of instructions in which it must be programmed, generically known as *machine instructions* or *machine language*.

To simplify their job, programmers have developed languages that are easier to use than machine language. These languages, such as FORTRAN, COBOL, and Ada, are known as *high level languages*, and require the programmer to know less about how a particular computer works than do machine languages. The language in which a program is written is known as the *source language* for the program, and the text of the program is called the *source program* or *source code*.[16] A program whose source language is a high level language must be translated into machine language before being loaded into the computer's memory for execution. Some lines of text in a source program may be translated into many machine instructions, some into just a few.

There are several measures of program size. One measure is the number of lines in the text of the source program, also known as *lines of source code* (LOC), or number of machine language instructions. Size is greatly variable: a simple program to add a list of numbers may require 10 or fewer instructions, while a word

[12]An early analysis of the problem can be found in Donald W. Kosy, "Air Force Command and Control Information Processing Requirements in the 1980s: Trends in Software Technology," Rand Report R-1012-PR, June 1974.

[13]Ronald L. Enfield, "The Limits of Software Reliability," *Technology Review*, April 1987.

[14]Eastport Study Group Report, op. cit., footnote 4.

[15]To protect them from change, and to enhance their performance, some programs are loaded into memories that are either unchangeable or that must be removed from the computer to be changed. However, most of the memory in nearly all computer systems is of a type that is reloadable while the computer is running.

[16]Instructions and data are encoded into a computer's memory as numbers, and programs are sometimes known as codes.

processing program may take 10,000 LOC (10 KLOC). The Navy's AEGIS ship combat software consists of approximately 2 million instructions.

Size alone is not a good measure of program difficulty. Large programs can be simple, small ones very complex. The size of a program is influenced by the language, computer, programmer's expertise, and other factors. A more important question is, "How complex is the problem to be solved by the program and the algorithms used to solve it?"[17] Compounding the problem is the lack of a standard method for measuring complexity.

Failures and Errors in Computer Programs

Since a computer can only execute the instructions that are stored in its memory, those instructions must be adequate for all situations that may arise during their execution.[18] Incorrect performance by a computer program during its operation is known as a failure. Failures in computer programs result from:

- the occurrence of situations unforeseen by the computer programmer(s) who wrote the instructions,
- a misunderstanding by the programmer(s) of the problem to be solved (including misunderstandings among a group of programmers), or
- a mistake in expressing the solution to the problem as a computer program.

Each of these situations can cause errors in the instructions making up computer programs, errors manifested as failures when particular inputs occur.[19] The effects of errors in

programs range from minor inconveniences (e.g., misspelled words in the program's output) to catastrophic failures—e.g., the cessation of all processing by the computer, wrong answers to problems like computing missile tracks, or overdoses of radiation to devices controlled by the computer.[20] [21]

Tolerating Errors

Errors in large computer programs are the rule rather than the exception. Freedom from errors cannot be guaranteed and is extremely rare. Since correcting an error requires changing the list of instructions that make up the program, the process of removing an error may, and often does, introduce a new error. For large software, the process of correcting errors is so time consuming and expensive that modifications to the software are distributed only a few times a year. As a result, lists of known errors are often published and distributed to users.[22] Where there is a high degree of human interaction with the program during its operation, the human user can usually circumvent situations where the program is known to fail—often by restricting the data input to the program or by not using features of the program known to be failure-prone.

The more critical the task(s) of the program and the smaller the degree of human intervention in the program's operation, the smaller the tolerance for errors. Accordingly, large, critical programs commonly include consistency checks whose goal is to try to detect failures, prevent them when possible, and recover from them when not. This approach is

---

[17]See chapter 8 for a discussion of algorithms.

[18]Some programs, known as self-modifying programs, add to or modify their own instruction sequences and then execute the resulting instructions. Nonetheless, the response of the program to input data is completely determined by the instructions that are initially stored in its memory.

[19]Errors in programs are often called bugs, although the term originally meant any cause of incorrect behavior. The origin of the term is described in John Shore, *The Sachertorte Algorithm*, (New York, NY: Penguin Books, 1986).

[20]For a sample of the variety of problems involving computers and software, see *ACM SIGSOFT Software Engineering Notes* 11(5):3-35, October 1986.

[21]The occurrence of a failure condition is sometimes known as an *incident*. The software may contain instructions that permit it to recover from such an incident. If the software successfully corrects the condition, it remains no more than an incident. Successful recovery from incidents requires good understanding of their causes and corrections, and requires that not too many occur at once.

[22]Manual pages describing programs used with the UNIX operating system, developed and sold by AT&T Bell Laboratories and a currently popular operating system, contain as standard sections a description of the known bugs in the programs.

discussed in more detail in a later section on fault tolerance.

Tolerating Change

As previously noted, change is both the blessing and the curse of the software engineer. Software is expected to be flexible, and his designs must accommodate change. Without its flexibility, software would be as useful. Although software does not wear out in the sense that hardware does, **complex software systems apparently tolerate only a certain amount of change.** The critical point occurs when changes introduce more errors than they fix, i.e., each change, on the average, introduces more errors than it removes.[23] It appears likely that increasing the rate of change decreases the time to reach the critical point. Brooks devotes a chapter to a discussion of the effects of changes in complex systems, concluding with:

> Program maintenance is an entropy-increasing process, and even its most skillful execution only delays the subsidence of the system into unfixable obsolescence.[24]

Although Brooks's discussion is more than 10 years old, it is still valid. Systems that tend to be very long-lived, e.g., 20 years old or more, undergo complete software redevelopment every few years. As an example, the Navy's Naval Tactical Data System, first built in the early 1960s, has undergone at least five major rewrites.

Traditional Reliability Measures

Reliability is one measure of system behavior. In engineering, reliability is often expressed as the average time between failures. For inexpensive consumer items, such as light bulbs, it is defined as the expected lifetime of the item, since such items are completely replaced when they fail. Complicated, expensive systems, such as automobiles, computer

systems, and weapon systems, are designed to outlive any particular component by allowing repair or replacement of components when they fail. Failure of a windshield wiper blade only requires the quick, inexpensive replacement of the blade by another that meets the same specifications as the failed one.

Reliability of complicated systems is traditionally measured in mean time between failure (MTBF), or an equivalent measure such as failure rate. MTBF is measured by counting failures during operation and then dividing by the length of the observation period. For systems with no operational history, MTBF must be predicted on the basis of estimates of the MTBF of each of the system's components. Usually such an estimate is made using the assumption that component failures are random, statistically independent events. Without such an assumption, the analysis is much more difficult and often impractical for complex systems.

Reliability as measured by MTBF is useful for systems with the following characteristics:

- the time to repair the system is unimportant to the user, perhaps because a temporary replacement is available or the user has no need of the system for a while; or
- the time to repair the system is important, but can be kept very short compared to the MTBF, perhaps by keeping a stock of replacement parts on hand; and
- there are no failures so serious as to be unacceptable, e.g., failures that could result in human deaths.

Traditional Reliability Measures Applied to Software

The concept of MTBF has historically been of limited use for critical software. For applications such as BMD, repair time is extremely important. If the system, or parts of it, were to fail, the user would have either no response or a weakened response to an ICBM attack. Accordingly, the concept of MTBF alone is not sufficient to judge whether or not the system would behave as desired. Furthermore, the

---

[23]M. Lehman and L. Belady, "Programming System Dynamics," *ACM SIGOPS Third Symposium on Operating System Principles*, October 1971.

[24]Frederick P. Brooks, Jr., *The Mythical Man-Month: Essays on Software Engineering*, (New York, NY: Addison-Wesley, 1975).

models often used for predicting MTBF are based on assumptions that are invalid for software. Many models assume that component failures are independent and that they are random, i.e., unrelated to system inputs and states. Software components do not fail randomly: they contain errors that cause failures in the event of particular inputs and particular states. The failure of one component often causes others to fail because software components tend to be closely interrelated.

Replacing a software component by a copy of itself will cause exactly the same failure under the same conditions that caused the original to fail. Remedying a failure consists of modifying a component to remove an error in its list of instructions, not replacing a failed component with a copy. Once modified, the component can no longer be considered to be the same as the original, and previous failure data do not apply to it. Finally, a failure in one com-

ponent is likely to lead to failures in others. Consequently, a stock of replacement components cannot be kept on hand in hopes of reducing repair time.

Regardless of whether MTBF were used to indicate software or hardware reliability for a BMD system, some failures would be clearly more disastrous than others. To be useful, MTBF would have to be calculated for different classes of failures.

In recent work, researchers have shown that if inputs are characterized in statistically sound ways, it is possible in testing to determine with high confidence a meaningful MTBF for a program.[25] Nonetheless, MTBF remains inadequate as the sole means of characterizing software dependability.

---

[25]Allen Currit, Michael Dyer, and Harlan D. Mills, "Certifying the Reliability of Software," *IEEE Transactions On Software Engineering*, SE-12(1), January 1986, pp. 3-11.

SOFTWARE DEPENDABILITY

Computer scientists and software users have devised a variety of ways to evaluate software dependability. As in deciding which automobile to buy, the buyer's concerns should determine which qualities are emphasized in the evaluation. Qualities commonly considered are:

- *correctness*—whether or not the software satisfies its specification;
- *trustworthiness*—probability that there are no errors in the software that will cause the system to fail catastrophically;
- *fault tolerance*—either failure prevention, i.e., capability of the software to prevent a failure despite the occurrence of an abnormal or undesired event—or failure recovery, i.e., capability of the software to recover from a failure when one occurs;
- *availability*—probability that the system will be available for use;
- *security*—resistance of the software to unauthorized use, theft of data, and modification of programs;
- *error incidence*—number of errors in the

software, normalized to some measure of size; and
- *safety*—preservation of human life and property under specified operating conditions.

For critical software, correctness and trustworthiness are important indicators of dependability. Fault tolerance assumes importance when the system must continue to perform—as in the midst of a battle—even if performance degrades. Security is important when valuable data or services may be stolen, damaged, or used in unauthorized ways. Safety is important in applications involving risk to human life or property. Error incidence is important in assessing whether or not a piece of software should stay in use.

OTA's characterization of BMD software dependability will include all of the above-listed qualities because:

- national survival may depend on the proper operation of BMD software;

- such software would have to be trusted to operate well during the entire course of a battle; and
- it would have a long lifetime.

Early versions of a BMD system may not have goals as ambitious as later, more capable versions. Nevertheless, we still would want to be confident that the software would operate well during the course of a battle, would do so without undue pause for failure recovery, would be secure, and would be safe to operate. In addition, since it would surely undergo continual modification during its lifetime, we would need to be sure that it was being maintained without repeated introduction of new errors.

Dependability needs to be attended to from the beginning of software development, for it is not easily added on later. Software designs often must be redone after system delivery when performance has been emphasized at the cost of such factors as correctness, fault tolerance, or security. The cost of redoing software may greatly exceed the original cost. Software designed for dependability may contain mechanisms for later improving its correctness, trustworthiness, fault tolerance, security, and safety later. For example, fault tolerance was strongly considered in the design of the SAFEGUARD software. During tests of the prototype system engineers realized that the wrong set of faults had been accommodated. Because the mechanism for detecting and responding to faults had been incorporated into the design, the set of faults tolerated by the system was changed in a matter of only a few weeks. This change involved perhaps 10 percent of the lines of code in the operational software.[26]

Figures of Merit

No single figure of merit can indicate dependability. Single figures of merit generally focus on some single characteristic, such as the cost to discover a password that would permit entry to a computer system. Because software

engineering is a young discipline, software engineers do not yet know very well how to evaluate software quantitatively. And because information permitting numerical evaluation of software is usually considered proprietary, few data are available anyway for such analysis. Accordingly, we would not expect a useful quantitative evaluation of BMD software dependability to be available for many years. Therefore, only a brief analysis of each software property contributing to dependability follows.

Trustworthiness is probably the most important quality for BMD software. The application is critical. Software engineers are unable to produce complex software that is correct and error-free at the current state of the art. Although BMD software should still be as nearly correct, highly available, error-free, secure, and safe to use as possible, we must above all know whether or not it could be trusted.

Correctness

Software developers work from specifications, both written and verbal, that are intended to convey the desired system behavior. The specifications are frequently developed by people with little familiarity with software, e.g., a Naval officer untrained in software development who writes specifications for a ship's combat management system. "Correct" software exhibits exactly the behavior described by its specifications. To convince himself and his customer that he has done his job, the software developer must somehow demonstrate that his software is correct.

Mathematical Correctness

Because no single technique has proved completely effective to demonstrate program correctness, software developers use a variety of techniques try to demonstrate that their software adequately approximates its specifications. Computer scientists, in recognition of the problems involved, have devoted considerable research to such techniques. They have investigated formal and informal, mathematical and non-mathematical ideas. Much of the

---

[26]Victor Vyssotsky, personal communication, 1987.

research attention has been focused on developing "program verification"—mathematical techniques to verify that a computer program is correct with respect to properties required of it. Some progress has been made in mathematically proving that programs are correct. It is unlikely, though, that a sudden breakthrough will occur leading to order-of-magnitude gains in productivity and greatly improved dependability. Brooks analyzed this possibility:

> Can both productivity and product reliability be radically enhanced by following the profoundly different strategy of proving designs correct before the immense effort is poured into implementing and testing them?
>
> I do not believe we will find productivity magic here. Program verification is a very powerful concept, and it will be very important for such things as secure operating system kernels. The technology does not promise, however, to save labor. Verifications are so much work that only a few substantial programs have ever been verified.
>
> Program verification does not mean error-proof programs. There is no magic here, either. Mathematical proofs can also be faulty. So whereas verification might reduce the program-testing load, it cannot eliminate it.
>
> More seriously, even perfect program verification can only establish that a program meets its specification. The hardest part of the software task is arriving at a complete and consistent specification, and much of the essence of building a program is in fact the debugging of the specification.[27]

Although mathematical techniques for demonstrating correctness are not frequently applied, other techniques—such as design reviews, code reviews, and building software in small increments—are. The one technique *always* used by software developers, however, is testing.

Testing

Program developers test a program by placing it in a simulated operating environment.[28]

The simulation supplies inputs to the program, and the testers examine its output for failures.[29] They report any failures to the programmers, who correct the relevant errors and resubmit the program for testing. The sequence continues until the developers agree that the program has passed the test. The final stage of testing developmental software for large and critical systems, especially military software, is acceptance testing. A previously agreed-upon test is run to show that the software meets criteria that make it acceptable to the user.

It has been shown that testing of every possible state of the program, known as exhaustive testing, is not practical even for simple programs. To illustrate this point, John Shore calculated the amount of time required to test the addition program used by 8 digit calculators to add 2 numbers. He estimated that, at the rate of one trial per second it, would take about 1.3 billion years to complete an exhaustive test.[30]

For large, complicated programs, the number of tests that can be run practically is small compared to the number of possible tests. Therefore, developers apply a technique called scenario testing. They observe the program's behavior in an operational scenario that the program would typically encounter. They may establish the scenario by simulating the operational environment, such as an aircraft flight simulator. Alternatively, they may place the software in its actual environment under controlled conditions. For example, a test pilot may put an aircraft with new avionics software through a series of pre-determined maneuvers. In the former case, the simulator must first be shown to be correct before the results can be considered valid. If the simulator itself relies on software, showing the validity of the simulation may be as difficult or more difficult than showing the correctness of the program to be tested.

---

[27]Frederick P. Brooks, Jr., "No Silver Bullet, Essence and Accidents of Software Engineering," op. cit., footnote 5, p. 16.

[28]For presentation purposes, the discussion of testing here is simplified, omitting, e.g., component testing. Appendix A contains a more complete discussion.

[29]Good testers carefully determine the inputs to be used in advance, often including some tests using random inputs, and some using nonrandom, so as to get representative coverage of the expected operational inputs.

[30]John Shore, op. cit., footnote 19, pp. 171-172.

For systems like aircraft, such tests are so expensive that only relatively few scenarios can be flown. Flight tests of the avionics software for the Navy's A-7 aircraft, including land- and carrier-based tests, cost approximately $300,000. Scenario tests for the SAFE-GUARD system consisted of installing a test version of the system at Kwajalein missile range and firing one or two missiles at a time at it.

Since exhaustive testing is not practical, testing cannot be relied upon to show that a computer program completely and exactly behaves according to its specifications or even that it contains no errors. As stated by computer scientist Edsger Dijkstra:

> Program testing can be used to show the presence of bugs, but never to show their absence![31]

The deficiencies of testing as a means of showing correctness and freedom from errors have moved software engineers to seek other methods, such as mathematical. They have also sought means of measuring error incidence. In addition, they are developing methods for random testing that permit statistical inferences about failure rates.[32]

Error Incidence

Some assert that error incidence—measured, for example, by the number of errors found per thousand lines of source code—measure program correctness. Those making this assertion assume that it is possible to count errors unambiguously and that the more errors a program has the less its behavior will conform to its specifications. They then portray the debate over BMD software dependability as hinging on the question of whether or not the software would contain errors, and how many it would contain.

Both critics and proponents of an attempt to build SDI software agree that any such software would contain errors. As put by the Eastport Group:

> Simply because of its inevitable large size, the software capable of performing the battle management task for strategic defense will contain errors. All systems of useful complexity contain software errors.[33]

Ware Myers notes:

> The whole history of large, complex software development indicates that errors cannot be completely eliminated.[34]

David Parnas asserts that:

> Error statistics make excellent diversions but they do not matter. A low error rate does not mean that the system will be effective. All that does matter is whether software works acceptably when first used by the customers; the sad answer is that, even in cases much simpler than SDI, it does not. What also matters is whether we can find all the "serious" errors before we put the software into use. The sad answer is that we cannot. What matters, too, is whether we could ever be confident that we had found the last serious error. Again, the sad answer is that we cannot. Software systems become trustworthy after real use, not before.[35]

Trustworthiness

Since correctness and error rates are not the real issues in the software debate, trustworthiness has become the focus. The issue is whether or not BMD software could be produced so that it would be trustworthy despite the presence of errors. In common usage, reliability and trustworthiness are often considered to be the same. In engineering usage, reliability has become associated with specific measures, such as MTBF. There have been few attempts to quantify trustworthiness, despite

---

[31]J. Dahl, E.W. Dijkstra, and C.A.R. Hoare, "Notes on Structured Programming," *Structured Programming* (London: Academic Press, 1972), p. 6.

[32]See the discussion on the cleanroom method in appendix A for more details.

[33]Eastport Study Group Report, op. cit., footnote 4.

[34]Ware Myers, "Can Software for the Strategic Defense Initiative Ever Be Error-Free?" *IEEE Computer* XX:61-67, November 1986.

[35]David L. Parnas, "SDI Red Herrings Miss the Boat," (Letter to the Editor), *IEEE Computer* 20(2):6-7, February 1987.

the desirability of trustworthy systems. One possible reason may be that trust is determined qualitatively as much as quantitatively: people judge by past experience and knowledge of internal mechanisms as much as by numbers representing reliability. Another possible reason is that most systems in critical applications are safeguarded by human operators. Although the systems are trusted, the ultimate trust resides in the human operator. Nuclear power stations, subway systems, and autopilots are all examples.[36]

As noted in chapter 7, a BMD system would leave little time for human intervention: trust would have to be placed in the system, not in the human operator. Accordingly, it is important to be able to evaluate the trustworthiness of BMD software. One suggested definition is that trustworthiness is the confidence one has that the probability of a catastrophic flaw is acceptably low.[37] Trustworthiness might be described by a sentence such as "The probability of an unacceptable flaw remaining after testing is less than 1 in 1,000."[38] (This measure of trustworthiness has only recently been suggested, and no data have yet been published to support it.) Estimating trustworthiness consists of testing the software in a randomly selected subset of the set of internal states with a randomly selected subset of the possible inputs. The set of possible inputs and internal states must be known. It must be possible to recognize a catastrophic test result, i.e., the expected operating conditions must be well-understood. For BMD systems, this means understanding the expected threat and countermeasures as well as testing under conditions closely simulating a nuclear environment.

[36]Even when human operators are aware of a problem they sometimes do not or cannot react quickly enough, or with the proper procedures, to prevent disaster.

[37]David L. Parnas, "When Can We Trust Software Systems?" (Keynote Address), *Computer Assurance, Software Systems Integrity: Software Safety and Process Security Conference*, July 1986.

[38]David L. Parnas, personal communication, 1987.

Fault Tolerance

Realizing that errors in the code and unforeseen and undesired situations are inevitable, software developers try to find ways of coping with the resulting failures. Software is considered fault-tolerant if it can either prevent or recover from such failures, whether they are derived from hardware or software errors or from unanticipated input. Techniques for fault tolerance include:

- back-up algorithms,
- voting by three or more different implementations of the same algorithm,
- error-recovery programs, and
- back-up hardware.

Program verification techniques, discussed above, attempt to prove correctness by mathematical analysis of the code. In contrast, fault-tolerant techniques attempt to cope with failures by analyzing how a program behaves during execution.

Since a BMD system would have to operate under widely varying conditions for many years, its software would have to incorporate a high degree of fault tolerance. Unfortunately, there are no accepted measures of fault tolerance, and design of fault-tolerant systems is not well understood. As an example, space shuttle flight software is designed in a way thought to be highly fault-tolerant. Four identical computers, executing identical software, vote on critical flight computations A fifth, executing a different flight program, operates in parallel, providing a backup if the other four fail. On an early attempted shuttle launch, this flight system failed because the backup program could not synchronize itself with the four primary programs. The failure, occurring just 20 minutes before the scheduled lift-off, caused the flight to be postponed for a day. It was a direct result of the attempt to make the software fault-tolerant.

The price for fault tolerance is generally paid in performance and complexity. A program incorporating considerable code for the purpose of detecting, preventing, and recovering from failures will be larger and operate more slowly than one that does not. A successful fault-tolerant design will result in a system with higher availability than a corresponding system built without regard for fault tolerance. Producers of non-critical software may not care to pay the price. Those concerned with critical systems that must operate continuously often feel that they must.

Availability

Systems that are intended to maintain continuous operation are often evaluated by calculating their availability, i.e., the percent of time that they are available for use. Availability is easily measured by observing, for some interval, the amount of time the system is unavailable (the "down" time) and available (the "up" time) and then calculating (up time)/(up time + down time). As with other figures of merit, availability figures are useful when the conditions under which they were measured are well-known. Extrapolation outside of those conditions is risky. Since prediction of availability is equivalent to prediction of MTBF and mean time to repair (MTTR)—measures of up- and down-times, respectively—availability is at least as difficult to predict as MTBF and MTTR are individually.

Security

Computer users concerned with preserving the confidentiality of data and the effectiveness of weapon systems, such as banks or the military, consider security a necessary condition for dependability. Breaches of security that concern such users include:

- knowledge by an opponent of the algorithms implemented in a computer controlling a weapon system, allowing him to devise ways of circumventing the strategy and tactics embodied in those algorithms;
- access by unauthorized users to sensitive or classified data stored in a computer;
- denial of access by authorized users to their computers, thereby denying them the capabilities of the computer and the data stored in it; and

- substitution of an opponent's software for operational software (changing even a few instructions may be potentially disastrous), allowing the opponent to divert the computer to his own uses.

Many of the preceding concerns only apply if a computer must use a potentially corruptible communications channel to receive data or instructions from another computer or from a human.[39] Any BMD system would contain such links. (The possibility that a link could be corrupted and measures for preventing such corruption are discussed in ch. 8.) Over these channels one might:

- load revised programs into the memories of the BMD computers;
- correct errors in existing programs;
- change the strategy incorporated into existing programs; or
- accommodate changes to software requirements, such as might be caused by the introduction of new technology into the BMD system.

In addition, any BMD architecture would contain communications channels for the exchange of data between battle management computers and sensors and among battle management computers.

Since the 1960s, when computers started to be used on a large scale in weapon systems, the DoD has expended considerable effort to find ways of making computer systems secure. As yet, no way has been found to meet all the security requirements for computers used in the design, development, and operation of weapon systems. As Landwehr points out in a discussion of the state of the art in developing secure software:

At present, no technology can assure both adequate and trustworthy system performance in advance. Those techniques that have been tried have met with varying degrees of success, but it is difficult to measure their success objectively, because no good measures ex-

---

[39]Physical security, i.e., control of physical access to computing equipment, is a problem as well, generally unsolvable by technical means and outside the scope of this report.

ist for ranking the security of various systems.[40]

Although there is no quantifiable measure of the security of a computer system, the DoD has developed a standard for evaluating the security of computer systems.[41] The evaluation consists of matching the features provided by a system against those known to be necessary, albeit not sufficient, to provide security. For example, the second highest rating is given to those systems that let users label their data according to its security level, e.g., Confidential or Secret, then protect the labels against unauthorized modification. Furthermore, the developer must show the security model used in enforcing the protection and show that the system includes a program that checks every data reference to ensure that it follows the model. As with fault tolerance, incorporating security features into software exacts penalties in performance and complexity.

Safety

A software engineering journal distinguished between safety and reliability:

> Safety and reliability are often equated, especially with respect to software, but there is a growing trend to separate the two concepts. Reliability is usually defined as the probability that a system will perform its intended function for a specified period of time under a set of specified environmental conditions. Safety is the probability that conditions which can lead to an accident (hazards) do not occur whether the intended function is performed or not. Another way of saying this is

that software safety involves ensuring that the software will execute within a system context without resulting in unacceptable risk.[42]

Interest in software safety has increased markedly in recent years. Formal publications specifically addressing software safety issues started appearing in the early 1980s.[43] As yet, there are no standard measures or ways of assessing software safety. Nonetheless, it is important that BMD software be safe so as to prevent accidents that are life-threatening and costly. An unsafe BMD system might, for example, accidentally destroy a satellite, space station, or shuttle.

Appropriate Measures of Software Dependability

As should be clear from the preceding discussion, software dependability cannot be captured in any single measure. Correctness, trustworthiness, safety, security, and fault tolerance are all components of dependability. All should be considered in the development of software for a BMD system. Attempts to quantify them in a clear-cut way require specifying too many conditions on the measure to allow useful generalization. Estimates of the dependability of BMD software would always be suspect, since in large part they would always be subjective. Until we can quantify software dependability we cannot know that we have developed dependable BMD software. The following sections discuss the factors involved in developing dependable software.

[40]Carl Landwehr, "The Best Available Technologies For Computer Security," *IEEE Computer*, July 1983, p. 93.

[41]"DoD Standard 5200.28, Department of Defense Trusted Computer System Evaluation Criteria," (Washington, DC: Department of Defense, Aug. 15, 1983).

[42]*IEEE Transactions on Software Engineering: Special Issue On Reliability And Safety In Real-Time Process Control*, SE-12(9):877, September 1986.

[43]Nancy Leveson and Peter Harvey, "Analyzing Software Safety," *IEEE Transactions on Software Engineering*, SE-9(?), September 1983, pp. 569-579, was one of the first papers to discuss software safety.

CHARACTERISTICS OF DEPENDABLE SYSTEMS

Despite the lack of ways of quantifying confidence in software, people trust many computerized systems. Further, people are willing to undertake development of many systems

with confidence that they will be reliable when finished. In this section we discuss why systems come to be trusted and give some examples of trusted systems. We divide methods of gaining trust into two classes: those based on observations of the external behavior of the system, and those based on understanding how the system operates internally.

Observations of External Behavior

A system, whether containing software or not, may be considered to be a black box with connections to the outside world. One may observe the inputs that are sent to the box and the outputs it produces. The next few sections discuss methods of gaining confidence in software and systems based on black-box observations of the software.

Extensive Use and Abuse

Perhaps the most important factor inspiring confidence in software is that the software has been used extensively. A good analogy is the automobile. Confidence comes from familiarity with cars in general and frequent use of one's own car. Having seen that the engine will start when the key is turned hundreds of times gives one the feeling that it will start the next time the key is turned. Automatic teller machines, electronic calculators, word processors, and AT&T's long distance telephone network are all examples of systems controlled by software that are trusted to work properly. The trust is built on extensive experience: one has high confidence that the telephone will work the next time it is tried because it usually has in the past.

Confidence is considerably enhanced when a system continues to work even though abused. A car that starts on cold and rainy days inspires increased confidence that it will start on mild and sunny days. Observing that calls still get through under heavy calling conditions (albeit not as quickly), that dialing a non-existent number produces a meaningful response, and that calls can still be made when major trunk circuits fail boosts one's confidence that nearly all one's calls will get through under normal conditions. Conversely, system failure detracts from confidence. Having observed that issuing a particular command to a word processor sometimes results in mean-

ingless text being inserted into a document leads one to refrain from using that command.

It is important to note that extensive confidence comes from extensive use and not from testing that incompletely simulates use. No one would consider granting a license to a pilot who had spent extensive time in a flight simulator but had never actually flown an airplane. Simulated use inspires confidence to the degree that the simulation approximates operational conditions. Real-world complications are often either too expensive or too poorly understood to simulate. In testing systems, simulators are useful for convincing ourselves that the gain from putting the system into its operating environment is worth the attendant cost and risks. They allow the jump to actual use with some confidence that disaster will not result.

Predictable Environments

Confidence in software also comes from being able to predict the behavior of the software in its operational environment. If the environment itself is predictable, the job of designing and testing the software is considerably eased. For example, engineers can predict and mathematically analyze the number of telephone calls per hour that a particular switching center will receive at any time of day. The number and type of signals that will be received on the telephone lines (e.g., the 7 digits in a local telephone number) are known because their specifications form part of the requirements for the telephone system and are determined by the designers. The software and hardware may then be designed to cope with the telephone traffic and the signal types based on the specifications.

Engineers can observe the system in operation to verify predictions before new software is placed into operation. Finally, they can observe the behavior of new software in terms of number of calls handled, number of calls rerouted, and other parameters for different traffic loads. Observing that behavior matches predictions builds confidence in the operation of the system. Nonetheless, even when the developers have extensive experience with a well-controlled environment, they sometimes make mistakes in prediction and do not discover those mistakes until the system goes into use.

Low Cost of a Failure

Although extensive use and environmental predictability both strongly influence the amount of confidence placed in a system, they are not sufficient to induce users to continue using a system after significant failures. Large, complicated software systems inevitably experience software failures. Therefore, users don't have confidence in the software unless the risk associated with a failure is smaller than the gain from using the software. A word processor that loses documents may go unused because the cost of re-creating the document is greater than the effort saved by using the word processor.

If, however, an easy method of recovering from such losses is available, perhaps by including a feature in the word processor that automatically saves back-up copies of documents, then the cost to the user of the failure becomes acceptably low: he can recover his document when it is lost. Similarly, the cost of recovering from a misconnected phone call is small to the dialer and to the telephone company. (Although a misdialed phone call is not really a system failure, the same principle applies: users can recover quickly and easily.) The ability to recover from a failure at low cost increases confidence in and willingness to use a system.

Systems With Stable Requirements

A desire for flexibility is a prime motive for using computer systems. The behavior of a computer can be radically altered by changing its software. Radical changes may be made to a computer program throughout its entire lifetime. Because there is no apparent physical structure involved, the impact of change may not be readily appreciated by those who demand it without having to implement it. No one would ask a bridge builder to change his design from a suspension to an arch-supported bridge after the bridge was half built without expecting to pay a high price. The equivalent

is often demanded of software builders with the expectation of little or no penalty in schedule, cost, or dependability.

An example is the combat system software for the first of the Navy's DD 963 class of destroyers. During the development of the software, which cost less than 1 percent of the cost of building the ship, the customers imposed major changes on the software developer. The original requirements specified that the combat system need only provide passive electronic warfare functions. One year into development the buyers added a requirement for active electronic warfare. A year later they removed the requirement for active electronic warfare. On the ship's maiden voyage its commander issued a casualty report on the software: the ship could not perform its function because of deficiencies in the software. Although the major requirements changes were probably not the only reason for the deficiencies, they were certainly a prime contributing factor.

The B-1B bomber is another example of a system where deficiencies have resulted from too much change during development. According to a report on the B-1B bomber,

> Defense officials blame many of the program's problems on the decision to begin producing the aircraft at the same time that research and development efforts were under way, forcing engineers to experiment with some systems before they were completely developed.[44]

Conversely, a system whose requirements change little during the course of development is more likely to work properly. Developers have a chance of understanding the problem to be solved: they need not continually reanalyze the problem and revise their solution. Stability of requirements is particularly important for software because of the many decisions involved in software design. Each subdivision of a program into subprograms involves decisions about the functions to be performed by the subprograms and about the interfaces be-

---

[44]"New Weapon Suffers From Major Defects," *Washington Post*, Jan. 7, 1987, p. A1.

tween them. Writing each subprogram further involves decisions on the algorithm to be used, the way data are to be represented, the order of the actions to be performed, and the instructions to be used to represent those actions.

Decisions made early in the process are more difficult to change than those made later in the process because later decisions are often dependent on earlier ones. Furthermore, the process of change is more expensive in later phases of a project because there are more specifications and other documentation. Using data from SAFEGUARD software and software projects at IBM, GTE, and TRW, one expert has shown that, as a result of the preceding factors, error correction costs (and costs to make other software changes) increase exponentially with time. In Boehm's words:

> These factors combine to make the error typically 100 times more expensive to correct in the maintenance phase than in the requirements phase.[45]

Clearly then, for systems where requirements change little during development, not only can one have increased confidence in the software, but one can also expect it to cost less. Among the developers of large, complex systems who attended OTA's workshop on SDI software, there was unanimous agreement that BMD software development could not begin until there were a clear statement of the requirements of the system.[46]

Systems Based on Well-Understood Predecessors

As with other human engineering projects, successful software systems are generally the result of slow, evolutionary change. Where radical changes are attempted, failure rates are high and confidence in performance is low. This rule can be seen in endeavors such as bridge building[47] as well as software design.[48]

With the example and experience of a previous solution to a problem, a software developer can have the confidence that a system to solve a small variation on the problem can be correctly produced. The structure of the previous solution and the associated algorithms may be applied again with small variations. A good example is the software used by NASA to compute the orientation of unmanned spacecraft. The orientation, also known as attitude, is computed by ground-based computers while the spacecraft is in operation. Attitude is determined from the readings of sensors on board the spacecraft. The sensor readings are telemetered to earth and supplied as input to an attitude determination program for the spacecraft. The algorithms for computing orientation are well known and have been used many times. The design of the attitude determination software that incorporates the algorithms is also dependable.

The design of an attitude determination program for a new spacecraft starts with the design of an earlier program and consists of modifying the design to take into account sensor and telemetry changes. Many of the subprograms from the earlier program are reused intact, some are modified, and some new subprograms are written. A typical attitude determination program of this type is 50,000 to 125,000 lines of code in size and takes about 18 months to produce. It must be produced before the launch of the associated satellite, and must work when needed so that the satellite may be maneuvered as necessary. The de-

---

[45]Barry W. Boehm, *Software Engineering Economics* (Englewood Cliffs, NJ: Prentice-Hall, 1981), figure 4-2, p. 40.

[46]Attendees at the workshop included software developers who participated in the development of SAFEGUARD, Hard Site defense, telephone switching systems, digital communication networks, Ada compilers, and operating systems.

---

[47]As stated by Henry Petroski in *To Engineer Is Human: The Role of Failure in Successful Design*, (New York, NY: St. Martin's Press, 1985), p. 219.

. . . departures from traditional designs are more likely than not to hold surprises.

[48]Early compilers for the new Ada language have been so slow, unwieldy to use, and bug-ridden that they have been worthless for real software development. This situation has occurred despite the fact that compilers for older languages such as FORTRAN, for which there have been compilers since the mid-1950s, are considered routine development tasks. The main contributing factors were the many features, especially the many new features, incorporated into Ada.

veloper's confidence in his ability to meet these criteria is based on the success of the previous attitude determination programs.

The developers of the SAFEGUARD software believed they could solve the problem of defending a small area from a ballistic missile attack because similar, but somewhat simpler, problems had been solved in the past. The history of missile defense systems can be traced back to World War II anti-aircraft systems, starting with the T-10 gun director. Next came: the M-9 gun director, which ultimately attained a 90 percent success rate against the V-1 flying bombs; the Nike-Ajax missile interceptor system; then, the Nike-Hercules, improved Hercules, Nike-Zeus, Nike-X, and Sentinel ABM systems.[49] Each system typically involved some mission changes and a change of one or two components over the previous one. Although the last few of these were never used in battle, constraining judgments of success in development, the evolutionary process is clear.

Note that the evolutionary approach requires the availability of experience gained from the earlier systems. Experience may take the form of personal memories or of documentation describing earlier programs. In other words, most of the problem must be well-understood and the solution clearly described. As Parnas put it, following a series of observations on what makes software engineering hard,

> The common thread in all these observations is that, even with sound software design principles, we need broad experience with similar systems to design good, reliable software.[50]

Observations of Internal Behavior

The above approaches to gaining confidence in software are based on observing the external behavior of the software without trying to determine how it behaves internally. That is, the software is tested by observing the effects of executing computer programs rather than the mechanisms by which those effects are produced. The next few sections discuss methods based on observing the internal behavior of programs—methods that may be called "clear box" to denote that the internal mechanism used to produce behavior may now be observed.

Simple Designs

It is not practical to give mathematical proofs that software performs correctly. Given a simple design and a clear specification of requirements, it is sometimes possible to give a convincing argument that each requirement is satisfied by some component of the design. Similarly, a convincing argument can be given that a simple design is properly implemented as a program. As with reliability measures, how convincing the argument is depends on subjective judgment. Where only a weak argument can be given that the design properly implements the requirements and that the code properly implements the design, there would be little reason to trust the software, especially in its initial period of operation. As one expert puts it,

> . . . the main principle in dealing with complicated problems is to transform them into simple ones.[51]

Put another way, each complication in a design makes it less trustworthy. Simplicity, is, of course, relative to the problem. The inherent complexity of a problem it may require complex solutions. The designer's job is to make the solution as simple as he can. As Einstein said:

> Everything should be as simple as possible, but no simpler.[52]

Disciplined Development

The software development process comprises a variety of activities. Describing software cost estimation techniques, Boehm iden-

---

[49]The history of missile defense systems given here was supplied in a 1987 personal communication by Victor Vyssotsky, responsible for development of SAFEGUARD software.
[50]David L. Parnas, op. cit., footnote 1.

[51]T.C. Jones, *Design Methods, Seeds Of Human Futures*, (New York: John Wiley & Sons, 1980).
[52]Personal communication, P. Neumann.

tifies 8 different major activities occurring during software development and 15 different cost drivers.[53] Other estimators use different factors. (One early study introduced more than 90 factors influencing the cost of software development.) Fairley lists 17 different factors that affect the quality and productivity of software.[54] There is general agreement that many factors affect software development. There is still considerable doubt over how to identify the factors that would most significantly affect a new project—particularly if there is little experience with the development environment, the personnel involved, or the application. Appendix A describes the typical software development process and some of the complicating factors.

Development of large, complicated software must be a carefully controlled process. As the size and complexity of the software increases, different factors may dominate the cost and quality of the resulting product. Based on personal observations, Horning conjectured that:

> . . . for every order of magnitude in software size (measured by almost any interesting metric) a new set of problems seems to dominate.[55]

Although it is early to expect an accurate estimate of the size of BMD software, current estimates of the size of SDI battle management software range from a factor of 2 to a factor of 30 larger than the largest existing systems (and the the accuracy of some estimates is judged to be no better than a factor of 3).[56] If Horning's statement is correct, then there is reason to suspect that currently unforeseen problems would dominate BMD software development. Solving these problems would add to the time and expense involved in producing the software, and may undermine judgments of its reliability.

The development process must be geared to controlling the effects of the dominating factors. An example is the procedures by which changes are made. Most software development can be viewed as a process of progressive change. At every phase, ideas from the previous phase are transformed into the products of the current phase. For very small projects, the changes may be kept in the mind of one person. For moderately small projects, verbal communication among the project members may suffice to keep track of changes.

For larger projects, the number of people involved and the length of time of the project require that changes be approved by small committees and that written lists of revisions be distributed to all project personnel at regular intervals. Revised products of earlier phases are also distributed to those who need them. For very large projects, formal change control boards are established and all changes to baseline designs must be approved before they are implemented. A library of approved documents and programs is maintained so that all personnel have access to the same version of all project products. The process of controlling change becomes a source of considerable overhead, but is necessary so that all project members work from the same assumptions.

Factors Distinguishing DoD Software Development

There are some similarities between DoD and commercial software. The environments where DoD uses software are also found outside of DoD. Commercial and NASA avionics systems perform many of the same functions as military avionics, and must also work in life-threatening situations. Furthermore, the software must ultimately be produced in the same form, i.e., as a computer program, often in the same or a similar language for the same or a similar computer. But the DoD development process, as described in appendix A, is often

---

[53]*Software Engineering Economics*, op. cit., footnote 45, p. 98.

[54]Richard Fairley, *Software Engineering Concepts*, (New York, NY: McGraw-Hill, 1985).

[55]Jim Horning, "Computing in Support of Battle Management,"*ACM SIGSOFT Software Engineering Notes* 10(5):24-27, October 1985.

[56]Barry Boehm, author of *Software Engineering Economics*, and deviser of the most popular analytical software cost estimation model in use today, estimated, in a personal communication, that estimates of the size of SDI battle management software with which he was familiar could easily be in error by a factor of 3.

quite different from commercial software development.

Several factors, *in combination*, distinguish DoD software from commercial software. Elements of all of these factors are found in commercial software applications, but the combination is usually not.

- *Long lifetime.* Military command and control software often has a lifetime of 20 or more years. The Naval Tactical Data System was developed in the early 1960s and is still in use.
- *Embedded.* New DoD systems must interface with other, existing DoD systems. The interfaces are not under the control of the developer, and the need for the interface was often not foreseen when the existing system was developed. Commercial software developers are generally free to develop their own interfaces, or build stand-alone systems.
- *Operating in Real Time.* Command and control systems must generally respond to events in the outside world as they are happening. A delayed response may result in human deaths and damage to material.
- *Life-critical.* Command and Control and weapon systems are designed to inflict death or to prevent it from occurring.
- *Large.* DoD systems containing hundreds of thousands of lines of code are common. The larger systems contain as many as 3 million lines of code.
- *Complex.* Command and control systems perform many different functions and must coordinate the actions of a variety of equipment based on the occurrence of external events.
- *Machine-near.* The programmers of command and control systems must understand details of how the computer they are using works, how the equipment that it controls works, and what the interface between the two is. Many such details are transparent to commercial programmers because of the standardization of equipment, such as printers, for which already existing software handles the necessary details. The same is not true for new weap-

ons, sensors, and computer systems specially tailored to particular DoD applications. As an example, the computers used on board the A-7 aircraft, in both the Navy and Air Force versions, were designed for that aircraft and rarely used elsewhere. The use of non-standard equipment often means that standard programming languages cannot be used because they provide no instructions that can be used to control the equipment. The current DoD trend is toward standardization of computers and languages, but programmers still must deal with specialized equipment.

- *Facing Intelligent Adversaries.* DoD battle management and command, control, and communications systems must deal with intelligent adversaries who actively seek ways to defeat them.

The DoD software development process is often characterized as cumbersome and inefficient, but is a significant improvement over the situation of the early 1970s when there was no standard development process. It provides some protection, in the form of required documentation, against software that is either unmaintainable or unmaintainable by anyone except the builders. Minimal requirements for the conduct of acceptance tests also provides some protection against grossly inadequate systems. Nonetheless, the process often still produces systems that contain serious errors and are difficult to maintain.[57] [58] The complexity of BMD software development would probably require significant changes in the process, both in management and technical areas.[59] The Fletcher Study concluded that:

Although a strong concern for the development of software prevails throughout the civil and military data-processing community,

---

[57]For examples of problems in such systems as the SGT YORK Division Air Defense Gun, see *ACM SIGSOFT Software Engineering Notes*, op. cit., footnote 20.

[58]Upgrade of the A-7E avionics software, which is small (no more than 32,000 instructions), but quite complex (to accommodate a new missile cost about $8 million).

[59]Appendix A contains a further discussion of the DoD software development process and recent technical developments that might contribute to improving it.

more emphasis needs to be placed on the specific problem of BMD:

- Expanded efforts to generate software development tools are needed.
- Further emphasis is needed on simulation as a means to assist the design of battle management systems and software.
- Specific work is needed on algorithms related to critical battle management functions.[60]

Improving the Process

Software development, a labor-intensive process, depends for its success on many different factors. Improvements tend to come from better understanding of the process. Furthermore, improvements tend to be made in small increments because of the many factors influencing the process. To produce a system successfully requires, among other things:

- availability of appropriate languages and machines,
- employment of properly trained people,
- good problem specification,
- stable problem specification, and
- an appropriate methodology.[61]

Current efforts in software engineering technology development concentrate on providing automated support for much of the process. Software engineering tools may contribute to small incremental improvements in the process and the product. Such tools may help programmers produce prototypes, write and check the consistency of specifications, keep track of test results, and manage development

Software Dependability and Computer Architecture

Variations in computer design can have a strong effect on the software dependability. Some architectures are well-suited to certain

applications and make the job of developing and testing the software easier. As an example, some computer systems allow programs to act as if they each had their own copy of the computer's memory. This feature permits several programs to execute concurrently without risk that one will write over another's memory area. The computer detects attempts to call on memory areas beyond a program's own and can terminate the program. The computer provides the programmer with information about where in the program the failure occurred, thus helping him find the error. This memory sharing technique makes the programmer's development job easier and allows the computer to be be used for several different purposes simultaneously.

Other systems permit the programmer to define an area of the computer's memory whose contents are sent at regular intervals to an external device. This feature could be used in conjunction with a display device to ensure that the display is properly maintained without the programmer having to write a special program to do so. Such a feature simplifies the job of developing software for graphics applications. Also, at the cost of added hardware, it improves the performance of the computer system when used with graphic displays.

Features built into the computer may make the software development job easier, the software more dependable, and the system performance better. The penalty for this approach may be to make the computer designer's job harder and the hardware more expensive. Further, the gain in software dependability is, as in many other cases, not quantifiable. Chapter 8 contains a more detailed discussion of various computer architectures and their potential for meeting the computational needs of BMD.

Software Dependability and System Architecture

Just as an appropriate computer architecture may lead to improved software dependability, so may an appropriate system architecture. A BMD architecture that simplified

---

[60]James C. Fletcher, Study Chairman and Brockway McMillan, Panel Chairman, op. cit., footnote 11.

[61]It is only in the last few years that the job title "software engineer" has been used. There is no qualification standard for software engineers, and no standard curriculum. Few universities or colleges yet offer an undergraduate major in software engineering, and there is only one educational institution in the country that offers a master's degree in software engineering.

coordination and communication needs among system components, such as different battle managers, would simplify the software design and might lead to improved software dependability. As with computer architecture, there would be a penalty: decreased coordination usually leads either to decreased efficiency or to more complex components. The increase in complexity is caused by the need for each component to compensate for the loss of information otherwise obtained from other components. As an example, if battle managers cannot exchange track information with each other, then they must maintain more tracks individually to do their jobs as efficiently. They may also have to do their own RV/decoy discrimination. Note that an architecture that requires exchange of a small amount of track information would be nearly as difficult to design and implement as one that required exchange of a large amount. The reason is that the communications procedures for the reliable exchange of small quantities of data are about the same as those for large quantities.

The Eastport group estimated that for an SDI BMD system the penalty for not exchanging track information among battle managers during boost phase would be about a 20 percent increase in the number of SBIs needed.[62]

The improvement in software dependability that might be obtained by architectural variations is not quantifiable.

Software Dependability and System Dependability

It is desirable to find some way of combining software and hardware dependability measures. As indicated earlier, MTBF, a traditional hardware reliability measure, is not appropriate as a sole measure of dependability of BMD software. Certainly it will still be desirable to measure hardware reliability in terms of MTBF in order to schedule hardware maintenance and to estimate repair and replacement

inventory needs. The only components of both hardware and software dependability for which there may be some common ground for estimation are trustworthiness and availability. However, there have been few or no attempts to estimate trustworthiness for systems that are composites of hardware and software.

In summary, there are no established ways to produce a computer (hardware and software) system dependability measure. Furthermore, there are few good existing proposals for potential system dependability measures.

Software Dependability and the SDI

Although it is not possible to give a quantitative estimate of achievable software dependability for SDI software, it is possible to gain an idea of the difficulty of producing BMD software known to be dependable. We can do so by comparing the characteristics of a BMD system with characteristics of large, complex systems that are considered to be dependable. In an earlier section those characteristics were described. We apply them here to potential SDI BMD systems, using the architecture described in chapter 3 as a reference. Table 9-1 is a summary of the following sections. It shows whether or not each characteristic can be applied to SDI software, and provides a comparison with SAFEGUARD and the AT&T telephone system software, both often mentioned as comparable to SDI BMD software.[63]

SAFEGUARD and telephone system software represent different ends of the spectrum of large systems that could reasonably be compared to SDI BMD systems. The telephone system:

- is not a weapon system,
- has evolved over a period of a hundred years,

---

[62]Eastport Study Group Report, op. cit., footnote 4. The analysis and assumptions behind this claim have not been made available.

[63]Cf. Dr. Solomon Buchsbaum, Executive Vice President for Customer Systems for AT&T Bell Laboratories and former chair of the Defense Science Board and the White House Science Council:

> . . . most if not all of the essential attributes of the BM/C³ system have, I believe, been demonstrated in comparable terrestrial systems.
>
> S. Hrg. 99-933, op. cit., footnote 3, p. 275.

The system most applicable to the issue at hand is the U.S. Public Telecommunications Network.

Table 9-1.—Characteristics of Dependable Systems Applied to SDI, SAFEGUARD, and the Telephone System

Characteristic	SDI	SAFEGUARD	Telephone system
Extensively used & abused	No	No	Yes
Predictable environment	No	No	Yes
Low cost of a failure	No	No	Yes
Stable requirements	No	Yes	Yes
Well-understood predecessors	No	Yes	Yes
Simple design	Unknown	?	Yes
Disciplined development	Unknown	Yes	Yes

SOURCE: Office of Technology Assessment, 1988.

- operates in a predictable environment with well-understood technology,
- is kept supplied with spare hardware parts that can be quickly installed, and
- is not designed to be resistant to an attack aimed at destroying it (although it can be reconfigured in hours by its human operators to circumvent individual damaged switching centers).

The SAFEGUARD system was a missile defense system that used well-understood technology, was never used in battle, would have had to operate in an environment that was not easily predictable, and was designed to make its destruction by an enemy attack costly.

Several other systems lie within the spectrum defined by SAFEGUARD and the telephone system. Examples are NASA flight software systems, such as the Apollo and Space Shuttle software, and weapon systems such as AEGIS. All have some of the characteristics of BMD systems. Nearly all are autonomous within clearly defined limits, must operate in real time, and are large. Some that are viewed as successful developments, such as AEGIS, have only been used under simulated and test conditions, but are thought to be sufficiently dependable to be put on operational status.

None of the examples known to OTA have been developed under the combined constraints imposed by SDI requirements, i.e., an SDI system would have to:

- control weapons autonomatically;
- incorporate new technology;

- be partly space-based, partly ground-based;
- defend itself from active and passive attacks;
- defend against threats whose characteristics cannot be well-specified in advance;
- operate in a nuclear environment, whose characteristics are not well-understood;
- be designed so that it can be changed to meet new threats and add new technology; and
- perform successfully in its first operational use.

Even a system such as AEGIS, which is perhaps DoD's most technologically advanced deployed system, was not developed under such stringent constraints, and its success is not yet fully determined.

Extensively Used and Abused

Although it might undergo considerable testing in a simulated environment, a BMD system cannot be considered to have been used in its working environment until it has been used in an actual battle. The working environment for a BMD system would be a nuclear war. Thus, the first time it would be used would also likely be the only time. In the telephone system, components that are put into use even after extensive testing often fail. A letter to Congress from designers and maintainers of AT&T Bell Laboratories switching systems stated:

> Despite rigorous tests, the first time new equipment is incorporated into the telephone network, it rarely performs reliably.

> Adding new equipment is just the tip of the iceberg; even the simplest software upgrade introduces serious errors. Despite our best efforts, the software that controls the telephone network has approximately one error for every thousand lines of code when it is initially incorporated into the system. Extensive testing and simulation cannot discover these errors.[64]

---

[64] A copy of the letter also appears as "SDI Software, Part II: The Software Will Not Be Reliable," *Physics and Society*, 16(2), April 1987.

Predictable Environment

Two aspects of the BMD battle environment will remain unpredictable until the outbreak of war. The first is the effect of the nuclear background caused by the battle and the second is the type and extent of the countermeasures employed against the system. In contrast, the telephone system environment is well-known and predictable. Call traffic can be measured and compared to mathematical models. Furthermore, much of the environment, such as the signals used in calling, is controlled by the designers of the system, so they are well-acquainted with its characteristics. Those who seek to defeat telephone systems want to use the environment for their own ends, and generally do not try to disrupt it. Therefore, although countermeasures are not all known in type and extent, neither are they intended to destroy the operation of the system.

Low Cost of a Failure

Software errors manifested as failures during a battle would not be repairable until after the battle. Catastrophic failures could result in unacceptably high numbers of warheads reaching their targets; there is no way to guarantee or predict that catastrophic failures will not occur. Even minor failures may result in failure to intercept some enemy warheads, causing loss of human life. Telephone switching centers experiencing catastrophic software failures generally can be removed from service and the software repaired while calls are rerouted. Minor failures are at most likely to cause difficulties for a few subscribers.

Stable Requirements

As new threats arose, new strategies devised, new countermeasures found, and new technology introduced, the requirements for BMD systems would change, and change continually. Although some changes could be planned and introduced gradually, changing threats and, particularly, countermeasures would impose changes beyond the control of the system developers and maintainers. BMD countermeasures are not subject to close scrutiny by the opposition, and new ones might appear quickly, requiring rapid response. Because changes in threat and the development of countermeasures would depend on Soviet decisionmaking and technology, the rate at which the U.S. would have to make changes to its BMD software would partly depend on Soviet actions. Delays in responding to countermeasures might have serious consequences, including the temptation for the side that had a new, effective countermeasure to strike first before a counter-countermeasure could be devised and implemented.

Well-Understood Predecessors

Earlier BMD systems, such as SAFE-GUARD, can be characterized as terminal or late mid-course defense systems. The terminal and late mid-course defense part of an SDI BMD system could benefit from experience with these predecessors. There has been no experience, however, with boost phase and post-boost phase, and little experience with early mid-course defenses.[65] They are new problems that will take new technologies to solve. Most demanding of all, a system to solve these problems must be trusted to work properly the first time it is used. There have been approximately 100 years of experience with telephone switching systems. Each new system is a small change over its predecessor. If a newly-installed switching system does not work acceptably, it can be replaced by its predecessor until it is repaired.

Simple Design and Disciplined Development

Since the SDI BMD system has not yet proceeded to the point of a system design, much less a design for battle management or other software, one cannot judge whether or not the

---

[65]The Spartan missile, used by SAFEGUARD, can be considered a late mid-course defense component. However, SAFE-GUARD was designed to discriminate reentry vehicles from aircraft, satellites, aurora, and meteors, but not from decoys of the types expected to be available for use against BMD systems within the next 10-20 years. The only discriminators available to SAFEGUARD were phased-array radars. Potential countermeasures against modern BMD systems are discussed in chapters 10 and 11, and discriminators in chapter 4. Options considered for both include technologies considerably different from anything available for or against SAFEGUARD.

design will be simple. Similarly, one cannot judge whether or not the development process will be appropriately disciplined.

Development Approaches That Have Been Suggested

In the middle ground between those who believe that an SDI BMD system could never be made trustworthy, and those who are sure that it could, are some software developers who are unsure about the feasibility. The view some of them take is that it would be worthwhile to try to develop BMD software, given that one were prepared to abandon the attempt if the system could not be shown to be trustworthy. The approaches they suggest have the following characteristics:

- The purpose of the system would have to be clearly stated so that the requirements were known before development started.

- The development would have to start with what was best known, i.e., should build upon the knowledge and results of earlier U.S. efforts to build BMD systems.
- The development would have to be phased, so that each phase could build upon the results of the previous one. The system architecture would have to be consistent with such phasing.
- Simulation would be needed at every stage, and the simulations would have to be extremely realistic.
- Realistic tests would have to be performed at each stage of development.

Because failure is a clear possibility, those who advocate this approach recognize that options to deal with the possibility must be left open. If this approach were adopted, and failed, the cost of the attempt, including maintaining other options, could be high.

SUMMARY

Estimating Dependability

Most of the indices of dependability for large, complex software systems would be missing in BMD software systems. In particular, the telephone switching system, often cited as an example of a large, complex system, is quite unlike BMD systems.

The characteristics associated with dependability in large, complex systems include:

- a history of extensive use and abuse,
- operation in a predictable environment,
- a low cost of failures to the users,
- stable requirements,
- evolution from well-understood predecessor systems,
- a simple design, and
- a disciplined development effort.

The absence of many of these factors means that technology beyond the present state of the art in software engineering might have to be developed if there is to be a chance of producing dependable BMD software. It might

be argued that such technology will be invented, but traditionally progress has been slow in software engineering technology development. It appears that the nature of software causes progress to be slow, and that there is no prospect for making a radical change in that nature.

There is no highly reliable way to demonstrate that BMD software would operate properly when used for the first time. One of the long-term purposes of the National Test Bed is to provide a means of simulating operation of BMD software after deployment. Such tests could simulate a variety of threats and countermeasures, as well as the conditions existing in a nuclear environment. On the other hand, actual environments often exhibit characteristics not reproduced in a simulator. Simulations of battles involving BMD would have to reproduce enemy countermeasures—a particularly difficult task. The usual technique for validating simulations—making predictions based on the simulation and then verifying their accuracy—would be particularly difficult to use. This would especially be true when one considers the complexity of the atmospheric effects of nuclear explosions and the speculation involved in determining countermeasures. Repeated failures in simulation tests would demonstrate a lack of dependability. Successful performance in a simulation would give some confidence in the dependability of the system, but neither the dependability nor the confidence could be measured. Subjective judgments based on simulations would probably be highly controversial.

Traditional Reliability Measures

Traditional measures of reliability, such as mean time between failure, are insufficient to characterize dependability of software. Appropriate software reliability measures have yet to be fully developed. Furthermore, in the debate over BMD software dependability there is often confusion over the meaning of reliability. Error rate, e.g., number of errors per KLOC, is often misapplied as a definition of software reliability. There is no single figure of merit that would adequately quantify the dependability of BMD software. A potentially useful view is that dependability can be considered to be a combination of qualities such as trustworthiness, correctness, availability, fault tolerance, security, and safety. Unfortunately, there are no good ways of quantifying some of these properties and dependability would have to be a subjective judgment.

Technology for Preventing Catastrophic Failure

OTA found no evidence that the software engineering technology foreseeable in the near future would make large improvements in the dependability of software for BMD systems. In particular there would be no way to ensure that BMD software would not fail catastrophically when first used. It might be argued that the most important part of dependability is fault tolerance, and that there exist large, complex systems that are fault-tolerant, such as the telephone switching system. On the other hand, the fault tolerance of such systems is small compared to what would be needed for

BMD, since they are not under attack by an intelligent adversary interested in destroying their usefulness. A further complication of the argument over fault tolerance is that quantifications of software fault tolerance are not easily translated into measures of performance. At the same time, there is no generally accepted subjective standard of fault tolerance.

Confidence Based on Peacetime Testing

Confidence in the dependability of a BMD system would have to be derived from simulated battles and tests conducted during peacetime. Getting a BMD system to the point of passing realistic peacetime tests would most likely require a period of stability during which there were few changes made to the software. Unfortunately, the system developers and maintainers would have to respond to changes in threats and countermeasures put into effect by the Soviets. That is, the Soviets would partly control the rate at which changes would have to be made to the system. As changes were made, the system would again have to pass tests in order for the United States to maintain confidence in it.

Accommodating Changes During Peacetime

Experience with complex systems shows that changes eventually start introducing errors at a rate faster than they can be removed. At such a point all changes must be stopped and new software developed. The extent to which changes could be made would depend on the foresight of the developers during the design of the software. The better the requirements were understood at that time, and the better the potential changes were predicted, the more the chance that the software could accommodate changes as they occurred. The appearance of an unforeseen threat or countermeasure, or simply the advent of new, unexpected technology, might require redevelopment of all or substantial parts of the software. In a sense, the useful lifetime of the software would be determined by how well the software developers understood the requirements initially.

Establishing Goals and Requirements

Explicit performance and dependability goals for BMD have not been established. Consequently, one cannot set explicit software dependability goals. Even when BMD goals have been set, it will be difficult to derive explicit software dependability goals from them; there is no clear mapping between system dependability and software dependability. All agree that perfect software dependability is unattainable. Only arguments by analogy, e.g., as dependable as an automobile or telephone, have been proposed. There is no common agreement on what the dependability needs to be, nor how to measure it, except that it must be high.

There is common agreement that standard DoD procedures for developing software are not adequate for producing dependable BMD software in the face of rapidly changing requirements. There are few convincing proposals as yet on how to improve the procedures. The developers should not be expected to produce an adequate system on the first try. As Brooks says in discussing large software systems:

> In most projects, the first system built is barely usable. It may be too slow, too big, too awkward to use, or all three. There is no alternative but to start again, smarting but smarter, and build a redesigned version in which these problems are solved. . . . all large-system experience shows that it will be done. Where a new system concept or new technology is used, one has to build a system to throw away, for even the best planning is not so omniscient as to get it right the first time. . . .
>
> Hence plan to throw one away: you will, anyhow.[66]

BMD software may be an order of magnitude larger than any software system yet produced. Early estimates of software size for projects are notoriously inaccurate, often by a factor of 3 or more. Some argue that the use of an appropriate systems architecture can make SDI software comparable in size to the largest existing systems. On the other hand, none of the intermediate or far-term architectures yet proposed would appear to have this effect, and previous experience with large software systems indicates that the size is likely to be larger than current estimates. Such an increase in scale could cause unforeseen problems to dominate the development process.

---

[66]Frederick P. Brooks, Jr., *The Mythical Man-Month: Essays on Software Engineering* (New York, NY: Addison-Wesley, 1975), p. 116.

SDIO INVESTMENT IN BATTLE MANAGEMENT, COMPUTING TECHNOLOGY, AND SOFTWARE

SDIO's battle management program serves as the focus for addressing many of the communications, computing, and software technology problems discussed in chapters 7, 8, and 9. Based on funding and project description data supplied by SDIO, this section analyzes how SDIO is spending its money to try to solve these problems. The battle management program is organized into eight areas:

1. *software technology program plan*: developing and implementing a software technology program for the SDIO;
2. *algorithms*: development of algorithms for solving battle management problems such as resource allocation, track data handing over, discrimination, and coordination of actions within a distributed system;
3. *communications*: identifying the requirements and technology for establishing a communications system to link SDI components together into a BMD system;
4. *experimental systems*: proposing and evaluating system and battle management architectures and the technologies for implementing them;
5. *networks*: the design and development of distributed systems and of communications networks that could be used to support BMD;

6. *The National Test Bed*: procurement of hardware and software needed for the National Test Bed;

7. *processors*: development of computers that would be sufficiently powerful, radiation-hardened, fault-tolerant, and secure for BMD needs, and of the software required to operate them; and

8. *software engineering*: the technology for developing and maintaining software for SDI, including techniques and tools for requirements specification, design, coding, testing, maintenance, and management of the software life-cycle.

Table 9-2 is a snapshot of the funding for these areas as of June 1987. Rather than showing the fiscal year 1987 SDIO battle management budget, it shows money that at that time had been spent since the inception of the program, that was then under contract, or that was expected soon to be under contract. It is a picture of how the SDIO was investing its money to solve battle management problems over the first few years of the program. Not shown is money invested by other agencies, such as the Defense Advanced Research Projects Agency, in joint projects. The leverage attained by SDIO in some areas is therefore greater than might appear from the table.

The SDIO battle management program clearly emphasizes experimental systems. Examination of the individual projects in this area shows a concentration on the development and maintenance of simulations and simulation facilities, such as the Army's Strategic Defense Command Advanced Research Center Test Bed, used to run battle simulations; on architecture analyses, such as the phase I and II battle management/C³ architecture studies; and on the first two Experimental Validation 88 (EV88) experiments.

The funding categories shown in table 9-2 permit considerable overlap; projects in each category could easily be assigned to a different category. To try to draw clearer distinctions among categories and to try to identify funding targeted specifically at the problems discussed in chapters 7 through 9, OTA reorganized the funding data supplied by SDIO. Table 9-3 shows just those funds aimed at exploring solutions to some of the more significant problems noted in chapters 7 through 9. It does not include all funds shown in table 9-2, but does show percentages of total funding. The categories are defined as follows:

1. *battle management and system simulations*: the development of particular simulation algorithms or specialized hardware for battle management simulations;

2. *simulation technology development*: the development of the hardware and software for bigger, faster simulations, and for improving techniques for evaluating the results of simulations;

3. *automating existing software engineering technology*: the development of software and hardware that would be used to improve the software development and maintenance process, which is now based on existing manual techniques;

Table 9-2.—SDIO Battle Management Investment

Area	Funding ($M)	Percent of total
Software technology program plan ..	2.5	1
Algorithms.......................	25.3	9
Communications..................	8.1	3
Experimental systems	117.5	42
National Test Bed	13.0	5
Networks	29.6	11
Processors......................	47.1	17
Software engineering..............	*32.8*	*12*
Total	275.9	100

SOURCE: Office of Technology Assessment, 1988; and SDIO.

Table 9-3.—Funding for OTA Specified Problems

Problem	Funding ($M)	Percent of total[a]
Battle management and system simulations	42.5	15
Simulation technology development	35.7	13
Automating existing software engineering technology	14.2	5
Computer security......................	10.3	4
Communications networks	7.8	3
Software verification	4.6	2
Fault tolerance (hardware and software)	3.1	1
Software engineering technology development....	*2.5*	*1*
Total..................................	120.6	44

[a]Percentage of total battle management funding, i.e., of $275.9M

SOURCE: Office of Technology Assessment, 1988; and SDIO.

4. *computer security*: techniques for detecting and preventing unauthorized access to computer systems;

5. *communications networks*: the organization of computer-controlled communications equipment into a network that could meet SDI communications requirements;

6. *software verification*: the development of practical techniques for mathematically proving the correctness of computer programs;

7. *fault tolerance (hardware and software)*: the development of hardware and software that continues to work despite the occurrence of failures; and

8. *software engineering technology development*: the development of new techniques for improving the dependability of software and the rate at which dependable software can be produced.

Table 9-3 shows that SDIO is investing considerably more in simulations and simulation technology than any of the other problem areas in battle management and computing identified by OTA. **Of some concern is the smallness of the investment in especially challenging areas such as computer security, communications networks, fault tolerance, and new software engineering technology development.**

CONCLUSIONS

Based on both the preceding analysis, and the further exposition in appendix A, OTA has reached eight major conclusions.

1. **The dependability of BMD software would have to be estimated subjectively and without the benefit of data or experience from battle use. The nature of software and our experience with large, complex software systems, including weapon systems, together indicate that there would always be irresolvable questions about how dependable the BMD software was, and also about the confidence to be placed in dependability estimates.** Political decision-makers would have to keep in mind that there would be no good technical answers to questions about the dependability of the software, and no well-founded technical definition of software dependability.

   It is important to note that the Soviets would have similar problems in trying to estimate the dependability of the software, and therefore the potential performance of the system. Technical judgments of dependability would rely on peacetime tests that would be unlikely to apply to battle conditions. Political judgments about the credibility of the defense provided would therefore rest on very uncertain technical grounds.

2. **No matter how much peacetime testing were done, there would be no guarantee that the** system would not fail catastrophically during battle as a result of a software error. Furthermore, experience with large, complex software systems that have unique requirements and use technology untested in battle, such as a BMD system, indicates that there is a significant probability that a catastrophic failure caused by a software error would occur in the system's first battle.

3. It is possible that an administration and a Congress would reach the political decision to "trust" software that passed all the tests that could be devised in peacetime, despite the irresolvable doubts about whether such software might fail catastrophically the first time it was used in an actual battle. **Such a decision could be based upon the argument that the purpose of strategic forces—even defensive strategic forces—is primarily deterrence, and that a defensive system passing all its peacetime tests would be adequate for deterrence.** If deterrence succeeded, we would never know, and never need to know, whether the system would function in wartime.

4. **The extent to which BMD software would differ from complex software systems that have proven to be dependable in the past raises the possibility that software could not be created that ever passed its peacetime tests. This a** possibility exacerbated by the prospect of

changing requirements caused by Soviet actions. We might arrive at a situation in which fixing problems revealed by one test created new problems that caused the software to fail the next test.

5. **No adequate models exist for the development, production, test, and maintenance of software for full-scale BMD systems.** Current DoD models of the software life-cycle and methods of software procurement appear inadequate for the job of building software as large, complex, and dependable as BMD software would have to be.

6. **The system architecture, the technologies to be used in the system, and a consistent set of performance requirements over the lifetime of the system must be established before starting software development.**[67] Otherwise, the system is unlikely even to pass realistic peacetime tests.

[67]Note that this does not preclude a phased system, with both capabilities and requirements growing over time, provided that the final architecture and final performance requirements are clear before initial software development begins. Even then, considering the uniqueness of BMD defense, one would expect to spend considerable time finding a workable design.

7. **As the strategic goals for a BMD system became more stringent, confidence in one's ability to produce software that would meet those goals would decrease as a result of the increased complication required in the software design.** Even for modest goals, such as improved deterrence, the United States could not have high confidence that the software would not fail catastrophically, whether faced with a modest threat or a severe threat. Put another way, there is no good way of knowing that BMD software would degrade gracefully rather than fail catastrophically when called on to face increasing levels of threat. Current techniques for identifying problems and detecting errors, such as simulations, would not help, although they could help to reduce the failure rate. **Furthermore, foreseeable improvements in software engineering technology would not change this situation.**

8. **The SDIO is investing relatively small amounts of money in software technology research in general, and in software engineering technology, computer security, communications networks, and fault tolerance in particular.** This investment strategy is of some concern, since particularly challenging BMD software development problems lie in these areas.

Chapter 10

Non-Destructive Countermeasures to Ballistic Missile Defense

The classified version of this chapter is available in the classified version of this report. As of this writing, the unclassified version continues to be withheld from release by the Department of Defense.

CONTENTS

Chapter 11
Defense Suppression and System Survivability

The classified version of this chapter is available in the classified version of this report. As of this writing, the unclassified version continues to be withheld from release by the Department of Defense.

CONTENTS

Chapter 12

Defense Suppression Scenarios

The classified version of this chapter is available in the classified version of this report. As of this writing, the unclassified version continues to be withheld from release by the Department of Defense.

CONTENTS